T0092686

Communications
in Computer and Information Science 1984

Editorial Board Members

Joaquim Filipe⬛, *Polytechnic Institute of Setúbal, Setúbal, Portugal*
Ashish Ghosh⬛, *Indian Statistical Institute, Kolkata, India*
Raquel Oliveira Prates⬛, *Federal University of Minas Gerais (UFMG), Belo Horizonte, Brazil*
Lizhu Zhou, *Tsinghua University, Beijing, China*

Rationale

The CCIS series is devoted to the publication of proceedings of computer science conferences. Its aim is to efficiently disseminate original research results in informatics in printed and electronic form. While the focus is on publication of peer-reviewed full papers presenting mature work, inclusion of reviewed short papers reporting on work in progress is welcome, too. Besides globally relevant meetings with internationally representative program committees guaranteeing a strict peer-reviewing and paper selection process, conferences run by societies or of high regional or national relevance are also considered for publication.

Topics

The topical scope of CCIS spans the entire spectrum of informatics ranging from foundational topics in the theory of computing to information and communications science and technology and a broad variety of interdisciplinary application fields.

Information for Volume Editors and Authors

Publication in CCIS is free of charge. No royalties are paid, however, we offer registered conference participants temporary free access to the online version of the conference proceedings on SpringerLink (http://link.springer.com) by means of an http referrer from the conference website and/or a number of complimentary printed copies, as specified in the official acceptance email of the event.

CCIS proceedings can be published in time for distribution at conferences or as post-proceedings, and delivered in the form of printed books and/or electronically as USBs and/or e-content licenses for accessing proceedings at SpringerLink. Furthermore, CCIS proceedings are included in the CCIS electronic book series hosted in the SpringerLink digital library at http://link.springer.com/bookseries/7899. Conferences publishing in CCIS are allowed to use Online Conference Service (OCS) for managing the whole proceedings lifecycle (from submission and reviewing to preparing for publication) free of charge.

Publication process

The language of publication is exclusively English. Authors publishing in CCIS have to sign the Springer CCIS copyright transfer form, however, they are free to use their material published in CCIS for substantially changed, more elaborate subsequent publications elsewhere. For the preparation of the camera-ready papers/files, authors have to strictly adhere to the Springer CCIS Authors' Instructions and are strongly encouraged to use the CCIS LaTeX style files or templates.

Abstracting/Indexing

CCIS is abstracted/indexed in DBLP, Google Scholar, EI-Compendex, Mathematical Reviews, SCImago, Scopus. CCIS volumes are also submitted for the inclusion in ISI Proceedings.

How to start

To start the evaluation of your proposal for inclusion in the CCIS series, please send an e-mail to ccis@springer.com.

Liliana Vale Costa · Nelson Zagalo ·
Ana Isabel Veloso · Esteban Clua ·
Sylvester Arnab · Mário Vairinhos · Diogo Gomes
Editors

Videogame Sciences and Arts

13th International Conference, VJ 2023
Aveiro, Portugal, November 28–30, 2023
Revised Selected Papers

Springer

Editors
Liliana Vale Costa [ID]
University of Aveiro
Aveiro, Portugal

Nelson Zagalo [ID]
University of Aveiro
Aveiro, Portugal

Ana Isabel Veloso [ID]
University of Aveiro
Aveiro, Portugal

Esteban Clua [ID]
Fluminense Federal University
Niteroi, Rio de Janeiro, Brazil

Sylvester Arnab [ID]
Coventry University
Coventry, UK

Mário Vairinhos [ID]
University of Aveiro
Aveiro, Portugal

Diogo Gomes [ID]
University of Aveiro
Aveiro, Portugal

ISSN 1865-0929 ISSN 1865-0937 (electronic)
Communications in Computer and Information Science
ISBN 978-3-031-51451-7 ISBN 978-3-031-51452-4 (eBook)
https://doi.org/10.1007/978-3-031-51452-4

© The Editor(s) (if applicable) and The Author(s), under exclusive license
to Springer Nature Switzerland AG 2024

This work is subject to copyright. All rights are reserved by the Publisher, whether the whole or part of the material is concerned, specifically the rights of translation, reprinting, reuse of illustrations, recitation, broadcasting, reproduction on microfilms or in any other physical way, and transmission or information storage and retrieval, electronic adaptation, computer software, or by similar or dissimilar methodology now known or hereafter developed.
The use of general descriptive names, registered names, trademarks, service marks, etc. in this publication does not imply, even in the absence of a specific statement, that such names are exempt from the relevant protective laws and regulations and therefore free for general use.
The publisher, the authors, and the editors are safe to assume that the advice and information in this book are believed to be true and accurate at the date of publication. Neither the publisher nor the authors or the editors give a warranty, expressed or implied, with respect to the material contained herein or for any errors or omissions that may have been made. The publisher remains neutral with regard to jurisdictional claims in published maps and institutional affiliations.

This Springer imprint is published by the registered company Springer Nature Switzerland AG
The registered company address is: Gewerbestrasse 11, 6330 Cham, Switzerland

Paper in this product is recyclable.

Preface: Videojogos 2023

The 13th Conference on Videogame Sciences and Arts – Videojogos 2023 – was held in Aveiro, Portugal, during November 28–30, 2023. The event was co-organized by the DigiMedia Research Center, the Portuguese Society of Video Games Sciences (SPCV) and the Departments of Communication and Art (DeCA) and Electronics, Telecommunications and Informatics (DETI), both from the University of Aveiro.

The annual conferences of the SPCV are an international event dedicated to promoting the scientific gathering of researchers and professionals in the expanded field of videogames, as a multidisciplinary domain assembling research from New Media, Culture, Technology, Education, Psychology, and the Arts.

The blending of all these scientific areas has contributed to the growth of scientific expertise and acceptance in academia but also to the increasingly clear alignment of highly relevant sub-areas, such as game experience, game learning, game development and game culture. As such, this year's conference is fully aligned with these macro developments in the field by proposing four sections that meet these four sub-areas.

Therefore, the first section of the conference was dedicated to Game Experience and Evaluation. Here we can find a series of articles that discuss models for evaluating the gaming experience, both at the level of automatic intra-game systems, as is the case of the article "Data Driven Agents for User Experience Testing" by Fernandes, Lopes and Prada, and at the level of the impacts on the players' experience, as in "Embraceable Virtual Paws: Player Experiences in Animal Shelter Simulators" by Lu and Hassan; "Psychological and Behavioural Effects of League of Legends rank system for Italian Competitive Players" by Gursesli, Masti, Duradoni, Bostan, Sungu, Zilbeyaz and Guazzini; "Comparing Performance and Experience in VR vs. Real-world through a Puzzle Game" by Berkman and Choeib; and "Livestreaming Games and Parenthood: Exploring the Experience of Portuguese Parent Streamers" by Assuncao, Scott and Summerley. At the same time, we can find in this section one article reflecting on experience and addressing perceptions and motivations, in the article "Videogame Students in Portuguese Higher Education: Perceptions, Motivations, and Playing Habits" by Barroso and Sousa; and a final one focused on the evaluation of cinematics as a design object, ""Looking Up the Camera to Play Right": An Interview Study of the Implications of Cinematic Storytelling in Game Design" by Passos, Vale Costa and Zagalo.

In section 2, you can find a series of articles dedicated to Game-based learning and Edutainment, starting with a set of three articles that work on the creation of games for the classroom, two of them focused on the study of maths – "From Concept to Classroom: Design and Deployment of a Configurable Math Educational Game for Elementary Students" by Jeri and Baldeón; "Math-Masters: An Educational Game to Practice the Mathematical Operations" by Marques, Ferreira and Silva - and a third proposing an extended model, in terms of subjects, "Extending Educational Games Across Product Lines" by Castro, Werner and Xexeo. Outside the classroom, but focused on specific learning processes, such as Computational Thinking, Architectural Design and Reading, we have the articles "How Players Develop Computational Thinking while Modelling Character Behaviors in Gameplay" by Moreira Pinto, Seiça and Roque; "A Videogame for Architectural Design? Minecraft for Young People to Imagine Desirable Climate Futures" by Andrade, Crowley, Cocco and McNally; and "A Framework for the Creation of a Reading Video Game for Children" by Boussejra. Lastly, we have a serious game designed to tackle environmental problems, particularly electronic waste, which is the result of technological innovation throughout contemporary society, in the article "Breaking the Wall of E-Waste Recycling Education by Means of a Digital Game" by Lopes, Brandão, de Marchi, Yasui, Vittori, Santos and Gama.

Since experience and learning are central to the process of studying video games, another dimension that is of great relevance and ends up being left out of more technologically orientated conferences is the field of Culture. In this third section, there are four articles divided into two main sections: game analysis, with "For a pragmatic study of the generic categorisation of video games: the case of survival horror" by Surinx and "Video Games and Adaptation: an Introduction" by Ristić and Kubik; and the politics of video games with "A Lantern Called Desire: Time Travel, Space Nostalgia, and Desiring-Machines in 'The Great Perhaps'" by Mejía-Alandia; and "Adolescent masculinity and the geek aesthetic: a study of gaming magazine imagery 1982 to 1993" by Bootes. While the first two provide a deeper understanding of the conventions that shape a game genre and adaptation conditions, the latter two analyze its societal, ideological and gender impacts.

To end this book, we have a section on the core subjects of game design and development, responsible for the creation of the artefacts that sustain the research in the field. Here we start with two chapters specifically on Game Design questions—"Cities: Skylines: the digital and analog game design lessons for learning about collaborative urban planning" by Sousa; "An Evolutionary Approach for PCG in a Cooperative Puzzle Platform Game" by Guimarães Rocha and Prada; and "Unlocking the Untapped Potential of Video Game Data: A Case Study of Aim Trainers" by Rejthar. This is followed by two articles on artificial intelligence, "Humans vs AI: An Exploratory Study With Online and Offline Learners" by Inácio, Fachada, Matos-Carvalho and Fernandes; and "Icarus, towards diplomatic agents in Diplomacy" by Araújo, Dias and Santos. And finally, a game centred on the use of Augmented Reality technologies to support design, in "ChemXP AR Edition, A Serious Game" by Bandeira, Vairinhos, Dias, Silva and Soengas.

The conference received 64 submissions, and each submission was at least reviewed by three reviewers in a double-blind review process. This book contains a selection of just 24 papers (18 long and 6 short), representing an acceptance rate of 37.5%. Authors belong to academia, research institutes, industry, and some are independent researchers from 17 countries (Austria, Belgium, Brazil, Czechia, Finland, France, Greece, Ireland, Israel, Italy, Norway, Peru, Portugal, Serbia, Spain, Sweden and UK). These contributions address the novel research and development outcomes in the videogame context, gathering in several different scientific areas.

To help the videogame community bridge the gap between industry and academia, Dirk Bosmans, the Director General of PEGI S.A. (Pan-European Game Information) was invited for the first keynote. A second keynote addressed the industry of translation, currently a hot topic in the Iberian industry, with José Ramón Calvo-Ferrer from the Universidad de Alicante, Spain. For the last keynote, we invited Professor Lynn Alves from the Federal University of Bahia, Brazil, a specialist in the development of educational games, particularly games based on regional culture.

We would like to thank the scientific board for their contribution to guaranteeing and delivering the highest scientific quality, allowing the outstanding relevance of this book. We would also like to thank the organisation team for their effort in arranging and setting up the 2023 Conference. We would also like to thank the Association of Portuguese Video Game Producers (APVP) and the Association of Video Game Producers and Distributors (AEPDV).

Finally, we would like to thank the DigiMedia Research Center, the Portuguese Society of Video Games Sciences, and the Department of Electronics, Telecommunications and Informatics from the University of Aveiro for all their support, and the Department of Communication and Art for hosting the event and making this conference possible.

November 2023

Nelson Zagalo
Liliana Vale Costa
Ana Isabel Veloso
Esteban Clua
Sylvester Arnab
Mário Vairinhos
Diogo Gomes

Organization

Committees

Conference Chairs

Liliana Costa	University of Aveiro, Portugal
Esteban Clua	Universidade Federal Fluminense, Brazil

Scientific Chairs

Ana Isabel Veloso	University of Aveiro, Portugal
Nelson Zagalo	University of Aveiro, Portugal
Sylvester Arnab	Coventry University, UK

Organizing Chairs

Diogo Gomes	University of Aveiro, Portugal
Mário Vairinhos	University of Aveiro, Portugal

Programme Committee

Ahu Yolaç	Lawrence Technological University, USA
Alan Carvalho	São Paulo State College of Technology, Brazil
Alexander Dockhorn	Gottfried Wilhelm Leibniz University Hannover, Germany
Anabela Marto	Polytechnic Leiria, Portugal
Anna Vvedenskaya	University of Amsterdam, The Netherlands
Antonio José Panells de la Maza	TecnoCampus, Spain
Barbara Göbl	Universität Wien, Austria
Beatriz Legeren Lago	University of Vigo, Spain
Belen Mainer Blanco	Francisco de Vitoria University, Spain
Bernard Perron	University of Montreal, Canada
Cameron Browne	Maastricht University, The Netherlands
Carme Mangiron	Universitat Autónoma de Barcelona, Spain
Carla Sousa	Lusófona University, Portugal
Carsten Möller	University of Cologne, Germany

Cristiano Max	Universidade Feevale, Brazil
Dan Golding	University of Melbourne, Australia
Daniela Karine Ramos	Federal University of Santa Catarina, Brazil
Davide Gadia	Università degli Studi di Milano, Italy
Elina Roinioti	University of the Peloponnese, Greece
Esteban Clua	Universidade Federal Fluminense, Brazil
Eva Brooks	Aalborg University, Denmark
Fanny Barnabé	University of Liège, Belgium
Filipe Luz	Lusófona University, Portugal
Francisco Perales López	University of the Balearic Islands, Spain
Frutuoso Silva	University of Beira Interior, Portugal
Gabriel Menotti Gonring	Queen's University, Canada
Hans-Joachim Bache	IT University of Copenhagen, Denmark
Igor Nedelkovski	University "St. Kliment Ohridski" in Bitola, North Macedonia
Jean-Michel Blottière	Games For Change Europe, France
Jennifer Jenson	University of British Columbia, Canada
Jesse Nery Filho	Instituto Federal Baiano, Brazil
João Jacob	Mindera Gaming, Portugal
João Victor Boechat Gomide	Universidade FUMEC, Brazil
John Edison Cardona	University of Waterloo, Canada
Jonne Arjoranta	University of Jyväskylä, Finland
José Ramón Calvo-Ferrer	Universidad de Alicante, Spain
José Luís Eguia Gómez	Universitat Politécnica de Catalunya, Spain
Jose Zagal	University of Utah, USA
Josep Blat	Universitat Pompeu Fabra, Spain
Jussi Pekka Holopainen	Blekinge Institute of Technology, Sweden
Hans-Joachim Bache	IT University of Copenhagen, Denmark
Licínio Roque	University of Coimbra, Portugal
Simone Hausknecht	Simon Fraser University, Canada
Leonel Morgado	Open University, Portugal
Luis Mañas Viniegra	Universidad Complutense de Madrid, Spain
Marko Suvajdžić	University of Florida, USA
Markus Wiemker	Hochschule Fresenius, Germany
Maxim Mozgovoy	University of Aizu, Japan
Mercedes García Betegon	U-tad, Spain
Micael Sousa	University of Coimbra, Portugal
Michael Rönnlund	Umeå universitet, Sweden
Mónica Aresta	University of Aveiro, Portugal
Óscar Mealha	University of Aveiro, Portugal
Panagiotis Fotaris	University of Brighton, UK
Patrícia Oliveira	University of Aveiro, Portugal

Pedro Cardoso   University of Aveiro, Portugal
Pilar Lacasa   Universidad de Alcalá, Spain
Piotr Siuda   Kazimierz Wielki University in Bydgoszcz,
                                    Poland
Raquel Echeandia Sánchez   Universidad de Alcalá, Spain
Ricardo Casañ Pitarch   València Polytechnic University, Spain
Ricardo Fassone   University of Torino, Italy
Roger Tavares   Polytechnic Institute of Bragança, Portugal
Rui Prada   IST, University of Lisbon, Portugal
Ruth S. Contreras-Espinosa   Universitat de Vic - Universitat Central de
                                    Catalunya, Spain
Salma ElSayed   Abertay University, UK
Samuel Silva   University of Aveiro, Portugal
Sanaul Hauque   LUT University, Finland
Siitonen Marko   University of Jyväskylä, Finland
Susana Tosca   IT University of Copenhagen, Denmark
Suzanne de Castell   Simon Fraser University, Canada
Teresa Piñeiro Otero   Universidade da Coruña, Spain
Valter Alves   Polytechnic Institute of Viseu, Portugal
Victor Navarro-Remesal   TecnoCampus, Spain
Xiaochun Zhang   University College London, UK
Wolfgang Müller   University of Education Weingarten, Germany

Organizing Committee

Bernardo Marques (Online Event   University of Aveiro, Portugal
  Support)
Cátia Silva (Demo and Workshop) University of Aveiro, Portugal
Cláudia Ortet (Event Manager)   University of Aveiro, Portugal
Dalila Martins (Demo and   University of Aveiro, Portugal
  Workshop)
Francisco Regalado (Web Design) University of Aveiro, Portugal
Maria Júlia Vieira (Social Media) University of Aveiro, Portugal
Pedro Reisinho (Demo and   University of Aveiro, Portugal
  Workshop)
Samuel Silva (Online Event   University of Aveiro, Portugal
  Support)
Sofia Ribeiro (Web Design)   University of Aveiro, Portugal
Silvino Martins (Demo and   University of Aveiro, Portugal
  Workshop)
Tânia Ribeiro (Event Image)   University of Aveiro, Portugal

Organizing Institutions

DigiMedia – Digital Media and Interaction
University of Aveiro - DeCA - DETI
Sociedade Portuguesa de Ciências dos Videojogos (SPCV)

Support

University of Aveiro
FCT - Fundação para a Ciência e a Tecnologia

Contents

Game Experience and Evaluation

Data Driven Agents for User Experience Testing 3
    Pedro M. Fernandes, Manuel Lopes, and Rui Prada

Embraceable Virtual Paws: Player Experiences in Animal Shelter Simulator . . . 19
    Chien Lu and Lobna Hassan

Livestreaming Games and Parenthood: Exploring the Experience
of Portuguese Parent Streamers 33
    Carina de Assunção, Michael James Scott, and Rory K. Summerley

Videogame Students in Portuguese Higher Education: Perceptions,
Motivations, and Playing Habits – A Case Study 49
    Ivan Barroso and Carla Sousa

Psychological and Behavioral Effects of League of Legends Rank System
for Italian Competitive Players 59
    Mustafa Can Gursesli, Federica Masti, Mirko Duradoni,
    Barbaros Bostan, Ertugrul Sungu, Pervin Cagla Zilbeyaz,
    and Andrea Guazzini

Comparing Performance and Experience in VR vs. Real-World Through
a Puzzle Game 72
    Ahmed Choueib and Mehmet İlker Berkman

"Looking up the Camera to Play Right": An Interview Study
of the Implications of Cinematic Storytelling in Game Design 86
    Ana Passos, Liliana Vale Costa, and Nelson Zagalo

Game-Based Learning and Edutainment

Breaking the Wall of E-Waste Recycling Education by Means of a Digital
Game 103
    Richard da Cruz Lopes, André Luiz Brandão, Alessio de Marchi,
    André Kazuo Yasui, Karla Vittori, Flávia de Souza Santos,
    and Sandra Gama

How Players Develop Computational Thinking While Modeling Character
Behaviors in Gameplay   118
    Valéria Moreira Pinto, Mariana Seiça, and Licínio Roque

Extending Educational Games Across Product Lines   134
    Diego Castro, Claudia Werner, and Geraldo Xexéo

A Videogame for Architectural Design? Minecraft for Young People
to Imagine Desirable Climate Futures   150
    Bruno Andrade, Saul Crowley, Chiara Cocco, and Brenda McNally

Math-Masters: An Educational Game to Practice the Mathematical
Operations   166
    João A. B. T. Marques, João L. A. P. Ferreira, and Frutuoso G. M. Silva

A Framework for the Creation of a Reading Video Game for Children   174
    Hakim Boussejra

Games and Culture

Video Games and Adaptation: An Introduction   187
    Tatjana Ristić and Darjan Kubik

A Lantern Called Desire: Time Travel, Space Nostalgia,
and Desiring-Machines in *The Great Perhaps*   202
    Diego A. Mejía-Alandia

Adolescent Masculinity and the Geek Aesthetic: A Study of Gaming
Magazine Imagery 1982 to 1993   217
    Robin Bootes

For a Pragmatic Study of the Generic Categorization of Video Games: The
Case of Survival Horror   238
    François-Xavier Surinx

Game Design and Development

Cities: Skylines: The Digital and Analog Game Design Lessons
for Learning About Collaborative Urban Planning   257
    Micael Sousa

Humans vs AI: An Exploratory Study with Online and Offline Learners   272
    *João Inácio, Nuno Fachada, João P. Matos-Carvalho,
    and Carlos M. Fernandes*

An Evolutionary Approach for PCG in a Cooperative Puzzle Platform Game ... 287
  José Bernardo Rocha, Nuno Martins, and Rui Prada

Icarus, Towards Diplomatic Agents in Diplomacy 300
  André Araújo, João Dias, and Pedro A. Santos

Unlocking the Untapped Potential of Video Game Data: A Case Study
of Aim Trainers 315
  Jan Rejthar

ChemXP AR Edition, A Serious Game 322
  Mário Bandeira, Mário Vairinhos, Paulo Dias, Raquel Soengas,
  and Vera Silva

Author Index 337

Game Experience and Evaluation

Data Driven Agents for User Experience Testing

Pedro M. Fernandes[✉], Manuel Lopes, and Rui Prada

INESC-ID and Instituto Superior Técnico, Univ. de Lisboa, Lisbon, Portugal
{pedro.miguel.rocha.fernandes,manuel.lopes,rui.prada}@tecnico.ulisboa.pt

Abstract. Testing User eXperience (UX) during the development of complex systems, such as games, often requires costly and time-consuming human involvement. To address this issue, we propose the use of modular UX testing agents capable of providing quick and on-demand UX estimates. These agents empower developers to efficiently assess UX design goals and understand user actions and preferences. We present two data-driven modules for creating a flexible UX testing agent: one for emotion prediction and another for generating persona-like behaviour. The agent enables the evaluation of various player types and their emotional responses within a game environment.

Keywords: UX Testing · Games · Player Modelling · Machine Learning

1 Introduction

In a world where agile software development is becoming the norm, entailing quick development sprints and a reliance on automatic testing, the testing of User eXperience (UX) is lagging behind. This is especially relevant for complex systems such as games. Currently, testing UX on such systems requires testing with humans, which is both money and time consuming. It becomes infeasible to test the implications to UX every time developers change something in the application as it would considerably slow down the development process. Having access to quick and on demand estimates of UX would allow developers to create better and more user friendly applications. It would also greatly benefit developers and designers to know what actions and paths users are most likely to take.

The creation of UX testing agents is our approach to begin solving these problems and allow UX concerns to be tested automatically during development, aiding the creation of better applications. Such agents must be capable of interacting with an environment and provide estimates of UX, allowing developers and testers to quickly and automatically have a better understanding of whether their UX design goals are being met or not. These agents could, for example, allow developers to automatically know which areas of an environment

This work was supported by national funds through Fundação para a Ciência e a Tecnologia (FCT) with references UIDB/50021/2020 and 2020.05865.BD.

© The Author(s), under exclusive license to Springer Nature Switzerland AG 2024
L. Vale Costa et al. (Eds.): VJ 2023, CCIS 1984, pp. 3–18, 2024.
https://doi.org/10.1007/978-3-031-51452-4_1

are not providing enough stimulus to users or which ones are too overwhelming. They could also give developers an idea of how different the playing experience would be for different users.

User experience (UX) is a broad, complex and multi-faceted concept. It encompasses many different components of human experience along with characteristics of the system itself and the surrounding environment. It is therefore unfeasible to have a single, uni-dimensional measure of UX. What can be done is the measurement or prediction of different components of UX according to what is most relevant to testers and designers. With this in mind, we argue that UX testing agents should be modular by design. This means that they should have the capability of being run with different modules, each endowing them with the ability to predict different components of UX or grant different behaviours to the agents.

In this paper, we present two such modules for the creation of a UX testing agent: one module for emotion prediction (Sect. 3) and one for the generation of persona like behaviour (Sect. 4). Together, these modules allow for the creation of UX testing agents capable of imitating the behaviour of different types of players and predicting the expected emotional outcome of such players interacting with a game level. Both the modules here proposed are data-driven, generating both the behaviour and the emotional prediction based on player traces and emotional reporting.

2   Related Work

This work brings together several areas of research. In this section, we'll give a quick overview of some works on the field of player modelling, player clustering and emotion prediction.

In previous work, we have proposed automated UX testing agents, yet used fully rule-based approaches for both behaviour generation and prediction of core affect [6].

When it comes to modeling players based on behavior, Inverse Reinforcement Learning (IRL) [16] has emerged as a relevant approach. Tastan et al. [20] employed IRL to generate policies for the competitive game Unreal Tournament, using rewards obtained from the IRL framework through a linear solver. Similar applications of IRL for learning different behaviors can be found in Lee et al. [10], Lee et al. [11], and Almíngol et al. [1].

In terms of generating behavior that is believably "human-like" Asensio et al. [2] used genetic and evolutionary algorithms to create agents capable of passing the Turing test based on observable behavior. Wang et al. [23] also explored methods to create agents with believable behavior.

For persona generation, Holmgård et al. [8] introduced an approach based on psychological decision theory to create procedural personas using the Monte Carlo Tree Search (MCTS) algorithm and manually defined heuristics. Stahlke et al. [19] developed an agent creation framework based on heuristics, incorporating human qualities and limitations, such as visibility and memory. Tychsen et al. [22] derived personas based on video game metrics obtained from player interactions with the game world. Holmgård et al. [9] explored three types of evolving models controlled by neural networks to generate human-like behavior: "personas," "clones," and "specialized agents."

In the realm of player clustering, an important aspect of learning or predicting player profiles is the ability to group players into clusters based on similar behaviors. Drachen et al. [5] conducted cluster analysis on the games "Tera" and "Battlefield 2: Bad Company 2," utilizing K-means and Simplex Volume Maximization algorithms. Thawonmas et al. [21] proposed a clustering method based on game world landmarks, using the Euclidean distance between players to determine their transition probabilities between these landmarks.

In the context of emotional component prediction, Melhart et al. [15] utilized player traces and emotional annotation to predict the level of arousal in different games from various genres. Other works focused on arousal prediction using sound and pixels [14].

Our work builds upon the several referenced areas by joining components from all of them to create testing agents that can both act on the game and predict UX.

3   Emotion Prediction

In this section of the paper, we explore emotional prediction using a 3-dimensional emotional model, the PAD model of emotion [18], which describes human emotions based on three dimensions: Pleasure; Arousal; and Dominance. We use machine learning to predict the expected emotional state of a user interacting with the system by creating a predictor for each of these dimensions.

3.1   The Game and Inputs

Acting as a test-bed for the developed UX testing agents, the game "Flower Hunter" was developed, inspired by old-school top-down 2D games like Legend of Zelda. It was designed to be easily modifiable, fast-running, compatible with Python machine-learning libraries, and ultimately entertaining enough to motivate users to play it. Screenshots of the game can be found in Fig. 1.

Pertaining the inputs, we decided to use numerical values related to the player and the different objects present in the game. The list of the inputs used is as follows:

- Distance to the closest enemy
- Distance to closest rice cake
- Distance to closest coin
- Number of enemies in view
- Number of rice cakes in view
- Number of coins in view
- Sum of value/distance of enemies
- Sum of value/distance of rice cakes
- Sum of value/distance of coins
- Time (in secs) since seeing an enemy
- Time since seeing a rice cake
- Time since seeing a coin
- Distance to objective
- Health Points
- Coins gathered
- Enemies killed
- Damage done

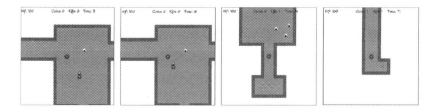

Fig. 1. Screen shots of the "Flower Hunter" game. The player, represented by a black and yellow ball, needs to traverse a field riddled with enemies, health-providing rice cakes, and coins, in order to find a pink flower (shown on the rightmost screenshot). Once the player finds this flower, the game is over and the player won. If the player loses all its health points by touching enemies, then the game ends and the player lost. The player can use a sword to fight and kill the enemies (shown in the second from the left screenshot). (Color figure online)

3.2 The Output

To train a machine learning model, we required information about the emotions of a player as she or he traversed the game. Additionally, we believe it is more meaningful to the testers and designers to know how the emotional dimensions evolved over time and space as opposed to only having a final estimate for the totality of the interaction between the player and the game. Furthermore, the closest to continuous this information could be, the better, as it would allow us to create a finely-grained model.

To achieve this close to continuous annotation, user questionnaires would be hard to apply, and physiological data was considered an intrusive method, requiring specialized equipment. Furthermore, we found no studies directly correlating physiological data with the 3 dimensions of the PAD model. As such, we decided to use continuous, after-the-fact annotation, inspired by such works as [13,15].

This annotation worked as follows. The users, after playing a given level of the "Flower Hunter" game, were asked to annotate one of the PAD emotional dimensions. They did so by seeing a recording of the level they had just played while using the up and down arrow keys on a computer keyboard to control a line on the screen, which represented the evolution of the emotional dimension throughout the traversal of the level. Two screenshots taken during the annotation process can be found in Fig. 2.

We chose to have each user annotate only one of the PAD dimensions. We did this both to spare the user 3 consecutive annotations after playing a single level and to ensure the user kept in mind the dimension that he was annotating without getting confused and inadvertently mixing the dimensions. By annotating a single dimension, the user only had to remember a single definition for

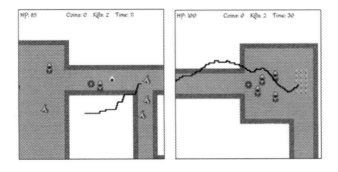

Fig. 2. Screenshots of the continuous annotation process used. The black line that is seen on the screen is controlled by the user, going up or down according to the perception the user has of the dimension being annotated increasing or decreasing, respectively.

the dimension being annotated, thus, in principle, ensuring more reliable annotations. This came, however, at the cost of having only one of the dimensions annotated for each user trace we had (Fig. 3).

3.3   Data Collection

We had 88 participants play three "Flower Hunter" levels and self report their levels of a given PAD dimension. Each participant was randomly assigned a dimension at the beginning of the experiment and given a definition of said emotional dimension. The participants could only proceed with the experiment once they confirmed that they understood the definition of their assigned emotional dimension. These participants were students of Psychology, which might enable them to more easily understand the definitions of the PAD dimension. The levels used for the experiment can be found in Fig. 4. These maps had the same topology but different distributions and quantities of objects and enemies. In the end, we collected 264 annotated traces.

3.4   Data Processing

The several input and output values were collected with a frequency of 8 Hz. To tackle the sequential nature of the data, we decided to translate the input and output into overlapping slices of 1 s each and use the variation of the values within that slice of time to train the model instead of the absolute values themselves. An exception was the input values related to the time elapsed since an event, which was fed to the model in their absolute form to allow the model to be aware of long periods of time where a given event didn't occur, for example, being aware that the player did not see an enemy in over a minute.

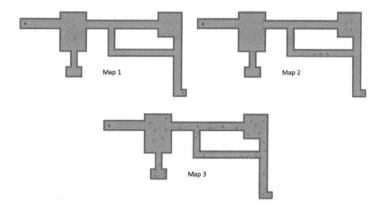

Fig. 3. The three maps used for the collection of data. As can be seen, all the maps had the same topology yet the location and amount of objects differed between them.

The output slices were further classified as "increasing" or "decreasing/stable", transforming a prediction problem into a classification one. The absolute values for the emotional dimensions varied greatly between different users and didn't provide much information by themselves. To know if an emotional dimension was increasing or not was, however, valuable information.

We then discarded all traces where there was no change to the emotional dimension throughout the entire play-through. These were the only traces that were discarded, all others being used.

Lastly, there were considerably more instances of the "decreasing/stable" class than of the "increasing" class. As such, the training data required balancing. From several methods tried, balancing using random over-sampling proved to give the best results.

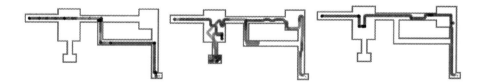

Fig. 4. Three examples of traces and self reporting for the Arousal dimension. These traces are for Map 2 and show how different users can have very different experiences depending on the traversal of the map and their own different perceptions of the reported dimension.

3.5   Prediction Results

After gathering and processing the data as described in the previous section, we were now faced with a traditional binary classification problem. We experimented with several different machine learning algorithms, such as neural networks, decision trees, and state vector machines. In the end, the random forests algorithm was the one that provided the best results.

A different predictive model had to be trained for each one of the PAD emotional dimensions. As such, we achieved a different accuracy for each dimension. The accuracy was based on the correct classification of 1-second slices using the "leave one out" method. For the Pleasure dimension, we were able to achieve an accuracy of 72.8%. For the Arousal dimension, we were able to obtain a slightly better 73.1% of accuracy. However, our approach fared considerably worse on predicting the Dominance dimension, which we were only able to predict with $\approx 60\%$ accuracy. We believe this resulted from the participants having different interpretations of what this dimension meant, leading to considerably different annotations and therefore a very noisy data set.

4   Persona-Like Behaviour for UX Testing

In the previous section, we described how we developed a model to predict emotion from a playtrace. To be able to automatically predict UX, we also need to be able to generate such playtraces automatically. We thus need to create agents that act like players. In this section of the paper, we focus on creating **persona agents**, that is, agents that represent the behaviour of a subset of players. To do so, we must first define these sub-sets of players, which will henceforth be called **persona clusters**.

A diagram of the pipeline for defining persona agents can be found in Fig. 5. To use this pipeline on any given game, four things need to be implemented: a behavioural distance metric, a clustering algorithm, a genetic agent, and an evolutionary algorithm. With these four components, player traces can be turned into persona agents. The quality and coverage of these persona agents will obviously depend on the implementation of the components as well as on the quantity and quality of collected player traces.

4.1   Behavioural Distance Metric

To define a behavioural distance metric, we must decide what constitutes similar behaviour, as the metric will attribute a value of similarity (or dissimilarity) to any given pair of player traces. It is not obvious, at least to the authors of this paper, how to define a behavioural distance metric that is the best for every single game and situation. It might be of interest to a designer to consider players that choose to go left instead of right as having different behaviours, whereas another designer, or even the same designer trying to evaluate a different thing, might prefer to consider them as the same behaviour as long as both players are "exploring".

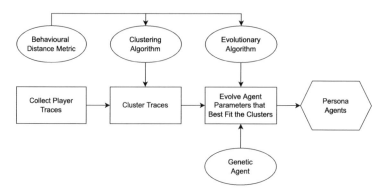

Fig. 5. Diagram of the persona agent pipeline, identifying the 4 main components that need to be implemented: a behavioural metric; a clustering algorithm; an evolutionary algorithm; and a genetic agent.

For this proof of concept, we decided to consider that players that take different routes and chose different actions when playing a level of the "Flower Hunter" game (Sect. 3.1) are behaving differently. Behaviour can then be seen as the sequence of low-level actions that a player does. We chose to consider the lowest action level, that is, the actions dictated by the keys being pressed at each of the game's time steps. A player game trace can therefore be represented by a string such as "dddwsd", meaning the player pressed the "d" key for the first three time steps, then the key "w" in the fourth, followed by the keys "s" and "d" in the fifth and sixth time steps respectively.

To match this decision, we implemented a distance metric based on the Levenshtein distance [12] between the string representation of the sequence of low-level actions. We therefore judged the similarity between two game traces based on the minimum number of edits, deletions and additions that are required to transform the string representation of one of the traces into that of another. For example, a trace represented by the string "dddwsd" has a Levenshtein distance of 4 from the trace represented by the string "wwddsdd".

4.2   Clustering Algorithm

Having settled on a metric of behavioural distance, we had now a foundation to choose the clustering algorithm we would be employing to find the persona clusters. We did not have previous knowledge that allowed us to predict the number of persona clusters we could expect to find. Therefore, we had preference for using a clustering algorithm that did not require the number of clusters to be given as a parameter. We also required clustering algorithms that did not rely on Euclidian distances and could be used with the behavioural distance metric we had previously defined. It would also be a bonus if the clustering algorithm could determine which player trace was the most representative of each persona cluster.

With the aforementioned in mind, we decided to use the affinity propagation clustering algorithm [7], as implemented by the scikit-learn python library [17]. This algorithm allows for any distance metric to be used, defines the number of clusters automatically, and returns the player trace that is most representative of each cluster. However, any other clustering algorithms that accepted the previously defined behavioural distance metric could be used instead.

4.3   Genetic Agent

A genetic agent, or parametric agent, is an agent whose behaviour is dictated by the values of a set of parameters, which can be thought of as the genome of the agent. Different sets of parameters will produce different behaviours. This encoding of the agent's behaviour into a set of parameters allows the use of evolutionary algorithms [3] as a way to find genetic agents that behave in a particular way. In this section, we will present our implementation of a genetic agent for the "Flower Hunter" game.

For the agent to represent player behaviour, we had to endow it with the ability to do that which players do. Namely, the agent had to be able to move and explore the map, fight enemies, collect items, and reach the final objective. To achieve this, we began by endowing the agent with the ability to navigate the map.

Since a player does not have access to the full map when playing a level of the "Flower Hunter" game, we decided not to give knowledge of the full map to the agent. The agent thus has to construct a map of the level as it explores. We use the game engine's collision detection to build a map for the agent as it traverses the game. We do so by creating a square object in the game of a set dimension. The dimension of this square corresponded to the granularity of the map we would generate. We then iterate this square over all non-overlapping positions on the field of view of the agent, checking at each iteration if the square collides with any object. If no collision is detected, the position of the square is added to a "free positions graph". All adjacent nodes of this graph are connected. In this way, the agent can run classical path-finding algorithms on this graph, like Dijkstra's algorithm [4], in order to navigate the level. The agent navigating the map and the generated internal navigational graph can be seen in Fig. 6.

Having a graph of the visited locations of the map, the agent is able to navigate by finding the shortest path to a given known location and following it. Having this, the agent can also reach any object it has found, including enemies. Endowing the agent with the ability to fight enemies was only a question of having the agent move toward the closest enemy and begin attacking when the enemy is within reach. Our agent is thus able to do everything required to play the game. It has no way, however, of knowing when it should do any of these things nor how it should explore the level. This will be solved by the genetic nature of the agent. Each genetic agent will have a set of parameters, the value of which will dictate the actions of the agent. The chosen parameters are the following:

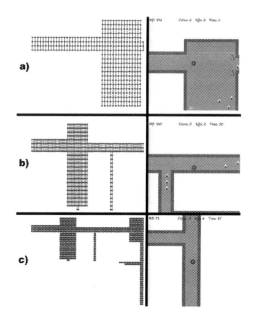

Fig. 6. A sequence of 3 moments of the agent's traversal of a level. On the left side, we can see the generated internal navigational graph of the agent, whereas, on the right side, we can see the actual position of the agent in the "Flower Hunter" game. As the agent traverses the level, it expands its navigational graph, as can be seen in the evolution from 1) to 2) to finally 3). In all of the shown navigational maps, there are still areas of the map left unexplored given that the agent has not yet visited them.

1. Objective Parameter - $\mathbf{O}_p$
2. Fighting Parameter - $\mathbf{F}_p$
3. Currency Parameter - $\mathbf{C}_p$
4. Health Item Parameter - $\mathbf{H}_p$
5. Exploration Method Parameter - $\mathbf{E}_p$

Each of these parameters can have a value $\in [0, 100]$. The first four parameters encode the preference the genetic agent will give to reaching the objective, fighting enemies, gathering currency, and gathering health items, respectively. The fifth parameter encodes the method of exploration that the agent will pursue. The remainder of this section will be dedicated to explaining how these parameters dictate the behaviour of the agent.

At any given moment, the agent can follow any of five macro-actions:

- **Reach Objective** - Go to the final objective (if the objective has been found).
- **Fight** - Fight the closest enemy (if any enemy is visible).
- **Gather Currency** - Move towards the closest currency item (if any currency item has been found and not gathered).

- **Gather Health Items** - Move towards the closest health item (if any health item has been found and not gathered).
- **Explore** - Continue exploring the level and finding new locations (if the level has not been fully explored).

Each one of these macro-actions is given a value according to the following equations:

$$V(\textbf{Reach Objective}) = \frac{\textbf{O}_p}{distance(objective)} \tag{1}$$

$$V(\textbf{Fight}) = \frac{\textbf{F}_p}{distance(enemy)} \tag{2}$$

$$V(\textbf{Gather Currency}) = \frac{\textbf{C}_p}{distance(currency)} \tag{3}$$

$$V(\textbf{Gather Health Items}) = \frac{\textbf{H}_p}{distance(health\_item)} \tag{4}$$

$$V(\textbf{Explore}) = \lambda \times \xi \tag{5}$$

with $distance(x)$ returning the distance to the nearest object of type x, λ being an exploration constant set as 0.5 for this implementation and:

$$\xi = \begin{cases} 0, & \text{if all locations in the map have been discovered} \\ 1, & \text{otherwise} \end{cases} \tag{6}$$

At each moment, the genetic agent will choose to pursue the macro-action with the greatest value, thus guided by the distance to the several game objects and its genome or set of parameters.

The only parameter not yet mentioned, $\textbf{E}_p$, dictates how the agent explores the level. When the agent decides to explore, it has to choose which of the boundary nodes on its internal map graph (Fig. 6) it should visit so as to expand its knowledge of the map. Boundary nodes are the nodes that lie at the limit of the agent's map graph whose neighbours have not been discovered, be them reachable positions, or walls. For example, in Fig. 6 a), the boundary nodes are the three rightmost nodes plus the last horizontal line of bottom nodes, since the agent still does not know what lies beyond them.

The agent will choose to explore the node that minimizes the following distance, d:

$$d = \sqrt{\left(i_x + \frac{p_x * \textbf{E}_p}{\frac{\textbf{MaxE}_p}{2}} - n_x\right)^2 + \left(i_y + \frac{p_y * \textbf{E}_p}{\frac{\textbf{MaxE}_p}{2}} - n_y\right)^2} \tag{7}$$

where (i_x, i_y) is the initial position of the player/agent on the level, (p_x, p_y) is the current position of the player, (n_x, n_y) is the position of the node that is being considered for exploration and $\textbf{MaxE}_p$ is the maximum value that $\textbf{E}_p$ can take.

In practice, if the value of $\mathbf{E}_p$ is close to 0, the agent will explore the node closest to the initial position, resembling a breadth first search algorithm. If $\mathbf{E}_p$ is close to 50, the agent will explore the node that is closest to itself. If $\mathbf{E}_p$ is close to 100, the agent will explore the node that is furthest away from both itself and the initial position.

We have thus described the genetic agent and how its genome dictates its behaviour. In the next section, we will describe the evolutionary algorithm used to find the sets of parameters that will be used for the persona agents.

4.4   Evolutionary Algorithm

Having a clustering algorithm that finds the persona clusters present on a set of player traces (Sect. 4.2) and a genetic agent that behaves differently according to its genome (Sect. 4.3), we now need a method of finding the set of parameters that dictate a behaviour that most resemble the traces found on each persona cluster. To do so, we will use an evolutionary algorithm.

For each persona cluster, we initialize a population of 300 genetic agents with random sets of parameters. At each generation, all of the agents play the same level of the "Flower Hunter" game. Their actions are recorded and compared to the action traces of the representative player trace of the persona cluster. This comparison is done using the behavioural distance metric described in Sect. 4.2. This distance is then turned negative and used to assign a fitness to each of the agents: this means that the greater the distance between the agent trace and the cluster representative trace, the lower the fitness of the agent. Once every agent has been assigned a fitness, the 30% with the highest fitness is chosen to reproduce and be a part of the next generation. The reproduction is done by randomly selecting two parent agents and randomly mixing their parameters to create a new child agent. With a 20% probability, each of the parameters can suffer a mutation take a random value. The top 30% of the population thus reproduces between itself until the population has once again 300 agents. This process is repeated for 60 generations. The agent with the set of parameters that allow it to have the best fitness in the last population is then chosen as the persona agent.

4.5   Behavioural Results

The first step of the persona agent pipeline was clustering the 88 player traces we had collected (Sect. 3.1) into clusters that represent different playing styles. Following the approach described in Sect. 4.2, we obtained 16 clusters. As can be seen in Table 1, some of these clusters have only one member, representing outliers that behaved in such a particular way that they could not be added to any of the other clusters. One of these players went around in circles multiple times whereas another went back and forth in the same corridor. We decided such traces should not be discarded from the data-set as they still represented player behaviour, however strange it might be. Other clusters have many members, like cluster number 10, which has 29 members and represents all players that went

Table 1. Persona clusters found by the clustering algorithm, along with their number of members, the fitness of the corresponding persona agent, and whether the persona agent was accepted as representing the behaviour of the cluster.

Cluster Nº	Members	Persona Agent Fitness	Accepted
1	1	−493	No
2	10	−138	Yes
3	2	−572	No
4	1	−682	No
5	10	−348	Yes
6	1	−1214	No
7	2	−536	No
8	3	−239	Yes
9	12	−185	Yes
10	29	−75	Yes
11	1	−8846	No
12	4	−377	Yes
13	1	−589	No
14	5	−190	Yes
15	8	−192	Yes
16	1	−879	No

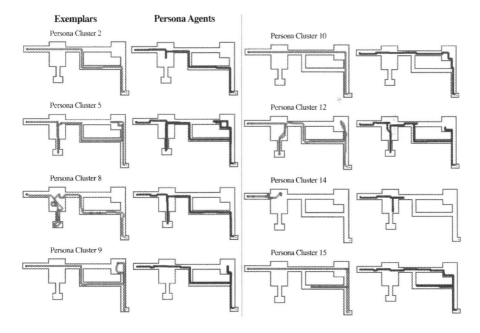

Fig. 7. Representation of the game paths taken by the persona cluster representative (left, in green) and the corresponding persona agent (right, in blue. (Color figure online)

in a straight line to the rightmost corner of the game and then straight down to the final objective (Fig. 7).

Having defined the persona clusters, we then evolved the parameters of 16 persona agents so that each one of them represented the behaviour of one of the persona clusters (Sect. 4.4). We thus obtained 16 persona agents, the fitness of which can be found in Table 1. Only agents with a fitness above −400 were considered acceptable as representatives of their persona cluster. This value was decided upon through observation: traces from agents with a fitness above −400 could not be visually spotted by the authors as outliers when compared to the player traces of the cluster they represented. The traces of the accepted persona agents can be seen next to the traces of the corresponding persona cluster representative in Fig. 7.

In the end, only half of the persona clusters were properly represented by a persona agent. However, the 8 persona agents that were accepted represented 89% of the player traces, as every cluster with more than 2 members was successfully represented. This was an unexpected result as the number of members in a cluster has no influence on the evolution of the agent, as the fitness is always calculated based only on the representative of the cluster. We believe that clusters with 2 or fewer members represent complex outlier behaviour that our agents were not able to reproduce.

5   Conclusion

In this paper, we propose two modules, one behavioural and one predictive. Used together, they create a UX testing agent that can both play a game representing different personas and predict the expected emotional outcome of such interactions.

Although the main goal is the creation of fully automatic UX testing agents, the approach here proposed still requires an initial round of data collection or data from previously done data collection rounds. Notwithstanding, once the persona agents and predictive models have been obtained, they can be used for the remainder of the game's life-cycle without requiring further data collection unless drastic changes are made to the game.

The agents developed cannot fully express all different human behaviours and the emotional prediction is still far from perfect. However, the UX testing agents here presented could already be used to gain many UX insights automatically and help developers and designers create better, more enjoyable games.

References

1. Almingol, J., Montesano, L., Lopes, M.: Learning multiple behaviors from unlabeled demonstrations in a latent controller space. In: International Conference on Machine Learning, pp. 136–144. PMLR (2013)
2. Asensio, J.M.L., Peralta, J., Arrabales, R., Bedia, M.G., Cortez, P., Peña, A.L.: Artificial intelligence approaches for the generation and assessment of believable human-like behaviour in virtual characters. Expert Syst. Appl. **41**(16), 7281–7290 (2014)
3. Bäck, T., Schwefel, H.P.: An overview of evolutionary algorithms for parameter optimization. Evol. Comput. **1**(1), 1–23 (1993)
4. Dijkstra, E.W., et al.: A note on two problems in connexion with graphs. Numer. Math. **1**(1), 269–271 (1959)
5. Drachen, A., Sifa, R., Bauckhage, C., Thurau, C.: Guns, swords and data: clustering of player behavior in computer games in the wild. In: 2012 IEEE Conference on Computational Intelligence and Games (CIG), pp. 163–170. IEEE (2012)
6. Fernandes, P.M., Lopes, M., Prada, R.: Agents for automated user experience testing. In: 2021 IEEE International Conference on Software Testing, Verification and Validation Workshops (ICSTW), pp. 247–253. IEEE (2021)
7. Frey, B.J., Dueck, D.: Clustering by passing messages between data points. Science **315**(5814), 972–976 (2007)
8. Holmgård, C., Green, M.C., Liapis, A., Togelius, J.: Automated playtesting with procedural personas through MCTS with evolved heuristics. IEEE Trans. Games **11**(4), 352–362 (2018)
9. Holmgård, C., Liapis, A., Togelius, J., Yannakakis, G.N.: Evolving models of player decision making: personas versus clones. Entertainment Comput. **16**, 95–104 (2016)
10. Lee, G., Luo, M., Zambetta, F., Li, X.: Learning a Super Mario controller from examples of human play. In: 2014 IEEE Congress on Evolutionary Computation (CEC), pp. 1–8. IEEE (2014)
11. Lee, S.J., Popović, Z.: Learning behavior styles with inverse reinforcement learning. ACM Trans. Graph. (TOG) **29**(4), 1–7 (2010)
12. Levenshtein, V.I., et al.: Binary codes capable of correcting deletions, insertions, and reversals. In: Soviet Physics Doklady, vol. 10, pp. 707–710. Soviet Union (1966)
13. Lopes, P., Yannakakis, G.N., Liapis, A.: RankTrace: relative and unbounded affect annotation. In: 2017 Seventh International Conference on Affective Computing and Intelligent Interaction (ACII), pp. 158–163. IEEE (2017)
14. Makantasis, K., Liapis, A., Yannakakis, G.N.: The pixels and sounds of emotion: general-purpose representations of arousal in games. IEEE Trans. Affect. Comput. **14**, 680–693 (2021)
15. Melhart, D., Liapis, A., Yannakakis, G.N.: The arousal video game annotation (again) dataset. IEEE Trans. Affect. Comput. **13**(4), 2171–2184 (2022)
16. Ng, A.Y., Russell, S.J., et al.: Algorithms for inverse reinforcement learning. In: ICML, vol. 1, p. 2 (2000)
17. Pedregosa, F., et al.: Scikit-learn: machine learning in Python. J. Mach. Learn. Res. **12**, 2825–2830 (2011)
18. Russell, J.A., Mehrabian, A.: Evidence for a three-factor theory of emotions. J. Res. Pers. **11**(3), 273–294 (1977)
19. Stahlke, S., Nova, A., Mirza-Babaei, P.: Artificial playfulness: a tool for automated agent-based playtesting. In: Extended Abstracts of the 2019 CHI Conference on Human Factors in Computing Systems, pp. 1–6 (2019)

20. Tastan, B., Sukthankar, G.: Learning policies for first person shooter games using inverse reinforcement learning. In: Proceedings of the AAAI Conference on Artificial Intelligence and Interactive Digital Entertainment, vol. 7, pp. 85–90 (2011)
21. Thawonmas, R., Kurashige, M., Chen, K.T., et al.: Detection of landmarks for clustering of online-game players. Int. J. Virtual Real. **6**(3), 11–16 (2007)
22. Tychsen, A., Canossa, A.: Defining personas in games using metrics. In: Proceedings of the 2008 Conference on Future Play: Research, Play, Share, pp. 73–80 (2008)
23. Wang, D., Subagdja, B., Tan, A.H., Ng, G.W.: Creating human-like autonomous players in real-time first person shooter computer games. In: Twenty-First IAAI Conference (2009)

Embraceable Virtual Paws: Player Experiences in Animal Shelter Simulator

Chien Lu[1]([✉]) [iD] and Lobna Hassan[2] [iD]

[1] Tampere University, Tampere, Finland
`chien.lu@tuni.fi`
[2] Lappeenranta-Lahti University of Technology, Lappeenranta, Finland

Abstract. This paper explores the intersection of companion animal welfare and video games by investigating the player experiences in *Animal Shelter Simulator*. A joint analysis of 925 player reviews and profiles on Steam is conducted to explore the potential of using video games to communicate sustainability in the context of companion animal welfare. Our findings reveal various aspects of player experiences and their implications including player agency, the role of achievements in the game, player-perceived emotions, and storification. Moreover, our analysis highlights the significance of interactivities and emotions in engaging players with the game's primary theme, as some players have reflected the game's theme to their real-life experiences. This connection indicates the effectiveness of using video games to communicate sustainability themes.

Keywords: Companion Animal Welfare · Player Experience · Player Typologies

1 Introduction

Games and play have become a primary cultural form of modern human society [9]. With their capabilities of storytelling and engaging players, video games have been used not only for entertainment but as an effective tool to communicate issues regarding sustainability and encourage taking real-life actions [41]. Numerous games have been widely implemented to communicate a diverse range of sustainability-related issues including climate change [48] and resource management [33]. These sustainability-theme games have been increasing in popularity.

However, anecdotal evidence suggests that players differ in their reception of these relatively new sustainability themes in games. Some highly appreciate the educational potential whereas others argue that the storification [18] of play unnecessarily imposes additional expectations of learning and teaching on players. This suggests that personalities and player types can significantly influence and determine the communication of sustainability themes in video games. Nevertheless, limited research has specifically explored whether player experiences in games have led to reflections on sustainability in the real world. Furthermore, it remains unclear which player types are more likely to engage in these reflections.

© The Author(s), under exclusive license to Springer Nature Switzerland AG 2024
L. Vale Costa et al. (Eds.): VJ 2023, CCIS 1984, pp. 19–32, 2024.
https://doi.org/10.1007/978-3-031-51452-4_2

As one crucial aspect of sustainability, animal welfare has recently gained an increasing attention as public concern over the treatment of animals has increased over time [16]. In particular, concerns regarding companion animal welfare [35] carry unique implications. Companion animals are *"an integral part of the human family and this aspect has many social and emotional implications"* [45], particularly in the context of their evolving societal roles in human-animal interactions.

This research investigates the use of games to communicate animal welfare in the context of companion animals. More specifically, we aim to understand player experiences and how they are associated with various player typologies. We aim to answer: what profiles of players are most likely to have what experiences while playing an animal welfare game? In other words, who will the game theme most resonate with? We focus on *Animal Shelter Simulator* [21], a video game that embeds companion animal welfare as its main theme. The primary task of the player is to receive rescued animals, take care of them, and finally match them to suitable adopters. A computational analysis of 925 Steam reviews and their corresponding player profiles was conducted to understand the playful experiences. Our analysis explores player experiences through the lens of player typologies, aiming to gain a deeper understanding [12]. Specifically, it examines how player characteristics are associated with their perceptions and identifies what kind of settings or content can interest certain types of players.

This paper is organized as follows. Section 2 describes the research background, including the notion of companion animal welfare, and highlights the importance of incorporating player typologies when studying player experiences; Sect. 3 describes the data collection process and the employed analytical method; Sect. 4 displays the results and Sect. 5 discusses the implications of our findings. Finally, Sect. 6 summarizes this study.

2   Background

This section offers the necessary background information for this work. We first describe the relevance of the selected game *Animal Shelter Simulator* to the focused theme of this work. The notions of player experiences and player typologies are later introduced.

2.1   Companion Animal Welfare, Video Games, and Animal Shelter Simulator

Described as *"definitely part of the social responsibility pillar of sustainability"* [22], animal welfare has been recognized as an essential component of sustainability in modern society [10,43]. While much academic effort has been focused on farm or agricultural animals for food production [7,10,43], concerns related to companion animals, or domestic pets, as well as stray animals, have gradually received an increasing attention [42]. One essential distinction of companion animals from others is that they are animals with which *"people tend to form strong anthropomorphic, attachment-based relationships*" [40]. Despite the biases resulting from anthropomorphism, it is further suggested that such anthropomorphism also has the positive potential to raise greater sensitivity to perceived welfare problems in animals, preventing the oversight of those issues.

Moreover, in the context of building sustainable cities and communities [15] and considering their impact on the environment [8], the primary challenge falls within the realm of human responsibility for enhancing animal welfare. This challenge centers around sheltering and facilitating the adoption of abandoned or unwanted companion animals [44,45]. Recently, there has been a growing emphasis on various innovations to facilitate the adoption process of rescued animals with the aim of addressing these issues [2,13,15].

Several relevant serious games have been introduced. For example, *Pet Welfare* [26] has been developed and used to educate children and promote positive child-animal interactions. *Rabbit Rescue* [47] is another playful intervention designed to educate children about rabbit behavior and their welfare needs. It's worth noting that these games are used for specific educational programs, are not commercialized, and are primarily targeted at children. Thus, they have limited access to the general public.

We empirically investigate one solution to address the aforementioned companion animal welfare issues: the use of video games to communicate to the masses about these issues to raise concerns and potentially, encourage real actions. *Animal Shelter Simulator*, released on Steam in March 2022, has been chosen in this research as the subject of our analysis. In this simulation game, the player plays the role of a rescuer-vet working in an animal shelter. The overall gameplay involves a range of tasks, such as caring for the rescued animals and finding them suitable adopters (see an example screenshot in Fig. 1). The game also contains typical features that can be found in common simulation games, including expanding the shelter and managing budgets. We selected this particular game for our study due to its well-positioned theme and its distinct focus on the welfare of rescued animals.

2.2   Player Experiences and Factorized Player Typologies

Player experience can be generally understood as what the player goes through when they play the game [19], i.e., thoughts, emotions, and meaning-making that the players have. Player experiences can vary widely and are highly personal [3], therefore, when investigating player experiences, it is worth noting that it is not sufficient if the investigation of player experiences is without considering player typologies. Player experiences can differ from one another, or at least different within player groups/types, even when they are experiencing the same game design and elements [12], different perceptions can arise from a diversity of players [25]. The notion of player typologies was originally used as a tool to segment customers (or players) based on their experiences and preferences. [5]. However, as players can and do have overlapping motivations and traits, the notion of classification has received criticism for being dichotomous and overtly simplified [23,27]. Alternative player typology frameworks have been

Fig. 1. A gameplay screenshot of *Animal Shelter Simulator* showing the main tasks at the moment (hand over the animal to new family), player action (petting the dog), and the adaptability of the dog (its health condition and level of trust in the human player).

proposed based on computational factor models, in which player typologies are considered as latent dimensions (underlying factors) of the observed variables (player behavior and experience). Hence, each player can be a composition of several different factors [20,49].

This research focuses on players on Steam as it is not only a popular digital game distribution platform but also a virtual space for online gaming communities. Besides gaming, players can also create profiles, review and rate games, and join online player groups. Various research has been conducted using the abundance of data that Steam offers [28,30]. Game reviews written by players on Steam are a valuable resource that can be utilized to understand players' experiences [31]. Apart from game reviews, Steam user profiles which contain the personal gameplay history, preferences, and game-related activities (e.g., level, badges, collected games and DLCs, shared guides, screenshots, etc.) of a player can be used to extract player typologies through the previously described factorization of players' online behavior [29].

3 Methods

This section describes an overview of the research methods used in this paper. The data collection process is first described. The Cross-structural Topic Model (CFTM) [32], which is used for analyzing the collected data is also introduced.

3.1 Data Collection

We collected data from Steam and conducted a joint analysis of game reviews and player profiles. Steam Web API[1] was used to collect game reviews and the corresponding user IDs. Later, a web crawler based on the R package `rvest` [46] was developed to collect player profiles associated with those user IDs. Data collection took place on the 10th of June, 2023. We removed excessively short reviews and 925 reviews written by players who have made their profiles public remained and were analyzed. After web parsing, each player profile contained 2 playtime variables, 12 profile variables and 42 showcase variables across 16 showcase areas such as Video ([V]), Artwork ([A]).

3.2 Data Analysis

To analyze this large amount of collected data, a computational approach called topic modeling [6] was employed. It has been a widely used method for analyzing text data to identify underlying themes or topics that are present in the collection of documents. In this study, a recently developed method called the Cross-structural Topic Model (CFTM, [32]) was used to jointly analyze player profiles and review texts. The key advantage of CFTM is that it identifies both the underlying topics and player factors from player profiles. Moreover, the interactions between the extracted topics and factors were also modeled, which provided essential aspects in our analysis.

CFTM represents each document as a mixture of latent topics and each topic is a distribution over words . The probability of a word w occurring in a document d is modeled as a sum over K topics such that $p(w|d) = \sum_{k=1}^{K} p(k|d)p(w|k)$ and $p(k|d)$ are probabilities of each topic k in the document d and $p(w|k)$ are probabilities of the words w of the topic k. CFTM further models the topic prevalences $p(k|d)$ of all K topics in a document d with a vector $\theta_d = [p(1|d), \ldots, p(K|d)]^\top$ drawn from a distribution that depends on the document-level, L-dimensional factor loadings Λ_d, so that $\boldsymbol{\theta}_d = \text{softmax}(\boldsymbol{\eta}_d)$ and

$$\boldsymbol{\eta}_{d,1:(K-1)} \sim \boldsymbol{N}(\boldsymbol{\Gamma}^\top \boldsymbol{\Lambda}_d, \boldsymbol{\Sigma}_\eta) , \tag{1}$$

where $\boldsymbol{\Sigma}_\eta$ is a covariance matrix, and $\boldsymbol{\Gamma}$ is a $L \times K$ coefficient matrix that governs the interaction between topic prevalence and document-level factor loading. The same document-level factor loading Λ_d also governs the generation of the document-level covariates, with a factorization structure such that $x_d \sim N(\Phi^\top \Lambda_d, \Sigma)$ where x_d denotes a P-dimensional covariate vector of the document d, the coefficient matrix Φ is a $L \times P$ matrix where each column Φ_p is a vector of feature weights on the L factors, and Σ is a covariance matrix.

To reduce unnecessary noise, stop words (such as "is", "this", "etc.") and rare words (words that only appear once in the corpus) were first removed. The documents were then lemmatized (e.g., "play" and "played" are lemmatized to their common lemma "play"). These pre-processing steps help improve

---

[1] https://steamcommunity.com/dev.

the performance of the model by reducing the unnecessary noise in the data and ensuring that the words are in a consistent form. The final model was decided by the value of Normalized Pointwise Mutual Information (NPMI, [1]), which measures how strongly the top words in each topic co-occur over documents. A higher NPMI value implies a better consistency between extracted topics and analyzed documents. To address the problem that common words appear in multiple topics, both the top word lists with the highest probabilities and Frex values which emphasize the exclusivity of each topic were examined. The Frex value for each word v in topic k is computed as $FREX_{k,v} = \left(\frac{\omega}{ECDF(\beta_{k,v}/\sum_{j=1}^{K} \beta_{j,v})} + \frac{1-\omega}{ECDF(\beta_{k,v})} \right)^{-1}$ where $ECDF(\cdot)$ denotes the empirical cumulative distribution function (proportion of items smaller than the value inside the parentheses). The parameter ω, is used to balance the frequency and exclusivity of the word, and here is set to $\omega = 0.5$.

4   Results

After the model training and selection, we arrived at 5 topics and 5 factors that achieved the highest NPMI value. These are presented in this section.

Table 1. Extracted topics. Pr (%) is the average topic probability over documents.

Topic (Pr%)	Top 10 Words
Updates & Fixes (31.2)	[P]update fix file steam week suggest folder patch issue thank
	[F]update fix file steam issue patch save release thank suggest
Interactions & Emotions (27.6)	[P]worker bother stuff hello candidate send adorable stray cute sad
	[F]worker stuff adorable cute send candidate sad love bother perfect
Tasks in Gameplay (19.1)	[P]bag cleanliness dirty stack result enclosure adopter trash brush hygiene
	[F]enclosure cleanliness adopter building clean completely kennel bag toy place
Limits & Suggestions (13.4)	[P]fat sun limit aspect ability owner set size loop reptile
	[F]fat sun limit aspect owner ability set breed lol reptile
Review Template (8.5)	[P]good bad spare paint average hear audience potato grind audio
	[F]good bad spare average paint hear grind audience potato audio

4.1   Extracted Topics

Table 1 shows the 5 extracted topics, with the top 10 words with the highest probabilities ([P]) and Frex values ([F]) for each topic. Topic labels were given by examining the word lists and example documents (reviews with a high prevalence of a topic). This process is similar to "coding" procedures in Thematic analysis [17].

Among the extracted topics, **Updates & Fixes** (with words "update", "fix', and "issue", etc.) is the most prevalent topic, which primarily reflects encountered problems and issues during gameplay. As a game review mentioned: "*I waited a few more updates before playing it again. They have fixed the lag issues...2 updates ago you couldn't even play it without frame drops, and other game-breaking bugs...*". The comment expressed the concerns about the game's playability.

On the other hand, the topic **Limitations & Suggestions** reveals players' expectations of improved freedom in the game. For example, one player wrote: "*...Essentially the building aspect is very limited at the moment and needs more customization and more building types...ability to customise those buildings and more complex animal types...*". This quote mentioned the limitation and expressed the expectations of more opportunities for customization in the game.

The topic **Interactions & Emotions** reflects the process of meaning-making, emotional response to the game, and its potential real-life impact on the player. E.g., One player wrote in the review: "*I liked how cute the animals are and it is so much fun to take care of the animals but just don't get to attached to them because it gets really sad when they go...*", which illustrates how the game engaged the player and created the bond between the player and the rescued animals in game. Another player also alleged: "*Super cute game but I am emotional...sad for all the real-life animals that are in shelters needing adopted...*". This player's reflection has gone beyond gaming and has extended to the reflection on real-life concerns regarding animal welfare.

The topic **Tasks in Gameplay** with top words including "cleanliness", and "enclosure", reflects the core game mechanic of actual gameplay in *Animal Shelter Simulator*. As a player detailed: "*If your animal uses the bathroom in their enclosure you'll need to clean it...disposed of with a poop bag...Being in a dirty enclosure with bathroom waste will cause their hygiene to decline much faster...*". Lastly, the topic **Review Template** of the lowest prevalence (8.55%) contains common words such as "good", "bad", "audio" represent reviews that use standardized, off-the-rack templates for game reviews.

4.2   Extracted Player Factors

Table 2[2] displays the 5 extracted player factors and their corresponding weights on different profile variables. The average prevalence (%) of factors in players'

---

[2] Abbreviations in Table 2: [PT] Playtime [GC] Game Collection [F] Favorite Game [A] Award [AC] Achievement [C] Completionist [B] Badge [S] Screenshot [AR] Artwork [FA] Featured Artwork [W] Workshop [V] Video [FI] Favorite Items [I] Items [IT] Items for Trade [G] Guide [FG] Favorite Guide [FG'] Favorite Group.

profiles is also provided. Each player's profile is a combination of various factors, the average prevalence of a factor is its average weight in the combinations across players.

The name of each factor is given by analyzing the weights on the profile variables. Specifically, the player factor **Collector** represents players who are into possessing and trading items and games. **Perfectionist** depicts players who are active in perfecting their profiles and achievements. **Elite** describes players who put more effort maintaining and accumulating profile capitals (e.g., Level, Badges, etc.) The primary distinction between **Perfectionist** and **Elite** is that **Perfectionist** focuses more on the personal perfection, whereas **Elite** emphasizes overall records in their profile, especially social aspects (e.g., Friends, Guides, etc.) **Social Artist** further represents players who are into artworks and interacting with other players (e.g., participating in groups and creating guides). Finally, **Enthusiast** factor characterizes players that have spent more time on *Animal Shelter Simulator* than others.

4.3 Topics Vs. Player Factors

As mentioned, CFTM is able to model the interactions between the extracted topics and player types. Figure 2 displays the influences of player types on topic prevalence. In particular, **Social Artist** and **Enthusiast** are associated with topic **Updates & Fixes**. Player factors **Perfectionist** and **Elite** are associated with the topic **Interactions & Emotions**. Player factors **Social Artist** and **Elite** are associated with the topic **Tasks in Gameplay**. Player factors **Collect** and **Perfectionist** are associated with the topic **Limitations and Suggestions**. Finally, player factors **Collect** and **Enthusiast** are associated with topic **Review Template**.

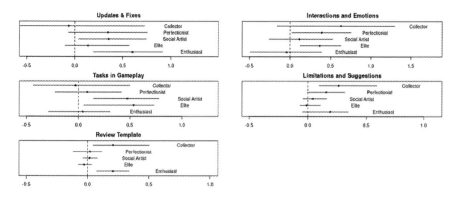

Fig. 2. Factor Influences on Topic Prevalence. The posterior mean (dot) and credible interval (line) are simulated following a standard process [39] to highlight how much the topic prevalence is affected by the player factors in game reviews.

Table 2. Feature weights on factors

Factor	Collector	Perfectionist	Social Artist	Elite	Enthusiast
(Pr%)	(17.5)	(19.2)	(17.73%)	(20.1)	(25.4)
[PT] At Review	−16.07	−3.95	−0.29	4.46	10.80
[PT] Total	−17.14	−2.95	0.27	4.02	10.74
Level	1.46	4.68	4.05	10.69	−15.85
Profile Awards	−3.66	4.97	4.75	4.27	−7.93
Badges	−1.30	−3.20	1.34	19.16	−12.76
Games	11.49	−1.83	10.62	1.23	−14.97
Screenshots	−7.00	−11.46	−1.21	18.88	−0.55
Reviews	6.46	−2.43	−4.94	16.69	−12.37
Groups	−4.30	−3.69	15.23	6.78	−10.24
Games	11.36	−3.55	−5.94	18.46	−15.62
Friends	−8.68	−6.20	9.02	14.07	−6.72
Workshop Items	0.08	−13.83	0.53	21.39	−6.85
Artwork	5.60	−5.43	10.99	4.21	−10.77
Guides	−8.30	−7.32	0.69	15.56	−1.48
[GC] Games Owned	10.81	−4.12	−6.74	19.47	−15.04
[GC] DLC Owned	5.55	7.16	−1.81	6.74	−13.33
[GC] Reviews	5.12	−2.46	−5.66	17.63	−11.66
[GC] Wishlisted	2.60	9.23	−4.43	4.89	−9.57
[FG] Hours played	−6.40	−0.50	3.91	5.91	−2.59
[FG] Achievements	−1.38	5.57	0.43	4.42	−7.07
[A] Awards Received	−13.17	−4.59	5.95	15.88	−4.12
[A] Awards Given	−12.17	−13.51	16.39	14.98	−4.62
[AC] Achievements	−5.78	4.55	−0.24	8.41	−5.93
[AC] Perfect Games	−9.99	7.52	1.23	7.19	−5.34
[AC] Avg. Game Completion Rate	−5.07	7.61	3.43	4.04	−7.86
[C] Perfect Games	−11.46	6.81	1.99	6.97	−4.12
[C] Achievements in Perfect Games	−11.71	3.49	2.64	8.27	−2.92
[B] Total Badges Earned	−11.19	−4.83	2.23	20.47	−6.33
[B] Game Cards	−2.57	9.68	−4.56	5.11	−6.41
[B] Foil Badges Earned	−10.68	−8.94	12.08	10.20	−2.33
[S] Up Votes	4.29	−0.67	12.39	0.03	−11.14
[S] Number	−4.60	5.81	8.29	−1.62	−5.74
[S] Comments	−3.46	7.73	6.88	−4.36	−4.82
[S] Favorites	−5.25	7.69	9.93	−4.40	−5.67
[AR] Up Votes	1.50	−5.38	13.16	3.89	−9.23
[AR] Number	−10.56	−10.44	13.33	9.64	−1.71
[AR] Comments	−5.94	−7.46	19.56	0.93	−4.64
[AR] Favorites	−10.89	−9.70	12.11	9.33	−0.94
[FA] Up Votes	−4.31	−2.35	8.03	7.17	−6.51
[FA] Comments	−10.31	−11.13	15.70	9.08	−2.58
[FA] Favorites	−5.67	−6.72	18.31	0.22	−3.95
[FA] Number	−4.99	−6.76	18.81	0.26	−4.78
[W] Submissions	3.38	2.14	1.58	−0.05	−5.03
[W] Followers	−1.14	3.85	−0.80	2.11	−3.24
[V] Up Votes	−10.30	−13.96	−1.51	23.33	0.33
[V] Number	−14.53	−13.74	10.14	17.55	−0.48
[V] Comments	−15.16	−14.41	8.53	19.82	−0.21
[I] Items Owned	29.12	−5.90	−6.03	9.91	−19.31
[IT] Items Owned	30.62	−7.65	−7.21	9.97	−18.24
[IT] Trades Made	35.37	−8.17	−6.78	6.15	−18.42
[IT] Market Transactions	34.34	−8.54	−6.76	7.40	−18.42
[G] Guides	−10.48	−12.11	−2.09	23.07	−0.34
[G] Followers	−10.19	−9.47	−2.46	21.56	−1.09
[FG] Stars	−0.22	5.09	8.76	−2.78	−7.64
[FG] Ratings	0.60	2.15	6.57	−2.28	−4.84
[FG'] Members	−1.50	6.86	−4.30	2.99	−3.52

5   Discussion

5.1   Player Agency in Games

Player agency can be understood as *"the satisfying power to take meaningful action and see the results of our decisions and choices"* [34]. It has long been recognized as a prominent element in game studies, especially when it comes to understanding player experiences [14]. The topic **Limitations and Suggestions** can be seen as supporting the importance of player agency in the overall players' experiences of *Animal Shelter Simulator*. It indicates that players have sought better agency in gameplay and have positively received game improvements in this regard. Its association with player factors **Collector** and **Perfectionist** can be attributed to these player characteristics being more mastery-motivated with intentions to seek more ways to exercise their agency and master the game.

On the other hand, the high prevalence of the topic **Updates & Fixes** which reflects the dissatisfaction of players, could be due to the game still being in its early stage of development. It also indicates that the game may have undergone a series of updates and patches to reach a certain level of playability. Since the game is still undergoing continuous development, there might still be room for incorporating player feedback to improve the game in future updates. This topic is associated with the player factor **Enthusiast**, suggesting that players that are more experienced in the game tend to be more passionate about suggesting such improvements.

5.2   The Role of Achievements

Tasks and missions are the core gameplay elements in *Animal Shelter Simulator*. From maintaining the shelter, and taking care of animals, to arranging adoptions, players are essentially required to complete a variety of achievement activities [38]. It is worth noting that successfully matching rescued animals to potential adopters is the key achievement a player can attain in the game, and they earn the reputation and money required to progress in the game through the process. To make a successful match, players have to carefully process the information provided in the adoption applications and decide if the traits of the rescued animal fit the potential adopter. The process can be seen as a process of cultivating animal-oriented empathy [37].

The topic **Tasks in Gameplay** indicates that players have reflected on the process of running a virtual shelter which was designed to simulate the operations of a real-life shelter. Achievement seems to motivate the players to examine the shelter tasks more closely to figure out how to master them and attain achievements. This process potentially leads to players learning about real-life animal welfare. Besides, the association with player types **Elite** and **Social Artist** may reflect the characteristics of the tasks in the game. Those tasks are not only about individual-level success but bear a resemblance to the notion of social responsibilities. Thus, they can impress or resonate with players who are motivated by relatedness or a sense of belonging.

5.3   Beyond 'Having Fun': Emotions, Meaning Making, and Storification

The topic **Interaction and Emotions** illustrates how emotional narratives play a crucial role in engaging players with the game's theme. It is worth noting that emotionally engaging players have also been employed as a strategy in communicating other issues related to sustainability-related issues [36]. We can not make informed decisions on whether the theme in the game was utilized to intentionally communicate about animal welfare through a "serious game"-like design, or if the theme was merely out of the developers' interests. Nevertheless, we can read this game as an attempt to incorporate storification of companion animal welfare. Storification is an approach that wraps an activity (in this case learning about animal welfare) in a story (running a shelter) [18], and can often be a part of games [24]. Empirical evidence from classrooms shows that such storification can create an emotional connection and active engagement, leading to better learning outcomes and a lasting impact [4].

Indeed, within this study, we have empirically observed that reviews mention emotional reactions to the game and explicitly connect these emotions to real-world animal shelters. Notably, previous studies on farm animal welfare have also emphasized the importance of empathy and compassion [11]. Our analysis further corroborates the findings that interactive activities can enhance welfare knowledge and promote positive human-animal interactions [26,47]. This study shows that similar results may be expected from games, as previously theorized [24], given that players often express emotional reactions associated with reflections on real-world issues related to animal welfare.

The association of this topic with the extracted typologies further suggest that the length of time players spend with the game may not necessarily make an impact on their internalization of the game's "key messages", as **Enthusiast** is not positively associated with this topic. Instead, it is associated with player factors **Perfectionist** and **Elite**. One possible explanation can be related to the link between animal-oriented empathy and pet ownership. Previous research has discovered a positive association between animal-oriented empathy and pet ownership [37]. As both factors tend to have higher ownership-driven variables (e.g., DLC owned, Wishlisted, etc.), this motivation can possibly be connected to the ownership of the "virtual animals" in the game. However, the discovered associations can also indicate that other potential factors, such as a drive towards achievement and completion that may be better predictors or contributors of such engagement with the sustainability theme. Overall, although the player experiences reflected in the reviews indicate that such transference communication results have taken place, the reasons and a more detailed mechanism still need more investigation in future research.

6   Conclusion, Limitation and Opportunities

This study investigates player experiences of *Animal Shelter Simulator* to explore the potential of using games to communicate companion animal welfare. The game focuses on rescuing animals and matching them to suitable adopters, making it a highly relevant example for studying the use of digital games in communicating such issues. By leveraging the player profile data, we further incorporate the notions of player typologies and achieve a more granular understanding of player experiences.

Our analysis indicates that players have expressed their emotions resulting from their interactions with the virtual animals in the game and reflected on real-world animal welfare issues. Overall, this research sheds light on the promising potential of using a commercialized video game to communicate sustainability issues.

However, as the game is still in its early stage, the analysis can provide a limited understanding of the overall player experiences. Another limitation is that player profiles were collected at a single time point. Since player profiles can change and evolve dynamically, the extracted factors can be only interpreted as proxies but are insufficient to capture the complexity of player typologies.

Nevertheless, our analysis has discovered meaningful aspects of discussions in the game reviews, highlighting the importance of player agency, in-game achievements, and the emotional impact of storification on active reflection on animal welfare issues. We expect this study can offer insights for future game design and research in terms of communicating animal welfare through games and the important role emotional narrative can play in this regard.

References

1. Aletras, N., Stevenson, M.: Evaluating topic coherence using distributional semantics. In: Proceedings of the 10th International Conference on Computational Semantics, IWCS 2013, Long Papers, pp. 13–22 (2013)
2. Alsuwailem, R., Almobarak, R., Aboali, R., Alrubaiea, S., Aldossary, J.: Leen: web-based platform for pet adoption. In: 2022 IEEE IAS Global Conference on Emerging Technologies (GlobConET), pp. 775–780. IEEE (2022)
3. Arrasvuori, J., Boberg, M., Holopainen, J., Korhonen, H., Lucero, A., Montola, M.: Applying the PLEX framework in designing for playfulness. In: Proceedings of the 2011 Conference on Designing Pleasurable Products and Interfaces, pp. 1–8 (2011)
4. Aura, I., Hassan, L., Hamari, J.: Teaching within a story: understanding storification of pedagogy. Int. J. Educ. Res. **106**, 101728 (2021)
5. Bartle, R.: Hearts, clubs, diamonds, spades: players who suit muds. J. MUD Res. **1**(1), 19 (1996)
6. Blei, D.M., Ng, A.Y., Jordan, M.I.: Latent Dirichlet allocation. J. Mach. Learn. Res. **3**, 993–1022 (2003)
7. Broom, D.M.: Animal welfare: an aspect of care, sustainability, and food quality required by the public. J. Vet. Med. Educ. **37**(1), 83–88 (2010)
8. Broom, D.M.: Animal welfare complementing or conflicting with other sustainability issues. Appl. Anim. Behav. Sci. **219**, 104829 (2019)
9. Buckingham, D., Burn, A.: Game literacy in theory and practice. J. Educ. Multimedia Hypermedia **16**(3), 323–349 (2007)
10. Buller, H., Blokhuis, H., Jensen, P., Keeling, L.: Towards farm animal welfare and sustainability. Animals **8**(6), 81 (2018)

11. Burich, L., Williams, J.M.: Children's welfare knowledge of and empathy with farm animals: a qualitative study. Anthrozoös **33**(2), 301–315 (2020)
12. Busch, M., et al.: Using player type models for personalized game design-an empirical investigation. IxD&A **28**, 145–163 (2016)
13. Campanilla, B.S., Etcuban, J.O., Maghanoy, A.P., Nacua, P.A.P., Galamiton, N.S.: Pet adoption app to free animal shelters. J. Positive Sch. Psychol. **6**(8), 5993–6006 (2022)
14. Carstensdottir, E., Kleinman, E., Williams, R., Seif El-Nasr, M.S.: "naked and on fire": examining player agency experiences in narrative-focused gameplay. In: Proceedings of the 2021 CHI Conference on Human Factors in Computing Systems, pp. 1–13 (2021)
15. Chang, M., Cañarte, G.: Agapet: supporting a responsible adoption process for stray and abandoned pets in urban areas. In: Extended Abstracts of the 2023 CHI Conference on Human Factors in Computing Systems, pp. 1–5 (2023)
16. Clark, B., Stewart, G.B., Panzone, L.A., Kyriazakis, I., Frewer, L.J.: A systematic review of public attitudes, perceptions and behaviours towards production diseases associated with farm animal welfare. J. Agric. Environ. Ethics **29**(3), 455–478 (2016)
17. Cooper, H.E., Camic, P.M., Long, D.L., Panter, A., Rindskopf, D.E., Sher, K.J.: APA Handbook of Research Methods in Psychology, Vol 1: Foundations, Planning, Measures, and Psychometrics. American Psychological Association (2012)
18. Deterding, S.: Make-believe in gameful and playful design. In: Turner, P., Harviainen, J.T. (eds.) Digital Make-Believe. HIS, pp. 101–124. Springer, Cham (2016). https://doi.org/10.1007/978-3-319-29553-4_7
19. Ermi, L., Mäyrä, F.: Fundamental components of the gameplay experience: analysing immersion. In: DiGRA Conference. Citeseer (2005)
20. Fritz, B., Stöckl, S.: Why do we play? Towards a comprehensive player typology. Games Culture, 15554120221094844 (2022)
21. Games Incubator: Animal Shelter Simulator (2022)
22. Grandin, T.: Improving Animal Welfare: A Practical Approach. CABI (2020)
23. Hamari, J., Tuunanen, J.: Player types: a meta-synthesis (2014)
24. Hassan, L., Deterding, S., Harviainen, J.T., Hamari, J.: Fighting post-truth with fiction. Storyworlds J. Narrative Stud. **11**(1), 51–78 (2019)
25. Hassan, L., Rantalainen, J., Xi, N., Pirkkalainen, H., Hamari, J.: The relationship between player types and gamification feature preferences (2020)
26. Hawkins, R., Scottish Society for the Prevention of Cruelty to Animals, Williams, J.M.: The development and pilot evaluation of a 'serious game' to promote positive child-animal interactions. Hum. Anim. Interact. Bull. **8**, 68–92 (2020)
27. Kallio, K.P., Mäyrä, F., Kaipainen, K.: At least nine ways to play: approaching gamer mentalities. Games Cult. **6**(4), 327–353 (2011)
28. Kang, H.N., Yong, H.R., Hwang, H.S.: A study of factors influencing helpfulness of game reviews: analyzing steam game review data. J. Korea Game Soc. **17**(3), 33–44 (2017)
29. Li, X., Lu, C., Peltonen, J., Zhang, Z.: A statistical analysis of steam user profiles towards personalized gamification. In: 3rd International GamiFIN Conference, GamiFIN 2019. CEUR-WS (2019)
30. Lin, D., Bezemer, C.P., Zou, Y., Hassan, A.E.: An empirical study of game reviews on the steam platform. Empir. Softw. Eng. **24**(1), 170–207 (2019)
31. Lu, C., Li, X., Nummenmaa, T., Zhang, Z., Peltonen, J.: Patches and player community perceptions: analysis of no man's sky steam reviews. In: Proceedings of the 2020 DiGRA International Conference, DiGRA 2020. DiGRA (2020)

32. Lu, C., Peltonen, J., Nummenmaa, T., Nummenmaa, J., Järvelin, K.: Cross-structural factor-topic model: document analysis with sophisticated covariates. In: Asian Conference on Machine Learning, pp. 1129–1144. PMLR (2021)

33. Mittal, A., Scholten, L., Kapelan, Z.: A narrative review of serious games for urban water management decisions: current gaps and future research directions. Water Res. **215**, 118217 (2022)

34. Murray, J.H.: Hamlet on the Holodeck, Updated Edition: The Future of Narrative in Cyberspace. MIT Press (2017)

35. Odendaal, J.: Science-based assessment of animal welfare: companion animals. Revue scientifique et technique-Office international des épizooties **24**(2), 493 (2005)

36. Ouariachi, T., Olvera-Lobo, M.D., Gutiérrez-Pérez, J., Maibach, E.: A framework for climate change engagement through video games. Environ. Educ. Res. **25**(5), 701–716 (2019)

37. Paul, E.S.: Empathy with animals and with humans: are they linked? Anthrozoös **13**(4), 194–202 (2000)

38. Pekrun, R.: The control-value theory of achievement emotions: assumptions, corollaries, and implications for educational research and practice. Educ. Psychol. Rev. **18**, 315–341 (2006)

39. Roberts, M.E., Stewart, B.M., Tingley, D.: stm: an R package for structural topic models. J. Stat. Softw. **91**, 1–40 (2019)

40. Serpell, J.A.: How happy is your pet? The problem of subjectivity in the assessment of companion animal welfare. Anim Welf. **28**(1), 57–66 (2019)

41. Stanitsas, M., Kirytopoulos, K., Vareilles, E.: Facilitating sustainability transition through serious games: a systematic literature review. J. Clean. Prod. **208**, 924–936 (2019)

42. Steiger, A.: Pet animals: housing, breeding and welfare. In: Animal Welfare, pp. 111–133 (2006)

43. Tucker, C., Mench, J., Keyserlingk, M.v.: Animal welfare: an integral component of sustainability. In: Sustainable Animal Agriculture, pp. 42–52. CABI, Wallingford, UK (2013)

44. Turner, P., Berry, J., MacDonald, S.: Animal shelters and animal welfare: raising the bar. Can. Vet. J. **53**(8), 893 (2012)

45. Verga, M., Michelazzi, M.: Companion animal welfare and possible implications on the human-pet relationship. Ital. J. Anim. Sci. **8**(sup1), 231–240 (2009)

46. Wickham, H.: rvest: easily harvest (scrape) web pages (2022). https://rvest.tidyverse.org/. https://github.com/tidyverse/rvest

47. Williams, J.M., Cardoso, M.P., Zumaglini, S., Finney, A.L., SSPCA, Knoll, M.A.: "Rabbit Rescuers": a school-based animal welfare education intervention for young children. Anthrozoös **35**(1), 55–73 (2022)

48. Wu, J.S., Lee, J.J.: Climate change games as tools for education and engagement. Nat. Clim. Chang. **5**(5), 413–418 (2015)

49. Yee, N.: Motivations for play in online games. Cyberpsychol. Behav. **9**(6), 772–775 (2006)

Livestreaming Games and Parenthood: Exploring the Experience of Portuguese Parent Streamers

Carina de Assunção[1]([⊠]) [iD], Michael James Scott[1] [iD], and Rory K. Summerley[2] [iD]

[1] Falmouth University, Falmouth, UK
carina.assuncao@falmouth.ac.uk
[2] London South Bank University, London, UK
summerlr@lsbu.ac.uk

Abstract. Streaming games is increasingly popular amongst people of childbearing age. So, what happens when streamers become parents? There are few accounts, scarce advice and a dearth of research. Streaming seems incompatible with parenting due to its tensions with familial responsibilities. However, it is also conceivable that parent and gamer identities can be reconciled to yield successful outcomes. This exploratory study investigates the identity and experience of parent streamers. Six parent streamers, mothers and fathers from an online Portuguese community, were interviewed. Thematic analysis revealed several foci: (i) the difficulty of managing time effectively; (ii) the tension between work and play; (iii) the parent streamer identity (particularly, differences between mothers and fathers); (iv) the criticality of familial support; (v) the increasingly complex relationship between parents and games; (vi) children's interference in streaming practices; and (vii) the benefits of streaming including communal connection and improved mental health. These findings highlight how online media increasingly challenges the way in which modern parents navigate parenthood and their own personal lives. They also pave the way for evidence-led guidance that can support parent steamers.

Keywords: Streaming · Parent gamer · Twitch

1 Introduction

There is a perception that, normally, parenting and playing video games are mutually exclusive; particularly, in the early months of a child's life. Becoming a parent is a life-changing event. Leisure time is typically sacrificed to the demands of parenthood [8]. There is also a moral responsibility to protect youths from violent media [6], even if the underlying concerns are mired in controversy and perhaps overstated [17]. However, these norms of parents themselves could now be brought into question with a new generation of *parent streamers* [20].

Streamers are people who broadcast themselves and activity on their computers in real-time across social multimedia platforms such as YouTube and

© The Author(s), under exclusive license to Springer Nature Switzerland AG 2024
L. Vale Costa et al. (Eds.): VJ 2023, CCIS 1984, pp. 33–48, 2024.
https://doi.org/10.1007/978-3-031-51452-4_3

Twitch [18]. Typically, they convey their own content, which may consist of them playing a game. Since the technology enables viewers to perceive what the streamer is experiencing and communicate with them via text, they can interact with their viewers in a live fashion. Many streamers monetise their channel, receiving commissions or donations. Success correlates with the size of the audience a streamer can attract [12], and given the scalable nature of these platforms it can be lucrative [19].

There is an increasing number of people, of childbearing age, setting up streams [14] and many such established social media influencers are now becoming parents [2]. Hence, the term: *parent streamers*. However, parenting and streaming yield an apparent contradiction. Reportedly, feelings of guilt are common amongst parent gamers [11], and it could be presumed that such feelings would inhibit the decision to play or stream. Yet, investment in digital identity and incentives to cultivate a following [16] potentially spur further streaming.

With little literature exploring their experience, there is scarce guidance and few accounts to learn from. Given the increasing prominence of the medium, and its ease of setup as an at-home business [18], the present investigation is timely. As such, this initial study explores how parent and gamer identities are being negotiated and reconciled (if at all) in the context of gameplay live streaming and content creation.

2   Literature Review

Prior work on the relationship between games and family seems to assume that parents seldom play games recreationally themselves [7]. It is, understandably, a difficult site to navigate. Finding a moment to play is a challenge. Furthermore, many societies subscribe to the convention that video games are a negative influence. For example, games are often a candidate in scrutinising disruptive behaviour [4].

Whilst the justification for play has been a persistent social question, given an ageing population that played video games as young children, there seems to be a shift towards permissiveness. More nuanced discussions about the effects of video games paint a picture of effects that can be beneficial as well as detrimental [10]. It is the content that matters. This raises interesting questions about whether parents who stream the games they play gravitate towards particular content. For example, would parents stream a game they consider to be child-friendly whilst their family is present and potentially able to interrupt a stream? Would parents stream a game with mature content when this risk is very low? This plays into guilt as a potential factor in parents' decision-making process [11]. It is reflective of a potential conflict between advocating and blaming play in different situations.

It also relates to the notion of what a "good" parent does, with Aarsand's research [1] suggesting that gatekeeping playtime is a key facet to this end. If the parent plays a lot by themselves, this may be in conflict with a common conceptualisation of bad parenting. Notionally, they ought to exemplify resilience in the face of temptation rather than encouraging media consumption. However, parenting and streaming are not necessarily only compatible in the absence of moral fibre. Many parents now inform and discuss media consumption with their children. Nevertheless, striving to be a good role model likely weighs on decisions around play as well as streaming play.

Many people stream for fun or a sense of community. However, many also aim to derive an income, whether full-time or supplementary. Johnson and Woddcock [14] identify two major routes into streaming. These are: (i) esports, engaging in professional competition to provide content for fans; and (ii) variety stream-ing, playing different types of games on a regular basis. Typically, on Twitch. Other routes include participating in online communities that overlap but aren't exclusively gaming, such as creating content for YouTube or Reddit.

Tension between leisure and labour is a prevalent concern for most streamers. Streaming can be managed around a full-time job, and while exhausting, some report being driven to do it for passion. However, a typical parent's schedule, especially with young children, is prohibitive. A similar tension exists between the competing social and commercial motivations of parent influencers in blog-ging or social media contexts [3]. Torhonen et al. [22] have examined 'playbour' in more detail including its risks to the streamer's own wellbeing when juggling full-time work or studies:

> This level of work-like activity may lead to negative effects such as exhaus-tion and even depression, which have already been reported by some pop-ular YouTubers and live-streamers

The perception of streaming as casual entertainment focused around play may sometimes obscure this nature. A considerable amount of labour goes into streaming. It is a type of attention economy where audience members are scarce and fickle for all but the well-established career streamers. It becomes a commit-ment that streamers feel invested in. This likely changes as audiences become sufficiently large to facilitate going full-time as approaches to streaming are adapted in terms of the time spent per week and the expectations of income generated from it.

For a parent streamer, this labour is presumably intensified. Time is a more precious resource. Streaming thus brings pressures which are likely magnified through a parental identity and responsibility. Johnson [13] notes that there is still relatively little knowledge about the off-camera labour of streamers and this is particularly true of parent streamers. It may be that of a neoliberal work ethic where hard work is rewarded [14].

In their study on Norwegian 'gamer-parents', Sørenssen et al. [20] categorise the identity of gamer-parents into three domains: outsiders, involved, and repre-sentatives of game culture. Gamer-parents are seen as inheriting general gamer identity traits such as those associated with being outside of the mainstream. This is balanced by the parental identity which often leads them to be involved with their child's play of video games as well as being considered a relative expert by non-gaming parents. As a result, gamer-parents are not primarily gamers who happen to be parents or parents who also play games but have a distinct hybrid identity. One which practices parenting in a self-identified distinct way due to the benefit of their experience and prior identity as a player.

There are famous streamers who achieved fame and success on platforms like Twitch and Youtube who then much later became parents e.g. Maximillian'MaximillianDood' Christensen or Felix'PewDiePie' Kjellberg. These cases tend to be considered for their streaming identity primarily and even they do not feature in case studies that place the emphasis on parental identity. Career streamers who later became parents are also typically much more financially stable and not representative of the norm for most parent streamers. Another comparable example is influencers who involve children/family as part of their work though this tends to be cases where parents involve their adult children in a traditional family business model that has a media component [2], or more dubious cases where an influencer extensively documents the daily activities of their young child on social media [3].

Given the performance skills and work-life balance requirements inherent to streaming, it is likely that streaming complicates the hybrid identity of parent-gamers further as they become parent streamers'. Parent streamers presumably feature traits, considerations, and practices that reflect their unique life situations. From the initial review of how parental, streaming, and gaming identities intersect with labour and leisure, it is clear more research is needed to understand the unique challenges and contexts parent streamers face.

3   Method

To understand the experience of parent streamers, primary engagement is crucial. This research adopted a qualitative approach, examining the identity, motivation, and experience of parent streamers. The authors interviewed six parent streamers (three fathers and three mothers, none related) who were recruited via virtual [5] snowball sampling [9] from a relatively small online community of Portuguese gamers. The method was adapted to use Discord servers[1] rather than Facebook. Initially, known parent streamers who featured the fact they were parents as part of their outward-facing brand were contacted. These initial contacts were with Portuguese streamers. Given that the Portuguese gaming scene is understudied [23], the work thus focused on this population, as recruitment evolved through snowball sampling. Only one of the authors was able to conduct the interviews in Portuguese and thus translate the data. Due to this, and to the small sample size, intercoder reliability testing was not performed. Each interview lasted between 45 min to an hour and ten minutes.

The interviews were semi-structured to facilitate a free-form exchange whilst providing anchors to enable comparison, such as their motivation to play and stream. Thematic analysis [21] was used to explore and identify themes. The coding was a mix of deductive and inductive coding. This is because some themes

---

[1] Discord is an instant messaging and VoIP platform which many streamers use to create communities around their practice.

could be presumed ahead of time which were covered in the literature review. Labour and leisure issues were common for many streamers and gamer parents relating to their own parent-gamer identity as well as the logistics of time management were unavoidable talking points for most participants. Meanwhile other topics were inductively coded as the goal of the research is primarily exploratory, to examine what new information might be revealed by interviewing this specific group. Given the small dataset and more exploratory qualitative goals, reliability testing was not done to verify quantitative assessment of what were clearly prevalent themes in the corpus.

Interviewees were anonymised in accordance with institutional guidelines and recommendations from ethical review. A brief biography for each participant is provided below:

- PT1 is a 39-year-old married father of two children (11 and 4-years-old). He has a full-time job and he started streaming during the covid-19 pandemic as a way to stay connected with friends and meet new people to play with. His channel has the word 'dad' in it.
- PT2 is a 37-year-old married father of a four-year-old girl, with a Twitch channel of the same age. He is unemployed and emigrated to another country within Europe. He and his daughter have a rare heart disease. The illness causes fatigue and tiredness and due to this, his streaming is inconsistent.
- PT3 is a 33-year-old father of a four-year-old boy. He has a full-time job and has been creating gameplay content and livestreaming on Youtube for about a year. The branding has the term 'pai' ('father' in Portuguese) in it. He got inspired by his partner who, besides having a full-time job, is also a content creator.
- PT4 is a 35-year-old married mother of a 12-year-old boy and she works full-time. She's been a streamer on Twitch for two and a half years. She decided to start her channel, encouraged by her husband, because she couldn't find Portuguese Twitch streamers who played the games she enjoys (casual video games).
- PT5 is a 34-year-old married mother of a six-year-old girl. Until recently she worked full-time alongside streaming on Twitch for the past two years and on YouTube before that. She's left her job to become her daughter's full-time carer. PT5 shared that her daughter suffers from severe sensory crises and has therapy four times weekly; this impacts PT5's ability and consistency in live-streaming.
- PT6 is a 39-year-old single mother with an 18-year-old daughter. She has been a Twitch streamer for about a year while working full-time. She has always been a gamer but decided to start the channel as a way to cope with a period of mental instability and to meet like-minded people.

4   Analysis

Discussion in the interviews was varied and led the research team to topics such as: the choice of streaming platforms; the labour involved in preparing a stream;

the tension between labour and leisure; personal identity; and balancing familial responsibilities. Subsequent analysis of the corpus revealed seven substantive themes. It can be seen that time management, the transition from streaming being a hobby to a form of work, and the conflict in the parent streamer identities are the most prominent themes appearing in all of the interviews. The relationship between family and gaming habits and support from the family was also prominent, appearing in most of the interviews. Half of the participants reported that children influenced their practice in some way. A few interviews were able to delve more deeply into the perceived benefits of streaming. The following sections describe these themes, with quotations from the underlying interviews.

4.1   Time Management

Time management is clearly a persistent issue for most parent streamers and the degree to which one has to sacrifice free time' for the pursuit is all-encompassing, bordering on impossible for some. Either to stream, to finish day-job-related tasks, or to advertise their content, reducing sleep hours was a common habit: "Having the stream and having the kid I can say that there's a lot of working through the night, until 3am, doing work that was left to do because I had to start the stream at 6pm." (PT5) and "If you ask any content creator they'll tell you the same - we just sleep [for] less time" (PT3). PT3 and PT4 mention rigorous time management. Being shift workers, they take advantage of being home without the children. PT3 uses their night shift to edit videos. PT4, however, concedes that household chores place considerable pressure on her time management, "depending on what I'm making for lunch if it's something that takes longer, I won't have time to stream [before work]". If instead, she is on a morning shift, she will stream in the afternoon until it is time to start cooking dinner, "but sometimes my husband tells me he'll cook lunch or dinner [...] he's a huge support".

Followers and viewers sometimes ask PT3 how it is possible for a parent to have time to play and record YouTube videos, "The trick is to use up all the free time [...] to have the maximum amount of content possible recorded because that's what takes longer [...] so if I have a lot of content in advance, then I can edit [...] on the free time."

PT4 is sometimes asked (by friends) how she is able to manage time for her streaming channel, being a mom, "given that I have a home, I have a family". But she reiterated that if she had a more traditional work schedule, it would be impossible for her to livestream. "It takes a lot of time. Can you manage work and this? Yes. Is it tiring? Yes. Having a full-time job and having a stream and creating content regularly is very hard [...] but it is doable." (PT5) This difficult management of family life, work, and creating content has had a toll on PT5, "I've already had three burnouts since starting to create content. Because it's a lot." Given that her daughter's crises are unpredictable, her plan for consistency is changed daily, "I can't make a plan".

4.2   From Hobby to Work

The approach to streaming as a form of labour is varied and income is not always an expectation or actively sought, yet there are pressures to consider this aspect of streaming from both streaming audiences and family members. PT2 sees the stream as a hobby. He sees the channel as leisure, as an escape from normal everyday life. He also mentions fatherhood as a reason for the inconsistency in streaming, "depending on how life is going... my life as a dad... my objective in life is always to be the best dad I can be for my daughter and Twitch is not my priority [...] [I don't want] to have an obligation to Twitch". Specifically, PT2 justifies seeing Twitch as a hobby due to his daughter's poor health, "me and my wife dedicate ourselves a thousand per cent to our daughter." Although PT2 engages with Twitch as a hobby, the both playful and serious nature of this activity is conveyed: "[...]doing it with gusto. If we have 20 or 30 people watching... of course it will always be important to us as streamers... but I think the most important is that we have fun, and we pass that on to the audience".

The link between PT1's leisure time and the livestreaming, however, denoted a tension between seeing Twitch as a hobby or as a potential source of income. This was discussed in relation to the types of games PT1 likes to play versus the ones more amenable to growing the channel,

> [...] it is the time I have to play so I'm going to play what I like. [...] If suddenly I stop playing what I like, then I wouldn't want to play anymore. [...] It'd be almost like I'm forced to live stream as a job [but] this is my free time to play and I simply turned on the live streaming and I'm here... relaxing with other folks while we chat about life, the game we're playing... football... whatever it is...

PT1 made another reference to Twitch as a job when asked about how his hobby could influence his children. That is, it would only make sense for his children to become inspired to follow his footsteps as a streamer if the channel became his career—privileging the idea of streaming as labour over leisure as a preference for his children. PT1 consistently identified his efforts to grow the channel while acknowledging there is a ceiling of investment, both in terms of time and money, until it becomes "part of the family budget". In terms of income, this mention of schedules and not letting down followers and subscribers seemed to cause uncomfortable feelings, "sometimes my wife gets a little upset as if she were saying 'if you're 5 min late it's not that big a deal'' because "[the stream] isn't part of our family budget, there's no money coming in that would affect it...".

Both PT1 and PT6 commented that anyone who starts a Twitch stream wants it to grow and, presumably, become profitable. Being the oldest interviewee, and the one with the most recent channel, PT6 acknowledges that it will not be easy to start a Twitch career at her age but "I'm not going to be a hypocrite and say I didn't start a channel to see if it [a career] could be a possibility."

PT3 treated streaming similarly, planning it as a potential form of income as he relates: "[Before starting] I studied YouTube thoroughly, how it works and how [the] algorithm works [...] one year has passed and given that I've achieved one of the goals to monetise the channel, I already see it as a part-time job. I'm a lot more professionally focused on the channel[...]". This means striving for consistency, "that's what YouTube's algorithm likes, and what helps with growth". This means sometimes his partner has had to take over childcare for PT3 to record some gameplay to keep releasing content consistently.

Meanwhile PT4, is more relaxed about streaming as a form of income: "I don't have ambitions [...] it's one day at a time and then we'll see because it is a hobby to me ... I don't have that anxiety about [money]" Even though she has a partnership with a gaming e-commerce platform, she does not "see my channel as a way to make money". She has had other partnership proposals that she rejected because "they didn't make any sense to me". She recalls one of them was a sportswear brand that wanted her to promote sports jerseys. PT4 reiterated that she does not promote games just to monetise her audience. This caring for her viewers was also reflected on how PT4 described her stream, "my channel is my home, it's where I welcome my friends". While it is said as an analogy to the type of stream she creates, "I've opened up my home to welcome [the viewers] and for us to have a good time", it may also be related to the fact that she streams from her bedroom and her bed is in full view.

PT4 has never thought about turning her streaming into a full-time job. Her reasoning is related to longevity: "if I were told I was gonna be able to make the jump and keep myself afloat with this... but how long would it last? I don't see this lasting forever, you know". She likes her life as it is, with herself and her family being the priority. Nonetheless, "it's a good feeling to get to the end of the month and see that I've reached the goal for Twitch to pay me [...] especially as we have a bunch of costs with games and stuff we have to buy in order to play." Still, the priority, from PT4's perspective, is for her viewers to be active on the chat, and engage with the stream, rather than support her financially, "for me the people who watch me daily are much more important, making the stream active [with their participation], because the stream doesn't make itself."

PT5's idea to start creating gaming content came from the perception of some Portuguese Youtubers as millionaires. Her love for communicating and entertaining led PT5 to realise that brands are investing in content creators, which makes this work a possibility of forming a long-lasting career, "even though it is a hobby because I don't earn a salary [...] the time I invest here is thinking about the future. I see it happening maybe in 5 years, not tomorrow." She's not naïve to the fact that it is a long journey until one can live off this type of work. "I don't think it's possible to live off only donations and [subscriptions...] I believe it's possible to live off this by becoming an influencer in gaming". PT5 is business-minded and has her eyes set on becoming such an influencer.

4.3   Parent Streamer Identity

There was a clear difference between how mothers and fathers navigated the parent streamer identity despite the small sample size. Fathers felt much freer to express their parental identity as part of the stream whereas mothers had to actively keep the two distinct in order to navigate sexism online as well as their own sense of independence from their identity as a parent.

PT1's channel name was chosen during a brainstorming session with his wife. The lore' of the channel, i.e. private jokes, emotes, and nicknames for subscribers and followers all follow the parenting theme by adopting names such as *filhotes*[2]. The parenting theme, however, does not go as far as his streaming persona where he does not like to sound like a parent to his audience, "Obviously I'm not going to 'scold them' if... if they don't eat their soup [laughs]."

PT1 sometimes gets comments regarding his age and him being a parent, viewers wishing their own fathers also played video games, wondering what it is like being a father, and saying he must be a wonderful one to which PT1 says "Maybe my own kids don't think that. I don't know." Being open about one's identity as a parent on a stream may characterise the parasocial relationship formed with audience members [15].

PT2 shares his parental status in the 'about' section on their channel. When asked if this was a conscious choice or a consequence of his daughter appearing on camera accidentally, PT2 said "nowadays people don't know what it means to be a father" and mentions having to sometimes discipline his daughter during live streams: "I have to be ready, at any moment, for her to show up here [...] and I have to be firm and [...]say 'look... don't do this, or don't do that'[...]" as she interferes with the stream. Even though he tries to avoid showing her face on stream, he has accepted that this sometimes happens.

PT3 chose to have the word father' (in Portuguese) in his channel's branding. He and his partner were brainstorming and wanted to come up with something catchy. Their son was already a gamer by then and PT3 was thinking about recording a gameplay video in which they both participated so the name, including the term 'father', came up.

Unlike the male participants, PT4, PT5 and PT6 deliberately keep their gamer and mother identities separate from their stream's branding. PT4 does not hide the fact that she is a mother from her viewers. Her son sometimes participates in the stream and also has his own channel. However, she does not want to label herself as a mother on the Twitch channel, as, for her, the two are completely separate: "I don't have to put a label on saying that I'm a wife, that I'm a mom [...] the goal is to show myself playing games, me as a gamer". PT4 was not always a gamer. She used to be self-conscious about her gaming skills but now can "make that my own 'trademark' [laughs]". She sees her channel as a shop window, as she's "there only to introduce the games, not to show great gameplay or to even finish games!" PT5's parental status is sometimes a shock to some of her viewers,

"[...] especially as I'm someone who looks younger, carefree, and I talk about things in a carefree way, people don't associate me with motherhood [...] So when they find out they go like 'What?! You?! What do you mean? Who's that child?' [laughs] they are shocked and surprised, 'but you're .

---

[2] An endearing way of expressing "my children".

such a chill and fun person, how are you a mother?' they can't see it, they don't understand it [...]"

This denotes a view that motherhood is incompatible with a relaxed, entertaining, and fun persona. "They compare me with their nagging moms... I'm also nagging! Just not to them."

Even though PT5 does not feel gender-discriminated, she acknowledges sometimes getting negative comments "I've gotten playful comments which I know are playful but I know I wouldn't receive them if I were a man [...] 'go make me a sandwich' [...] or 'if you're a woman and a mother... what are you doing here? [...]"; or even asking whether she produces explicit content. The comments are mostly ignored or the users who send them are banned. Other negative comments were about her knowledge of video games.

Having recently become her daughter's full-time carer, PT5 is wary of losing her sense of identity, "I don't want to lose my identity in this process because it's very complicated to be home taking care of a child with these special needs". The stream and her online persona are an important part of the process of maintaining her sense of identity beyond motherhood. She rarely shares her parental status, mainly when it comes up in conversation or when she has to interrupt the stream due to childcare. "Because I'm a mother, and then I'm a streamer. I can't see the two as the same thing. [...] they're two different people." PT5 mentions protecting her daughter's privacy but also wanting to avoid pity, "I don't want people to see me as a martyr, 'oh poor her, she's a mom of a disabled child'. No. I want them to see me as the one who entertains them, who makes them laugh, who plays games."

PT6 exclusively plays The Sims 4 (Electronic Arts, 2014) on her Twitch channel, "I've been playing since the first game. By now it's not just a game I like, it's my personality, it's a lifestyle [laughs]". In the context of her life-long gaming hobby, PT6 mentioned that, for a while, she stopped playing The Sims due to motherhood. Accepting societal expectations that now she was "a mother, an adult woman, I have to take care of the home, the child, and the husband." PT6 mentions that when she got pregnant she "ceased being [herself] and was just mom"'. To have a hobby, and especially a gaming hobby seems to be incompatible with motherhood but for PT6 it is about more than leisure, "If I'm not ok with myself, I'm not going to be ok with [my daughter]. So at that point, I'm probably not going to be a great mom." Her gaming hobby and now her streaming channel is thus linked to a regained sense of self and identity separate from motherhood: "[After the divorce] I realised I have to be more myself [...] it doesn't mean abandoning my responsibilities, [...] I still have time for my daughter, but I'm also a person and I didn't stop being that person just because I'm a mother."

4.4   Family Support

A supportive family environment seems to be critical to keeping up streaming activities. Besides helping to manage time, PT4's husband also helps with, "the technical part of the channel [...] because I have no idea about it [laughs]". Her husband also has a Twitch channel that he mostly uses to test things for PT4 to use in hers. PT5's husband also support her stream by helping her with the technology involved. Even though PT1 only livestreams after the children are asleep, his wife is there, "looking out for them. [...]even now with the youngest being four, he doesn't sleep through the night, so he needs one adult there for him when he wakes up. So that's a really big help, for me to be online."

PT1 emphasizes the family dynamics and management that is done through good communication, both for his own case and for others. Streamers will sometimes livestream new games at launch as a way of piggybacking off of the marketing interest generated by prominent releases. PT1 reports the following agreement with his wife:

> Recently [...] because of [a famous new game release] I told my wife 'look, I'm going to take a day off work and I'm going to stream Friday, Saturday, and Sunday all day. So, if you don't mind taking care of the kids this weekend, the following weekend is my turn. So, then, if you feel like going out, you could go out then. And I'll take care of them.'

PT2's wife has a pivotal role in his Twitch channel. Even though she does not appear on camera, she supports him by taking care of their daughter while he streams. She also supports him with ideas for the channel and with challenges he sometimes faces during the course of livestreaming, "[...]she supports me like, 'well if that's what you like to do, do it, and I'm here don't worry [...] about anything you see on the [Twitch] chat, or what they may tell you, you're not alone...". When probed to expand on this, PT2 explained that the Twitch audience sometimes advises him not to show his daughter's face on stream. As a four-year-old, she sometimes sneaks in, especially as PT2 does not have an isolated room to livestream from.

PT2 also reported that he tries not to speak too much about his and his daughter's illness. The hesitancy is described not so much as a privacy concern but as a worry about being misunderstood: "I've sometimes spoken a little bit about it but I should avoid it because then you get presumptions and you get judged [...] and people don't know you at all [...] and they think they know you...". PT2 explained this happens due to his illness being hidden. Some people have doubted he actually suffers from it because the symptoms are not visible.

PT5's husband was, at first, against her starting to create content: "Are you crazy? What are you gonna do? You're insane. You're gonna have even less time [for yourself]". Nowadays, without her husband, PT5's channel would not be possible. Besides taking care of their daughter, "he's the pillar of my sanity". There are days when PT5 is unmotivated and does not want to stream but her husband reminds her she can do it.

4.5 Family Gaming

PT1's wife, a non-gamer, has trouble understanding the benefits of (their child) playing video games. He reflected on this by mentioning his knowledge of research studies that show such benefits. In addition, as a gamer, he understands the content and age ratings. PT1 said his wife gets upset when their eldest cries at losing: "My wife does not like him [their son] to play [violent first-person shooter games] because she thinks it's too realistic", so he's able to step in and suggest alternatives. This echoes some of the concerns parents have when children act out while playing games.

PT2's daughter "[...] already has a lot of [gaming] apps... we were forced to pay for an app she downloaded [laughs]". When it comes to streaming, PT2 considers it possible for his daughter to livestream if she so desires one day, "she's going to decide for herself if she wants to do some streaming. As her dad, I'll keep a watchful eye [...] but that's something for her to choose." This was not the only instance where PT2 considered this possibility. Indeed, regarding their child watching his channel, he said: "[...]if one day my daughter sees the stream, which she will, then she can decide if she wants to follow her father's footsteps in this platform."

When speaking about PT3's channel branding, he mentions his son was already a gamer at the time. Realising it meant his son had started to play games at a young age, he justified himself by saying "he was already used to games [laughs] maybe he started a little too early." To expand this point further, PT3 explained that both he and his partner are shift workers. One weekend his partner had been working a night shift so PT3 had to care for his, at the time, two-year-old. To avoid the child being noisy and allow the mother to sleep, PT3 had to resort to a tablet game to entertain the child, "it was like his mind was opening up, at that age... the discovery, he loved it." PT3 was remorseful "it sounds like I'm a really bad father".

PT3's son influences the games he plays on his channel to an extent. His son stars in a video series where they play Sackboy [Sackboy: A big adventure] cooperatively: "it isn't a game I would normally play by myself [...] but since I have my son, I play with him and bring him to the channel [...] if I weren't a dad I wouldn't play it." Recording gameplay with his son is not only something he likes to do but also a business strategy, "within the gaming niche people have different tastes [...] some people really like watching the interaction in more family-oriented games, the type of family fun [...] so I have a little bit of everything". This has an impact on the type of persona he performs on his videos, depending on the game, and thus the audience, he is recording for. Due to exposure to games and game characters, PT5's daughter has taken up a special interest in Super Mario, "she has a hyperfocus on Super Mario. Everything is Supermario". Even though the child does not play a lot due to poor motor coordination, she enjoyed PlayStation 5's haptic feedback as mother and daughter played Astro Playroom (Team ASOBI, 2020), "it's one of the best memories I have of us, playing the Astro bot together".

4.6 Children Affecting Practice

Two situations can stop PT1 from livestreaming: his wife having to travel for work or both his children falling ill at the same time. These situations are seen by

PT1 as him missing out on his leisure time, when this happens he "basically lose[s his] free time to play." Although she strives for consistency, PT5's livestreaming depends mainly on her daughter's disposition,

> If she's well and I'm up for it... the plan stays the same and I stream daily on weekdays. [...] If there's any complications, which has happened often, I can't stream because I won't have the physical or psychological capacity to.

Having to interrupt the stream to care for her daughter has also happened: "She started having a sensory crisis [...] so I go 'friends, I'll see you tomorrow' and the door closes and mom mode is on."

For PT3, the unpredictable mood of a 4-year-old seems to be more compatible with a YouTube channel where he pre-records and edits captured gameplay. For instance, he's already had to record a video twice, "I would like to make more content with him [...] but he is a child, it is very complicated to record with him." Even though the child sometimes asks to play and record videos with his father, he can change his mind halfway through it: "He's either in a really good or a really bad mood".

4.7   Perceived Benefits of Streaming

Due to being emigrated, streaming allows PT2 to reconnect with a Portuguese audience and reinforce his national identity. Being physically removed from the Portuguese gaming community also impacts how much PT2 can grow his Twitch channel,

> "If I were in Portugal and if I had the opportunity to go to [gaming] events I would; [...] I don't have that chance to go to another streamer's home to livestream. In Portugal, there's a large community of gamers that get together in each other's homes and do livestreaming just hanging out and it is beautiful [...] because it's that family that is created and who has that opportunity of really being close with those streamers".

PT2 started streaming in part to leave it as a legacy for his daughter "[...] something for my daughter later in life, to watch her dad. How her dad was, what her dad did, etc". When prompted to expand on this point, PT2 said "it is all recorded when you start to stream. Everything you say and everything you do and all your reactions [...] so as a father, for my daughter to one day say, 'this was my dad'... for me this is way more important: we savour the precise moment we're on stream as much as possible". He seems to view the stream as a diary or photo album, which will live on after he passes. He never mentioned his passing explicitly even though he talks often about his illness and its associated symptoms.

PT5 meanwhile spoke fondly of the positive impact the stream has on her mental health: "At the end of a work day, or a day spent taking care of her [...] if I'm not OK and I turn on the stream, then I end up feeling great." She mentions this impact also helps her manage childcare with more patience and creativity for playtime.

5 Concluding Discussion

The research presented in this paper is an initial step towards understanding the identity and experience of parent streamers, a relatively under-studied population. It contributes new insight into the challenges faced by people who play games and choose to stream their gameplay, identifying seven themes: (i) the difficulty of managing time effectively, balancing family responsibilities with streaming; (ii) the tension between work and play, further complicated by the interplay between a sense of parental moral responsibility and economic incentives to provide; (iii) the parent streamer identity and how this shapes the role of children in the stream. The qualitative data seems to underpin the notion that these identities are in conflict, hinting at substantive differences between mothers and fathers; (iv) the criticality of familial support; (v) the increasingly complex relationship between parents and games, and the influence this has on play habits within the family group; (vi) sources of interference that affect streaming practices in the home environment; and (vii) the benefits of streaming including communal connection and mental health.

It also suggests that, despite the struggle, many parent streamers are successfully navigating the challenges they encounter; including the tensions caused by competing demands for attention as well as the conflict in identity between parent and streamer. The incentives and underlying drive to create content are not always explicit but seem to be a force that many families are willing to sacrifice free time for. Thus, further work would do well to focus on understanding the motivations for parents to stream.

It is important to acknowledge that this is only an initial exploratory study that involved six participants. Further work is necessary to improve representativeness and synthesise accounts into a coherent narrative, particularly given the differences observed in how fathers and mothers navigate the parent streamer experience with regards to gender and audience perception. But, hopefully, such work will pave the way towards guidance and accounts that serve to support parents and the streaming community; particularly, for parents who may be considering whether to pursue streaming or soon-to-be parents who are already streamers.

A   Appendix on Interview Questions

The interviews conducted were semi-structured, with scripted questions asked in varied order and form tailored around the interviewees' context:

- What made you start your channel?
- How do you see your channel, as work or as a hobby?
- How do you balance your time between your channel and your parenting responsibilities?
- How do you deal with the unpredictability of parenting and how it can affect your channel?
- Do you share your 'parenting status' on your channel?

– Does your audience comment anything about the fact that you're a parent?
– Do you talk about parenting in your channel?
– What's your children's relationship with the channel? What do they say about your channel? Do they appear on it?
– How does the fact that you're a parent influence the content of your channel?
– How would you say having the channel/being a streamer influences your child?
– How are the logistics at home for your channel?
– What's your partner's role in your streaming/content creation?

References

1. Aarsand, P.: Parenting and digital games: on children's game play in us families. J. Child. Media **5**(3), 318–333 (2011)
2. Ågren, Y.: Branded childhood: Infants as digital capital on Instagram. Childhood **30**(1), 9–23 (2023)
3. Archer, C.: How influencer 'mumpreneur' bloggers and 'everyday' mums frame presenting their children online. Media International Australia **170**(1), 47–56 (2019)
4. Ask, K., Sørenssen, I.K., Moltubakk, S.T.: The struggle and enrichment of play: domestications and overflows in the everyday life of gamer parents. Nordicom Rev. **42**(s4), 107–123 (2021)
5. Baltar, F., Brunet, I.: Social research 2.0: virtual snowball sampling method using facebook. Internet Res. **22**(1), 57–74 (2012)
6. DeCamp, W.: Parental influence on youth violent video game use. Soc. Sci. Res. **82**, 195–203 (2019)
7. Dralega, C.A., Seddighi, G., Corneliussen, H.G., Prøitz, L.: From helicopter parenting to co-piloting: models for regulating video gaming among immigrant youth in norway. In: Modeller: Fjordantologien 2019, pp. 223–241. Universitetsforlaget (2019)
8. Flood, S., Meier, A., Musick, K.: Reassessing parents' leisure quality with direct measures of well-being: Do children detract from parents' down time? J. Marriage Family **82**(4), 1326–1339 (2020). https://doi.org/10.1111/jomf.12647, https://onlinelibrary.wiley.com/doi/abs/10.1111/jomf.12647
9. Goodman, L.A.: Snowball sampling. In: The Annals of Mathematical Statistics, pp. 148–170 (1961)
10. Greitemeyer, T.: The dark and bright side of video game consumption: effects of violent and prosocial video games. Curr. Opin. Psychol. **46**, 101326 (2022)
11. Heaselgrave, F., Bogkvist, A.: "i prefer to play alone to recharge my social battery": parent gamer identities in Australia. In: DiGRA23. in press (2023)
12. Jodén, H., Strandell, J.: Building viewer engagement through interaction rituals on twitch. tv. Inf. Commun. Soc. **25**(13), 1969–1986 (2022)
13. Johnson, M.R.: Behind the streams: the off-camera labour of game live streaming. Games Cult. **16**(8), 1001–1020 (2021)
14. Johnson, M.R., Woodcock, J.: 'it's like the gold rush': the lives and careers of professional video game streamers on twitch. tv. Inf. Commun. Soc. **22**(3), 336–351 (2019)
15. Leith, A.P.: Parasocial cues: the ubiquity of parasocial relationships on twitch. Commun. Monographs **88**(1), 111–129 (2021). https://doi.org/10.1080/03637751.2020.1868544

16. LeLaurin, A.: Twitch Affiliation: A Rite to Cultivate Digital Identity and Community. Ph.D. thesis, Harvard University (2023)
17. Mathur, M.B., VanderWeele, T.J.: Finding common ground in meta-analysis "wars" on violent video games. Perspect. Psychol. Sci. **14**(4), 705–708 (2019)
18. Ruberg, B., Lark, D.: Livestreaming from the bedroom: Performing intimacy through domestic space on twitch. Convergence **27**(3), 679–695 (2021)
19. Scullion, C.: Twitch leak reveals the site's highest paid streamers (2021)
20. Sørenssen, I.K., Ask, K., Moltubakk, S.T.: Gamer-parent identity: positioning parenthood between fun screentime and ideals of responsibility. In: Proceedings of the 2022 Conference on Games+Learning+Society (2022)
21. Terry, G., Hayfield, N., Clarke, V., Braun, V.: Thematic analysis. In: The SAGE Handbook of Qualitative Research in Psychology, vol. 2, pp. 17–37 (2017)
22. Törhönen, M., Hassan, L., Sjöblom, M., Hamari, J.: Play, playbour or labour? The relationships between perception of occupational activity and outcomes among streamers and youtubers. In: Proceedings of the 52nd Hawaii International Conference on System Sciences (2019)
23. Urbaneja, J.S., Mendoça, C.N., Coelho Teixeira, M.: El gamer portugués: caracterización y hábito deportivo (perspectiva de género) (the portuguese gamer: characterization and sports habit (gender perspective)). Retos **47**, 352–358 (2023). https://doi.org/10.47197/retos.v47.94508, https://recyt.fecyt.es/index.php/retos/article/view/94508

Videogame Students in Portuguese Higher Education: Perceptions, Motivations, and Playing Habits – A Case Study

Ivan Barroso and Carla Sousa(✉)

Universidade Lusófona, CICANT, Lisbon, Portugal
carla.patricia.sousa@ulusofona.pt

Abstract. Recognizing the growing importance of videogames as a multifaceted medium in contemporary society, this study focuses on the perceptions, motivations, and playing habits of students enrolled in game design and game development courses at Portuguese higher education institutions. Data was collected from three educational institutions in Portugal offering game-related courses. The participants consisted of 233 students, with a majority of males (81.50%) and varying age groups. Data collection occurred over two years through online forms. This study examines Portuguese students enrolled in game design and development programs. It highlights a significant gender disparity in the country's videogame higher education, reflecting limited female representation, with consistent age and gender distributions across institutions. Students emphasize the importance of diverse creative references in their future careers but undervalue AAA games while showing limited awareness of indie titles. Motivation to pursue these programs primarily stems from a desire to create games, with parental and peer recommendations holding little influence. Regarding habits, students spend substantial time gaming but tend to acquire games through illegal means, underscoring the prevalence of such practices. Content creators on platforms like YouTube and Twitch play a pivotal role in shaping students' game choices and perceptions, mirroring their societal relevance among contemporary youth. Extending the temporal and even transnational scope of studies of this kind could be crucial in the future, considering that the characteristics and preferences of students is critical for designing effective educational programs and fostering ethical gaming practices in the rapidly evolving sector of videogames.

Keywords: Games · Students · Higher Education

1 Introduction

Videogames are a multifaceted medium, central in contemporary society, framing them as a mass cultural phenomenon. Moreover, it is estimated that, in 2020, the videogame industry had a revenue of around €145 billion, compared to the €39 billion of the movie industry, according to the Council of Europe (CoE) [1]. Considering this factor, promoting quality higher education in the field of game design and game development becomes a priority.

© The Author(s), under exclusive license to Springer Nature Switzerland AG 2024
L. Vale Costa et al. (Eds.): VJ 2023, CCIS 1984, pp. 49–58, 2024.
https://doi.org/10.1007/978-3-031-51452-4_4

Based on the relevance of student inquiry for pedagogical relevance and adequacy [2, 3], the aim of this study is to explore the perceptions, motivations and playing habits of young people enrolled on game design and game development courses at Portuguese institutions.

2 Method

2.1 Participants

For this case study, data was collected from three educational institutions in Portugal with courses in game design and game development for two academic years (2021/22 and 2022/23). *Escola de Tecnologias Inovação e Criação* (ETIC) – henceforth referred to as Institution 1 – which at the time of data collection was not yet an autonomous higher education course, but allowed the completion of a degree with the support of a foreign institution. *Instituto Politécnico de Leiria* (IPL) – Institution 2 – with a Degree in Digital Games and Multimedia. *Universidade Lusófona - Centro Universitário de Lisboa* - Institution 3 - with a degree in Videogames. Institutions 1 and 2 are private, while institution 2 is public.

Non-probabilistic convenience sampling was adopted. The different representation of each institution in the sample is due to the different number of places and, consequently, students enrolled at each one.

A total of 233 students participated in the different data gathering moments, both during 2021 ($n = 124$; 53.20%) and 2022 ($n = 109$; 46.80%), from which 190 were males (81.50%), and 43 females (18.50%). Regarding age, most students were between 17 and 20 years old ($n = 169$; 73.50%), followed by students between 21 and 24 years old ($n = 49$; 21.00%), as well as students between 25 and 28 years old ($n = 14$; 6.00%). One student (0.40%) belonged to the age group between 29 and 33 years old. The detailed distribution of the sample, considering the different institutions, is presented in Table 1.

2.2 Procedure

The data was collected during two different years – 2021 and 2022 – as part of specific subjects, within classes on each of the courses. For this purpose, online forms were used, and applied at six different times during the semester. This form was made up of generic demographic data and items – which will be presented in section three – aimed at the respondents' perceptions, motivations and playing habits.

Given the complexity of collecting data in six different phases, and the impossibility of ensuring that all the students attended all the classes, there were almost always several missing values, which were taken into account for statistical analysis purposes.

The anonymised data obtained was analysed using descriptive statistics using SPSS, version 26. Questions that allowed multiple response options were analysed as dichotomous variables.

Table 1. Sample detailed distribution ($n = 233$).

	Institution 1 ($n = 32$)	Institution 2 ($n = 129$)	Institution 3 ($n = 72$)	Total ($n = 233$)
Age Group[1]	17–20 = 20 (62.50%)	17–20 = 101 (78.29%)	17–20 = 48 (66.67%)	17–20 = 169 (73.50%)
	21–24 = 9 (28.13%)	21–24 = 22 (17.05%)	21–24 = 18 (25.00%)	21–24 = 49 (21.00%)
	25–28 = 3 (9.37%)	25–28 = 5 (3.88%)	25–28 = 6 (8.33%)	25–28 = 14 (6.00%)
	29–33 = 0 (0.00%)	29–33 = 1 (0.78%)	29–33 = 0 (0.00%)	29–33 = 0 (0.00%)
Gender[2]	M = 23 (71.88%)	M = 106 (82.17%)	M = 61 (84.72%)	M = 190 (81.50%)
	F = 9 (28.12%)	F = 23 (17.83%)	F = 11 (15.28%)	F = 43 (18.50%)

[1]The other age groups were omitted because there were no participants in them; [2]M = Male; F = Female

3 Results

3.1 Perceptions

Regarding the participants' perceptions, as videogame students, a central question was asked – "What is more important and adequate to become a game developer?" – allowing two possible answers: (a) Play longer game sessions to be very proficient in a specific genre, achieving superior ranks or similar; or (b) Play lot of different games to get more exposed to different experiences and have a richer creative pool. The total of 184 valid answers showed that students, almost unanimously, believed in the relevance of enhancing their framework of creative references through diverse play ($n = 183$; 99.46%), with only one student (0.54%) stating the opposite.

In the assessment of game-related perceptions, the students showed that the game they knew the least about or were least able to express an opinion on was *Fez* [4] ($n = 12$; 6.40%), followed by *Gris* [5] ($n = 106$; 56.70%), as opposed to *Among Us* [6] ($n = 4$; 2.10%), *League of Legends* [7] ($n = 12$; 6.40%), and *Fortnite* [8] ($n = 12$; 6.40%). *Candy Crush Saga* [9] was the game that most students were indifferent to ($n = 63$; 33.70%), followed by *Clash of Clans* [10] ($n = 52$; 27.80%). On the other hand, the games *The Last of Us - Part II* [11], *Hollow Knight* [12] ($n = 14$; 7.50%), and *Gris* [5] ($n = 18$; 9.60%) were the ones to which students were least indifferent. *FIFA 21* [14] was the most disliked game ($n = 85$; 45.50%), followed by *Fortnite* [8] ($n = 63$; 33.70%). On the opposite side, *Hollow Knight* [12] ($n = 0$; 0.00%) and *Fez* [4] ($n = 1$; 0.50%) were the least disliked games.

On the positive spectrum, ninety-three students (49.70%) classified *Among Us* [6] as "good", and eighty-nine (47.60%) reported similarly for *Overwatch* [13]. On the opposite hand, *FIFA 21* [14] ($n = 21$; 11.20%) and *Fez* [4] ($n = 30$; 16.00%) were the least perceived as "good games" by the students. *The Legend of Zelda: Breath of the*

Table 2. Students' game-related perceptions ($n = 187$).

	No opinion/Don't know it	Indifferent	Dislike	Good	Excellent
League of Legends [7]	12 (6.40%)	39 (20.90%)	39 (20.90%)	62 (33.20%)	35 (18.70%)
Destiny 2 [17]	57 (30.50%)	42 (33.50%)	21 (11.20%)	50 (26.70%)	17 (9.10%)
Among Us [6]	4 (2.10%)	35 (18.70%)	14 (7.50%)	93 (49.70%)	41 (21.90%)
The Last of US – Part II [11]	54 (28.90%)	14 (7.50%)	13 (7.00%)	42 (22.50%)	64 (34.20%)
Fortnite [8]	12 (6.40%)	35 (18.70%)	63 (33.70%)	60 (32.10%)	17 (9.10%)
Clash of Clans [10]	28 (15.00%)	52 (27.80%)	31 (16.60%)	56 (29.90%)	20 (10.70%)
Warframe [18]	51 (27.30%)	40 (21.40%)	15 (8.00%)	53 (28.30%)	28 (15.00%)
Gris [5]	106 (56.70%)	18 (9.60%)	0 (0.00%)	29 (15.50%)	34 (18.20%)
The Legend of Zelda: BotW[1] [15]	41 (21.90%)	14 (7.50%)	2 (1.10%)	42 (22.50%)	88 (47.10%)
Fez [4]	113 (60.40%)	19 (10.20%)	1 (0.50%)	30 (16.00%)	24 (12.80%)
Animal Crossing: New Horizons [19]	37 (19.80%)	33 (17.60%)	12 (6.40%)	73 (39.00%)	32 (17.10%)
Hollow Knight [12]	45 (24.10%)	14 (7.50%)	0 (0.00%)	47 (25.10%)	81 (43.30%)
Rust [20]	53 (28.30%)	44 (23.50%)	12 (6.40%)	56 (29.90%)	22 (11.80%)
Call of Dutty: CW[2] [16]	52 (27.80%)	47 (25.10%)	29 (15.50%)	47 (25.10%)	12 (6.40%)
Overwatch [13]	18 (9.60%)	34 (18.20%)	18 (9.60%)	89 (47.60%)	28 (15.00%)
FIFA 21 [14]	26 (13.90%)	45 (24.10%)	85 (45.50%)	21 (11.20%)	10 (5.30%)
Candy Crush Saga [9]	24 (12.80%)	63 (33.70%)	45 (24.10%)	42 (22.50%)	13 (7.00%)
Genshin Impact [21]	28 (15.00%)	37 (19.80%)	31 (16.60%)	65 (34.80%)	26 (13.90%)

[1]BotW = Breath of the Wild; [2]CW = Black Ops - Cold War

Wild [15] ($n = 88$; 47.10%) and *Hollow Knight* [12] ($n = 81$; 43.30%) were the most frequently considered as "excellent" games, while *FIFA 21* [14] ($n = 10$; 5.30%) and *Call of Duty: Black Ops - Cold War* [16] ($n = 12$; 6.40%) were the least frequently classified in such way. Detailed results are presented in Table 2.

According to the detailed results on Table 3, to build the above-described perceptions, most students played all the listed games – or at least the ones they knew ($n = 154$; 81.90%). Watching youtubers or streamers playing those games was also a very relevant strategy for the sample ($n = 142$; 75.50%). Reading online reviews was, on the other hand, the least relevant way of building perceptions about a game for the inquired students ($n = 48$; 25.50%).

Table 3. Ways of building the perceptions about the games ($n = 188$).

Adopted strategy (multiple choice)	Yes	No
I played them all (or at least, the ones that I know)	154 (81.90%)	34 (18.10%)
I saw Youtubers or Streamers playing them	142 (75.50%)	46 (24.50%)
I read reviews online	48 (25.50%)	140 (74.50%)
I was introduced to them on social media	68 (36.20%)	120 (63.80%)
My friends recommended them	114 (60.60%)	74 (39.40%)

3.2   Motivations

Students' motivations to study computer games as a profession were assessed through multiple choice items and the obtained results are presented in Table 4.

From the 195 students answering to this question, the will to make computer games was the most reported ($n = 183$; 93.80%), while parents recommendation was the least reported motivational source ($n = 7$; 3.60%).

Table 4. Motivation to study computer games as a profession ($n = 195$).

Reason (multiple choice)	Yes	No
Proximity to your home address	9 (4.60%)	186 (95.40%)
After being proficient in playing games, it seems like a good second step	65 (33.30%)	130 (66.70%)
From all the available courses in the institution, this area seems the more interesting one	33 (16.90%)	162 (69.50%)

(*continued*)

Table 4. (*continued*)

Reason (multiple choice)	Yes	No
I want to learn how to make games	183 (93.80%)	12 (6.20%)
Employment	50 (25.60%)	145 (74.40%)
Parents recommendation	7 (3.60%)	188 (96.40%)
Friends recommendation	9 (4.60%)	186 (95.40%)
I have no idea/Application mistake	8 (4.10%)	187 (95.90%)

Regarding the genres of games students were more motivated to create, during their academic journey, Role-Playing Games (RPG) were the most reported (n = 123; 66.80%), followed by platformers (n = 113; 61.40%), while sports games (n = 22; 12.00%) were the least mentioned in this sense. Detailed results for these variables are presented in Table 5.

Table 5. Genres that the students are more motivated to create.

Genre (multiple choice)	Yes	No
Sports Game	22 (12.00%)	162 (88.00%)
MMO[1]	39 (21.20%)	145 (78.80%)
RPG[2]	123 (66.80%)	61 (33.20%)
Platformer	113 (61.40%)	71 (38.60%)
FPS[3]	68 (37.00%)	116 (63.00%)
Dungeon Crawler	83 (45.10%)	101 (54.90%)
Competitive Game	62 (33.70%)	122 (66.30%)
Puzzle Game	81 (44.00%)	103 (60.30%)
Top-Down Explorer	73 (39.70%)	111 (60.30%)
Something with an online component	50 (27.20%)	134 (72.80%)

[1]MMO = Massively Multiplayer Online; [2]RPG = Role-Playing Games; [3]FPS = First-Person Shooters

3.3 Playing Habits

Seventy-six students from the sample (38.19% of the valid answers to this question) played either around two, or around four hours per day, being this the most frequent case. On the other hand, sixteen students (8.04%) played around eight or more hours per day, as detailed in Table 6.

Table 6. Gaming hours per day ($n = 199$).

Gaming hours per day	n	%
Around 2 h	76	38.19
Around 4 h	76	38.19
Around 6 h	31	15.58
Around 8 or more hours	16	8.04
Total	199	100.00

Regarding their buying habits, as players, most students reported to adopt non legal methods to access games, through the statement "Piracy" ($n = 41$; 22.40%), followed by the ones that spend between one and 4.99€ per month ($n = 40$; 21.90%). On the opposite side, only five students (2.70%) reported to spend between 26 and 34.99€ per month on games. Full results are presented in Table 7.

Table 7. Money spent on games, monthly ($n = 183$).

Money spent on games, monthly	n	%
1–4.99€	40	21.90
6–9.99€	34	18.60
11–14.99€	31	16.90
16–19.99€	15	8.20
21–24.99€	6	3.30
26–34.99€	5	2.70
More than 35€	11	6.00
Piracy	41	22.40
Total	183	100.00

Table 8 presents the different methods adopted by students to discover games online, from which it is possible to highlight the relevance of youtubers and streamers ($n = 170$; 90.90%), as well as friends and family recommendations ($n = 165$; 88.20%). Magazines ($n = 13$; 7.00%) and television commercials ($n = 18$; 9.60%) represent the least relevant methods to this extent.

Table 8. Methods to discover games online ($n = 187$).

Method (multiple choice)	Yes	No
Friends and family recommendations	165 (88.20%)	22 (11.80%)
Youtubers and streamers	170 (90.90%)	17 (9.10%)
Internet search	141 (75.40%)	46 (24.60%)
Websites	100 (53.50%)	87 (46.50%)
Online ads	70 (37.40%)	117 (62.60%)
Magazines	13 (7.00%)	174 (93.00%)
Television commercials	18 (9.60%)	169 (90.40%)
Social Media	127 (67.90%)	60 (32.10%)

4   Discussion

The objective of this case study is to investigate the perceptions, motivations, and gaming habits of young individuals who are currently enrolled in game design and game development programmes at institutions in Portugal. In demographic terms, the obtained results reinforce those of previous studies – as the one from Lima & Gouveia [22] - regarding the very small presence of the female gender in videogame sector, in Portugal. In addition, both in terms of gender and age, the distributions do not seem to show notable differences between institutions.

In terms of perceptions, the students believe in the relevance of a wide range of creative references for their future as game designers and game developers. However, their perceptions of the games on the market seem to emphasise a devaluation of AAA or more lucrative games (e.g. *FIFA 21* [14] or *Fortnite* [8]). Paradoxically, there seems to be a lack of awareness of titles that have been very important on the indie circuit in recent years, such as *Fez* [4] or *Gris* [5]. As expected, playing is the most relevant way to build perceptions about these games, and contact with content on Youtube or streams is also very relevant.

In motivational terms, the desire to play games is the biggest reason for entering a course in the area, as expected. On the other hand, the low recommendation of parents and friends in this regard emphasises less positive views of this area of study. In line with the perceptions of existing games explored, the Portuguese students also showed little motivation to create sports games. On the other hand, RPGs and platformers seem to fulfil the students' creative preferences.

As players, these Portuguese videogame students have habits that allow us to categorise them, considering other demographics of young people, as heavy gamers. For example, if we consider the most prevalent reported gaming time – around two hours per day – our sample would be tendentially playing more hours per week than the youth studied by Barr [23], Connolly et al. [24], and Pontes & Griffiths [25] – who specifically studied the Portuguese context.

Even as heavy gamers, the sample of these Portuguese videogame students tend to spend low amounts to no money on buying games, heavily relying on illegal strategies to acquiring them. These results emphasize the relevance of illegal downloads and related phenomena in the study of digital games [26], as well as the relevance of promoting the moral and ethical dimensions of digital life [27].

The obtained results, regarding the relevance of youtubers and streamers both in selection of games and in the development of perceptions around them, for Portuguese videogame students, are also aligned with the societal relevance attributed to these actors in the social cognition of contemporary youth [28], as well as in their overall identities [29].

4.1 Limitations and Future Directions

The research on students' perceptions, motivations, and gaming habits has faced several challenges. One of the main issues is missing values, which could lead to skewed conclusions. To address this, robust data collection methods should be implemented. Response bias is another concern, as self-reported data can introduce socially desirable or inaccurate responses. To mitigate this, multiple data sources and validation methods should be considered. The study also lacks a thorough exploration of the cultural context of gaming in Portugal, which can significantly influence students' perceptions and motivations. The study also only briefly mentions illegal game acquisition but does not extensively examine its ethical and legal implications.

Longitudinal studies offer valuable insights into the evolving nature of the gaming industry and its impact on the target demographic. A more thorough cultural analysis of gaming in Portugal is warranted, as it can provide a deeper understanding of the subject. Ethical considerations should also be a central focus of future studies. Comparative research, relating findings from Portuguese students with those from other countries, could reveal cross-cultural differences and similarities in perceptions and habits.

Acknowledgments. This project has received funding from the European Union's Horizon Horizon Europe research and innovation programme under grant agreement No 101095058 (EPIC-WE).

References

1. Council of Europe.: Educating for a Video Game Culture – a Map for Teachers and Parents. Council of Europe, Strasbourg (2021)
2. McLoughlin, C., Lee, M.J.W.: The Three P's of pedagogy for the networked society: personalization, participation, and productivity. Inter. J. Teach. Learn. Higher Educ. **20**(1), 10–27 (2008)

3. VanHaitsma, P.: New pedagogical engagements with archives: student inquiry and composing in digital spaces. Coll. Engl. **78**(1), 34–55 (2015)
4. Polytron Corporation: Fez (2012). https://fezgame.com/, (Accessed 1 Sep 2023)
5. Nomada Studio.: Gris (2018). https://nomada.studio/, (Accessed 1 Sep 2023)
6. InnerSloth: Among Us (2018). https://www.innersloth.com/games/among-us/, (Accessed 1 Sep 2023)
7. Riot Games: League of Legends (2009). https://www.leagueoflegends.com/, (Accessed 1 Sep 2023)
8. Epic Games.: Fortnite (2017). https://www.fortnite.com/, (Accessed 1 Sep 2023)
9. King: Candy Crush Saga (2012). https://www.king.com/game/candycrush, (Accessed 1 Sep 2023)
10. Supercell: Clash of Clans (2012). https://supercell.com/en/games/clashofclans/,(Accessed 1 Sep 2023)
11. Naughty Dog: The Last of Us – Part II (2020). https://www.imdb.com/title/tt6298000/, (Accessed 1 Sep 2023)
12. Team Cherry: Hollow Knight (2017). https://www.hollowknight.com/, (Accessed 1 Sep 2023)
13. Blizzard Entertainment: Overwatch (2016). https://overwatch.blizzard.com/, (Accessed 1 Sep 2023)
14. Electronic Arts: FIFA 21 (2020). https://store.playstation.com/pt-pt/concept/100 00278, (Accessed 1 Sep 2023)
15. Nintendo Entertainment Planning & Development.: The Legend of Zelda: Breath of the Wild (2017). https://www.nintendo.pt/Jogos/Jogos-para-a-Nintendo-Switch/The-Legend-of-Zelda-Breath-of-the-Wild-1173609.html, (Accessed 1 Sep 2023)
16. Treyarch: Call of Duty: Black Ops Cold War (2020). https://www.callofduty.com/pt/blacko pscoldwar, (Accessed 1 Sep 2023)
17. Bungie.: Destiny 2 (2017). https://www.bungie.net/7/en/destiny/newlight, (Accessed 1 Sep 2023)
18. Digital Extremes: Warframe (2013). https://www.warframe.com/, (Accessed 1 Sep 2023)
19. Nintendo Entertainment Planning & Development.: Animal Crossing: New Horizons (2020). https://www.nintendo.pt/Jogos/Jogos-para-a-Nintendo-Switch/Animal-Crossing-New-Hor izons-1438623.html , (Accessed 1 Sep 2023)
20. Facepunch Studios: Rust (2013). https://rust.facepunch.com/, (Accessed 1 Sep 2023)
21. miHoYo: Genshin Impact (2020). https://genshin.hoyoverse.com/, (Accessed 1 Sep 2023)
22. Lima, L., Gouveia, P.: Gender asymmetries in the digitalGames sector in Portugal. In: Proceedings of DiGRA 2020, Tampere, Finland (2020)
23. Barr, M.: A cross-sectional study of video game play habits and graduate skills attainment. Res. Learn. Technol. **28**, 1–22 (2020)
24. Connolly, T.M., Boyle, E.A., Stansfield, M.H., Hainey, T.: A survey of students' computer game playing habits. Adv. Technol. Learn. **208** (2007)
25. Pontes, H.M., Griffiths, M.D.: Portuguese validation of the internet gaming disorder scale–short-form. Cyberpsychol. Behav. Soc. Netw. 1–6 (2016)
26. Drachen, A., Bauer, K., Veitch, R.W.D.: Distribution of digital games via BitTorrent. In: MindTrek 2011: Proceedings of the 15th International Academic MindTrek Conference: Envisioning Future Media Environments, Tampere, Finland, pp. 233–240. (2011)
27. Flores, A., James, C.: Morality and ethics behind the screen: young people's perspectives on digital life. New Media Society **15**(6), 813–1002 (2013)
28. Soo Lim, J., Choe, M.-J., Zhang, J., Noh, G.-Y.: The role of wishful identification, emotional engagement, and parasocial relationships in repeated viewing of live-streaming games: a social cognitive theory perspective. Comput. Hum. Behav. **108**, 106327 (2020)
29. Vilasís-Pamos, J., Pérez-Latorre, Ó.: Gamer identity and social class: an analysis of barcelona teenagers' discourses on videogame culture and gaming practices. Int. J. Commun. **16**, 5864–5884 (2022)

Psychological and Behavioral Effects of League of Legends Rank System for Italian Competitive Players

Mustafa Can Gursesli[1,2]([✉]), Federica Masti[2], Mirko Duradoni[2], Barbaros Bostan[3], Ertugrul Sungu[3], Pervin Cagla Zilbeyaz[4], and Andrea Guazzini[2,5]

[1] Department of Information Engineering, University of Florence, 50139 Florence, Italy
mustafacan.gursesli@unifi.it
[2] Department of Education, Literatures, Intercultural Studies, Languages and Psychology, University of Florence, 50135 Florence, Italy
[3] Department of Game Design, Bahcesehir University, 34353 Istanbul, Turkey
[4] Department of Humanities and Social Sciences, Okan University, 34959 Istanbul, Turkey
[5] Centre for the Study of Complex Dynamics, University of Florence, 50019 Sesto Fiorentino, Italy

Abstract. This study presents the relationships between levels of toxicity, validation-seeking behavior, emotional affectivity, and desire to quit at higher ranks in the popular multiplayer online battle arena (MOBA) game, namely League of Legends. Analysis of data collected from Italian participants ($N = 370$) supports positive correlations between rank and toxicity, rank and validation-seeking behavior, and rank and positive emotion affectivity. In addition, higher ranks are associated with a reduced desire to quit the game caused by toxic behavior. These findings underline the importance of supporting positive interactions between players and intervention programmes to tackle toxic behavior in competitive gaming environments.

Keywords: MOBA · League of Legends · Rank · Toxicity

1 Introduction

Technology has become increasingly important in meeting people's needs, and it has brought about significant changes in various domains of our lives [1]. One of the areas that have been profoundly affected by technology is the entertainment industry, where it plays a crucial role in delivering innovative and satisfying experiences [2–5]. "Video games", one of the important industries where technological developments and the need for entertainment melt in one pot, has achieved a rapid acceleration in recent years, reaching up to 2.69 billion people in 2020 and 158$ billion in revenue [6]. With the effect of this large revenue and the growth rate of the industry, game producers ensure that the game market is home to numerous genres in order to provide that the games reach more people [7]. Moreover, games today, with the help of these numerous genres, have

© The Author(s), under exclusive license to Springer Nature Switzerland AG 2024
L. Vale Costa et al. (Eds.): VJ 2023, CCIS 1984, pp. 59–71, 2024.
https://doi.org/10.1007/978-3-031-51452-4_5

introduced the concept of eSports to the world by considering the competitive playing of video games as a sport [8]. In fact, eSports has been nominated for inclusion in the 2020 Olympics Games [9].

"Multiplayer Online Battle Arena" (MOBA), one of the most popular of these game genres today, is estimated to exceed \$490 million in annual sales revenue by 2025 [10]. The first steps of the MOBA adventure of the gaming world began in 1998 with the "fan-made" custom map developed by players in Blizzard's real-time strategy (RTS) game Aeon of Strife [11]. In 2003, "Blizzard's Warcraft III: Reign of Chaos" game, Defence of the Ancients (DOTA), which also appeared as a custom map, enabled the MOBA style to reach people by completely creating it [11]. In 2009, Riot Games introduced League of Legends (LoL), the first stand-alone game of the MOBA genre [12]. In 2022, it is known that 152 million people are actively playing LoL [13]. MOBA is defined by Xia, et. al. as "A hybrid of the massively multiplayer online game and real-time strategy (RTS) genres" [9]. Games in this genre are shaped around two small teams (usually 5 versus 5, with players taking on different roles) competing against each other [14].Games end when one team destroys the other team's "basement".

Multiplayer gaming is a popular pastime that could provide many benefits to gamers, such as providing social support [15], combating loneliness [16], and improving well-being [17]. However, multiplayer games and their competitive contexts represent also an environment in which players may be exposed to the toxic behaviors of other players. In fact, while the element of competition increases enjoyment [18] and could lead to a greater player experience, it has also been associated with an increase in negative behavior, such as cyberbullying [19], griefing [20], cheating [21] (See Table 1. For further definitions). These negative behaviors are grouped together and referred to as toxic behavior. However, the definition of toxic behavior is often unclear, in part because of the specific set of social norms and rules of the game, and so game communities vary in terms of netiquette and habits [22]. Consequently, there are a variety of behaviors that could be considered toxic across the different contexts and games, based on different norms, rules, and player expectations of each community. In general, toxicity refers to various types of negative behaviors including verbal or in-game behaviors intended to provoke and antagonize other players (i.e., trolling), aggressive or derogatory language [23] or verbal abuse directed towards other players, and disruptive gameplay that violates the norms of the game or play styles that intentionally disrupt the gaming experience of another player, such as griefing or feeding [20]. In conclusion, toxic behavior is a subset of deviant behavior including sending offensive messages and intentionally helping the opposing team: toxicity impacts strongly on game development, consumption and maintenance, but also on player health and well-being, also representing a form of cyberbullying [24].

In order to understand the diffusion of toxic behavior, in particular in the video game context, it is possible to analyze the phenomenon from two different points of view, focusing on the virtual context or on the social aspects.

a) Adopting the first point of view, the causes of the perpetration of toxic behavior could be found in the characteristics of virtual environments and their effects on the individual. Online environments have been often associated with negative behavior, in part because of the disinhibition effect [25]: individuals are more willing to show

Table 1. Online misconducts definitions

Negative Behavior	Definition	Sources
Cyberbullying	An aggressive and intentional act (by one or more individuals) meant to harm someone who is not able to defend themselves, carried out via electronic medium (e.g. blog, websites, emails, chats etc.…). This can comprise of verbal aggression, mockery, non-consensual photo sharing and other intentional aggressive behaviors	[19, 22]
Griefing	The act of intentionally disrupt other players' enjoyment by using game dynamics to create discomfort (e.g. destroying another ally player's construction)	[20, 22]
Cheating	Use of "cheats", namely softwares that facilitate game performance by breaking its rules (e.g. automatically targeting another player), thus resulting in lack of fairplay and enjoyment for other players	[21]
Toxic Behavior	Umbrella term comprising of the aforementioned in-game misconducts, aimed to elicit negative reactions and antagonize other players	[23, 24]

disruptive attitudes characterized by toxic connotations [24, 26] due to increased anonymity and invisibility, expressing themselves without restrictions or inhibitions. These effects are particularly accentuated in MOBA games, in which people do not feel accountable for their toxic behavior thanks to the anonymity and increase their aggressive behavior [27].

b) It is possible to adopt another point of view or a so-called social lens. Once a negative behavior is ignored or does not get appropriate reaction in the community it becomes a normative standard and will be followed by both old members and newcomers, who try to integrate with others following the common norm.

In this way, trying to outline the social psychological concepts behind this toxicity in MOBA games, an explanation of the spread of toxic behavior could be found in the bystander effect [28], which describes the tendency for observers to avoid helping a victim, particularly when they are immersed in a group. In this way, in this anonymous environment, the bystander effect can influence how other players react to a toxic player, leading the observer to not report the toxic player even though they directly witnessed the abuse. However, this could contribute to generating a toxic environment in which toxic behaviors are accepted and normalized.

In particular, Kwak et al. found that in the context of League of Legends, there is relatively low participation in reporting toxic behavior (confirming the impact of anonymity and bystander effect), but also that an explicit request to report toxic behavior significantly increases the amount of reporting. Furthermore, recent studies show League of Legends toxicity level is tragically increasing [29–31]. According to this, in the presented study, we directly asked the participants to report if they had suffered or perpetrated toxic behaviors.

In League of Legends, teams are often made up of strangers who will never play together again. However, effective communication and teamwork are essential points for winning a match: this need for cooperation and communication with teammates causes a strong dependence on social interactions with other players. As in MOBA games, players need to cooperate and those who are not sufficiently able to or refuse to collaborate are targeted. Consequently, communication channels can be misused to verbally assault other players, leading to a fragmented team and to unsatisfied players who could aim to quit the game. Grandprey-Shores et al. [32]found that interactions with toxic players decrease the retention rates of new players, while the same effect is not applicable to those who have been playing longer, i.e., expert players, or high ranked players. One possible explanation could be that exposure to toxic behavior leads to the perpetuation of them, since it has been proven that being a victim of toxic abuse in MOBA games increases the chance of perpetuating toxic behavior [33]. As a result, due to the normalization of toxic behaviors in games, a vicious circle is established: engaging in toxic behaviors will normalize players' beliefs about toxicity, and those with normalized beliefs will be more approving of toxic behaviors.

Consequently, experienced and skillful players are more likely to commit toxic behaviors [34], likely due to continuous exposure to toxicity [35]. In this way, Kordyaka et al. [33] found that past victimization experiences of toxicity led to higher levels of toxic disinhibition: thus, being the target of toxicity in the past leads to acceptance of toxic behaviors, which can consequently lead to an acceptance and perpetration of the same behaviors [33, 36].

Recent studies show that games belonging to the MOBA genre display very high toxic behavior tendencies in its players. Research shows that 66% of young players have reported having fallen victim to toxic behaviors, especially in MOBA environments [37]. Furthermore, 70% of League of Legends matches get disrupted by toxic behaviors [31]. A report carried out by the Anti-Defamation League (ADL) in 2019 displays how MOBAs context highly elicitates toxic behavior, specifically in DOTA 2 and League of Legends communities [38].

Rank can be an important metric of both skill level and player characteristics from the perspective of a player. In fact, in the videogame communities, and in particular in the League of Legends' community, stereotypes are formed around the different ranks [29], concerning the game modes, players interaction, in-game collaboration or cooperation, and so on. In addition, an important finding was that higher ranks supplied players' sense of achievement and gratification [29]. These kinds of achievements are central to players' experience and are usually obtained through a quite long gaming career studded with many victories and defeats, and in this sense, it assumes an important meaning and value for the player, who begins to experience complicated feelings for their rank. In fact, it becomes an indicator of skills and motivation, a reason to be proud but also something to keep, also causing frustration and fear of being unable to maintain a high rank [29].

Overall, this study aims to explore how toxic behavior and exposure to this have effects on players. In particular, we aimed to understand why experienced players are more likely to engage in toxic behavior [34], and why even if they are in a toxic context they do not leave the game. We assumed that rank was a critical variable in this process, and in this way, several hypotheses were formulated.

First, we expect that the acted toxicity would increase at a higher rank. Indeed, prolonged exposure to toxic behaviors may cause a normalization of these behaviors, and this can facilitate the assumption of these due to compliance or due to an interiorization of that pattern of behavior.

Hypothesis 1 (H1): The acted toxicity increases at higher ranks due to a higher exposure to toxicity and a consequent introjection of the norm.

Second, we expect that at higher ranks the game becomes more important to the player, which tries to satisfy his validation needs through the competitive game. In this way, due to the higher importance of the game and the validation seeking, we expect that the player perceives less desire to quit the game, developing a resistance to leave it and resilience in receiving or observing toxicity.

Hypothesis 2 (H2): At higher ranks the game becomes more salient for the players' identity, and so it influences and defines self-esteem. Therefore, we expected a positive correlation between ranks and self-esteem validation through the game.

Third, it is expected that players with higher ranks will have higher positive emotion activation because of LOL, given that they value the game more than other players (Self-esteem).

Hypothesis 3 (H3): At higher ranks, given the more competitive and challenging nature of the matches, as well as the number of successes required to reach a high rank, we expect to observe a higher level of positive emotions in players.

Considering the value that players with high ranks attach to winning and ranking, leaving the game, in any case, means that they will definitely lose. They are expected to be able to ignore many variables in order not to lose the game/rank.

Hypothesis 4 (H4): Highranked players are expected to be less likely to quit the game when exposed to toxic behavior.

2 Methods

2.1 Participants

A total of 370 participants from the Italian gaming community who could speak Italian ($N = 370$) participated to the experiment. Participants ranged in age from 14 to 38 years ($M = 22.70$; $SD = 4.09$). The majority of participants identified as cisgender men (83.8% of the sample), followed by cisgender women (12.4%). A smaller percentage identified as non-binary (2.7%), while 1.1% of participants did not provide an answer regarding their gender identity. In terms of educational status, more than half of the participants (64.1%) had completed high school. In terms of relationship status, 56.2% of participants reported being single, while 35.9% reported being in a relationship.

2.2 Procedure

The recruitment of participants for this study involved sending a message that contained a survey Google form link. This link was disseminated via various channels, including the web, and social media platforms such as Facebook and Discord, as well as mailing lists, to ensure that all potential participants had access to it. Prior to commencing the survey, participants were provided with a disclaimer form that outlined the study's objectives and assured the full anonymity of their responses. To proceed with the questionnaires, participants were required to acknowledge and accept the study's terms and conditions, which were in compliance with various ethical guidelines, including the Helsinki Declaration, Italian legal requirements of privacy and informed consent (Law Decree DL-101/2018), EU regulations (2016/699), and American Psychological Association (APA) guidelines. The survey's completion time was approximately 10 min.

2.3 Measures

Demographic Information Form. The study requested participants to complete a form containing demographic information. The form consisted of several inquiries about various aspects, including their gender, age, marital status, language ability, and educational qualification.

Gaming Activity. This section contains 5 ad-hoc items created to measure the participants' gaming activity and their relationship with rank in LoL. Examples of these items are: "What is the competitive rank you feel you belong to based on your skills?", "What competitive rank would you like to get to?".

Positive and Negative Affect Schedule (PANAS). In this study, positive and negative affect schedule was used to measure how the participants felt in the last 30–60 days during their competitive gaming activities. The Italian version of the PANAS and the measure consists of 20 adjectives graded from 1 (very slightly or not at all) to 5 (extremely) on a five-point Likert scale and asks to indicate how the participant generally felt [39]. PA (10 items; $\alpha = 0.72$): the positive affect scale reflects the level of pleasant engagement, that is, the extent to which a person feels enthusiastic, excited, or active; NA (10 items; $\alpha = 0.83$): the negative affect scale reflects a general dimension of unpleasant engagement and subjective distress that subsumes a broad range of aversive effects including fear, nervousness, guilt, and shame [39]. The original PANAS also has acceptable internal reliability is $\alpha = 0.76$ [40].

Toxicity in Game. In order to measure the toxic behaviors that the participants were exposed to or exhibited in the game, 12 ad-hoc items were prepared and added to this section. The participants were provided with an introduction that included the definitions of toxic behaviors, namely verbal abuse, and griefing, to read. They were asked if they had performed in, exposed, or observed such behaviors. Based on this, queries were posed concerning these behaviors. Examples of these items are: "How often have you wanted to stop playing LoL because of the toxic behavior you have been subjected to?", "What toxic behavior have you been subjected to?".

Gaming-Contingent Self-Worth Scale (GCSW). The scale comprises 29 items and is organized into four subscales, namely validation seeking, reward orientation, competition focus, and detachment. To obtain a total score, the subscale scores are summed up with a 5-point Likert scale running from "Strongly Disagree" to "Strongly Agree" [41]. In terms of overall reliability, the GCSW Scale demonstrated acceptable consistency as an all-encompassing measure, with a Cronbach's alpha coefficient of 0.94 across all 29 items. In the research conducted, 13 items were selected from GCSW, adapted to LoL and used in the research, of which seven were from the validation seeking sub-scale and six from the detachment sub-scale. Examples of the items used are: "My self-esteem would decrease if I stopped playing LoL", "I play LoL when I feel bad about myself to feel better", "Criticism from other players affects my overall sense of self-worth" [41]. In particular, we used only the selected items because the GCSW scale was developed mainly for RPG games, and so some items were referred to specific characteristics or mechanics of these games and were not transferable to the context of League of Legends.

3   Results

3.1   Descriptive Statistics

In the rank structure, the majority of participants are Gold (23.0%), the next ranks are Silver (18.4%) and Bronze (17.8%). The Iron rank represents 5.9% of the participants, while the Platinum and Diamond ranks are held by 17.3% and 10.0% respectively. There is a remarkable group of Master, Grand Master and Challenger ranks, representing 7.6% of the participants. In terms of the GCSW Validation Seeking scores, the results show a mean of 15.90 and a standard deviation of 5.63, indicating a moderate level of external validation seeking among the participants. In addition, participants' scores on the Positive and Negative Affect Schedule (PANAS) show a mean of 30.56 for positive affect and 18.44 for negative affect, with standard deviations of 8.06 and 7.64.

Table 2. Descriptive statistics of the collected variables

Variables	M (s.d.) N = 370
Current Rank	3.88 (1.64)
Acted Toxicity (yes)	40.3%
GCSW Validation Seeking	15.90 (5.63)
PANAS Pos	30.56 (8.06)
PANAS Neg	18.44 (7.64)
Quit desire	3.43 (0.90)

Moreover, the mean quit desire of the participants is 3.43 with a standard deviation of 0.90, indicating a pretty consistent level of desire to quit among the respondents. Lastly, it is important to highlight that toxicity level was reported among participants, with approximately 40.3% of respondents reporting toxic behavior during the gameplay (See Table 2.).

3.2   Inferential Analysis

We conducted hypothesis testing using Pearson correlation. Consistent with Hypothesis 1, we found that participants' toxicity levels increased with higher ranks, demonstrating a significant effect size that approached the "relatively large" threshold recommended by Gignac and Szodorai [42] (r = 0.27; p <0.001). Similarly, Hypothesis 2 was supported, revealing a positive and moderately strong association between validation-seeking scores and rank (r = 0.20; p <0.001). Furthermore, the results pertaining to Hypothesis 3 indicated a statistically significant and positive correlation between positive affectivity and rank, displaying a typical effect size (r = 0.20; p <0.001). In contrast, no significant relationship emerged between negative affectivity and rank (r = −0.01; p > 0.05). Lastly, we observed a meaningful association between the desire to quit the game due to experienced toxicity and rank, although with a more modest effect size (r = -0.12; p <0.05). Higher ranks were associated with a reduced inclination to abandon the game.

Despite the normal distribution of the variables of interest, which suggests the suitability of parametric analysis like Pearson's correlation, we aimed to examine potential non-linear relationships through the use of ANOVA and Fisher's Least Significant Difference (LSD) Test. Furthermore, we visually portrayed the changing patterns of the dependent variables in relation to competitive rank. Consistent with our expectations, the levels of Validation Seeking (Italy: $F(3;369) = 3.67$; p. = 0.001), PANAS positive (Italy: $F(3;369) = 5.37$; p. < 0.001), and Quit desire (Italy: $F(3;343) = 2.83$; p. = 0.01) appear to vary in a statistically significant way across different ranks. Subsequent post hoc analysis revealed significant inflection points in the distributions of the variables of interest, indicating noteworthy changes in their levels as represented in Fig. 1.

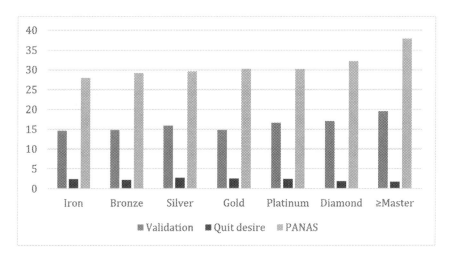

Fig. 1. Validation, Quit Desire, and PANAS mean values across participants' rank.

In general, as highlighted by the post hoc analysis, levels of validation seeking tend to remain stable and then increase dramatically from the Gold ranks onwards, reaching the highest level of validation seeking in the Master and above ranks. When it comes to positive affect (PANAS Positive), it is noteworthy that players at the Master rank and beyond consistently display the highest scores. There is a significant surge in positive affect observed only among players from the Master rank onwards, although a preliminary upward trend can be discerned even at the Diamond rank. Eventually, players ranked Master and above demonstrate the lowest desire to quit playing League of Legends in response to toxicity from other players. Moreover, players starting from ranked Diamond exhibit increased "resilience".

4 Discussion

Video games have become easily accessible through various devices in the modern digital world, attracting a wide range of age groups. Online video games, the most popular genre among those, provide players with a variety of experiences and opportunities for social interaction with other players. Although these opportunities for social interaction have many positive effects in contemporary society the negative effects are also too numerous to be ignored. Particularly in competitive online games, the competitive environment has been associated with various toxic behaviors among players.

Toxic behavior in online games is shown to be related to numerous conditions, such as anxiety, depression, internet gaming disorder and anger rumination issues [37]. The content of toxic behavior in MOBAs tends also to touch salient topics, like stereotypes and discrimination through racist, sexist, and homophobic hate speech [29, 43], thus contributing to other systemic structures of violence.

Toxicity in MOBAs appears to stem from various reasons, the most salient ones being competitiveness [29] and team performance dissatisfaction [24, 29]. Players, in fact, seem to find competitiveness and poor team performance perception as substantial eliciting factors to engage in toxic behaviors. The ranking system in MOBAs is a strong competitive motivation and might elicit stronger reactions and affection toward performance in players. For this reason, it appears fundamental to understand how these aforementioned design choices can affect people's behavior and psychology.

In line with the first hypothesis of this study, the results showed a significant positive correlation between rank and level of toxicity, and our findings supported (H1). This is consistent with previous studies of toxicity in online gaming, which have shown that higher ranked players are more likely to engage in toxic behavior [44]. This may be due to a number of factors, including the nature of competitive video games and performance expectations [18].

Our second hypothesis (H2) was also confirmed, showing positive correlation between validation-seeking behavior and rank. Since competitive gaming has high salience to the player and the ranking system involves player's skill evaluation, this correlation could be explained by the key role rank plays in defining the player's perceived worth and identity [45]. This may be caused by the fact that higher-ranked players are more often seen as successful and skilled, which can raise their status and affirm their self-esteem [46].

Next, our findings showed support for H3, exploring the positive relationship between rank and positive affectivity. Players with higher ranks therefore showed more positive affection towards the game. This can be explained by the positive feedback and satisfaction the players get from the competitiveness of the game itself and their ability to succeed in "climbing the rank ladder" [47].

Lastly, our fourth Hypothesis (H4), which stated that high rank players are less likely to quit the game when exposed to toxic behavior, was supported by our findings. Higher ranks players were associated with a reduced tendency to quit. A relevant hypothesis to this correlation could be related to the amount of effort and time dedicated to the game: acting almost as an effort justification bias, higher rank individuals might develop higher resistance to toxicity in order to keep focus and not lose their hard-earned rank.

Overall, the findings of this study provide important evidence regarding the dynamics of toxicity, validation-seeking, emotions, and quitting desire in the context of League of Legends. The results support the argument that higher ranks in the game influence players' attitudes, emotions, and behaviors, leading to increased toxicity, higher validation-seeking, and a decreased desire to quit the game. These findings indicate a specific psychological perspective (Gamer psychology, [48]) for understanding competitive gaming environments and emphasize the importance of supporting positive and respectful interactions between players, especially at higher ranks where toxicity tends to be more common.

There are several limitations of this study that need to be mentioned. The study was designed as an exploratory and cross-sectional approach, which does not provide direct indications of causality between the variables. The participants were only the Italian population, and which limits the generalizability, together with the non-probability sampling technique we relied on to collect the data. Moreover, the criterion variables were measured using ad hoc items (measurement bias), which is not a valid standard in terms of validity. Future research should consider intervention and enlightenment programs to prevent this situation in competitive online games, especially in genres where toxicity is high. Unfortunately, although game developers continue to impose various penalties against players for toxic behavior, the low functionality of the penalty system is evident in the toxicity statistics of the players.

5   Conclusions

Our study revealed that higher ranks in League of Legends are associated with increased toxicity, increased validation seeking, and decreased desire to quit the game. These findings highlight the importance of encouraging positive relationships in competitive gaming environments.

References

1. Guazzini, A., Gursesli, M.C., Serritella, E., Tani, M., Duradoni, M.: Obsessive-compulsive disorder (ocd) types and social media: are social media important and impactful for ocd people? Euro. J. Invest. Health, Psychol. Educ. **12**, 1108–1120 (2022). https://doi.org/10.3390/ejihpe12080078
2. Martucci, A., Gursesli, M.C., Duradoni, M., Guazzini, A.: Overviewing gaming motivation and its associated psychological and sociodemographic variables: a prisma systematic review. Hum. Behav. Emerg. Technol., e5640258 (2023). https://doi.org/10.1155/2023/5640258
3. Cheok, A.D.: Art and Technology of Entertainment Computing and Communication: Advances in Interactive New Media for Entertainment Computing. Springer, London (2010). https://doi.org/10.1007/978-1-84996-137-0

4. Pantano, E., Naccarato, G.: Entertainment in retailing: the influences of advanced technologies. J. Retailing Cons. Serv. 17. New Technol. Retailing: Trends Direct. 200–204 (2010). https://doi.org/10.1016/j.jretconser.2010.03.010

5. Gursesli, M.C., Martucci, A., Duradoni, M., Mattiassi, A., Guazzini, A.: Gaming Motivation: Developing a New Tool to Measure Psychological Motivations to Play Video Games (2023). https://doi.org/10.22492/issn.2187-4743.2023.5

6. Wijman, T.: The World's 2.7 Billion Gamers Will Spend $159.3 Billion on Games in 2020; The Market Will Surpass $200 Billion by 2023. Newzoo (2022)

7. Wolf, M.: Genre and the Video Game. The medium of the video game (2001)

8. Reitman, J.G., Anderson-Coto, M.J., Wu, M., Lee, J.S., Steinkuehler, C.: Esports Research: A Literature Review. Games Culture **15**, 32–50 (2020). https://doi.org/10.1177/1555412019840892

9. Xia, B., Wang, H., Zhou, R.: What Contributes to Success in MOBA Games? An Empirical Study of Defense of the Ancients 2. Games Cult. **14**, 498–522 (2019). https://doi.org/10.1177/1555412017710599

10. LLC, FN Media Group. Multiplayer Online Battle Arena (MOBA) Industry Estimated to Exceed $490 Million in Annual Sales By 2025. GlobeNewswire News Room. February 23 (2022)

11. Mora-Cantallops, M., Sicilia, M.-Á.: MOBA games: a literature review. Entertain. Comput. **26**, 128–138 (2018). https://doi.org/10.1016/j.entcom.2018.02.005

12. Donaldson, S.: Mechanics and Metagame: Exploring Binary Expertise in League of Legends. Games Cult. 12, 426–444 (2017). https://doi.org/10.1177/1555412015590063

13. Susic, P.: 2022 How Many People Play League of Legends & Average LoL Player Stats (2023)

14. Kahn, A.S., Williams, D.: We're all in this (game) together: transactive memory systems, social presence, and team structure in mbultiplayer online battle arenas. Commun. Res. **43**, 487–517 (2016). https://doi.org/10.1177/0093650215617504

15. Trepte, S., Reinecke, L., Juechems, K.: The social side of gaming: How playing online computer games creates online and offline social support. Comput. Hum. Behav. **28**, 832–839 (2012). https://doi.org/10.1016/j.chb.2011.12.003

16. Depping, A.E., Johanson, C., Mandryk, R.L.: Designing for friendship: modeling properties of play, in-game social capital, and psychological well-being. In: Proceedings of the 2018 Annual Symposium on Computer-Human Interaction in Play, CHI PLAY 2018, pp. 87–100. . Association for Computing Machinery, New York (2018). https://doi.org/10.1145/3242671.3242702

17. Mandryk, R.L., Frommel, J., Armstrong, A., Johnson, D.: How passion for playing world of warcraft predicts in-game social capital, loneliness, and wellbeing. Front. Psychol. 11 (2020)

18. Vorderer, P., Hartmann, T., Klimmt, C.: Explaining the enjoyment of playing video games: the role of competition. In Proceedings of the Second International Conference on Entertainment Computing, ICEC 2003, pp. 1–9. . Carnegie Mellon University, USA (2003)

19. Smith, P.K., Mahdavi, J., Carvalho, M., Fisher, S., Russell, S., Tippett, N.: Cyberbullying: its nature and impact in secondary school pupils. J. Child Psychol. Psychiatry **49**, 376–385 (2008). https://doi.org/10.1111/j.1469-7610.2007.01846.x

20. Foo, C.Y., Koivisto, E.M.I.: Defining grief play in MMORPGs: player and developer perceptions. In: Proceedings of the 2004 ACM SIGCHI International Conference on Advances in Computer Entertainment Technology, ACE 2004, pp. 245–250. Association for Computing Machinery, New York (2004). https://doi.org/10.1145/1067343.1067375

21. Blackburn, J., Kourtellis, N., Skvoretz, J., Ripeanu, M., Iamnitchi, A.: Cheating in online games: a social network perspective. ACM Trans. Internet Technol. 13: 9:1–9:25 (2014). https://doi.org/10.1145/2602570

22. Chesney, T., Coyne, I., Logan, B., Madden, N.: Griefing in virtual worlds: causes, casualties and coping strategies. Inf. Syst. J. **19**, 525–548 (2009). https://doi.org/10.1111/j.1365-2575.2009.00330.x

23. Lapidot-Lefler, N., Barak, A.: Effects of anonymity, invisibility, and lack of eye-contact on toxic online disinhibition. Comput. Hum. Behav. **28**, 434–443 (2012). https://doi.org/10.1016/j.chb.2011.10.014

24. Kwak, H., Blackburn, J., Han, S.. Exploring Cyberbullying and other toxic behavior in team competition online games. In: Proceedings of the 33rd Annual ACM Conference on Human Factors in Computing Systems, CHI 2015. pp. 3739–3748. Association for Computing Machinery, New York (2015). https://doi.org/10.1145/2702123.2702529

25. Phillips, W.: This Is Why We Can't Have Nice Things: Mapping the Relationship Between Online Trolling and Mainstream Culture. MIT Press (2015)

26. Fryling, M., Cotler, J.L., Rivituso, J., Mathews, L., Pratico, S.: Cyberbullying or normal game play? Impact of age, gender, and experience on cyberbullying in multi-player online gaming environments: Perceptions from one gaming forum. Journal of Information Systems Applied Research **8**, 4 (2015)

27. Christopherson, K.M.: The positive and negative implications of anonymity in Internet social interactions: "on the Internet, Nobody Knows You're a Dog." Comput. Hum. Behav. 23. Including the Special Issue: Education and Pedagogy with Learning Objects and Learning Designs: 3038–3056 (2007). https://doi.org/10.1016/j.chb.2006.09.001

28. Barlińska, J., Szuster, A., Winiewski, M.: Cyberbullying among adolescent bystanders: role of the communication medium, form of violence, and empathy. J. Comm. Appli. Soc. Psychol. **23**, 37–51 (2013). https://doi.org/10.1002/casp.2137

29. Kou, Y.: Toxic behaviors in team-based competitive gaming: the case of league of legends. In: Proceedings of the Annual Symposium on Computer-Human Interaction in Play, CHI PLAY 2020, pp. 81–92. Association for Computing Machinery, New York (2020). https://doi.org/10.1145/3410404.3414243

30. Sengün, S., Salminen, J., Mawhorter, P., Jung, S., Jansen, B.: Exploring the relationship between game content and culture-based toxicity: a case study of league of legends and MENA Players. In: Proceedings of the 30th ACM Conference on Hypertext and Social Media, HT 2019, pp. 87–95. Association for Computing Machinery, New York (2019). https://doi.org/10.1145/3342220.3343652

31. Aguerri, J.C., Santisteban, M., Miró-Llinares, F.: The Enemy hates best? toxicity in league of legends and its content moderation implications. Euro. J. Criminal Policy Res. (2023). https://doi.org/10.1007/s10610-023-09541-1

32. Grandprey-Shores, K., He, Y., Swanenburg, K.L., Kraut, R., Riedl, J.: The identification of deviance and its impact on retention in a multiplayer game. In: Proceedings of the 17th ACM Conference on Computer Supported Cooperative Work & Social Computing, CSCW 2014, pp. 1356–1365. , NY, USA: Association for Computing Machinery, New York (2014). https://doi.org/10.1145/2531602.2531724

33. Kordyaka, B., Jahn, and Bjoern Niehaves. 2020. Towards a unified theory of toxic behavior in video games. *Internet Research* 30. Emerald Publishing Limited: 1081–1102. https://doi.org/10.1108/INTR-08-2019-0343

34. Beres, N.A., Frommel, J., Reid, E., Mandryk, R.L., Klarkowski, M.: Don't you know that you're toxic: normalization of toxicity in online gaming. In: Proceedings of the 2021 CHI Conference on Human Factors in Computing Systems, CHI 2021, pp. 1–15. Association for Computing Machinery, New York (2021). https://doi.org/10.1145/3411764.3445157

35. Shen, C., Sun, Q., Kim, T., Wolff, G., Ratan, R., Williams, D.: Viral vitriol: predictors and contagion of online toxicity in world of tanks. Comput. Hum. Behav. **108**, 106343 (2020)

36. Cook, C., Schaafsma, J., Antheunis, M.: Under the bridge: An in-depth examination of online trolling in the gaming context. New Medi Society **20**, 3323–3340 (2018). https://doi.org/10.1177/1461444817748578

37. Zsila, Á., Shabahang, R., Aruguete, M.S., Orosz, G.: Toxic behaviors in online multiplayer games: Prevalence, perception, risk factors of victimization, and psychological consequences. Aggressive Behav. **48**, 356–364 (2022). https://doi.org/10.1002/ab.22023

38. Free to Play? Hate, Harassment, and Positive Social Experiences in Online Games | ADL. 2023. https://www.adl.org/resources/report/free-play-hate-harassment-and-positive-social-experiences-online-games. 20 Accessed July

39. Terraciano, A., McCrae, R.R., Costa, Jr., O.T.: Factorial and construct validity of the Italian positive and negative affect schedule (PANAS). Euro. J. Psychol. Assessment **19**, 131–141 (2003). https://doi.org/10.1027/1015-5759.19.2.131

40. Watson, D., Clark, L.A., Tellegen, A.: Development and validation of brief measures of positive and negative affect: The PANAS scales. J Personal. Soc. Psychol. **54**, 1063–1070. https://doi.org/10.1037/0022-3514.54.6.1063

41. Beard, C.L., Wickham, R.E.: Gaming-contingent self-worth, gaming motivation, and Internet Gaming Disorder. Comput. Hum. Behav. **61**, 507–515 (2016). https://doi.org/10.1016/j.chb.2016.03.046

42. Gignac, G.E., Szodorai, E.T.: Effect size guidelines for individual differences researchers. Personality Individ. Differ. **102**, 74–78 (2016). https://doi.org/10.1016/j.paid.2016.06.069

43. Liu, Y., Agur., C.: After all, they don't know me" exploring the psychological mechanisms of toxic behavior in online games. Games Cult. **18**, 598–621. https://doi.org/10.1177/15554120221115397

44. Monge, C.K., O'Brien, T. C.: . Effects of individual toxic behavior on team performance in Leaguoe of Legends. Media Psychol. 25, 82–105 (2022). https://doi.org/10.1080/15213269.2020.1868322

45. Padilla-Walker, L.M., Nelson, L.J., Carroll, J.S., Jensen, A.C.: More than a just a game: video game and internet use during emerging adulthood. J. Youth Adolesc. **39**, 103–113 (2010). https://doi.org/10.1007/s10964-008-9390-8

46. Cruz, C., Hanus, M.D., Fox, J.: The need to achieve: Players' perceptions and uses of extrinsic meta-game reward systems for video game consoles. Comput. Hum. Behav. **71**, 516–524 (2017). https://doi.org/10.1016/j.chb.2015.08.017

47. Rieger, D., Wulf, T., Kneer, J., Frischlich, L., Bente, G.: The winner takes it all: The effect of in-game success and need satisfaction on mood repair and enjoyment. Comput. Hum. Behav. **39**, 281–286 (2014). https://doi.org/10.1016/j.chb.2014.07.037

48. Bostan, B. (ed.): : Gamer Psychology and Behavior. International Series on Computer Entertainment and Media Technology. Cham: Springer International Publishing. (2016). https://doi.org/10.1007/978-3-319-29904-4

Comparing Performance and Experience in VR vs. Real-World Through a Puzzle Game

Ahmed Choueib⬡ and Mehmet İlker Berkman$^{(\boxtimes)}$ ⬡

Bahcesehir University, Istanbul, Türkiye
`ilker.berkman@bau.edu.tr`

Abstract. The study aims to explore the VR gaming experience in comparison to real-world gameplay. User performance and experience is compared in an HMD VR puzzle game and its real-world toy replica, with 28 participants in a within-subjects experimental design. Mean comparisons on task time and success rate do not have a significant difference, as well as the subjective task load and task performance obtained through NASA-TLX. The subjective game user experience measures also did not reveal any significant difference between the toy and VR gameplay, except the Enjoyment measures via Game User Experience Satisfaction Scale. Findings suggest that the VR gaming experiences can replace with the real-world gameplay, within the context of a cognitive tasks in a limited representation of spatial surrounding. The interactions with the nearby objects in an HMD-based virtual environment and real-world lead to very similar measurements of user performance and experience.

Keywords: virtual reality · task load · presence · user experience · puzzle · game · real-world

1 Introduction

This study compares real-world and VR task performance on a predominantly mental puzzle-solving task. It investigates differences in objective performance, perceived self-performance, and game user experience. While previous studies had mixed results regarding objective performance, we anticipate similar user performance in both conditions, especially if VR controls are user-friendly. We expect users to find VR tasks more challenging due to unfamiliarity with the VR environment, but also more engaging because of the novelty effect. We are uncertain about applying presence, a key aspect of the VR user experience, to the real world, so we let participants decide on its applicability.

The VR task selected for this study is "Keep Talking and Nobody Explodes" [1], available on PC and mobile platforms. Unlike previous studies, we recreated in-game digital elements and environments in the real world, instead of emulating the real world in a digital format. We fabricated a toy bomb with an electronic circuit board, replicating the digital asset from the game.

© The Author(s), under exclusive license to Springer Nature Switzerland AG 2024
L. Vale Costa et al. (Eds.): VJ 2023, CCIS 1984, pp. 72–85, 2024.
https://doi.org/10.1007/978-3-031-51452-4_6

2   Related Work

2.1   Puzzle Games in VR

While some VR puzzle games focus on exploring virtual spaces [2–7], others revolve around real-world object manipulation [8–14], decomposed images [15–17], or abstract geometrical shapes [18–21]. Studies comparing real-world and virtual performance cover various aspects, such as spatial tasks like wayfinding [22], locomotion [23], and orientation [24], along with objective efficiency and effectiveness measures [25–27].

Slater et al. [28] found that in a word puzzle game, social interactions were better in a real-world setting, but they didn't provide performance metrics. Heldal et al. [29] compared task completion times for a 3D cube puzzle in face-to-face and various virtual conditions, revealing no significant difference. Axelsson et al. [30] presented a more complex task, with only six of 22 participants achieving it in the VR condition, while all succeeded in the face-to-face condition.

Oren et al. [31] showed no significant difference in task completion times between virtual and real-world users for a cube puzzle after training. Subjective evaluations revealed no significant differences in task difficulty, realism, or learning helpfulness, but physical assembly was easier in the real-world.

Some studies used NASA-TLX for self-assessment. Stone et al. [32] found mental demand similar for real-world and VR welding trainees, despite shorter training times in VR. Kamaraj et al. [33] reported lower mental demand and frustration in VR for a wheelchair driving task. Mouraviev et al. [34] showed similar raw NASA-TLX scores for VR and robotic surgery, except for frustration, which was higher in VR. Narasimha et al. [35] found better performance scores in VR despite a lower NASA-TLX score. George et al. [36] observed worse performance in VR for a smart home door authentication task, with no significant NASA-TLX score difference. Chang et al. [37] noted higher scores for temporal demand, frustration, and performance in VR for pediatric resuscitation. Rizzuto et al. [38] found no differences in joint angles but better pointing accuracy in the real world, with higher Task Load Index scores in one virtual condition. A throwing task [39] showed no significant NASA-TLX differences, but real-world accuracy was better. For a golf putting comparison, Harris et al. [9] reported better real-world putting performance, with no significant distance estimation difference. The SIM-TLX Index [25] showed no differences except for perceptual strain. Pontonnier et al. [40] reported higher discomfort in VE and increased muscular activity for the same real-world task.

2.2   Game User Experience

Studies comparing digital gaming and real-world toys mainly focus on social interaction [41, 42] and learning outcomes [43] rather than the game user experience. Notably, there is no study comparing the gaming experience on an electro-mechanical artifact with its digital counterpart.

On the topic of presence, Usoh et al. [44] found that assessing "sense of being there" differently in real-world and virtual reality can lead to varying interpretations. They suggest that participants interpret the question differently for the real world, emphasizing the sense of involvement, lack of isolation, and comfort, whereas virtual presence is understood as being in a computer-generated environment and the ability to act within it. Recent research shows similar brain activities in HMD-based VR and the real world [45].

Visual fidelity in representing virtual objects affects presence, but other factors like head tracking, frame rate, sound, and interaction methods play a more significant role [46–48]. Presence is a perceptual phenomenon observed in virtual reality, where individuals respond to events, feel their bodies, and even change body ownership based on the virtual representation they see. Presence is not a cognitive illusion; it's a rapid, automatic reaction of the brain-body system [49].

Weber et al. [51] argue that presence should encompass both spatial presence (being there) and perceived realism. Spatial presence is influenced by the allocation of attentional resources and place illusion, while perceived realism is a subjective judgment of stimulus fidelity. This broader sense of presence acknowledges that engaging with a toy can induce a similar altered state of consciousness as in VR, affecting volitional behaviors and non-conscious psychophysiological responses.

3 Methodology

3.1 Procedure

Participants play either the VR or toy version of "Keep Talking and Nobody Explodes," aiming to replicate a similar experience. The physical toy mimics the virtual bomb's components and design, with the only difference being the randomized positions of elements in the VR version as seen Fig. 1. The goal is to defuse the bomb in 5 min, guided by a moderator following instructions from a provided booklet [54].

The game's level includes three modules: a 5-min countdown, a module with six differently colored wires, another with four symbols on a keypad, and a bomb deactivation button. The moderator, always the same person with prior game experience, communicates with participants via VoIP.

Fig. 1. The physical toy bomb (on the left) replicated from the virtual bomb (on the right). Female participant defusing the toy bomb and male participant defusing the virtual bomb

After the first gameplay session, participants complete a questionnaire including personal questions and gameplay-related items. They rest for at least 10 min and then play on the other platform, followed by the same questionnaire but with gameplay-related items.

3.2 Participants

A total of 28 participants (14 males, 14 females), aged 18 to 27 (M = 23.11, SD = 3.1), were recruited among the researcher's social circle for this within-subjects study. They were divided into VR-at-first and toy-at-first groups to alternate the play sequence and minimize bias. Participants' gaming exposure was measured, with an average weighted gameplay score of 3.22 out of 7 (SD = 1.59) over the last 3 months, measured via items adapted from LTE [72]. Male participants (M = 3.76, SD = 1.31) had higher gaming frequency than females (M = 2.69, SD = 1.7), as depicted in Fig. 2.

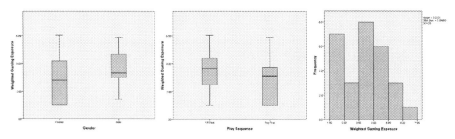

Fig. 2. Weighted gaming exposure of participants by gender, play sequence groups, number of participants regarding their scores.

In terms of prior VR experience, 17 had none, six tried it once, three a couple of times, one more than 10 times, and one was a regular user. Female participants had limited VR experience compared to males. Participants had moderate interest in the game's subject (M = 3.9, SD = 1.04), an enduring personality factor that influences attention allocation. VR-at-first and toy-at-first groups had similar interest scores (M = 3.90, SD = .97 and M = 3.91, SD = 1.16, respectively). Visual-Spatial Imagery scores, another enduring personality factor affecting the player's experience, were close for VR-at-first (M = 3.91, SD = .69) and toy-at-first (M = 3.79, SD = .77) groups.

Independent samples t-tests showed no significant differences between VR-at-first and toy-at-first groups regarding prior VR experience, gaming habits, domain interest, and spatial abilities (all p > .05). Participants were evenly represented in both groups based on these factors.

3.3 Measures and Data Collection

Task Performance. Task performance is evaluated based on objective indicators of game success, such as defusing the bomb within 5 min and the time remaining after successful defusal. Subjective assessment employs the NASA-TLX (National Aeronautics and Space Administration – Task Load Index) [55, 9] to measure the workload perceived by the player handling the bomb. NASA-TLX comprises six subscales assessed on a 20-point horizontal line scale and originally scored through a two-step process, encompassing Physical Demand, Mental Demand, Temporal Demand, Performance, Frustration, and Effort spent. Although the SIM-TLX is a recent alternative [56] for performance assessment specific to VR, we chose NASA-TLX for two reasons. First, it can be benchmarked with a worldwide collection of 556 studies [57]. Second, given the differences between adjusted and raw NASA-TLX scores, reflecting the perceived importance of task loads, we believe that this issue should be further explored through a real-world to VR comparison.

Game User Experience. GUESS (Game User Experience Satisfaction Scale) [58] is a 55-item scale with 9 factors for evaluating user satisfaction with various video games. We used the last three factors in our study: Usability/Playability assesses user interface, controls, and goal understanding; Enjoyment gauges pleasure and delight, while Personal Gratification focuses on motivational aspects.

Additionally, we used the Attention/Allocation and Involvement dimensions from the MEC-SPQ short version [52]. Attention/Allocation queries perceptual focus, and Involvement addresses higher cognitive processes. Other presence-related MEC-SPQ dimensions are also employed, as explained below.

Presence. Considering prior research on real-world versus virtual environment presence (as discussed in Related Studies), assessing a real-world toy experience's presence and comparing it to a virtual environment might initially seem implausible. However, the bomb used in our study is essentially a "toy," a non-real artifact by definition. Engaging with a toy parallels a VR experience, where users are aware that the toy isn't real at a cognitive level. Furthermore, conscious interaction with the toy mirrors behavior in VR, potentially eliciting unconscious psychophysiological responses [59]. As presence is a mediated experience, we argue that the "toy bomb" can also serve as a medium for enabling presence. Therefore, we allowed participants to decide whether the presence-related MEC-SPQ [52] items were applicable to the toy condition before answering them.

Despite numerous questionnaires for assessing spatial presence [60], we chose SPES [7] because it evaluates spatial presence within the Self-Location and Possible Actions dimensions and evolved from MEC-SPQ, which also considers realism and flow-related measures as components of presence. Moreover, SPES [] and MEC-SPQ [52] are known to be sensitive to different media and content [61,]. We also utilized the Suspension of Disbelief and Spatial Situation Model items from the short version of MEC-SPQ []. Suspension of Disbelief items inquire about errors and inconsistencies in the medium, while Spatial Situation Model items assess the precise understanding of the spatial surroundings.

3.4 Data Analysis

The performance data and the survey data were analyzed through a series of paired samples t-tests, assessing the scores obtained with the VR compared to the toy condition for each participant where the sample size is enough and the mean differences between the pairs are assumed to be normally distributed, regarding the results of Shapiro-Wilk tests. Some of the participants did not respond to the SPES [61] items for the toy condition, as they thought that they are not applicable for the real-world. For Spatial Presence dimension, 11 participants respondent for both toy and VR conditions, where there were 10 responses for Possible Actions dimension. Due to the small sample size, we executed non-parametric Wilcoxon signed-rank tests for these scores. In addition, the null hypothesis of normal distribution cannot be rejected for mean differences of MEC-SPQ [52] Attention/Allocation, Involvement, and raw NASA-TLX [55, 56] performance scores, which are also explored via non-parametric Wilcoxon signed-rank tests.

4   Results and Discussion

4.1   Performance and Task Load

Objective performance was assessed by task completion success and remaining task time. All 28 participants successfully disarmed the bomb in their trials, except one participant who exploded it in the first VR trial. Paired samples t-tests showed no significant difference in the time remaining (p > .05) with an average of 125.3 s (SD = 52.24) in VR and 147.4 s (SD = 57.49) in the toy condition, as in Fig. 3.

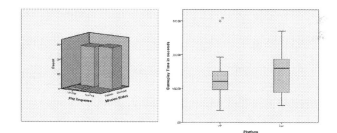

Fig. 3. Task completion and time on task

Subjective task load was explored using NASA-TLX assessments (raw and adjusted scores) in Table 1. When adjusted TLX scores were evaluated with percentile ranks, the VR condition showed higher Mental Demand, Temporal Demand, Effort, Frustration, and Overall scores than the toy condition. The lower VR Performance percentile rank may indicate that participants perceived their performance as poorer. Physical Demand had equal percentile ranks, with some participants perceiving higher Physical Demand in the toy condition. Paired sample t-tests did not reveal significant differences between the conditions for any NASA-TLX scores (p > .05). The Wilcoxon signed rank test also showed no significant difference in raw Performance score (p = .045).

As given in Table 1, benchmarking raw VR results with reference values from 72 VR studies showed that all raw scores exceeded mean reference values. Physical Demand, Temporal Demand, and Frustration were notably above the upper bounds of benchmarked studies, indicating a high workload for the VR task. While the benchmarked VR applications were for education and healthcare, the puzzle game in this study intentionally designed to be challenging. Hertzum's [57] reference values did not include a category comparable to the toy condition results. Comparing both toy and VR scores with reference values from 93 studies in Asia revealed higher scores for all dimensions except Effort for the toy condition. The Mental Demand score for the toy condition was similar to scores obtained in Asia. In comparison to 556 studies, all conditions for all dimensions were above the average NASA-TLX scores, except for the Effort score in the toy condition (50th percentile). These comparisons suggest a task load above average for the system evaluated in this study, considering the percentile correspondence of the scores.

Table 1. NASA TLX scores, benchmark values and mean comparisons

		Mean		SD		t(27)		Benchmark (Raw)			
NASA - TLX	Condition	Raw	Adj	Raw	Adj	Raw	Adj	VR	Asia	General	Perc
Mental Demand	VR	63.57	198.21	29.02	130.9	1.57	1.72	47 ± 20	55 ± 19	49 ± 17	70th
	Toy	56.07	156.43	30.98	128.5						60th
Physical Demand	VR	51.25	85.54	26.09	95.9	0.36	1.11	26 ± 13	42 ± 18	32 ± 16	80th
	Toy	48.93	117.14	31.57	127.5						80th
Temporal Demand	VR	66.25	217.32	25.73	145.4	1.73	1.28	40 ± 17	47 ± 19	42 ± 16	90th
	Toy	56.43	178.57	28.89	145						70th
Performance	VR	56.61 62.5[1]	153.21	28.77	115.2	.94 -2[2]	.95	47 ± 24	49 ± 21	45 ± 19	70th
	Toy	63.04 80a	181.25	33.26	133.9						80th
Effort	VR	64.64	138.75	25.05	110.5	1.97	0.50	48 ± 19	55 ± 19	50 ± 16	80th
	Toy	53.04	127.86	31.01	111.3						50th
Frustration	VR	59.11	157.86	22.77	131.1	1.52	1.37	34 ± 18	40 ± 18	36 ± 14	90th

The results indicate that workload is similar when the bomb disarming puzzle task is executed in a real-world or VR setting. This aligns with previous findings in many studies that do not reveal a difference between real-world and VR tasks or even show lower task loads for VR.

The higher changes in values for adjusted mental and temporal scores suggest that participants found the task more challenging in these aspects in both conditions. Although the raw score for physical demand is lower in the toy condition, the adjusted score is higher than in VR, indicating that participants perceived physical demand as more important in the real-world task. This finding is expected as participants needed to interact with the bomb mechanisms in the real-world setting using a physical wire-cutter.

4.2 Game User Experience

From the game user experience perspective, the Enjoyment dimension of GUESS [58] showed a significant but small difference, with a mean score of 5.55 (SD = .65) for VR compared to 5.19 for the toy condition (t(25) = 3.11, p < .05). The playability/usability and Personal Gratification scores obtained via GUESS items for both conditions were very similar, as shown in Table 2.

---

[1] Median values since the mean differences cannot be assumed as normally distributed.

[2] Score obtained for Wilcoxon signed rank test.

The Attention Allocation score of MEC-SPQ [52], assessed through a Wilcoxon signed rank test, did not reveal a significant difference between the VR (Mdn = 5) and Toy (Mdn = 4.75) conditions ($z = 1.73$, $p = .083$). Similarly, the MEC-SPQ Involvement scores showed no significant difference ($z = -1.5$, $p = .148$).

Table 2. Mean comparison of GUESS scores

UX metrics	Condition	Mean Score	SD	T-Test
Playability / Usability (GUESS)	VR	5.61	0.86	$t(26) = -.07$, $p = 0.95$
	Toy	5.62	0.87	
Enjoyment (GUESS)	VR	5.55	0.65	$t(25) = 3.11$, $p = .005$
	Toy	5.19	0.67	
Personal Gratification (GUESS)	VR	6.23	0.67	$t(25) = 2.05$, $p = .05$
	Toy	6.02	0.60	

The nearly identical score on the Playability/Usability dimension suggests that the VR equipment no longer poses an obstacle or additional workload for users. The real-world environment was aligned with the VR condition, resulting in similar attention allocation and involvement scores. Regardless of the bomb being a digital artifact in VR or an electromechanical toy in the real world, participants focused on the mental task of solving the puzzle in both conditions. Personal Gratification scores indicated a similar sense of achievement in both gameplay media. While the enjoyment scores exhibited a significant difference, it was relatively small. Given that most participants had limited or no VR experience, the higher VR score may be attributed to the novelty effect of VR, consistent with previous studies [63–65]. In conclusion, using VR did not significantly enhance the game user experience in the context of a bomb puzzle game compared to the toy version.

4.3 Presence

Presence related metrics of MEC-SPQ [52] were also led to very similar scores for both conditions, as given in Table 3. The Spatial Situation Model score, where the participants are queried for their mental image of the medium regarding to its arrangements, size and surroundings were almost equal for VR and toy experiences. The four Suspension of Disbelief items where the participants reflect on the inconsistences, errors, contradictions, and their attention on these issues also led to a very similar score for both conditions.

Presence-related metrics from MEC-SPQ yielded nearly identical scores for both conditions, detailed in Table 3. The Spatial Situation Model and Suspension of Disbelief scores showed very little difference between VR and toy experiences.

Regarding the Spatial Situation Model score, it seems participants could clearly perceive and understand the bomb in both conditions, with the bomb design appearing equally plausible, as indicated by the Suspension of Disbelief score. The puzzle-like

Table 3. Comparison of mean scores for presence-related measures

UX metrics	Condition	Mean Score	SD	T-Test
Spatial Situation Model (MEC-SPQ)	VR	4.04	0.90	$t(27) = -0.16, p = .87$
	Toy	4.06	0.84	
Suspension of Disbelief (MEC-SPQ)	VR	2.93	0.87	$t(27) = 0.14, p = .89$
	Toy	2.91	0.76	

design of the bomb may have seemed irrelevant to participants, leading to medium-level scores around 3 out of 5 for both conditions.

For the SPES items, many participants found them inapplicable to the toy condition. However, over one-third of participants believed they could respond to these questions within the context of their toy experience. The Wilcoxon Signed Rank Test analysis with this small sample size showed no significant difference between the toy (Mdn = 4.38) and the VR (Mdn = 4.5) conditions for the Self-Location dimension of SPES, which assesses participants' actual and physical presence in the environment.

The Possible Actions score, concerning interactions with objects, displayed no significant difference between the toy condition (Mdn = 4.5) and the VR condition (Mdn = 4.19).

These results align with Usoh et al. [43], where the real-world office space was compared with its VR representation using presence questionnaires [66, 67]. While higher presence scores in the real-world experience were expected, the difference turned out to be marginally significant or similar. It's worth noting that both the VR and toy conditions occurred in dark rooms with limited surrounding details. Despite a very high median score for "Self-Location," indicating users felt "being there," the VE environment was not well-defined and largely left to the user's imagination.

While the Possible Actions score was not significantly different, it was slightly higher for the toy condition, where more potential actions were available. Users could break apart the toy bomb, throw it outside the room, or engage in various actions within the physical world's limitations. Curiously, users scored the Possible Actions items similarly for both conditions, indicating they may have imposed restrictions on themselves based on the rules of "the game" rather than design limitations.

5   Conclusion

The results presented and discussed above reveal that a gaming task that highly depends on cognitive processes such as solving a puzzle do not lead to significant differences in user performance, workload, user experience or presence either it is executed through a physical toy, or an HMD based VR environment. That is in line with the findings of studies conducted after 2015, which report that workload for VR is comparable or lower than real-world settings; due to the advancements in displays quality, motion tracking and controllers after 2015.

While we observed only a minor difference just for the Enjoyment rating by the participants, that can be explained through a novelty effect since our participants had some very limited prior experience with HMDs.

The subjective workload is higher than NASA-TLX benchmark results of other VR studies, studies executed in Asia and worldwide. Since the evaluated task is a gameplay that is deliberately designed to be challenging, these results are not unexpected.

While the results obtained regarding the user experience and presence are very similar in both real-world and virtual environment tasks as well as performance metrics, our findings suggest that the VR gaming experiences can replace with the real-world gameplay. However, it should be noted again that this study is conducted through a puzzle game, in which the task has a mental and temporal demand rather than being physical. In our experiment, the tasks were applied by a handful of mechanics that manipulate the basic object of a box, ranging from wire cutting, pressing the buttons, and rotating the bomb, which is a different system all together than the type of experiences such as racing, or jet flying games where the user becomes surrounded by the interactive environment. The application evaluated in our study has a minimal spatial surrounding which does not affect the gameplay. On the other hand, our study provided evidence that the interactions with the nearby objects are very similar in a HMD-based virtual environment and real-world, within the context of a cognitive task. This conclusion can be reflected further beyond the gaming context, to claim that VR experience is not different from the real-world experience where the task has a non-spatial mental nature.

The primary goal of this study was not exploring the concept of presence beyond the virtual environments. On the other hand, our results imply that real-world experiences such as engaging with a toy can also invoke sense of presence as a consequence of mediated interaction.

References

1. Steel Crate Games (2015) Keep Talking and Nobody Explodes. Video Game (VR). https://www.igdb.com/games/keep-talking-and-nobody-explodes
2. Gonzalez, J., Pham, C., Umejiaku, A., Benjamin, J., Dang, T.: SkeletonVR: educating human anatomy through an interactive puzzle assembly. In The 12th International Conference on Advances in Information Technology, pp. 1–5, June 2021. https://doi.org/10.1145/3468784.3471605
3. Krekhov, A., Emmerich, K., Rotthaler, R., Krueger, J.: Puzzles unpuzzled: towards a unified taxonomy for analog and digital escape room games. Proc. ACM Human-Comput. Interact. 5, 1–24 (2021). https://doi.org/10.1145/3474696
4. Nyyssönen, T., Smed, J.: Exploring virtual reality mechanics in puzzle design. Comput. Games J. 10, 65–87 (2021). https://doi.org/10.1007/s40869-020-00120-6
5. Berkman, M.I., Bostan, B., Yalcin, B.: Controllers in VR game user experience: perceived user performance on a VR puzzle game. In: Contemporary Topics in Computer Graphics and Games, pp. 17–28. Peter Lang Publishing Group (2019)
6. Calabrese, L., Flangas, A., Harris, F.C.: Multi-user VR cooperative puzzle game. In: Latifi, S. (ed.) 17th International Conference on Information Technology–New Generations (ITNG 2020), pp. 293–299. Springer International Publishing, Cham (2020). https://doi.org/10.1007/978-3-030-43020-7_39

7. Khiew, J.B., Tan, P.H., Lin, F., Seah, H.S.: VR puzzle room for cognitive rehabilitation. In: International Forum on Medical Imaging in Asia 2019, vol. 11050, pp. 182–189. SPIE, March 2019. https://doi.org/10.1117/12.2518591

8. Berkman, M.I., Catak, G., Eremektar, M.C.: Comparison of VR and desktop game user experience in a puzzle game: "keep talking and nobody explodes." AJIT-e: Online Acad. J. Inf. Technol. **11**(42), 180–204 (2020). https://doi.org/10.5824/ajite.2020.03.008.x

9. Harris, D., Wilson, M., Vine, S.: Development and validation of a simulation workload measure: the simulation task load index (SIM-TLX). Virtual Real. **24**(4), 557–566 (2020). https://doi.org/10.1007/s10055-019-00422-9

10. Jeong, S., Yun, H.H., Lee, Y., Han, Y.: Glow the buzz: a VR puzzle adventure game mainly played through haptic feedback. In Extended Abstracts of the 2023 CHI Conference on Human Factors in Computing Systems, pp. 1–6, April 2023

11. Katsantonis, M.N., Manikas, A., Mavridis, I.: Design of a cultural heritage gesture-based puzzle game and evaluation of user experience. Appl. Sci. **13**(9), 5493 (2023). https://doi.org/10.3390/app13095493

12. Lee, P.W., Wang, H.Y., Tung, Y.C., Lin, J.W., Valstar, A.: TranSection: hand-based interaction for playing a game within a virtual reality game. In: Proceedings of the 33rd Annual ACM Conference Extended Abstracts on Human Factors in Computing Systems, pp. 73–76, April 2015. https://doi.org/10.1145/2702613.2728655

13. Pohlandt, D., Preim, B., Saalfeld, P.: Supporting anatomy education with a 3D puzzle in a VR environment-Results from a pilot study. In: Proceedings of Mensch und Computer 2019, pp. 91–102 (2019). https://doi.org/10.1145/3340764.3340792

14. Roumana, A., Georgopoulos, A., Koutsoudis, A.: Developing AN educational cultural heritage 3d puzzle in a virtual reality environment. Int. Arch. Photogramm. Remote. Sens. Spat. Inf. Sci. **43**, 885–891 (2022). https://doi.org/10.5194/isprs-archives-XLIII-B2-2022-885-2022

15. Araújo, J.D.F.O., Ribeiro, E.H., de Paiva Guimarães, M., Brega, J.R.F., Brandão, A.F., Dias, D.R.C.: Immersive Brain Puzzle: a virtual reality application aimed at the rehabilitation of post-stroke patients. In: 2021 16th Iberian Conference on Information Systems and Technologies (CISTI), pp. 1–6. IEEE, June 2021. https://doi.org/10.23919/CISTI52073.2021.9476311

16. Pan, Y., Steed, A.: The impact of self-avatars on trust and collaboration in shared virtual environments. PLoS ONE **12**(12), e0189078 (2017). https://doi.org/10.1371/journal.pone.0189078

17. Vercelli, G.V., Iacono, S., Vallarino, M., Zolezzi, D.: Puzzle battle 2.0: a revisited serious game in VR during pandemic's period. In: de Rosa, F., Schottman, I.M., Hauge, J.B., Bellotti, F., Dondio, P., Romero, M. (eds.) Games and Learning Alliance: 10th International Conference, GALA 2021, La Spezia, Italy, December 1–2, 2021, Proceedings, pp. 252–257. Springer International Publishing, Cham (2021). https://doi.org/10.1007/978-3-030-92182-8_25

18. Besoain, F., Jego, L., Arenas-Salinas, M.: Implementation of a gamified puzzle based on pro-origami protein structure cartoons: an experience in virtual reality. In 2018 IEEE Biennial Congress of Argentina (ARGENCON), pp. 1–7. IEEE, June 2018. https://doi.org/10.1109/ARGENCON.2018.8646202

19. Gugenheimer, J., Stemasov, E., Frommel, J., Rukzio, E.: ShareVR: enabling co-located experiences for virtual reality between hmd and non-hmd users. In: Proceedings of the 2017 CHI Conference on Human Factors in Computing Systems, pp. 4021–4033, May 2017. doi: https://doi.org/10.1145/3025453.3025683

20. Horst, R., NaraghiTaghi Off, R., Diez, S., Uhmann, T., Müller, A., Dörner, R.: FunPlogs – a serious puzzle mini-game for learning fundamental programming principles using visual

scripting. In: Bebis, G., et al. (eds.) Advances in Visual Computing: 14th International Symposium on Visual Computing, ISVC 2019, Lake Tahoe, NV, USA, October 7–9, 2019, Proceedings, Part I, pp. 494–504. Springer International Publishing, Cham (2019). https://doi.org/10.1007/978-3-030-33720-9_38

21. Liu, Y., Stamos, A., Dewitte, S., van Berlo, Z.M., van der Laan, L.N.: Development and evaluation of a virtual reality puzzle game to decrease food intake: randomized controlled trial. JMIR Ser. Games **10**(1), e31747 (2022). https://doi.org/10.2196/31747

22. Skorupka, A.: Comparing human wayfinding behavior in real and virtual environment. In: Proceedings of the 7th International Space Syntax Symposium, vol. 104, pp. 1–7. Stockholm: KTH Royal Institute of Technology, June 2009

23. Agethen, P., Sekar, V.S., Gaisbauer, F., Pfeiffer, T., Otto, M., Rukzio, E.: Behavior analysis of human locomotion in the real world and virtual reality for the manufacturing industry. ACM Trans. Appl. Percept. (TAP) **15**(3), 1–19 (2018). https://doi.org/10.1145/3230648

24. Kimura, K., et al.: Orientation in virtual reality does not fully measure up to the real-world. Sci. Rep. **7**(1), 18109 (2017). https://doi.org/10.1038/s41598-017-18289-8

25. Pontonnier, C., Samani, A., Badawi, M., Madeleine, P., Dumont, G.: Assessing the ability of a VR-Based assembly task simulation to evaluate physical risk factors. IEEE Trans. Visual Comput. Graphics **20**(5), 664–674 (2014). https://doi.org/10.1109/TVCG.2013.252

26. Kenyon, R.V., Afenya, M.B.: Training in virtual and real environments. Ann. Biomed. Eng. **23**(4), 445–455 (1995). https://doi.org/10.1007/BF02584444

27. Ovaskainen, H.: Comparison of harvester work in forest and simulator environments. Silva Fennica **39**(1), 89–101 (2005). https://doi.org/10.14214/sf.398

28. Slater, M., Sadagic, A., Usoh, M., Schroeder, R.: Small-group behavior in a virtual and real environment: a comparative study. Presence **9**(1), 37–51 (2000). https://doi.org/10.1162/105474600566600

29. Heldal, I., Steed, A., Schroeder, R.: Evaluating collaboration in distributed virtual environments for a puzzle-solving task. In: HCI International, July 2005

30. Axelsson, A.-S., Abelin, Å., Heldal, I., Schroeder, R., Wideström, J.: Cubes in the cube: a comparison of a puzzle-solving task in a virtual and a real environment. Cyberpsychol. Behav. **4**(2), 279–286 (2001). https://doi.org/10.1089/109493101300117956

31. Oren, M., Carlson, P., Gilbert, S., Vance, J.M.: Puzzle assembly training: real world vs. virtual environment. In: 2012 IEEE Virtual Reality Workshops (VRW), pp. 27–30. IEEE, March 2012. https://doi.org/10.1109/VR.2012.6180873

32. Stone, R.T., Watts, K.P., Zhong, P., Wei, C.S.: Physical and cognitive effects of virtual reality integrated training. Hum. Factors **53**(5), 558–572 (2011). https://doi.org/10.1177/0018720811413389

33. Kamaraj, D.C., Dicianno, B.E., Mahajan, H.P., Buhari, A.M., Cooper, R.A.: Stability and Workload of the virtual reality-based simulator-2. Arch. Phys. Med. Rehabil. **97**(7), 1085-1092.e1 (2016). https://doi.org/10.1016/j.apmr.2016.01.032

34. Mouraviev, V., et al.: Urology residents experience comparable workload profiles when performing live porcine nephrectomies and robotic surgery virtual reality training modules. J. Robot. Surg. **10**(1), 49–56 (2016). https://doi.org/10.1007/s11701-015-0540-1

35. Narasimha, S., Scharett, E., Madathil, K.C., Bertrand, J.: WeRSort: preliminary results from a new method of remote collaboration facilitated by fully immersive virtual reality. Proc. Human Factors Ergon. Soc. Ann. Meet. **62**(1), 2084–2088 (2018). https://doi.org/10.1177/1541931218621470

36. George, C., Khamis, M., Buschek, D., Hussmann, H.: Investigating the third dimension for authentication in immersive virtual reality and in the real world. In: 2019 IEEE Conference on Virtual Reality and 3D User Interfaces (VR) 23–27 March 2019, Osaka, Japan, pp. 277–285, March 2019. https://doi.org/10.1109/VR.2019.8797862

37. Chang, T.P., Beshay, Y., Hollinger, T., Sherman, J.M.: Comparisons of stress physiology of providers in real-life resuscitations and virtual reality-simulated resuscitations. Simul. Healthcare **14**(2), 104–112 (2019). https://doi.org/10.1097/SIH.0000000000000356

38. Rizzuto, M.A., Sonne, M.W., Vignais, N., Keir, P.J.: Evaluation of a virtual reality head mounted display as a tool for posture assessment in digital human modelling software. Appl. Ergon. **79**, 1–8 (2019). https://doi.org/10.1016/j.apergo.2019.04.001

39. Zindulka, T., Bachynskyi, M., Müller, J.: Performance and experience of throwing in virtual reality. In: Proceedings of the 2020 CHI Conference on Human Factors in Computing Systems, pp. 1–8, April 2020. https://doi.org/10.1145/3313831.3376639

40. Harris, D.J., Buckingham, G., Wilson, M.R., et al.: Exploring sensorimotor performance and user experience within a virtual reality golf putting simulator. Virtual Real. **25**, 647–654 (2021). https://doi.org/10.1007/s10055-020-00480-4

41. Ewin, C.A., Reupert, A., McLean, L.A., Ewin, C.J.: Mobile devices compared to non-digital toy play: the impact of activity type on the quality and quantity of parent language. Comput. Hum. Behav. **118**, 106669 (2021). https://doi.org/10.1016/j.chb.2020.106669

42. Ho, A., Lee, J., Wood, E., Kassies, S., Heinbuck, C.: Tap, swipe, and build: parental spatial input during i-Pad® and toy play. Infant Child Dev. **27**(1), e2061 (2018). https://doi.org/10.1002/icd.2061

43. Hinske, S., Lampe, M., Price, S., Yuill, N., Langheinrich, M.: Let the play set come alive: supporting playful learning through the digital augmentation of a traditional toy environment. In: 2010 8th IEEE International Conference on Pervasive Computing and Communications Workshops, pp. 280–285. (PERCOM Workshops) 29 March-2 April 2010 Mannheim, Germany IEEE, March 2010. https://doi.org/10.1109/PERCOMW.2010.5470654

44. Usoh, M., Catena, E., Arman, S., Slater, M.: Using presence questionnaires in reality. Presence **9**(5), 497–503 (2000). https://doi.org/10.1162/105474600566989

45. Petukhov, I.V., Glazyrin, A.E., Gorokhov, A.V., Steshina, L.A., Tanryverdiev, I.O.: Being present in a real or virtual world: a EEG study. Int. J. Med. Inform. **136**, 103977 (2020). https://doi.org/10.1016/j.ijmedinf.2019.103977

46. Slater, M.: Place illusion and plausibility can lead to realistic behaviour in immersive virtual environments. Philos. Trans. R. Soc. B Biol. Sci. **364**(1535), 3549–3557 (2009). https://doi.org/10.1098/rstb.2009.0138

47. SanchezVives, M.V., Slater, M.: From presence to consciousness through virtual reality. Nat. Rev. Neurosci. **6**(4), 332–339 (2005). https://doi.org/10.1038/nrn1651

48. Cummings, J.J., Bailenson, J.N.: How immersive is enough? A meta-analysis of the effect of immersive technology on user presence. Media Psychol. **19**(2), 272–309 (2016). https://doi.org/10.1080/15213269.2015.1015740

49. Kisker, J., Gruber, T., Schöne, B.: Behavioral realism and lifelike psychophysiological responses in virtual reality by the example of a height exposure. Psychol. Res. **85**(1), 68–81 (2021). https://doi.org/10.1007/s00426-019-01244-9

50. Slater, M.: Immersion and the illusion of presence in virtual reality. Br. J. Psychol. **109**(3), 431–433 (2018). https://doi.org/10.1111/bjop.12305

51. Weber, S., Weibel, D., Mast, F.W.: How to get there when you are there already? Defining presence in virtual reality and the importance of perceived realism. Front. Psychol. **12**, 628298 (2021). https://doi.org/10.3389/fpsyg.2021.628298

52. Vorderer, P, et al.: MEC Spatial Presence Questionnaire (MEC-SPQ): Short Documentation and In structions for Application. Report to the EuropeanCommunity, Project Presence: MEC (IS T-2001-37661) (2004). https://www.researchgate.net/publication/318531435_. Accessed 03 May 2022

53. Riddle, K.: Remembering past media use: toward the development of a lifetime television exposure scale. Commun. Methods Meas. **4**(3), 241–255 (2010). https://doi.org/10.1080/19312458.2010.505500

54. Bombmanual.com (n.d.). Bomb Defusal Manual for the game Keep Talking and Nobody Explodes. Website. web.archive.org/web/20220321124706. https://www.bombmanual.com/web/index.html

55. Hart, S.G., Staveland, L.E.: Development of NASA-TLX (Task Load Index): results of empirical and theoretical research. In: Advances in Psychology, vol. 52, pp. 139–183. North-Holland (1988). https://doi.org/10.1016/S0166-4115(08)62386-9

56. Hart, S.G.: Nasa-task load index (NASA-TLX); 20 years later. Proc. Human Factors Ergon. Soc. Ann. Meet. **50**(9), 904–908 (2006). https://doi.org/10.1177/154193120605000909

57. Hertzum, M.: Reference values and subscale patterns for the task load index (TLX): a meta-analytic review. Ergonomics **64**(7), 869–878 (2021). https://doi.org/10.1080/00140139.2021.1876927

58. Phan, M.H., Keebler, J.R., Chaparro, B.S.: The development and validation of the game user experience satisfaction scale (GUESS). Hum. Factors **58**(8), 1217–1247 (2016). https://doi.org/10.1177/0018720816669646

59. Hughes, M., Hutt, C.: Heart-rate correlates of childhood activities: play, exploration, problem-solving and day-dreaming. Biol. Psychol. **8**(4), 253–263 (1979). https://doi.org/10.1016/0301-0511(79)90007-3

60. Grassini, S., Laumann, K.: Questionnaire measures and physiological correlates of presence: a systematic review. Front. Psychol. **11**, 349 (2020). https://doi.org/10.3389/fpsyg.2020.00349

61. Hartmann, T., et al.: The spatial presence experience scale (SPES): a short self-report measure for diverse media settings. J. Media Psychol. **28**(1), 1–15 (2015). https://doi.org/10.1027/1864-1105/a000137

62. Yildirim, Ç., Bostan, B., Berkman, M.I.: Impact of different immersive techniques on the perceived sense of presence measured via subjective scales. Entertain. Comput. **31**, 100308 (2019). https://doi.org/10.1016/j.entcom.2019.100308

63. Elor, A., Powell, M., Mahmoodi, E., Teodorescu, M., Kurniawan, S.: Gaming beyond the novelty effect of immersive virtual reality for physical rehabilitation. IEEE Trans. Games **14**(1), 107–115 (2021). https://doi.org/10.1109/TG.2021.3069445

64. MacQuarrie, A., Steed, A.: Cinematic virtual reality: evaluating the effect of display type on the viewing experience for panoramic video. In 2017 IEEE Virtual Reality (VR), pp. 45–54. 8–22 March 2017, Los Angeles, CA, USA, March 2017. https://doi.org/10.1109/VR.2017.7892230

65. Richesin, M.T., Baldwin, D.R., Wicks, L.A.: Art making and virtual reality: a comparison study of physiological and psychological outcomes. Arts Psychother. **75**, 101823 (2021). https://doi.org/10.1016/j.aip.2021.101823

66. Witmer, B.G., Singer, M.J.: Measuring presence in virtual environments: a presence questionnaire. Presence Teleoper. Virtual Environ. **7**(3), 225–240 (1998). https://doi.org/10.1162/105474698565686

67. Slater, M., Usoh, M., Steed, A.: Depth of presence in virtual environments. Presence Teleoper. Virtual Environ. **3**(2), 130–144 (1994). https://doi.org/10.1162/pres.1994.3.2.130

"Looking up the Camera to Play Right": An Interview Study of the Implications of Cinematic Storytelling in Game Design

Ana Passos⬤, Liliana Vale Costa^(✉)⬤, and Nelson Zagalo⬤

Department of Communication and Art, DigiMedia Research Centre, University of Aveiro,
Aveiro, Portugal
{apassos,lilianavale,nzagalo}@ua.pt

Abstract. Game cinematics, consisting of filmmaking techniques, cutscenes, and animations, often play an essential role in the player's emotional attachment and relatedness with game storytelling. While extensive research has been carried out in game storytelling and design, very little attention has been paid to the role of cinematics in the gameplay experience. Using qualitative in-depth interviews with 16 scholars and practitioners in game experience and cinematics, this paper reports on recommended practices for designing game cinematics. A semi-structured interview was employed, and content analysis was performed. Although the interviewee's perspective on the use of cinematics in storytelling was not consensual, its use to set the game scene and progress in the narrative is generally recognized. The recommendations for game designers to use game cinematics include balancing narrative and cinematics goals; ensuring its coherence; considering its length and making it skippable, among others.

Keywords: Game cinematics · Digital Games · Storytelling · Game Experience

1 Introduction

Game Experience and Players' emotions during gameplay have been major topics of interest in the field of game studies [1, 2]. In fact, the identity and cultural functions of digital games have been highlighted [3], being filmmaking and the audiovisual language essential to establish the setting and time of a story [4], the atmosphere [5], and the characters' stability [6].

Game cinematics, also referred as cutscenes, are the interrelatedness of cinema and digital games to captivate the players' attention and create a sense of immersion in both the visual and sonic dimensions, while transmitting information about the story and the game world.

In addition, these may potentially help to recreate emotionally engaging experiences (from visceral to behavioral and reflective design [7]), being a growing trend toward immersive role-playing environments to explore aesthetically pleasing fictional universes [8]. Despite this mentioned potential, the use of cinematics in video game narratives has

© The Author(s), under exclusive license to Springer Nature Switzerland AG 2024
L. Vale Costa et al. (Eds.): VJ 2023, CCIS 1984, pp. 86–100, 2024.
https://doi.org/10.1007/978-3-031-51452-4_7

been frequently regarded as uninteresting from the player's point of view given that most of the time gameplay can be interrupted to show the progress in the story [9].

As consequence, the cinematics' investment in the game-playing experience is likely to be overlooked, often resulting in skipped material [10]. Moreover, the boundaries between video games and movies, and the multiple roles that gamers-viewers play, have been under focus in the discussions of gaming communities.

The purpose of this paper is to assess the strategies used in game cinematics and implications for storytelling mostly highlighted by scholars and practitioners in game experience and cinematics.

This paper is divided into six sections, including the Introduction and Conclusion. Section 2, Related Work, covers the topic of game cinematics. Section 3, The Interview Study, describes the interview procedures, interviewees' recruitment, selection criteria, background, interview structure, and analysis procedures. Finally, Sect. 4 subdivides into the pre-determined themes 'Use of game cinematics and digital game storytelling', 'Contribution to the game's visual and sonic immersion', 'Importance of cinematics in game-based learning or behavior change', 'Interviewee's perspective on the camera use', 'Player-viewer relation', and 'Recommendations.'

2 Related Work

Game cinematics often play an important role in advancing the game story. Beyond its usage to aid the players' progression in the story's events, these serve to establish the game levels and communicate the character's progress.

In a broader sense, game cinematics are allusive to a remediation process [11] in which digital games borrow from the filmmaking language through, for example, focalization (player's point of view), montage, and integration of a non-interactive scene-setting within gameplay [12] that can be either pre-rendered or rendered in real-time. In specific, these may integrate cut-scenes, in-game animations, or full-motion videos.

There have been three main strategies adopted in which the narrative-gameplay experience has been balanced through cinematics, i.e., (1) integration of interactive cutscenes as the main gameplay as the drama adventure cases of *Heavy-Rain* or *Detroit Become Human*; (2) balance between spectatorship-game-playing experience moments such as the case of *Uncharted* or *Assassin's Creed*; and (3) seamless cinematic experience with the absence of camera cuts like in the game *God of Wars*. It is, therefore, important to consider the purpose of cinematics before adopting such strategies and these may vary from capturing the player's attention to game events or challenges or rewarding to control the gameplay rhythm and creating the narrative tension [4].

Changes in game production technologies (e.g., graphic realism, art support, rigging, motion capture, and incorporation of lighting, camera, and visual effects [VFX] in game design) [9] have also impact the filmmaking language associated to games, being likely to affect the player-viewer's experience [13]. Nevertheless, game cinematics have also been subject of some criticism, claiming that these are likely to interrupt and not add value to the game-playing experience [10]. In this sense, understanding the articulation of the game narrative and gameplay and creating appealing scene compositions using color, scenery, *mise-en-scene*, and lighting [9] are of utmost importance.

In terms of game narratives, Jenkins [14] draws our attention that these can be divided into the following types: (a) Evoked, which are represented in the game space based on a specific theme and user-recognized references; (b) Enacted dependent on the character's navigation within the environment to advance the story; (c) Embedded to anticipate future activities through, for example, game events and *mise-en-scène*; and (e) Emergent determined by the players' decisions toward game actions.

It is worth mentioning that although two confronting perspectives have been persisting over the field of game studies (i.e., ludologists and narratologists), balancing these to ensure both gameplay-thinking and meaningful events is key. For that, there seem to be two approaches to create a dynamic game narrative:

- The gameplay unfolds the narrative: In this approach, a game challenge motivates the player's actions, and the player may use the necessary resources to progress and advance in the game world.
- The narrative unfolds gameplay: In this approach, part of the game world is presented, and the game world is revealed accordingly with the players' input. This approach is often followed in story-driven games.

For Lebowitz and colleagues [15], there are different narrative types, dependent on the level of interactivity and control. These are: (a) Fully traditional and Interactive Traditional Stories in which these do not change, being repeated; (b) Multiple Ending Stories and Branching Path stories in which the game endings are dependent on the player's choice-making and actions; and (c) Open-Ended Stories and fully driven stories in which the player determines the course of the story.

In view of these different modes of articulating narrative and gameplay, and the role of cinematics to enhance narrative comprehension, its impact, player-viewer relation to the game content and implications in game cinematic production are some of the challenges that are presented as the rationale for an interview study of the implications of cinematic storytelling in game design.

3   The Interview Study

This study seeks to assess the perspectives of scholars and practitioners in game experience and cinematics on the implications of cinematic storytelling in game design and recommended practices for designing game cinematics.

The interview is likely to be the most comprehensive data collection tool because it allows for questions that enable the interviewee to contribute with additional informative and reflective thoughts [16]. It generates a large amount of qualitative data and give the interviewer more control over the research question's objectives. The semi-structured interview was selected in this case because it contained a mix of open and closed questions that would let the interviewees freely express their opinions. So far, there has been lack of research in this domain and, as such, interviewing scholars and practitioners in the field constituted the most suitable procedure to meet the research purpose.

3.1 Interviewee's Recruitment Selection and General Information

A A total of 173 scholars and practitioners in the field were contacted via e-mail and LinkedIn platforms, in which 104 were Game Scholars and 69 were Game Industry Professionals. Out of this total, 32 responded to the emails sent, and 24 agreed and gave consent to the interview but were not able to schedule the interview. In total, 16 interviews were conducted. Relative to the geographic distribution of the interviewees, there were five from United States of America, three from Italy, two from Canada, two from Portugal, one from Germany, one from United Kingdom, one from Australia, and one from Spain.

The process of recruiting interviewees also interrupted when data saturation was achieved, and no new data has emerged during data analysis.

Table 1 shows the participants' general information.

Table 1. Participants' General Information

ID	Description
I1	Associate Professor with a Film History background. I1 worked in the game industry as a Translator and Script Assistant with a historical and theoretical knowledge of the relationship between video games and other media
I2	Writer and narrative designer for video games. I2 directed many commercials and voiceovers. I2 contributed to several digital games, including the real-time strategy role-playing game Dungeons & Dragons: Dragonshard. I2 has professional experience in voiceover, recording, acting, and scriptwriting
I3	I3 has been working as a producer for short films, branded content, advertising, and as a writer and director for 360o & VR projects since 2012. I3 began her career as a freelance translator and then as an interactive writer for the game and movie industries. I3 enjoys reading, videogames and interactive narrative, movies, and cinema
I4	Scholar in Media Arts specializing in digital game design and development. In GreyWolf Entertainment, he worked on VFX animations for the game "Dawn of Andromeda." I4 is interested in the impact of players' personal lives in video games, specifically how players bond with fictional characters and make decisions
I5	Researcher in rhetoric and new media. Creator of the massively distributed game archive - Learning Games Initiative Research Archive
I6	Game Studies researcher and educator. Prior to entering the scientific field, I6 was a journalist who worked as a game critic and editor of a computer game magazine
I7	Professor of Communication with a portfolio that includes many books on videogames and media studies. Founder of the Video Game Studies Scholarly Interest Group within the Society for Cinema and Media Studies
I8	Artist-researcher and critic working as indie game developer. Interest in Critical Historical Practices with Gaming

(continued)

Table 1. (*continued*)

ID	Description
I9	Background in cinema studies and games. Worked in game localization for the Electronic Arts. I9 has a book collection on game studies, characterizing its landscape
I10	I10 has graphic communication design experience and is interested in cinematic and sequential narratives. I10's interests focus on narrative design, i.e., affective narrative design
I11	Professor of media studies and game researcher. In addition to producing video game music, I11 also ran an independent games festival and worked as a part-time game journalist in 2008
I12	Academic and educator in the department of film and electronic arts. Beyond being a researcher in a Game Lab, I12 teaches digital culture, which includes videogames
I13	Associate professor in the art history and film studies department. Experience with narratives and game writing. Narratology and videogame studies writer
I14	Professor and researcher in games with a background in communication and media studies. I14 is interested in game freedom, Zen modes, Japanese videogames, and videogame preservation and history
I15	Professor of cinema and videogame studies, specializing in horror games. One of I15 first projects was about interactive cinema, and as university professor, I15 has been dealing with gameplay-centric research
I16	Associate professor of rhetoric digital media and games, being a director of a major in game design and development course. 16 is interested in researching how games are persuasive and how they use elements from other media such as cinema to create fictional words that instill messages

3.2 The Interview Procedure

The interviews were conducted and recorded on a videoconferencing platform, Zoom (https://zoom.us), from March to May, due to the internationality of the knowledgeable individuals select.

An interview procedure was developed. The procedures used aimed to identify cinematic strategies used in game genres and their impact on the narrative-gameplay experience cycle (RQ: How can cinematics engage young adults with game storytelling?). The protocol was broken down into four sections: 1. Introduction/Standard Instructions; 2. Ice-breaker Question; 3. 6/7 Questions; and 4. Thank you Statement.

Table 2 presents the questions posed and their intended use in data analysis.

Table 2. Data collection and analysis questions

Data Collection Questions	Data Analysis Questions
A. How do you see the use of cinematics in gameplay and digital game storytelling?	(i) How can cinematics impact on the narrative-gameplay experience?
B. In what way do you think cinematics can contribute to the game's visual and sonic immersion?	
C. How do you recognize cinematics to be important in game-based learning or/and behavior change?	
D. In your perspective, how can camera and story views affect the player's experience in different game genres (e.g., shooter, strategy, role-playing, vehicle)?	(ii) In what way can camera and story perspectives set different expectations towards a game genre?
E. How can we calibrate player-viewer relation to the game content in game-design and development?	
F. What core design recommendations would you give to cinematic designers to balance the narrative gameplay experience? What mistakes should be avoided?	(iii) What are the practices to consider when developing game cinematics?
G. In your perspective, what does the future hold for game cinematic producers?	

These questions relied on the definition of cinematics in which cinema and game design language combine, putting the challenge in transmitting the narrative, and using important elements such as camerawork beyond specific practices in its design and development.

3.3 Ethical Considerations

Data collected during the study followed the procedures: (a) consent form; (b) voluntary participation; and (d) confidentiality and anonymity. The interviewees' names used in this study were replaced by a unique code – e.g., I1, I2, I3. When answering the interview questions, interviewees were informed about the procedures and purposes for data collection and analyses.

3.4 Data Analysis

The semi-structured interviews were transcribed, and manual coding was performed considering the pre-determined codes:

- Use of game cinematics and digital game storytelling (A): This code refers to the interviewee's perspective on the articulation of cinematics and gameplay, and examples of its use.

- Contribution of cinematics to the game's visual and sonic immersion (B): This code refers to the way cinematics prevent/enhance visual and sonic immersion.
- Use of cinematics in game-based learning or/and behavior change (C): This code is related to the potential of cinematics in game-based learning or/and for behavior change purposes.

These codes A, B, and C enable to assess the possible impact that cinematics may have on the narrative-gameplay experience, whereas the following pre-determined codes (D and E) inform the role of camera and story perspective in setting expectations towards a game genre.

- Interviewees' perspectives on camera use (D): This code refers to the interviewee's perspective on the camera use in different game genres.
- Player-viewer's relation (E): This code is relative to the player-viewer's relation and balance in gameplay.

Finally, codes F, and G inform the practices in the development of game cinematics. For instance, these are the descriptions of the codes:

- Recommendations (F): This code refers to the recommendations for producing game cinematics and mistakes to be avoided.
- Trends (G): This code is relative to the trends for game cinematic producers.

It is worth noting that manual coding was used given that this facilitated the analytical process, although we recognize that it can be time-consuming in comparison with the use of computer-assisted analysis software that is worth to run matrix coding queries. The next section presents the findings of the conducted interviews to inform the recommendations for game designers to use game cinematics.

4 Results

The interviewee's statements about the impact of cinematics on the narrative-gameplay experience, the use of camera and story perspectives to set different expectations for a game, and practices to consider when developing game cinematics were analyzed.

4.1 Use of Game Cinematics and Digital Game Storytelling (A)

In response to the question 'How do you see the use of cinematics in gameplay and game storytelling', some interviewees were not fans of cinematics given the cut of agency, causing the player to stop playing, breaking interaction, and interfering with the player's immersion in the game world, potentially resulting in frustration (Interviewees I1, I5, I12, I13).

In a broader sense, interviewees emphasized that the use of cinematics is frequently misunderstood, both technically (I13) and in terms of game relevance (I14), which may often be perceived by the player as distracting and unappealing content (I3). As a result, it is understandable that multiple players may not all be apologists for the same type of content (I5, I3). Regardless of their respective points of view, all interviewees agreed that cinematics can be beneficial and useful for gameplay.

Some of the examples given for their utility referred to exposition, which introduces the player to the conflict and context (I2, I3, I6, I12, I14), as well as being useful to the progression of the game narrative (I2, I3, I4, I7), specifically for transitions, that is, an introduction or conclusion to the different levels of the game (I2, I6, I12).

Furthermore, cinematics can be used to create surprise by showing the player unique and impressive elements of the game (I3, I12). The cinematics can also reward players (I2, I4, I5, I6, I16) by allowing them to relax or rest after a period of intense gameplay.

Cinematics tend to add emotional value to the game (I2, I10), with advances in technology making it possible to characterize the environments and expressions of the characters more realistically (I9, I10), which can help the game provide a greater narrative depth while also aiding in the creation of empathy (I2, I3, I6). Finally, cinematics can be used in the conclusion to provide the player with closure on what occurred (I6).

Some interviewees stated that, while cinematics derive many of their principles from the medium of film, these are now an independent and distinct concept (I1, I11, I14). In brief, the perspectives relative to the use of cinematics in games diverge. If, on the one hand, these may interrupt the activity, on the other hand, these may be essential to set the scene and determine the game's pacing.

4.2 Contribution of Cinematics to the Game's Visual and Sonic Immersion (B)

In response to the question 'In what way do you think cinematics can contribute to the game's visual and sonic immersion?', different interviewees (I5, I6, I8, I16) noticed that cinematics, scientifically, are a break in immersion rather than a contribution, because gameplay and cinematics are two distinct modes of experience.

Following that, some interviewees suggested that the cinematics be visually smooth so that there is a seamless transition between the two sections of the game (I2, I6), while others stated that this approach is insufficient because it leaves the player unsure whether he/she is still in the gameplay or not (I5, I9).

In general, game cinematics should include visual and auditory cues that alert the player of being in a different section of the game, with images and sounds having different volumes and interpretations in each section (I5, I8, I16).

Cinematics, which show moments that cannot be shown when the player controls the gameplay, can be used to show specific details about characters and objects (I9, I10, I13), forcing the player to observe and listen to what is predefined, allowing the player to transpose important narrative information and establish the context, mood, and environment (I11, I13, I14, I16).

Finally, many interviewees compared cinematics to movies (I5, I12, I15), in terms of the images and sound shown/heard, due to the similarities in aesthetic values, technical production, and viewer immersion, with the difference being the agency required to complete a game.

Overall, games may borrow lessons from the cinema industry to enable the player's narrative immersion, setting the mood and the whole environment.

4.3   Importance of Cinematics in Game-Based Learning or Behavior Change (C)

In response to the question 'How do you recognize cinematics to be important in game-based learning or/and behavior change?' the interviewees placed themselves on different spectrums, each with a different view on the subject. Some questioned the concept of a "serious game," arguing that playing should be a voluntary, ludic, and spontaneous process rather than a lecture, and that players may not want to actively learn during the gaming experience (I1, I3, I9, I12).

Other interviewees stated that cinematics can be used to communicate pedagogical themes and that all games are intrinsically didactic, meaning that, for a player to be able to play, the game must be designed to teach him/her how to play (I5, I7, I13, I15, I16).

Another perspective was that serious games can help a certain subject to be better understood, through simulation, when we can see its effects, see the effects of our actions reflected in the game, more than seeing or hearing about the subject (I6, I8, I11, I15).

Despite the different perspectives, and assuming that the cinematics are just another toolset, which may or may not be used in the game, depending on the context thought of by the game designer (I1, I9, I10, I12, I13), different approaches on how to proceed in the creation of cinematics emerged.

On the one hand, cinematics may not be necessary for an educational game, and the educational part could be integrated into the gameplay systems of the game, being able to transmit the message through the action of play (I4, I6, I11, I13).

On the other hand, cinematics could be used to develop an emotional connection, include players in the dynamics created in the narrative, and create a visceral connection rather than to feed didactic information to the game (I2, I3, I10, I12).

Also, three of the interviewees mentioned that the educational elements should be spread throughout the game to balance and create cohesion between the game sections, whilst not having segments of the game exclusively focused on the teaching theme, which is something that can lead players to reject the game (I10, I11, I14).

Other aspect that was emphasized was that these kinds of games shouldn't depict a model that is like reality because the player's understanding of the message is also understandable by the depiction of a fictional universe (I5, I15).

Overall, the impact of cinematics on the narrative-gameplay can be either positive or negative. In specific, these can enable us to set the scene, introduce a conflict or context, provide details about characters and objects, progress in the game narrative, and establish the game pace, context, mood, and environment. By contrast, these can prevent player's sense of control over gameplay, interrupting the experience if misunderstood in terms of relevance, technical aspects, and content.

In a game-based learning context, cinematics may also reinforce the visceral emotional connections with the gameplay instead of merely feeding educational content.

4.4   Interviewee's Perspective on the Camera Use (D)

In response to the question 'In your perspective, how can camera and story views affect the player's experience in different game genres?,' some interviewees (I1, I7, I11) stated that there is similitude in the use of different camera perspectives both in games and the film industry. In addition, the aesthetics and emotional content of the game are likely to be affected by what the camera perspective shows (I7, I10, I11, I14).

First- and third-person perspectives differ in immersion and player's interaction (I5, I6, I8, I9, I11, I12, I16), and some interviewees added that the perspective may not always have the same effects on the goal that one is attempting to achieve. The depicted experiences, however, may vary from game to game (I6, I13, and I14) and from the players themselves, who may perceive concepts and camera perspectives in different ways. Thus, it appears that there are no set guidelines (I1, I5).

Still, some ideas were shared about the impact that each perspective can have, and in terms of immersion, it was stated that the first-person perspective can generate more and better this feeling (I2, I3, I6, I13), and many interviewees stated that the fact that a game is in first-person causes the player to live the experience as if it were his or her personal narrative, seeing it as if they were the character to whom all the interactions are happening (I2, I3, I4, I6, I9).

In terms of environment, the first-person perspective was highlighted to be better suited for horror games (I2, I9, I14) and for inducing a certain state of mind in the player, allowing for a higher presence and proximity to the items portrayed in the game (I6), but a lesser sense of the surrounding space (I5, I16) (I16). The third-person perspective was more akin to the cinematic medium, with a camera, a character, and the framing of game elements (I2, I15).

As in cinema, there is always a certain distance in relation to game events, because game events are likely to be experienced through a character and see them from an outside perspective (I2, I3, I6). As a result, a psychological distance is also generated owe to the fact that the character represented is someone different than the player (I3, I6, I11).

Most interviewers thought that this perspective was more suited for evoking empathy for the characters (I3, I8, I9).

Spatially, the third-person perspective gives players a wider field of view of the game world and gives them a sense of control over what they can see (I5, I16). In the first-person view, it was stated that players do not need to identify with the character because the character is themselves (I11). The argument made in the third-person perspective was that, despite the distance, the player tends identify more with the characters because he/she can see them and relate more to their mindset and experiences, connecting with what they are shown (I4, I11).

Additionally, it was stated that it might be appropriate to allow the player to view certain game portions from a different perspective than that of the cinematics to complete the game's objectives more effectively (I6, I10, I16).

Lastly, it was also mentioned that VR intensifies the sensation of being in a particular place more than any first-person or third-person game because the mere act of using a screen to play a game already creates some distance between the player and the environment in which they are playing (I5).

In all, the camera use is important to give the player's perspective and, as such, player's relation with game objects and environment may be represented (narrow or wide) with camera shooting types (e.g., extreme long shot, mid-shot, close-up), angles (e.g., low angle, high angle, eye-level), movement (e.g., panning, zooming, tilting, dolly) and focus (e.g., deep, shallow, soft).

4.5   Player-Viewer's Relation (E)

In response to the question 'How can we calibrate the player-viewer relation to the game content in game design and development?,' the majority of interviewees stated that there is no specific formula, no set of unchanging laws dictating how much gameplay and cinematics each game must contain, and that each game's experience is unique (I1, I2, I5, I6, I7, I8, I9, I11, I12, I13, I14). However, a few factors that influence how the experience is designed were identified.

Firstly, the experience should be tailored to the intended demographic (I1, I2, I8, I9, I12) given that the player's preferences can be diversified.

Another factor that can influence the player's experience is game genre, being this a concept that can also help to manage the player's expectations (I6, I9, I10, I12, I16).

The platform on which the game is played also has an impact on the overall experience (I1, I6). By contrast, a good narrative, should be adaptable to any condition (I6).

The balance of the game experience also depends on the purpose and the general objectives devised by the game designer, who must consider the intention, message, and emotions he/she wants to convey through the game (I7, I8, I14), being that each game can use different strategies (I14) and communicate in different ways (I8). Thus, a cinematic must have a plausible reason for being present in the game, i.e., it must be required for narrative structure and game progression (I4, I6, I10, I12, I14).

Some interviewees argued that gameplay and player performance should be prioritized, and that there should be more gameplay moments than cinematics (I2, I3, I7, I10), with gameplay moments intended for more repetitive actions and cinematics intended for more unique narrative moments in the game (I3, I6).

According to one of the interviewees, the player's experience should be anticipated to understand where the cinematics should be placed, depending on the proposed game activities (I6).

In line with this affirmation, another respondent gave the idea of developing dynamic cinematics that would change based on the player's performance. Therefore, if the player was feeling fatigued, cinematics would offer a moment of rest, and if they kept playing without getting bored, they might never see the cinematic, which would prevent them from getting frustrated if they had to stop playing to watch a cinematic (I5).

A further recommendation was to make the game's cinematic parts optional, allowing players to skip them without being visually affected (I7).

When analyzing these two codes, one may highlight the following practices in the development of game cinematics: (a) Consider the target group and expectations towards the game genre; (b) Borrow the lessons learned in the film industry; (c) Design the cinematics with the platform and the purpose into consideration; and (d) Provide the option to skip cutscenes. In the specific case of camera use, first-person perspective was pinpointed as the most suitable for creating the sense of immersion, higher presence, and proximity, whilst a third-person perspective gives a sense of control with a wider field of view in gameplay.

4.6   Recommendations (F)

The relevance that the cinematics should have for the game was brought up most frequently in responses to the question 'What core design recommendations would you give to cinematic game designers to balance the narrative gameplay experience? What mistakes should be avoided?.' For instance, it was emphasized that the cinematics should not be perceived as an external component to the game, therefore there should be a reason and significance in their existence (I1, I4, I6, I7, I8, I10, I12, I14, I15).

Also, it was suggested that the gameplay and cinematics should progress and work together with the gameplay, connecting the two parts of the game to create a cohesive experience and a natural game flow (I1, I3, I7, I10, I11, I12, I14).

To ensure the relevance of the cinematics, the game designer must be aware of the necessary messages to be conveyed, that is, know the narrative and the cinematics' respective objectives to guarantee their relevancy (I3, I4, I9, I13).

For players to be interested in the cinematics, the story should also be engaging throughout the entire game (I1, I10, I13). One of the suggested strategies for creating interest is to omit gameplay information inside the cinematics (I1). Another idea was to include micro-cinematics, which would captivate the player through the game's visual appeal or narrative suspense (I10, I12).

In between stages, cinematics was suggested to be used to break up monotonous gameplay sequences and to show brief videos to illustrate, otherwise, extensive tasks (I6).

One other idea suggested to make the cinematics' production more appealing was to build them similarly to film, using its visual language, so as not to make the player feel unusual (I3, I4, I13, I15).

When talking about the mistakes that should be avoided when producing cinematics, many of the respondents mentioned that the game shouldn't contain too many cinematics (I2, I4, I10) or too long cinematics (I3, I4, I7, I13, I16), as the act of playing a game implies agency and the lack of agency might lead to discontent or boredom.

Additionally, it was said that it was not advisable to show a player-possible action in cinematics (I2, I6, I9). Therefore, cinematics shouldn't rob the gamer of valuable gameplay time (I1, I11, I12).

Participants agreed that the player's choices during the action segments should be the source of the cinematics, which means that they would originate from the player's actions. In this manner, the player would adapt to and activate the cinematics rather than having them imposed upon them (I12, I13).

Interviewees also underlined the need for cinematics to be skippable when they weren't necessary for gameplay so that the player could watch what they wanted to see (I1, I7, I10, I13).

When creating cinematics, playtesting was also recommended as a helpful approach to determine the perspectives and preferences of the target audience (I9) (I5, I7, I9, I11).

In brief, one should account the length of the cinematics, its number, making it skippable and attending to the player's choices.

4.7 Trends (G)

When answering this question, the interviewees noted that traditional film and videogame formats will never cease to exist (I10, I15), but their expectations for the future include that the work of a cinematic producer will become more entwined with the work of a cinema producer because computer gaming and cinema now have common parallels blurring together due to the similarity of process and production engines (I1, I6, I10). As a result, in the future it might be possible to develop a hybrid language that connects the gaming and film industries (I3).

Some respondents predicted that cinematics would become less and less common, allowing for the incorporation of mood and visuals into the game's gameplay (I1, I7, I16).

Most interviewees mentioned that VR technology would be more used in cinematics in the future (I2, I3, I5, I8, I10, I11, I12, I14, and I16), and that this would enable the creation of a seamless and more immersive effect as well as a greater integration of the cinematics into gameplay (I2, I4, I5).

Since there is no longer a screen separating the player from the game, there was some skepticism about how the cinematics would function in virtual reality (I3, I11, I12).

Subsequently, some problems arose. One of them was the mention of the fact that, when games are played on screens, the game can cut into a cinematic and showcase what it is intended to, but this type of experience in VR might not work since the user stays in one location while the game takes him/her to another location (I14).

Additionally, the ability of AR technology to support cinematics was noted (I10). AI was also mentioned with the intention of producing unique responses in the NPCs (I10, I16), creating cinematics, through the formation of a pre-existing library that would have information about which cinematic elements were available for use. Thus, the cinematics would be created at the moment, arising from the game itself (I13). Likewise, game streaming would become more significant role.

In a nutshell, the practices in the development of game cinematics include a) Include cinematics in gameplay elements and in the game design process; b) Ensure coherence in cinematics; c) Establish the narrative and cinematic goals; d) Take into account micro-cinematics (only a few seconds long); e) Avoid having too many or long cinematics; and f) Reserve cinematics for special moments.

5 Conclusion

This study set out to assess the strategies used in game cinematics and implications for storytelling mostly highlighted by scholars and practitioners in game experience and cinematics.

From the interviews with 16 scholars and practitioners in game experience and cinematics, it was possible to gather their perspective on the use of game cinematics and digital game storytelling, its contribution to game's visual and sonic immersion, importance to game-based learning and behavior change, the role of camera use and player-viewer's relation, and design recommendations.

Cinematics on the narrative-gameplay can play an important role to set the scene, introduce a conflict or context, provide details about characters and objects, progress in the game narrative, and establish the game pace, context, mood, and environment. By contrast, these can prevent player's sense of control over gameplay, interrupting the experience if misunderstood in terms of relevance, technical aspects, and content.

Some of the recommendations for game designers to use game cinematics mostly cited were include balancing narrative and cinematics goals; ensuring its coherence; considering its length and making it skippable, among others.

A limitation of this study is that there is a convenience sample and, as such, findings should be interpreted with caution. Given the difficulty in knowledge systematization about cinematic storytelling and game experience, providing a framework for incorporating cinematic storytelling in gameplay is still lacking. Further work is being conducted to understand the specificities of cinematic recommending practices for each game type and the implications in using game engines to create videos with real-time rendering.

Acknowledgments. This work is financially supported by national funds through FCT –Foundation for Science and Technology, I.P., under the project UIDB/05460/2020. Thanks are due to FCT/MCTES for the financial support to DigiMedia, through national funds. This work was funded by DigiMedia under the project PLAYMUTATION Virus Epidemiologic-themed Digital Games and Youngsters' Attitudes to Viral Infection—DMPI/001/2022 and YO-MEDIA: Youngsters' Media Literacy in Times of Crisis European Media Fund (European University Institute & Gulbenkian).

References

1. Hemenover, S.H., Bowman, N.D.: Video games, emotion, and emotion regulation: expanding the scope. Ann. Int. Commun. Assoc. **42**(2), 125–143 (2018). https://doi.org/10.1080/238 08985.2018.1442239

2. Johnson, D., Gardner, M.J., Perry, R.: Validation of two game experience scales: the player experience of need satisfaction (PENS) and game experience questionnaire (GEQ). Int. J. Hum Comput Stud. **118**, 38–46 (2018). https://doi.org/10.1016/j.ijhcs.2018.05.003

3. Greenfield, P.M.: Video games as cultural artifacts. J. Appl. Dev. Psychol. **15**(1), 3–12 (1994). https://doi.org/10.1016/0193-3973(94)90003-5

4. Klevjer, R.: In defense of cutscenes. In: Mäyrä, F., (ed.) CGDC Conference on Proceedings of Computer Games and Digital Cultures Conference, Tampere: Tampere University Press, 2002, June 2002. https://folk.uib.no/smkrk/docs/RuneKlevjer_What%20is%20the%20Avatar_finalprint.pdf

5. Ribeiro, G., Rogers, K., Altmeyer, M., Terkildsen, T., Nacke, L.E.: Game atmosphere: effects of audiovisual thematic cohesion on player experience and psychophysiology. In: CHI PLAY 2020 - Proceedings of the Annual Symposium on Computer-Human Interaction in Play, pp. 108–120. Association for Computing Machinery (2020). https://doi.org/10.1145/341 0404.3414245

6. Fahlenbrach, K., Schröter, F.: Embodied avatars in video games. In: Fahlenbrach, K. (ed.) Embodied Metaphors in Film, Television, and Video Games: Cognitive Approaches, pp. 251–268. Routledge (2015). https://doi.org/10.4324/9781315724522-16

7. Norman, D.A.: Emotional design: why we love (or hate) everyday things. J. Am. Cult. **27**(2), 234 (2004). https://doi.org/10.1111/j.1537-4726.2004.133_10.x

8. Klevjer, R.: What is the Avatar? Media, 232 (2006). http://citeseerx.ist.psu.edu/viewdoc/download?doi=10.1.1.96.3804&rep=rep1&type=pdf

9. Newman, R.: Cinematic Game Secrets for Creative Directors and Producers: Inspired Techniques from Industry Legends. Routledge(2009)
10. Browning, B.: Should I Skip This?: Cutscenes, Agency and Innovation. Master thesis, Concordia University (2016). https://spectrum.library.concordia.ca/id/eprint/980988/
11. Bolter, J.D., Grusin, R.: Remediation Understanding New Media. The MIT Press, Cambridge (1999)
12. Walther, K.: Cinematography and Ludology: In Search of a Lucidography (2004). http://www.dichtung-digital.de/2004/1/Walther/index.htm. Accessed 27 Sept 2022
13. Priestman, C.: What does it mean when we call videogames cinematic? 28 March 2014. https://killscreen.com/previously/articles/what-does-it-mean-when-we-call-videogames-cinematic/. Accessed 27 Sept 2022
14. Jenkins, H.: Game Design as Narrative Architecture (2004). https://web.mit.edu/%7E21fms/People/henry3/games&narrative.html. Accessed 27 Sept 2022
15. Lebowitz, J., Klug, C.: Interactive Storytelling for Video Games: A Player-Centered Approach to Creating Memorable Characters and Stories (1st ed.). Focal Press (2011)
16. Quivy, R., Campenhoudt, L.: Raymond Quivy Manual de Investigação em Ciências Sociais. Gradiva, Lisboa, PT (1995)

Game-Based Learning and Edutainment

Breaking the Wall of E-Waste Recycling Education by Means of a Digital Game

Richard da Cruz Lopes[1], André Luiz Brandão[1,4(✉)] [iD], Alessio de Marchi[2],
André Kazuo Yasui[1], Karla Vittori[1], Flávia de Souza Santos[3,4],
and Sandra Gama[4]

[1] Universidade Federal do ABC, Santo André, Brazil
{lopes.richard,a.kazuo}@aluno.ufabc.edu.br, karla.vittori@ufabc.edu.br
[2] What Weee Are Project, Chieri, Italy
[3] Universidade de São Paulo, São Paulo, Brazil
flaviasantos@usp.br
[4] Universidade de Lisboa, Lisbon, Portugal
andre.brandao@ufabc.edu.br, sandra.gama@tecnico.ulisboa.pt,
brandao@daad-alumni.de

Abstract. Global E-waste monitoring has revealed a concerning surge
in e-waste generation, with millions of metric tons produced each year.
This underscores the urgent need for heightened awareness and responsible management of electronic waste (e-waste), given the continuous influx
of new information and communication technology (ICT) products, the
rapid obsolescence of older ones, and the associated environmental and
health hazards posed by improper disposal. In response, we developed
an innovative digital game, inspired by the Falling Walls Lab Conference, designed to engage players in learning about responsible e-waste
disposal and environmental justice, with the aim of breaking down barriers and raising awareness. The game can be used to stard discussions
about e-waste in schools to provide a context for teenagers to think
about recycling waste electrical and electronic equipment (WEEE). Furthermore, we conducted an evaluation of the game using the Cognitive
Walkthrough method to assess its effectiveness.

Keywords: E-waste · Responsible management · Game-based learning

1 Introduction

E-waste is primarily described as the waste generated by all parts and items of
electronic and electrical equipment (EEE) that have been discarded without the
intention of being reused [2]. It is also known as waste electrical and electronic
equipment (WEEE) and e-scrap in different parts of the world [22]. E-waste
encompasses a diverse range of electronic devices, such as telecommunications
and information technology equipment, large household items, lighting equipment, automatic dispensers, medical devices, monitoring, and control devices,

ⓒ The Author(s), under exclusive license to Springer Nature Switzerland AG 2024
L. Vale Costa et al. (Eds.): VJ 2023, CCIS 1984, pp. 103–117, 2024.
https://doi.org/10.1007/978-3-031-51452-4_8

as well as consumer electronics, including electronic and electrical tools, sports and leisure equipment, toys, mobile phones, and computers [13], [8].

E-waste has been regarded as an untreated treasure since it may contain a variety of natural and processed resources such as precious and platinum group metals, base metals, plastics, and other non-metals [24]. These metals, plastics, and other non-metals were either openly dumped or incinerated instead of processing at formal facilities to extend the life of resources by recovering them as secondary raw materials [28].

Recognizing the importance of engaging people in the process of learning about recycling waste, namely electrical and electronic equipment, we made the decision to develop a game that combines two groundbreaking ideas presented at the Falling Walls Lab Conference. Falling Walls Lab is an international conference and competition that fosters innovation and aims to overcome societal challenges. It was at this conference that the paths of two of the authors of this study crossed. They decided to collaborate on a digital game that combines computer science with environmental awareness. This project was a collaboration between a Computer Science Professor and the Head of the What Weee Are Project. As Falling Walls Lab alumni, they were inspired to break down barriers and create something innovative that could make a positive impact on society. The research question of this study is: How can researchers develop and evaluate a digital game to engage students in the learning process of e-waste recycling? Our game is designed to engage players in learning about the importance of responsible electronic waste disposal and environmental justice. Through this study, we aim to share our experience in developing this game, including the design process, technical implementation, and the impact we hope it will have on raising awareness about these critical issues.

The What Weee Are Project is dedicated to supporting schools in educating teenagers about e-waste recycling. In the educational environment, where computers often have limited processing power, we tailored our efforts to address the needs of our target audience –teenagers. The game design was thoughtfully chosen to align with the computational capabilities of the school machines. By using the game as a tool, we aim to encourage students to actively participate in discussions and learning about e-waste and recycling, fostering a greater awareness of environmental sustainability.

2   Game-Based Leaning

Education is a basic human necessity, as well as a critical component, of a country's development [12]. The selection of appropriate and effective teaching techniques to make the learning process helpful and to promote critical thinking abilities in learners is the most essential problem in the educational process [30, 32, 34].

New and advanced technologies have changed the learning style of students [11]. Among these technologies, we have the games, which refers to a rule-based system involving variable and quantifiable outcomes [16]. Defined by rules, games refer to the systems that encourage players to engage in an artificial conflict for quantifiable outcomes [31,36]. While experiencing the game where the consequences are optional and flexible, the participants exert efforts to influence the outcomes assigned corresponding values [16].

A learning process that utilizes game applications is called game-based learning (GBL) [15]. Game-based learning is designed to balance theoretical content and learning through the use of games [1]. Game-based learning allows students to explore rigorous learning environments and concepts and targeted learning outcomes [7].

The application of games in education can foster notable improvements in both learning and education outcomes [17,33]. According to Boctor [4], the process by which the game-based learning approach supports learning comprises two steps: first, games can motivate students to combine knowledge from various disciplines and utilize it in decision-making processes; and second, students can test how game outcomes change based on the choices and decisions they make. It also allows students to communicate with other participants and discuss game-related moves; this increases coordination which, in turn, improves social association skills [1]. Thus, integrating learning with a game-based approach can be an effective means of harmonizing teachers' and students' preferences. In short, game-based learning contributes to improving students' engagement, coordination, and creativity [1].

Digital game-based learning (DGBL) refers to the use of entertaining digital games to achieve educational goals [26,29]. In the aspect of education, instructors could use digital games created not with the primary purpose of pure entertainment to reinforce learning and improve training [20]. It has gained increasing attention in recent years as a way to engage and motivate learners, particularly in online and blended learning contexts. It enables students to engage in role playing, decision making, and problem solving by providing an immersive and interactive experience [18,27].

DGBL might promote not only academic achievement but also critical thinking [21], according to both problem-based learning and social conflict theories [25,35]. First, DGBL can simulate real-world problems without perfect information in a safe environment, allowing students to try to solve them with different strategies over time, receive feedback, evaluate their information use and decisions, and thereby improve their future critical thinking. For example, role-playing games in medical and nursing education allow students to ask a patient about symptoms, diagnose their illness, prescribe treatment, and receive immediate feedback on the treatment's effectiveness [14]. These students can then assess whether they properly obtained and assessed the symptoms to make the correct diagnosis, and if not, identify other needed steps or decisions-all of which can improve their future questions for patients and subsequent diagnoses [6].

Games should be designed to ensure that the students can repeat the cycles within the game context without becoming bored [1]. Further, a good educational game should, during such states of repetition, elicit desirable behaviors in students; this can be achieved through fostering certain emotional and cognitive reactions to interactions with and feedback received from the game [4]. Between games, a debriefing process and a review of learning outcomes should be implemented [23]. Post-game debriefings allow the teacher to establish a connection between the game and the real world. It also creates an association between occurrences within the game and those of real life, thereby connecting the students' understanding of the game to education [5].

3   The What Weee Are Project

"What Weee Are" is an independent artistic project that was founded in 2014 and integrates various fields of activity, including arts, science, education, and entertainment. The project originated in Torino, Italy, where its creators began collecting Waste Electric and Electronic Equipment (WEEE) discarded on the streets.

The project is a socio-cultural multimedia project that explores the complexities of the world through an inclusive and diverse approach. It aims to shed light on pressing global issues related to Environmental Justice and Dysfunctional Economy and inspire individuals to take action toward a more sustainable and equitable world. The project encourages individuals to question societal norms and values, fostering a deeper understanding of ourselves and our place in the world, and inspiring a sense of empathy and social responsibility.

What Weee Are uses a variety of media, including visual arts, film, field research, written and oral presentations, public panels, interactive workshops, and even a digital game, to create a multi-sensory and engaging experience for participants. The project explores complex themes related to electronic waste, encouraging reflection and critical thinking, and aims to foster a greater understanding of responsible e-waste management.

The What Weee Are project takes an inclusive and open-source approach, inviting proactive audience participation to promote responsible consumption and responsible citizenship with a focus on responsible e-waste management. The project aims to empower individuals to develop their own unique perspectives on these issues by applying their skills, capabilities, and knowledge. Through active involvement, the project inspires individuals to take action towards a more sustainable future while encouraging critical thinking and reflection.

The project has been showcased at international venues and has received recognition from institutions and the public. In 2015, the project was featured at Falling Walls Lab Berlin, leading to a collaboration with Universidade Federal do ABC. Professors and students developed a vintage-style video game as a graduation project using What Weee Are's visual materials. The project highlights the interconnectedness between human society and the natural world, emphasizing the importance of environmental sustainability.

The collaboration between the Federal University of ABC and the What Weee Are project was a crucial step towards raising awareness about the issue of e-waste and promoting environmental sustainability. By utilizing the project's visual materials to develop a vintage-style video game, the professors and students involved were able to engage with a younger audience and provide an interactive learning experience. The project not only served as a graduation project for students, but it also contributed to the What Weee Are project's mission of promoting responsible consumption and responsible citizenship. The collaboration highlights the potential for academic institutions to work with independent artistic projects to create innovative educational tools that address pressing social and environmental issues.

4   What Weee Are Computer Game

By focusing on WEEE, What Weee Are Game aims to raise awareness about the impact of electronic waste on the environment and encourage sustainable behavior among players. The project consists of a digital game that engages players in a fun and educational way, teaching them about the proper disposal and recycling of WEEE. Through its interdisciplinary approach, What Weee Are Game seeks to not only educate players about the importance of responsible e-waste management but also inspire creativity and promote a sense of social responsibility. The game is available in English, Italian, and Brazilian Portuguese. As we highlight in Sect. 1, the game is a starting point to contextualize teenagers in schools to contextualize discussions about e-waste and recycling. The target group is teenagers because the What Weee Are project have experienced valuable insights with this public in previous face-to-face activities. Those previous activities impacted game design decisions, such as a colorful virtual environment and the option to be a platformer game.

The video game is a nostalgic platformer that pays homage to the early '80 s era of gaming. It skillfully captures the essence of gaming history during that time. The game characters are meticulously crafted using stop-motion techniques, reminiscent of the iconic What Weee Are shorts. The animated sprites that breathe life into the characters are actually photographs of sculptures made from recycled Waste Electrical and Electronic Equipment, captured from various angles. In a similar fashion, everyday household objects serve as the inspiration for in-game items. Just as the actual What Weee Are sculptures are created by disassembling and reassembling electronic components found in common household items, players can also disassemble these in-game items to collect valuable resources. These resources can then be utilized to purchase upgrades for the main character, ranging from special abilities to powerful enhancements. We opted for a nostalgic platformer as our game choice, taking into consideration the limited processing power of computers in educational environments. By tailoring our efforts to meet the needs of school computers, we aimed to ensure a satisfactory performance during gameplay. The decision to create a 2-dimensional game was deliberate, as it significantly reduces the number of polygons to be processed, further contributing to the game's smooth performance on these machines.

The game's storyline loosely reflects real-life issues surrounding organized crime and improper waste disposal. It sheds light on the significant role insects play, emphasizing how they are often the first to bear the brunt of environmental disruptions such as contamination and pollution. By assuming the perspective of an insect, the game aims to remind players of the vulnerability of small creatures and their habitats to these environmental challenges.

During the user-centered design, we considered the co-design as an approach to make project decisions. The main tools that we used to develop the game were: Unity 2023.2 Game Engine with the packages TileMaps (for platforms) and Localization (for multi-language feature). The project is available for download[1].

4.1   Characters

"What Weee Are" Game features two main characters: Weee, the ant; and the Talking Cricket. Weee serves as our controllable character, guiding us through the game as we navigate and explore four distinct scenarios. Along the way, Weee has the ability to collect items, dismantle complex objects, assemble new items, acquire new skills, defeat enemies, and steadily advance through the game world.

The Talking Cricket serves as Weee's guide, providing narration and directing the playable character through the world, offering guidance on how to progress. The dialogues take place during the game and at the beginning of each scenario, where the Cricket appears to interact and communicate.

4.2   Scenarios and Phases

The game encompasses a quartet of distinct scenarios, with each scenario portraying a discrete phase of the gameplay. In the subsequent exposition, we shall explicate the distinctive attributes and characteristics exhibited by each phase, unveiling the diverse array of experiences they bestow upon the player.

Phase 1 – The Kitchen. In this phase of the game, we are introduced to the imminent challenges ahead and provided with fundamental gameplay mechanics. The Talking Cricket enlightens the player on the intricacies of movement and progression during the initial phase. It enlightens the player about the plight of electronic waste and the detrimental consequences arising from its improper disposal. Moreover, it unveils the Eco-InterCrim organization as a potential perpetrator behind this catastrophe. Figure 1 illustrates this scenario.

Throughout The Kitchen, the player will come across various collectible items and engage in encounters with both red and green ants that are enemies. The ultimate climax awaits as we confront the formidable Mechanical Spider, serving as the pinnacle of this enthralling journey.

Phase 2 – The Garden. During the Garden phase, the wise Talking Cricket will unveil a valuable insight to the player-an opportunity to obtain a new skill: the double jump. This newfound ability allows the player to delve deeper into the investigation of potential contaminations within the garden. Furthermore, the Cricket will emphasize the possibility of revisiting the kitchen to collect additional items that will aid in crafting and unlocking this empowering skill.

---

[1] https://github.com/iRitiLopes/WhatWeeAre.

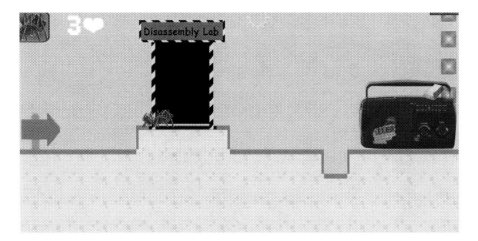

Fig. 1. Phase 1 – The Kitchen

Phase 3 – The Metro. As the player arrives at the metro, the sagacious Talking Cricket reveals crucial information: Eco-InterCrim is exploiting the railway network to advance their environmental crimes with their nefarious Toxicity plan. Initially, they have taken hold of the underground system and polluted it, intensifying the threat of groundwater contamination. Consequently, the mission pivots to prioritize the collection of a maximum number of waste items. Figure 2 illustrates the Metro.

Phase 4 – The Volcano. The ultimate challenge looms at the volcano, where the formidable stronghold of Eco-InterCrim resides. It is at this pivotal moment that the player can ultimately bring an end to their ceaseless onslaught against the environment. As Weee fearlessly conquers this final obstacle, their heroic achievement is rightfully celebrated. However, the journey is far from over, as we must now redirect our attention to mending the damages inflicted by this nefarious criminal organization. Figure 3 illustrates Phase 4.

Workshop: Assembling and Disassembling Objects. *Crafting* is a fundamental concept in the realm of electronic game design, specifically pertaining to the mechanics of construction and destruction. It offers users an interactive experience that fosters creativity and unraveling. Creating and destroying, actions commonly found within these games, serve as the foundation for this particular gameplay mechanic. By strategically employing this crafting system, it becomes possible to construct intricate and immersive storylines that not only provide a gratifying gaming experience but also delve into critical subjects such as environmental concerns, social justice, and public policies [10].

Fig. 2. Phase 3 – The Metro

In the What Weee Are game, players can control the Weee character who has the ability to collect various items. These items include:: (i) Board; (ii) Copper; (iii) Gear; (iv) Gold; (v) Battery; (vi) Iron; (vii) Mercury; (viii) Plastic; (ix) Silver; (x) Steel. The battery gives life to WEEE.

The game provides two different crafting environments: the Disassembly Laboratory (Fig. 4) and the Assembly Laboratory (Fig. 5). In the Disassembly Laboratory, players can dismantle the board into gold and iron, as well as the gear into silver. In the Assembly Laboratory, players can upgrade their character with the following enhancements: (a) Super Velocity - crafted using boards and gears; (b) Battery - crafted using steel and mercury; and (c) Double Jump - crafted using boards, gears, and iron. The player is also able to produce steel assembling irons.

5   Cognitive Walkthrough Game Evaluation

To assess users' interaction with the developed game, we implemented the Cognitive Walkthrough (CW) methodology in this evaluation. The Cognitive Walkthrough (CW) is a method for inspecting usability, focusing specifically on a user's cognitive processes and capabilities during interaction with a system, such as a video game [19]. Four primary tasks are encompassed within the CW methodology, as described by Barbosa et al. [3] and Dix et al. [9]:

(1)   Preparation: user profiles should be identified, tasks to be included in the evaluation should be defined, actions needed to perform each task should be described, and an executable (or non-executable) representation of the interface should be prepared to commence the actual inspection.

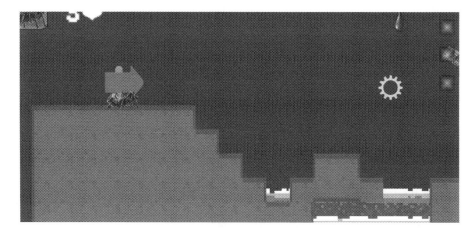

Fig. 3. Phase 4 – The Volcano

(2) Data Collection and Interpretation: The evaluator should navigate the interface according to the sequence of actions required to perform each task, and for each enumerated action, should assess whether the user would perform the action correctly, answering and justifying responses to the four fundamental CW questions (described in Table 1).

(3) Results Consolidation: The evaluator should synthesize the evaluation results on what the user needs to know beforehand to perform the tasks, what the user should learn while performing the tasks, and suggestions for correcting the problems found.

(4) Reporting of Results: A consolidated report should be generated detailing the problems found and suggestions for their rectification.

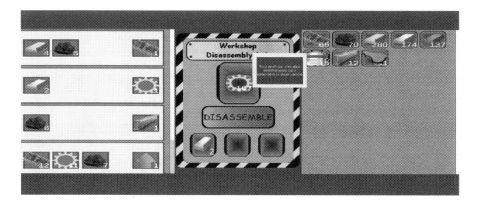

Fig. 4. Disassembly Laboratory

Fig. 5. Assembly Laboratory

Table 1. Cognitive Walkthrough (CW) questions

Q1:	Will the user try to achieve the right effect?
Q2:	Will the user notice that the correct action is available?
Q3:	Will the user associate the correct action with the effect they are trying to achieve?
Q4:	If the correct action is performed, will the user see that progress is being made toward the solution of their task?

These tasks are informed by a series of four critical questions, detailed in Table 1, designed to underscore the cognitive procedure, providing a clearer understanding of the user's learning experience when engaging with the interface.

In our evaluation, we enlisted the assistance of three experts proficient in Human-Computer Interaction and the Cognitive Walkthrough methodology to implement the CW approach. We considered 3 evaluators in this study because the main focus is to introducing the digital game. We adhered to the predefined procedures, initiating with the preparation phase. In this phase, we crafted a script that defined user personas, outlined the task to be assessed, and itemized the required actions for successful task completion (Table 2).

Each expert was then provided with the generated support material and access to the interface, allowing them to respond to each of the four questions (Table 1) while performing actions (Table 2) as if they were a user as depicted in the user profile. The user profile described for this evaluation are children aged between 10 and 11 years, who are elementary school students and use computers to access online games and videos.

The experts recognized eight potential concerns that might influence the users' cognitive processes. These concerns are delineated below in Table 3, paired with the ID of the corresponding action that they impact. No potential issues were observed in actions 1 and 2.

Table 2. Described actions to fulfill the task, and their IDs

Action ID	Action description
1	Click on the flag of the desired language (Brazil for Portuguese, Italy for Italian, and England for English)
2	Click on the New Game button
3	Follow the narrative and get information about the game context by pressing the'J' key to proceed
4	Navigate the level using the'space' key to jump,'a' to move left,'d' to move right,'j' to disassemble objects, and'w' to access the refinery when standing in front of it
5	Collect the items you find, generate new abilities (double jump, greater enemy damage), and find the exit
6	Repeat steps 3, 4, and 5 for the next levels

The issues associated with Task 3 center on the potential difficulty users might have in recognizing that they are expected to use the'J' key on the keyboard to progress in the task. This does not appear to be a natural or intuitive action, requiring a degree of cognitive processing and potentially some trial-and-error testing to successfully advance in the task. As a corrective suggestion for this issue, the experts propose that another key could be used, such as the spacebar, which might be more readily associated with this type of action. Alternatively, the possibility of using any available key (along with the on-screen information "press any key to continue") could also be considered.

The issue associated with Task 4 also pertains to the keys used, now specifically for controlling movements within the game. The experts believe that the

Table 3. Identified Issues

Action ID	Problem description
3	The key used is not intuitive for the player
3	The player might not realize that the expected key is'J', they might test several options before understanding what is expected
4	For an inexperienced player, there is no indication of the other keys that should be used for moving around in the game
5	The user may not realize that more combinations in the refinery are accessible after scrolling
5	It was not initially apparent to the player the need to generate skills, they may believe that the items are used to create new electronic items
5	Players might need to spend some time to look for the correct location
5	When creating a new ability, the player doesn't know if it's created or not until they leave the factory
6	It's possible that the perception that the correct action is available may only occur after some learning

chosen keys may not be easily discernible to an inexperienced player, especially since no in-game information indicates which keys should be used. This could lead to initial frustration and a high cognitive load as the player searches for the correct keys. As a corrective suggestion for this issue, the experts propose the commands could also be more intuitive, such as using the arrow keys or the AWD scheme, where the 'W' key is used for jumping, 'A' for moving left, and 'D' for moving right, as is the case in many platform games.

The issues related to Task 5 are tied to the fact that it's not readily apparent to the user which items can be generated from which combinations. As a result, players may not easily discern the intended use for the items collected during the game. As a corrective suggestion, we could highlight a change in the presentation of the list of items to be generated and their requirements.

The issue related to Task 6 is more about the user's perception of correct action in the game, which may only occur after some interactions with the game. However, it is perceived that this issue may be part of the game's dynamics.

6   Conclusion and Future Research

The digital game that we developed can provide an unique and interactive opportunity for individuals to learn about responsible e-waste management. In our approach of the system, What Weee Are Game, aims to inspire individuals to take action towards a more sustainable future while raising awareness about the pressing issue of electronic waste. This game is a starting point for teenagers students discuss about e-waste and recycling. By means of this game, teachers can address recycling contextualizing the students in this topic.

While we acknowledge that there are other game design options that could potentially enhance the game, such as virtual reality and augmented reality, our primary consideration was the limited processing power of computers in educational environments. Consequently, we deliberately chose to create a 2-dimensional game to minimize the number of polygons that need to be processed. This decision can significantly contribute to the game's overall performance on these machines. We also considered experiences in face-to-face activities that influenced the option for colorful environment and a 2D platformer.

Based on the evaluation, certain issues were identified in the game's tasks, including difficulties in recognizing the required keys, lack of intuitive controls, unclear item combinations, and uncertainty in user actions. Proposed solutions include using more familiar keys, providing in-game instructions, improving item presentation, and offering flexibility in key selection for progression. Notwithstanding these issues, the game remains engaging and successfully fulfills its intended purpose.

As part of future work, the technical game team can focus on implementing improvements based on the insights gained from the Cognitive Walkthrough evaluation. Some suggested enhancements include changing the assigned key "J" to a more intuitive alternative, replacing the WASD keys with arrow keys for character movement, and involving users as deputies in the game design process. In future works, we can detail how we apply game-based theory in the development of the system. We also include in future works the discussions of the game development and the inspection evaluation that we applied and lessons learned. We also consider tests with end-users, positive and negative learning outcomes that emerged from using this game in a GBL approach to e-waste reduction.

Overall, the What Weee Are project and its accompanying video game demonstrate the potential of gamification and interactive experiences to educate and inspire individuals towards sustainable practices. By addressing the identified issues and continually refining the game, the project can have a lasting impact on raising awareness and fostering responsible e-waste management in the future.

References

1. Adipat, S., Laksana, K., Busayanon, K., Ausawasowan, A., Adipat, B.: Engaging students in the learning process with game-based learning: the fundamental concepts. Int. J. Technol. Educ. **4**, 542–552 (2021). https://doi.org/10.46328/ijte.169
2. Baldé, C., Wang, F., Kuehr, R.: Transboundary movements of used and waste electronic and electrical equipment. Vice Rectorate in Europe - Sustainable Cycles Programme (SCYCLE), Bonn, Germany (2016)
3. Barbosa, S., Silva, B.: Interação humano-computador. Elsevier, Brasil (2010)
4. Boctor, L.: Active-learning strategies: the use of a game to reinforce learning in nursing education. a case study. Nurse Educ. Pract. **13**(2), 96–100 (2013). https://doi.org/10.1016/j.nepr.2012.07.010
5. Bundick, M., Quaglia, R., Corso, M., Haywood, D.: Promoting student engagement in the classroom. Teachers Coll. Record **116**(4), 016146811411600411 (2014)
6. Chang, C.Y., Kao, C.H., Hwang, G.J., Lin, F.H.: From experiencing to critical thinking: a contextual game-based learning approach to improving nursing students' performance in electrocardiogram training. Educ. Technol. Res. Develop. **68**(3), 1225–1245 (2020). https://doi.org/10.1007/s11423-019-09723-x
7. Chen, C.H., Liu, J.H., Shou, W.C.: How competition in a game-based science learning environment influences students' learning achievement, flow experience, and learning behavioral patterns. Educ. Technol. Soc. **21**, 164–176 (2018)
8. Chen, M., Huang, J., Ogunseitan, O.A., Zhu, N., min Wang, Y.: Comparative study on copper leaching from waste printed circuit boards by typical ionic liquid acids. Waste Manage. **41**, 142–147 (2015). https://doi.org/10.1016/j.wasman.2015.03.037. https://www.sciencedirect.com/science/article/pii/S0956053X15002317
9. Dix, A., Finlay, J., Abowd, G.D., Beale, R.: Human-computer interaction. Pearson Education (2003)
10. Grow, A., Dickinson, M., Pagnutti, J., Wardrip-Fruin, N., Mateas, M.: Crafting in games. Digit. Human. Quart. **11**(4), 350 (2017)
11. Hafeez, M.: Effects of game-based learning in comparison to traditional learning to provide an effective learning environment-a comparative review. Contemp. Educ. Res. J. **12**(2), 89–105 (2022). https://doi.org/10.18844/cerj.v12i2.6374
12. Hafeez, M., et al.: Impact of school enrolment size on student's achievements. J. Educ. Humaniora Soc. Sci. (JEHSS) **3**, 170 (2020). https://doi.org/10.34007/jehss.v3i1.170

13. Huang, J., Chen, M., Chen, H., Chen, S., Sun, Q.: Leaching behavior of copper from waste printed circuit boards with brønsted acidic ionic liquid. Waste Manage. **34**(2), 483–488 (2014). https://doi.org/10.1016/j.wasman.2013.10.027. https://www.sciencedirect.com/science/article/pii/S0956053X13005138

14. Hwang, G.J., Chang, C.Y.: Facilitating decision-making performances in nursing treatments: a contextual digital game-based flipped learning approach. Interact. Learn. Environ. **31**, 1–16 (2020). https://doi.org/10.1080/10494820.2020.1765391

15. Jin, G., Tu, M., Kim, T.H., Heffron, J., White, J.: Evaluation of game-based learning in cybersecurity education for high school students. J. Educ. Learn. (EduLearn) **12**, 150 (2018). https://doi.org/10.11591/edulearn.v12i1.7736

16. Juul, J.: The game, the player, the world: looking for a heart of gameness. In: Proceedings of the Level-Up: Digital Games Research Conference Proceedings, The Netherlands Utrecht, pp. 30–45 (2003)

17. Kula, S.S.: Mind games with the views of classroom teachers. Int. J. Res. Educ. Sci. **7**, 747–766 (2021). https://doi.org/10.46328/ijres.1471

18. Laine, T.H., Lindberg, R.S.N.: Designing engaging games for education: a systematic literature review on game motivators and design principles. IEEE Trans. Learn. Technol. **13**(4), 804–821 (2020). https://doi.org/10.1109/TLT.2020.3018503

19. Lewis, C., Polson, P.G., Wharton, C., Rieman, J.: Testing a walkthrough methodology for theory-based design of walk-up-and-use interfaces. In: Proceedings of the SIGCHI Conference on Human Factors in Computing Systems, pp. 235–242 (1990)

20. Loh, C.S., Sheng, Y., Ifenthaler, D.: Serious games analytics: theoretical framework. In: Loh, C.S., Sheng, Y., Ifenthaler, D. (eds.) Serious Games Analytics. AGL, pp. 3–29. Springer, Cham (2015). https://doi.org/10.1007/978-3-319-05834-4_1

21. Mao, W., Cui, Y., Chiu, M., Lei, H.: Effects of game-based learning on students' critical thinking: a meta-analysis. J. Educ. Comput. Res. **59**(8), 1682–1708 (2022). https://doi.org/10.1177/07356331211007098

22. Mary, J.S., Meenambal, T.: Inventorisation of e-waste and developing a policy – bulk consumer perspective. Procedia Environ. Sci. **35**, 643–655 (2016). https://doi.org/10.1016/j.proenv.2016.07.058. https://www.sciencedirect.com/science/article/pii/S1878029616301475. Waste Management for Resource Utilisation

23. Mozelius, P., Hettiarachchi, E.: Critical factors for implementing blended learning in higher education. Int. J. Inf. Commun. Technol. Educ. **6**, 37–51 (2017). https://doi.org/10.1515/ijicte-2017-0001

24. Murthy, V., Ramakrishna, S.: A review on global e-waste management: urban mining towards a sustainable future and circular economy. Sustainability **14**(2), 647 (2022). https://www.mdpi.com/2071-1050/14/2/647

25. Noroozi, O., Dehghanzadeh, H., Talaee, E.: A systematic review on the impacts of game-based learning on argumentation skills. Entertain. Comput. **35**, 100369 (2020). https://doi.org/10.1016/j.entcom.2020.100369

26. Nussbaum, M., Beserra, V.: Educational videogame design. In: Proceedings - IEEE 14th International Conference on Advanced Learning Technologies, ICALT 2014, pp. 2–3 (2014). https://doi.org/10.1109/ICALT.2014.9

27. Ott, M., et al.: Designing serious games for education: from pedagogical principles to game mechanisms. In: Proceedings of the 5th European Conference on Games Based Learning, vol. 2011. Athens, Greece (2011)

28. Perkins, D.N., Drisse, M.N.B., Nxele, T., Sly, P.D.: E-waste: a global hazard. Ann. Glob. Health **80**(4), 286–295 (2014)

29. Prensky, M.: Digital game-based learning. McGraw-Hill, New York 1 (2001). https://doi.org/10.1145/950566.950567

30. Saira, A.F., Hafeez, M.: Assessment of student's academic achievement by flipped classroom model and traditional lecture method. Global Educ. Stud. Rev. **V**, 10–19 (2020). https://doi.org/10.31703/gesr.2020(V-IV).02
31. Salen, K., Zimmerman, E.: Rules of play: game design fundamentals. Pról. de Frank Lantz, p. 672. MIT Press, Cambridge, Mass (2004)
32. Senthamarai, S.: Interactive teaching strategies. J. Appl. Adv. Res. **3**, 36 (2018). https://doi.org/10.21839/jaar.2018.v3iS1.166
33. Syafii, M., Kusnawan, W., Syukroni, A.: Enhancing listening skills using games. Int. J. Stud. Educ. **2**, 78–107 (2020). https://doi.org/10.46328/ijonse.21
34. Tavoosy, Y., Jelveh, R.: Language teaching strategies and techniques used to support students learning in a language other than their mother tongue. Int. J. Learn. Teach. **11**, 77–88 (2019). https://doi.org/10.18844/ijlt.v11i2.3831
35. Wu, W.H., Hsiao, H.S., Wu, P.L., Lin, C.H., Huang, S.H.: Investigating the learning-theory foundations of game-based learning: a meta-analysis. J. Comput. Assist. Learn. **28**(3), 265–279 (2012). https://doi.org/10.1111/j.1365-2729.2011.00437.x
36. Zhang, Q., YuChiu, Z.: Meta-analysis on investigating and comparing the effects on learning achievement and motivation for gamification and game-based learning. Hindawi Education Research International 2022 (2022). https://doi.org/10.1155/2022/1519880

How Players Develop Computational Thinking While Modeling Character Behaviors in Gameplay

Valéria Moreira Pinto[1]([✉]) [iD], Mariana Seiça[2] [iD], and Licínio Roque[2] [iD]

[1] Institute for Interdisciplinary Research, CISUC, University of Coimbra, Coimbra, Portugal
vamvp@dei.uc.pt
[2] Department of Informatics Engineering, CISUC, University of Coimbra, Coimbra, Portugal
{marianac,lir}@dei.uc.pt

Abstract. In this work we explore the potential of using a Petri Nets inspired graphic interface supporting a character action modeling mechanic to develop computational thinking skills in a game-based learning environment. We conceived a proof-of-concept paper prototype as a probe to perform gameplay rehearsals and distill insights on how young players would appropriate it. A qualitative research approach was used to study gameplay sessions and semi-structured interviews, coding player actions and dialogue. We were able to gain insights on how the design of the game components and its mechanics mimicking Petri Nets provided an accessible way for players to perform the game activities by modeling behaviors of game characters. The integration of an interface design for action modeling inspired by Petri Nets and the use of symbols for encoding conditions, actions and outcomes, allowed players to model complex sequences of behavior, recognize patterns, decompose in-game activities, and work with abstractions such as conditions, consequences and steps. This enabled players' articulation of cause-and-effect relationships, leading to the consolidation of computational thinking skills. This work provides insights for exploring similar design patterns in gameplay to enhance Computational Thinking.

Keywords: Player Modeled Actions · Computational thinking · Game Design · Petri Nets · STEAM

1 Introduction

The 21st century is being marked by an accelerated growth of technological development, which promoted a global interest in STEAM (science, technology, engineering, arts, and mathematics) from an educational and workforce perspective, offering more attractive career prospects [1, 2]. This growth in the STEAM areas led to the interest and legitimization of educational policies, thus investing in research, promoting higher education, and further development of educational programs [3, 4]. However, despite the existence of several education programs and the positive labor market outcomes, these areas only draw a smaller proportion of students, resulting in a general concern in many countries [5, 6]. Considering this, it is critical to identify ways to increase enrollment in STEAM fields to meet the demand for professionals in technological sectors.

© The Author(s), under exclusive license to Springer Nature Switzerland AG 2024
L. Vale Costa et al. (Eds.): VJ 2023, CCIS 1984, pp. 118–133, 2024.
https://doi.org/10.1007/978-3-031-51452-4_9

Research indicates that engaging students with STEAM concepts is beneficial once they expose students to real-world problems, fostering their interest in STEAM fields and preparing them for the evolving workforce. Establishing these connections at an earlier stage in their education could potentially increase interest in the students in pursuing careers in STEAM-related fields [7, 8]. For this, it is necessary to promote the motivation of individuals for STEAM subjects from an early age [9, 10].

Computational thinking (CT) is a problem-solving approach rooted in computer science with inherent value in these fields. CT is essential in STEAM due to its reliance on computational tools and problem-solving approaches. It is considered a vital twenty-first-century skill for solving complex problems [11, 12].

Games can be a strategy to make CT more available and attractive [13, 14]. A playful contact with CT creates opportunities for individuals to solve real-case problems, which can effectively engage individuals in STEAM learning [11, 12]. As such, an important approach to explore is the development of CT competences through a game that engages and promotes a playful contact during the learning process, which may impact motivation and career choices for the STEAM fields [12].

Petri Nets (PNs) are versatile tools used for modeling, analyzing, and designing the behavior of discrete event systems. Their graphic structure, composed of circles, squares/bars, and arcs, makes them easy to read and understand [15]. This simplicity allows their graphic structure to be used as a design artifact that can potentially enhance computational thinking (CT) skills. The flow representation of PNs can be adapted to represent algorithms, providing a step-by-step approach to solving tasks and promoting cause-and-effect understanding. We conjectured that by integrating PNs-based representations into the design of the game mechanics, we can enable players to develop CT skills as they create sequences of actions, define dependencies, play out and understand the consequences of their decisions within the game context. Considering this context, we will present a game design case study that explores how to enhance competencies associated with computational thinking by mimicking PNs in the game design to challenge players to define in-game characters' actions.

Over the next sections we will present this design case, the game design proposal, an evaluation and insights on how the game may promote CT skill development.

2 Background

2.1 Computational Thinking

The term Computational Thinking (CT) originated in the 1940s when scientists began exploring how computer technology could be applied in real-case situations, leading to the growth of computer science [16]. Jeannette Wing defined CT as "Computational thinking involves solving problems, designing systems, and understanding human behavior, by drawing on the concepts fundamental to computer science" [17]. Wing [18] argues that CT involves conceptualizing problems in abstract ways that combine mathematics and informatics engineering and is applied in various professions and disciplines, including economics, and the humanities.

CT is a way of exploiting computation for problem-solving or knowledge production. The process involves breaking down a problem into algorithmic steps or tasks, which can then be programmed into a computer to achieve the desired results. Although the concept originated in computer science as a way to design programs for specific tasks, CT is now being taught to students of all ages, as it provides a valuable framework for problem-solving in several areas [14, 18–21] and understanding the function of computerized devices in everyday life [16].

Considering that CT is a fundamental skill for everyone and is an analytical ability that all children could benefit to acquire, as CT involves solving problems, designing systems, and understanding human behavior, through the portrayal of fundamental concepts to computer science [17]. For that, diverse forms were explored to introduce CT, that include visual programming environments, robotics [22], and games [14, 23].

CT involves four components equally important for problem-solving, namely decomposition, abstraction, algorithms [16, 24, 25], and pattern recognition [16, 24]:

- Decomposition: The process of "breaking down" the problem, system, or task into smaller steps/parts;
- Abstraction: Identify critical information while ignoring irrelevant details;
- Algorithm: Develop a step-by-step process, or rules to follow, to solve a problem;
- Pattern recognition: Recognize the patterns in the process by searching for similarities among and within problems. Identifying patterns allows the individual to organize the information, which can then help with problem-solving.

2.2 Modeling with Petri Nets

Petri Nets are an abstract, formal model of concurrent information and computation flow which evolved from a representation initially developed by German mathematician Carl Adam Petri in 1962 to describe chemical processes and have evolved into a powerful tool for modeling and analyzing diverse kinds of systems [26, 27]. They are a graphical and mathematical tool for designing discrete event systems, understanding and describing information of complex systems that can involve concurrency, asynchrony, parallelism, non-determinism, and stochasticity [28].

As a graphical tool, PNs serve as an effective communication tool, enabling visual representation and understanding of systems. As a mathematical tool, PNs facilitate the formulation of formal models that govern system behavior [26, 27].

A Petri Net (PN) comprises places, transitions, arcs, and tokens. Visually, it is represented as a diagram, with places represented as circles, transitions as rectangles, arcs as directed arrows, connecting places and transitions, and tokens as small circles (Fig. 1). Each place can hold one or more tokens, signifying condition satisfaction, resources, or information required for an action to occur [15, 27–29]. The system state - a marking - is represented by a particular arrangement of tokens across the set of places. When required places (conditions, input/output, information, or resources) contain adequate tokens (resources, true or false), associated transitions can become enabled, and when triggered transitions are said to fire, lead the tokens to move from the origin places to the subsequent destination ones [15, 26–29] thus signifying a change in state.

Petri Nets (PNs) are a versatile modeling technique often used in game design, particularly for interactive storytelling. They offer graphical and formal representations, making them ideal for describing branching and parallel storylines.

Fig. 1. Petri nets representations showing before and after a transition has fired [27].

Researchers such as Brom et al. [30], Balas et al. [29], and Riedl et al. [31] have explored the application of PNs in storytelling and game design, emphasizing their clarity and adaptability for complex narratives. They highlight how PNs can represent and simulate various game elements and provide a foundation for game systems.

Araújo and Roque [27] proposed using PNs to model game systems and flow, highlighting the advantages of PNs over other modeling languages regarding scalability and effectiveness. PNs' formal semantics enable verification and simulation, aiding game designers in evaluating playtime characteristics early in the design process.

Muratet et al. [32] developed a domain-specific language and tool for modeling learning games using PNs, simplifying the creation of PNs that accurately represent player interactions. The combination of this tool and the Tina software environment (used for editing and analyzing PNs and Time PNs, allowing the construction of representations for PNs behavior [33]) streamlines the construction, inspection, and validation of PNs, offering a promising avenue for identifying design patterns applicable to various game mechanics.

Another application of PNs was demonstrated by Thomas et al. [34], that used them for tracking learning progress, recognizing the need to monitor player actions and provide analytical tools to understand knowledge acquisition using PNs.

3   Research Design

Our research design is loosely structured as a Design Science Research iteration [35]. A game design proposal was developed as part of a playful probing approach [36] focused on using play activities to collect data to investigate how participants engage with a process or artifact modeled in a playable context.

In this study, we created a cooperative multiplayer game activity that adapts the graphic structure of PNs to challenge players to define characters' behaviors and in the process, develop competences associated with CT.

We gathered data on how players explored the design to develop basic CT competences by performing the construction of the game characters' actions. For that, we conceived a proof-of-concept table-top paper prototype, as support for playful probing by performing gameplay rehearsals [36] as a data collection procedure to study and analyze modes of engagement.

The gameplay rehearsals were recorded for a qualitative approach focused on observing, coding, and analyzing action and verbal engagement. The axial coding was cross-checked, and issues were discussed among the three authors for consensus and consistent coding. At the end of the session, the players' testimonies were collected through individual semi-structured interviews.

3.1   Game Design Proposal

The probe design proposal began with understanding how the game could be designed, its main theme, features, and mechanics. Games with several activity modes become more attractive to a broad group of players since they offer multiple activities with distinct characteristics [37, 38]. Building educational games that respond broadly to individual needs and interests may increase engagement and improve student learning results.

With this in mind, we investigated motivational activity modes for school children [37, 38]. Grounded by these studies, for promoting players' engagement in a collaborative environment, our design embraces five activity modes: a) exploratory mode; b) problem-solving mode; c) creative mode; d) strategy mode; and e) social mode.

For the game's main theme, we focused on the bond children create with animals [39]. Taking into account the importance of collaboration in the game's mechanics, we searched for animal species with collaborative social organizations based on performing activities that aren't fixed or defined by sex but shared between community members to ensure the survival of the group.

We found that the meerkat has such a social structure and a generally appealing figure that seemed to fit the desired parameters. An analysis of this species' behavior served as the foundation for the game's development based on its behaviors, imagining or adapting them into actions for characters in the game, with the main goal of developing a colony. Three functions were defined as the basis of the game's mechanics: territory discovery and development, defense from predators, and member sustenance.

3.2   Defining Character Actions as CT Developing Game Mechanic

After defining the game theme, we designed a way for the players to specify character actions to develop computational thinking skills by mimicking the graphic structure of PN. We initiated this process by studying how programming concepts such as action sequencing, conditioned action, and resulting flow could be controlled and learned in this way. Instead of traditional coding methods (code or pseudocode, conditionals, loops, and function definition), we focused on the treatment of basic ideas such as the defining of possible actions, their dependencies and outcomes, enabling the possibility of chaining them. By abstracting or defining patterns, using symbols to encode information and places as messages or annotations, and by using actions as tools, and composing/decomposing them, players could act and develop basic algorithmic competences behind CT.

The basic competencies associated with CT would then be developed by the player through the definition of the behaviors (meerkat actions) in the game by coding action sheets with pre-condition signs, action signs, and post-condition signs (or results), as depicted in Fig. 2a. For that, we designed a simplified solution based on PNs models in games [27]. Players can not act before they define character actions. Considering this mechanic and the action sheet interface structure, the process of meerkat action construction is carried out by players through defining conditions that, when verified, enable players to take those actions assigned to their characters. Thus, producing results in the form of information or resources that can possibly satisfy other conditions, allowing the gameplay to advance and become more complex. The game's actions can only operate when the pre-conditions are satisfied through the availability of the element in the current game state, or the direct contact of the meerkat with the element (e.g., the player finds an element hidden in the game board).

3.3 Prototyping

The game prototype consists of a player panel (Fig. 2a) for coding the actions that meerkats can perform; and a main board (Fig. 2b) that defines the scenario where the meerkats enact the player's choices.

The player panel was designed to mimic the PNs' graphic structure: it is formed by a set of cards (action sheets), each with one main action to be performed, up to three conditions to trigger it, and up to three consequent results (Fig. 2a). This panel design gives the player the freedom to set various conditions for the action to be enabled, combining different condition-action-outcome pairings to implement their strategy.

Considering these mechanics, we developed the following action cards (Fig. 2d): *Walking; Excavate; Move to the burrow; Store food; Unload food; Bag sharing; Watch; Vocalize or warn; Run; Confront; Protect territory; Confront rat; Protect storage; Confront raccoon*, and the following elements to signify conditions or outcomes (Fig. 2e): *Directions; Steps; Favorable ground; Burrow; Tunnel; Meerkat in the burrow; Food; Meerkat with food; Empty bag; Bag with food; Full bag; Burrow with food; Snake; Wolf; Eagle; Rat; Raccoon; Question mark; Meerkat; Meerkat is watching; Meerkat is warned*.

We also created visual components for representing the colony (Fig. 2c), namely: 1) a card to hold colony members, 2) a card to hold the colony's storage of food, and 3) a meerkat inventory sheet. Five enemies were illustrated (Fig. 2f): the Snake, the Eagle and the Wolf as Predators, the Rat as Invader, and the Raccoon as Thief.

The main board consisted of two overlapping A3 paper sheets, with the upper sheet divided into 6x8 cell cuts to hide/reveal game elements within the cells, which can be activated through actions in the player's panel. Trees and shrubs were used to represent food rewards, encouraging the player to explore them.

3.4 Game Mechanics

Concerning the game mechanics, players can use up to eight action sheets; on each round, they define, collaboratively, the actions that the meerkats can perform on the main board by altering and combining conditions on the action sheets (Fig. 2a). Each player rolls a dice, and the sum of all players' dice rolls gives the total number of actions (in meerkat behavior steps) plus movements on the main board, which can be performed within each round and distributed through the players as they choose.

A round runs through three stages (Fig. 3): (1) defining the actions on the player panel; (2) rolling the dice, and (3) enacting actions with the characters on the main board, taking advantage of the behaviors currently defined. The game scenario exhausts its possibilities when all cells have been explored, all food (cells, trees, and bushes) has been collected, and the meerkats have confronted all enemies.

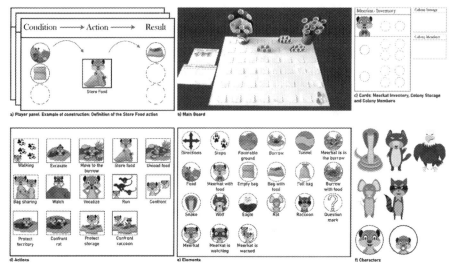

Fig. 2. Prototype of the Table-Top Paper Prototype Version.

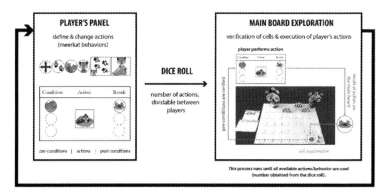

Fig. 3. Round operation.

3.5 Tracing Behavior Modeling with Petri Nets and Computational Thinking

After designing the dynamics of the game and player panel, we wanted to perform a qualitative study on how the promotion of CT could be achieved through action definition dynamics. This process resulted in the exploration and coding of associations between using the player panel and the four components of CT:

a) Decomposition involves breaking down a complex problem into smaller, more manageable parts. In the context of the player's panel, this skill is effectively applied through the use of action sheets, where each card represents a specific action. This allows players to decompose complex actions or challenges into smaller, more manageable actions. By creating sequences of action sheets, players engage in the process of decomposition, breaking down the larger problem (the game's objective) into smaller and more understandable tasks. As a result, players gain a deeper understanding of the hierarchical relationships between actions and their dependencies.

b) Pattern recognition involves identifying recurring patterns, elements, or sequences of actions that repeat in different situations. In the context of the player's panel, players can observe patterns in certain combinations of conditions and actions that lead to desired outcomes or efficient problem-solving. Players can create more efficient strategies by identifying patterns in the player's panel.

c) Abstraction involves focusing on essential details while ignoring unnecessary complexities. Using PNs, players abstract away unnecessary details while focusing on the essential elements of actions and their interconnections. Using symbols to encode information, this visual simplification enables players to identify key game elements and comprehend their significance.

d) Algorithms are well-defined instruction sequences describing how to perform a specific task. In the context of the game, the PNs visually represent step-by-step sequences. Players create algorithms by arranging transitions and places in the player panel, defining the action sheets with the pre-conditions, actions, and desired outcomes.

4   Gameplay Rehearsals

For this study, five gameplay rehearsal sessions (Table 1.) were performed: three sessions composed of mixed-gender groups with three individuals, one session with a group of three female individuals; and a session with a group of two female individuals. In total, the sample is composed of fourteen individuals (nine female individuals, five male individuals), aged between 6 and 11 years old, and enrolled between the 1st and 5th grades. For the analysis, the participants will be referred to as P1–14.

Table 1. Characterization of the study population

Rehearsal	1			2			3		4			5		
Grade	1st			2nd			4th		3rd			5th		
Player	P1	P2	P3	P4	P5	P6	P7	P8	P9	P10	P11	P12	P13	P14
Age	7	6	6	8	8	8	10	10	9	9	9	10	11	11
Gender	M	F	F	M	M	F	F	F	F	M	M	F	F	F

4.1   Probe Use and Data Collection Procedure

Explicit informed consent was obtained for audiovisual recording of the sessions for content analysis, with the camera focusing only on the board and pieces, and the audio transcribed and anonymized. At the beginning of each session, the researcher presented the game's theme, components, dynamics, and rules. An example card, demonstrating a condition-action-result construction, is also exemplified with the case of character movement. During the game session, the researcher acted as game master, clarified doubts and arising problems, arbitered decisions and calculated outcomes, with the least possible interference. In the end, the researcher collected the players' testimonies through individual semi-structured interviews.

The interview included a set of gameplay questions, such as: a)Tell us what was the most fun part of this game; b) Tell us what was the most boring/annoying part of this game; c) Tell us about an episode where you felt your friend helped you; d) Did you enjoy the game?; e) Do you think this game is for you?; f) Did the game become easier to play over time?.

4.2   Content Analysis

The content analysis involved the observation of the recorded videos, the selection of relevant player interaction and dialogue evidence over 30s segments, and coding for categories of interest. For this study, we focused on the content related to CT competence events and associated manipulations of the artifact.

Concerning the Computational Thinking competence category, three subcategories were defined: Reading and interpretation; Condition-action-result; and Action chaining.

The **Reading and Interpretation** subcategory focused on the individual's ability to read and understand the constructions already carried out in the player panel. This process involves the capacity to understand the illustrations and the way the game works in terms of dependencies and conditions, consolidating the knowledge necessary to construct the player panel. This subcategory is associated with the abstraction in CT, which involves the ability to focus on essential aspects of the representation. In the game, players must comprehend the symbols to encode information and make sense of game mechanics and instructions. By abstracting important information, players can understand how the relationship between game elements enables them to make decisions and elaborate actions. This abstraction comprehension also assists in identifying the useful actions to define in the player panel.

In the **Condition-Action-Result** subcategory, we retrieved and coded evidence corresponding to identifying the need for certain elements to enable the desired actions, and to obtain a desired result. This skill is the basis for motivating the player's panel construction in the game, in which they define the required elements to activate a specific action with useful outcomes. We associated this subcategory with the algorithmic competence in CT. Algorithms are sequences of instructions that specify how to perform a specific task. In the game context, players create algorithms by selecting and organizing the elements in action sheets, by defining the pre-conditions, actions, and post-conditions in the player panel.

Regarding the **Action Chaining** subcategory, in computational terms, it maps the need for developing an action to create (or calculate) the conditions to enable another action (or transition). This category helps to identify the chaining logic, leading players to think about the sequence of behaviors necessary to achieve a particular end. This subcategory is associated with the decomposition in CT, given the ability to break down the activity into steps, where players plan how to arrange actions in a specific order, considering the dependencies, to achieve the activity outcome.

Pattern Recognition is a CT competence that appears associated with all subcategories of competences. Since this component can be used in the player panel to identify symbol patterns, making dependencies, action sequences, and outcomes. By recognizing common combinations of conditions and actions allows the repetition of this pattern for combining conditions and actions, creating more efficient strategies that can be applied in various contexts of the game.

The category of **Artifact Manipulations** was divided into three subcategories, namely **cell exploration, collection of cell elements**, and **construction of actions** in the player panel. Considering the focus of this article, we will analyze the results of the construction of actions in the player panel subcategory. This subcategory focuses on identifying if the player has difficulties understanding the dynamic of the player panel, associating the necessary elements, and defining the desired behavior for the meerkat to execute on the main board. Through this subcategory, it is also possible to retrieve information about interaction with the simplified graphic structure of PNs for the player panel.

5   Discussion of Results

In this section, we present the results obtained from this study considering how the PNs representations in the artifact influence gameplay, as well as the development of competences associated with CT. We selected illustrative examples of evidence to expose and discuss findings.

5.1   Appropriating the Artifact Action Definition Mechanic

The evidence concerning interactions with the player panel indicates an initial difficulty that players feel when constructing the actions. The action construction mechanic first appears unfamiliar from the games that players were accustomed to, making them initially hesitant about defining game actions.

> *P8: "Yes, because at the beginning, it was a bit confusing. I had to put something here and there (on the panel). After doing it more, I managed (to do what I wanted)".*

> *P11: "(At the beginning) I didn't really know the meaning of the elements". (The researcher asked if constructing actions was difficult) "No, it was easy".*

Despite the initial difficulties, they are overcome through the players' own performance, by trial and error, as well as by the observation of the other's constructions. After developing some actions, players could easily identify the dynamics and construct them for the remaining gameplay. Some players mentioned, it was more difficult to understand the concepts at the beginning, but with the game's progression, it becomes easier and fun to realize the constructions on the player panel.

> *P12: "Yes (the game became easier to play over time). It was after deciding the actions on the player panel to move us around the board. When (have to perform) the store action, I had a bit of difficulty moving around there (on the main board)".*

Player stated that had a bit of difficulty executing actions on the main board, but not so much in defining the actions in the player panel.

P4: "I liked it! Sometimes we just put the actions together (on the panel) and I liked it".

However, in other cases, we verified that the player could understand and demonstrate to others how to perform the construction of the game's actions. The following evidence demonstrated that some players can easily indicate how to perform constructions during the initial explanation about the game in the player panel.

P4, P5 and P6: The players demonstrate the construction of the action excavate while the researcher explains the game. They point to the favorable ground element and associate it with the condition area on the player panel. Then, they point to the excavate action and associate it with the action area. Finally, they point to the burrow element and indicate the result area on the panel.

P6: A player demonstrates the construction of the action: "We have to pick up here (steps element)... I put it here (steps element in the condition area)... I put here (walk action) and this... (directions element in the result area) here!".

5.2   Manifestations of CT Competences During the Game

In this subsection, we present evidence of the development or manifestation of competences that are organized considering the association between the subcategory of competence and the four components of CT.

Evidence of Abstraction, Panel Reading and Interpretation Competence

We were able to identify 410 evidence entries that demonstrate the player's ability to read and understand the symbols used to encode gameplay state information. The individuals were engaged in reading, assisting others in the interpretation and understanding of action constructions that they developed during the game, explaining their relevance through cause-effect relationships. Illustrating this subcategory:

P5: "If there is food... Store!".

P12: "We need a favorable ground and a burrow, so we're going to excavate".

Our evidence so far already suggests a skillful use of abstraction, as players focus on essential elements of the game's actions (e.g., excavate) and conditions (e.g., favorable ground) they want to exploit in the gameplay context, while ignoring unnecessary details to the reading and understanding of the current player panel construction. As one player demonstrated:

P14: "If we find favorable ground, we excavate and make a tunnel. That makes sense!".

Algorithmic Condition-Action-Result Competence

Through the coding process, 1948 evidence entries were identified. Evidence showed that individuals possessed an understanding of condition-action-result relationships. Players indicate competence in identifying the necessary conditions to activate the actions to achieve the required result. Illustrating this subcategory:

> P2: "Eagle... Go kill it... Go warn". Player executes the action construction: inserts the element meerkat is warned in the condition area of the action confront. "And goes to kill it! Tauch! Tauch!" (Simulating hitting the eagle character on the main board).

The evidence coded suggests a quick development of a competent practice of the algorithmic component. Players follow a routine sequence of steps to construct the action, namely defining the a) pre-conditions, b) action and c) post-conditions on the player panel. This example demonstrates the player's ability to execute a step-by-step process to reach the desired outcome, which we observed to become routine for 2/3 of players after 1 h. A dialogue piece illustrating this sequence of steps:

> P5: Dialogue about the tunnels: "It's this one"- pointing to the action excavate on the player's panel. Action construction: inserts the element burrow in the condition area of the action excavate – "A tunnel... Excavate. The burrow to excavate tunnels". Player inserts the element tunnel in the result area of the action excavate.

Action Decomposition and Chaining Competence

Discourse about action sequences was identified, with 227 entries of evidence, highlighting the dependency between certain actions to achieve the desired effect. Players identified the dependency between the preventive actions (vigilance and vocalization) and the confrontation actions. The preventive actions allowed the reduction in the value of confronting predators. To use preventive actions, it was necessary to have both the watch and vocalize/warn actions activated simultaneously. To do that, players need to decompose these preventive actions into smaller, manageable tasks. Evidence indicates that players often decomposed the preventive actions into two distinct actions: watch and warn/vocalize. Players identify the hierarchical relationships between actions and their dependencies, demonstrating the decomposition competence. Illustrating these dependencies and decomposition:

> P14: "We need a guard to watch, and that one will warn". Player inserts the element meerkat is warned in the result area of the vigilance action.
>
> P4: Reacts to the preventive actions, "I want to (laughs), I want to vocalize. Because then we can call the others (meerkats), and they (points to the colony members) will go there and Papapapapaapaaa!".
>
> P5: Reacts, "I prefer vocalizing".
>
> P4: "Then let's first put the watching one". Inserts the action watch.
>
> P6: Inserts the action warn/vocalize.
>
> P5: Inserts the element meerkat is watching in the condition area of the warn/vocalize action.

Evidence of Pattern Recognition
During the gameplay, players demonstrate the ability to identify similarities in the process of defining some actions. It was possible to retrieve 28 entries of evidence related to pattern recognition. For example, players identify a pattern in the process of defining the "confront" and the "preventive" actions. They recognize that the steps to confront each predator are essentially the same, with minor variations based on the specific predator. Once they set up the action for one predator, they could easily apply a similar pattern to the others by changing the different predators into the condition area. This recognition of common patterns facilitates decision-making and allows players to efficiently handle multiple confrontations with different predators in the game.

6   Distilling Design Insights

In this research, we present an approach to develop CT competences through the design of a solution based on PNs. We designed a player panel mimicking the PNs graphic structure, where the players can define, by coding action sheets with pre-conditions, actions, and post-conditions (results) the meerkat behavior (actions). The adoption of graphic PNs as a means to define character behavior in the game carries significant implications for game design.

a) **The interface design for action definition inspired by PNs empowered players, provided an accessible and interpretable representation:** PNs provided an intuitive and visually accessible representation. The use of graphic PNs and the exploration of symbols as an encoder of information simplified the process of defining character actions, making it visual, learnable, and engaging. This visual adaptation for the player panel allowed the representation of cause-and-effect relationships in the actions that assist in the player's comprehension. By defining character behavior, simply by placing symbols in the condition, action, and result areas, most players could create complex sequences of behaviors, fostering problem-solving skills.

b) **A design of the action modeling mechanic with PNs fostered cooperative player dialogues that can lead to developing computational thinking skills:** By mimicking PNs, the design engaged players to construct game character behaviors, which differed from creating a way of practicing programming concepts. Coded evidence suggests the design appears aligned with developing the four components of CT: Decomposition, as players break down complex behaviors into smaller, manageable actions, by the existence of action sheets (composition of the player panel); Abstraction, as they focus on essential elements and patterns; Algorithm, as they sequence the action by define the necessary elements in a specific order (condition-action-result); and Pattern recognition, as they identify similarity in the sequences of actions in different contexts.

c) **This game design, while creating opportunities to develop CT skills proved to be a playful and enjoyable environment**. In addition, it revealed a promising way to promote critical cognitive abilities, by means of a game-based intervention. The current work also contributed with knowledge on a new perspective of player exploration of PN-inspired action definition interfaces in game design.

7   Conclusion

This paper discusses the applicability of PNs in developing CT competences. We propose an approach based on PNs models to design a player panel, allowing players to model meerkat behaviors by using symbols to code action sheets with pre-conditions, actions, and post-conditions or outcomes.

Five gameplay rehearsal exercises were conducted, videographed and axially coded for relevant categories, together with individual interviews. Content analysis focused on the manipulation of the player panel and the development of competence associated with CT. Based on the analysis, we could find evidence that the design of the player panel, mimicking the graphic structure of PNs, facilitated the players understanding of the process of action construction and led to the practice of activities associated with the development of CT. PNs inspired action definition interface provided an accessible representation, easy to understand, simplifying the process of defining character actions to solve the game's challenges, leading to evidence of the practice of decomposition, abstraction, algorithms, and pattern recognition.

This research highlights new forms and the potential of integrating PNs in the design of the game components and its mechanics to enhance CT skills for a game-based intervention to promote playful contacts that motivate the individual to ingress in STEAM fields, preparing them for the demands of the 21st century.

Acknowledgement. This work is funded by the FCT - Foundation for Science and Technology, I.P./MCTES through national funds (PIDDAC), within the scope of CISUC R&D Unit - UIDB/00326/2020 or project code UIDP/00326/2020.

References

1. Aktürk, A.A., Demircan, H.Ö.: A Review of Studies on STEM and STEAM Education in Early Childhood. Ahi Evran Üniversitesi Kırşehir Eğitim Fakültesi Dergisi (2017)
2. Leavy, A., Dick, L., MeletiouMavrotheris, M., Paparistodemou, E., Stylianou, E.: The prevalence and use of emerging technologies in STEAM education: a systematic review of the literature. J. Comput. Assist. Learn. (2023). https://doi.org/10.1111/jcal.12806
3. Hallinen, J.: STEM Encyclopedia Britannica (2023)
4. Tytler, R.: STEM education for the twenty-first century. In: Anderson, J., Li, Y. (eds.) Integrated approaches to STEM education: An international perspective, pp. 21–43. Springer International Publishing, Cham (2020). https://doi.org/10.1007/978-3-030-52229-2_3
5. Kwon, H., Vela, K., Williams, A., Barroso, L.: Mathematics and science self-efficacy and STEM careers: a path analysis. J. Math. Educ. **12**, 74–89 (2019)
6. OECD, Education at a Glance (2019). https://doi.org/10.1787/f8d7880d-en
7. Brown, R., Brown, J., Reardon, K., Merrill, C.: Understanding STEM: current perceptions. Technol. Eng. Teach. **70**(6), 5 (2011)
8. Merrill, C., Daugherty, J.: STEM education and leadership: a mathematics and science partnership approach. J. Technol. Educ. **21**(2), 21 (2010)
9. DeJarnette, N.: America's children: Providing early exposure to STEM (science, technology, engineering and math) initiatives, Education (Chula Vista) (2012)

10. Tuijl, C., WaMolenlma, J.H., Molen,: Study choice and career development in STEM fields: an overview and integration of the research. Int. J. Technol. Des. Educ. **26**(2), 159–183 (2015). https://doi.org/10.1007/s10798-015-9308-1

11. Govender, I.: Research status in computational thinking in STEM education. In: Advances in Research in STEM Education, IntechOpen (2022)

12. Shang, X., Jiang, Z., Chiang, F.-K., Zhang, Y., Zhu, D.: Effects of robotics STEM camps on rural elementary students' self-efficacy and computational thinking. Educ. Technol. Res. Dev. **71**(3), 1135–1160 (2023). https://doi.org/10.1007/s11423-023-10191-7

13. Ramadhan, D.G., Budiyanto, C.W., Yuana, R.A.: The role of game-based learning in developing students computational thinking skills: a review of the literature. In: AIP (2023)

14. Zhao, W., Shute, V.J.: Can playing a video game foster computational thinking skills? Comput. Educ. **141**, 103633 (2019)

15. Syufagi, M.A., Hariadi, M., Purnomo, M.H.: Petri net model for serious games based on motivation behavior classification. Int. J. Comput. Games Technol. **2013**, 1–12 (2013). https://doi.org/10.1155/2013/851287

16. Ungvarsky, J.: Computational thinking. Salem Press Encyclopedia (2023). https://shre.ink/UJrE

17. Wing, J.M.: Computational thinking. Commun. ACM **49**(3), 33–35 (2006)

18. Wing, J.M.: Computational thinking and thinking about computing. Philos. Trans. R. Soc. A Math. Phys. Eng. Sci. **366**(1881), 3717–3725 (2008). https://doi.org/10.1098/rsta.2008.0118

19. Barr, V., Stephenson, C.: Bringing computational thinking to K-12: What is involved and what is the role of the computer science education community? ACM Inroads **2**(1), 48–54 (2011). https://doi.org/10.1145/1929887.1929905

20. Mohaghegh, D.M., McCauley, M.: Computational thinking: The skill set of the 21st century (2016)

21. Papadakis, S.: The impact of coding apps to support young children in computational thinking and computational fluency. A literature review. In: Frontiers in Education (2021)

22. Wang, C., Shen, J., Chao, J.: Integrating computational thinking in STEM education: a literature review. Int. J. Sci. Math. Educ. **20**(8), 1949–1972 (2022)

23. Lee, T.Y., Mauriello, M.L., Ahn, J., Bederson, B.B.: CTArcade: computational thinking with games in school age children. Int. J. Child-Comput. Interact. **2**(1), 26–33 (2014). https://doi.org/10.1016/j.ijcci.2014.06.003

24. University of York, "What is computational thinking?" University of York

25. Yadav, A., Good, J., Voogt, J., Fisser, P.: Computational thinking as an emerging competence domain. In: Competence-Based Vocational and Professional Education: Bridging the Worlds of Work and Education, pp. 1051–1067 (2017)

26. Peterson, J.L.: Petri nets. ACM Comput. Surv. (CSUR) **9**, 223–252 (1977)

27. Araújo, M., Roque, L.: Modeling games with Petri Nets. In: Breaking New Ground: Innovation in Games, Play, Practice and Theory - Proceedings of DiGRA 2009, January 2009

28. Murata, T.: Petri nets: properties, analysis and applications. Proc. IEEE **77**(4), 541–580 (1989). https://doi.org/10.1109/5.24143

29. Balas, D., Brom, C., Abonyi, A., Gemrot, J.: Hierarchical petri nets for story plots featuring virtual humans. In: Proceedings of the 4th AIIDE (2008)

30. Brom, C., Šisler, V., Holan, T.: Story manager in 'Europe 2045' uses petri nets. In: Cavazza, M., Donikian, S. (eds.) Virtual Storytelling. Using Virtual Reality Technologies for Storytelling. ICVS 2007. LNCS, vol. 4871, pp. 38–50. Springer, Berlin, Heidelberg (2007). https://doi.org/10.1007/978-3-540-77039-8_4

31. Riedl, M., Li, B., Ai, H., Ram, A.: Robust and authorable multiplayer storytelling experiences. Proc. AAAI Conf. Artif. Intell. Interact. Digital Entertain. **7**(1), 189–194 (2011). https://doi.org/10.1609/aiide.v7i1.12450

32. Muratet, M., Carron, T., Yessad, A.: How to assist designers to model learning games with Petri nets? In: ACM International Conference Proceeding Series (2022)
33. Berthomieu, B., Ribet, P.O., Vernadat, F.: The tool TINA – construction of abstract state spaces for petri nets and time petri nets. Int. J. Prod. Res. **42**(14), 2741–2756 (2004). https://doi.org/10.1080/00207540412331312688
34. Thomas, P., Yessad, A., Labat, J.M.: Petri nets and ontologies: tools for the 'learning player' assessment in serious games. In: IEEE 11th ICALT (2011)
35. Vaishnavi, V.K., Vaishnavi, V.K., Kuechler, W.: Design Science Research Methods and Patterns: Innovating Information and Communication Technology, 2nd Edition. CRC Press (2015). https://doi.org/10.1201/b18448
36. Bernhaupt, R., Weiss, A., Obrist, M., Tscheligi, M.: Playful Probing: Making Probing More Fun. In: Baranauskas, C., Palanque, P., Abascal, J., Barbosa, S.D.J. (eds.) Human-Computer Interaction – INTERACT 2007, pp. 606–619. Springer Berlin Heidelberg, Berlin, Heidelberg (2007). https://doi.org/10.1007/978-3-540-74796-3_60
37. Kinzie, M.B., Joseph, D.R.D.: Gender differences in game activity preferences of middle school children: implications for educational game design. Educ. Technol. Res. Dev. **56**(5–6), 643–663 (2008). https://doi.org/10.1007/s11423-007-9076-z
38. De Jean, J., Upitis, R., Koch, C., Young, J.: The story of phoenix quest: how girls respond to a prototype language and mathematics computer game. Gender Educ. **11**(2), 207–223 (1999). https://doi.org/10.1080/09540259920708
39. Jalongo, M.R.: An attachment perspective on the child–dog bond: interdisciplinary and international research findings. Early Child Educ. J. **43**(5), 395–405 (2015)

Extending Educational Games Across Product Lines

Diego Castro[✉][ORCID], Claudia Werner[ORCID], and Geraldo Xexéo[ORCID]

Programa de Engenharia de Sistemas e Computação - COPPE,
Universidade Federal do Rio de Janeiro, Rio de Janeiro, Brazil
{diegocbcastro,werner,xexeo}@cos.ufrj.br

Abstract. Some students with limited class time have lost their all
interest in what is being taught. This may be a result of the current
teaching method, which is heavily centered on the instructor and slides.
Keeping this in mind, a large number of researchers are implementing
new teaching strategies that emphasize active techniques, such as task-
based learning, videos, and games. The majority of educational games
are built from previously established games, either by expiry or modification, which is referred to as Software Reuse (SR). Software Product
Line is one of the primary areas of SR, and it is a technique that seeks
to bring together systems that have a particular set of comparable functionality, such as a series of similar games. Considering this, the purpose
of this research is to develop a product line of educational games in order
to simplify game production in this field.

Keywords: Software Reuse · Software Product Line · Serious Games

1 Introduction

Educators are increasingly exploring creative learning methodologies that combine enjoyment with education to enhance student engagement and motivation.
Active Learning (AL) methodologies [1], such as Project-Based Learning [2] and
Flipped Classroom [3], empower students and give them a central role in their
learning journey, with reports that indicate good results [4].

Among AL methodologies, Game-Based Learning (GBL) [5], especially with
video games [6,7], plays a prominent role. According to Kalmpourtzis [8],
"Games have an amazing ability to change the presentation and delivery of problems to players, making them invisible to the eyes of players, while they are still
engaged in the game context." The use of games in education has been found to
improve knowledge acquisition, skill acquisition, perceptual and cognitive skills,
promote empathy, among other benefits [9].

Despite the benefits that educational games can provide, their design is complex, resource intensive and requires multiple sets of interdisciplinary skills [10–
12]. Furthermore, if they are digital, significant technical expertise and resources
are also required to support their development. Due to these obstacles, educational game designers frequently concentrate on adapting (modifying) existing

© The Author(s), under exclusive license to Springer Nature Switzerland AG 2024
L. Vale Costa et al. (Eds.): VJ 2023, CCIS 1984, pp. 134–149, 2024.
https://doi.org/10.1007/978-3-031-51452-4_10

games rather than creating new ones [13]. Similarly to the concept of opportunistic Software Reuse (SR) [14], this method involves modifying something that has already been created and altering it for a different function. This strategy reduces the experience required for game creation, as the ability to modify is based on recognizing/adapting game mechanics as opposed to designing/creating them. Adaptations are inevitable, but this strategy (modding) drastically reduces the experience and resources required to create an effective serious game [13].

SR is a subdiscipline of Software Engineering (SE) that seeks to create new products from existing ones. There are several areas of study within this field of study, including Componentization, Model Driven Development (MDD), and Software Product Line (SPL). SPL can be thought of as a collection of software that share similar characteristics and can be modified from the same base by adding and eliminating characteristics at "variation points" [15], with the main objective of increasing productivity and reducing production time [16]. From the analysis of games from large companies, it is possible to identify the SPL patterns that were used in the development of these games [17]; however, we do not observe that this technique is frequently used in the creation of educational games [18].

As previously mentioned, the process of creating educational games, from conception to execution, can be quite complex; therefore, it is unreasonable to expect a teacher with limited time to create educational games for his/her students. Scratch, eAdventure, Alice, Roblox Studio, a few engines, and the concept of modifying games are examples of tools and techniques that seek to facilitate this process and have already been used with success. However, even with these tools and concepts, creating educational games takes a significant amount of time and can be too much for a single teacher to manage [12]. The objective of this study is to investigate the characteristics of games in the context of an SPL, aiming to design an SPL system for educational games that encourages teachers to create multiple variations of a game efficiently and interactively. This system aims to expedite the game creation process, allowing teachers to develop their own games within a shorter period of time, as opposed to the traditional approach that may take days or even months.

The remainder of this paper is as follows: Section 2 briefly describes concepts for a good understanding of this work; Section 3 discusses some related works; Section 4 details some introductory works that have already been produced within the theme; Section 4 presents our work's proposal; and Section 5 concludes the paper with limitations, and future research.

2 Theoretical Foundation

2.1 Software Reuse

Multiple industries, such as manufacturing, automotive, and electronics, utilize reuse effectively. SR is defined as the process of developing systems from one or more existing ones, rather than starting from scratch; that is, it is the process of utilizing existing software artifacts and knowledge to create something new [15].

Based on the SWEBOK book, several applicable areas can be identified in SR, including Construction for and with Reuse, Software Product Lines, Component-Based Design, and Model-Driven Architecture [19].

The term Software Product Line (SPL) refers to a collection of strategies, techniques, and tools for the methodical development of comparable systems that have a common core but exhibit distinct characteristics. Utilization of these objects is predicted to result in a decrease in development time, simpler maintenance and evolution of systems, greater programmers' satisfaction and better code quality [15].

SPL is essentially divided into two stages: domain engineering, which entails the creation of shared assets, and application engineering, which entails the reuse of shared elements and the addition of unique ones. In contrast to other forms of reuse, these two methods contrast predictive and opportunistic approaches. Instead of stockpiling generic assets in anticipation of reuse, they only develop assets when their reuse in one or more products is expected [15,20]. Our work focuses on creating the application domain, developing the product line so that instructors can perform application engineering using the created instruments, thereby enabling the creation of various games. In this manner, the work seeks to define the domain and develop reusable codes.

Every SPL is categorized according to the similarities and differences of the products positioned on the line, beginning by a resource called root, which provides the starting point of the same, and is the only node that doesn't have a top node. The nodes are then branched by mandatory and optional features, also known as variation points, which is one of the basic characteristics that makes SPL as a large-scale development standard [16]. This is the purpose of the product line that will be demonstrated in this work: to provide the teacher with an application that exhibits an SPL where he/she can choose the attributes of his/her game.

2.2 Games in Education

The academic literature presents myriad definitions of play and games [21,22].

Huizinga provides a classical definition of *play*, that is widely cited as referring to games, as "a free activity standing quite consciously outside'ordinary' life as being 'not serious,' but at the same time absorbing the player intensely and utterly [23]. It is an activity connected with no material interest, and no profit can be gained by it. It proceeds within its own proper boundaries of time and space according to fixed rules and in an orderly manner. It promotes the formation of social groupings which tend to surround themselves with secrecy and to stress their difference from the common world by disguise or other means." [23].

On the other hand, definitions focused on game design often characterize games as systems with uncertain outcomes [24], emphasizing formalism through states, constraints, and goals, and underscoring players' decision-making related to resource management [21].

Although some definitions echo Huizinga's stance that games remain insulated from the real world within a "magic circle", contemporary perspectives like Juul's [25] argue that games produce "negotiable consequences" in real life. Consequently, modern discourse posits that the "magic circle", if it exists, is permeable [26]. This premise is essential to support the application of games in Education.

Games go beyond entertainment, passing messages and values [27]. This can be a side effect of some design choice in an entertainment game, such as adolescents learning Greek Mithology while playing "God of War". When the main objective of game design is not entertainment, but rather teaching, persuasion, or other objectives, they are termed serious games [28] or Games With a Purpose (GAWP).

Considerable part of serious games, educational and training games are used in Game-Based Learning (GBL) methods. These approaches explore game features like simulations, safety from undesirable consequences, immediate feedback, error-based learning, etc. to improve educational results to enhance learning experience. The term Digital Game-Based Learning (DGBL) narrows this down to digital games [5, 29].

Educational game designers, acknowledging the intricacies of game development, often adapt existing games [13]. This adaptation in the gaming community is termed **mod** [30]. However, in the context of game SPL, there are additional considerations. In this new context, games constructed by adding, removing, or modifying predetermined characteristics in the SPL are referred to as game variants [31], being different from the concept of mods in which these are recreated as a form of creative expression by the developers, having the ability to alter what their creativity permits.

There are several ways to organize or define a game, and one well-known formal approach for this purpose is MDA, which aims to divide the game into three main parts: **Mechanics**, which are the essential components of a game, such as actions and rules; **Dynamics**, which describe the behavior of the mechanic when performed by the player, and **Aesthetics**, which can be understood as the emotions felt by the player [32].

It is possible to argue, from an educational point of view, that how a user learns is fundamentally more essential than the environment through which learning occurs [33]. However, this step of how content will be taught is significantly influenced by the type of game and the mechanics used in its development, leading to recommendations for the types and mechanics for each objective [34, 35].

Bloom's Revised Taxonomy [36] can be understood as a hierarchical structure of educational objectives organized in ascending levels of complexity, that is, from the simplest to the most difficult learning level. This taxonomy categorizes the learning process into six levels: remember, understand, apply, analyze, evaluate, and create. There is a desired outcome or a detailed description associated with each of these categories. For instance, in the first level, the student must be able to recall the content being taught, and based on these objectives, it is possible to correlate the mechanics and the various game categories within these levels. Table 1 illustrates the recommended game categories and game mechanics for each level [35, 37, 38].

Table 1. Bloom's Taxonomy applied to games

Bloom's Taxonomy Level	Description	Recommended mechanics	Recommended game types
Remember	Lower level, aims to strengthen knowledge from memorization	Find, Select, Match, Cascading information. Feedback	Quiz and matching games are better for pushing students to attempt to recall the material in order to solve a problem or answer a question.
Understand	Giving meaning to something through an experience	Tutorial, Participation, Cascading information, progression, Feedback	Adventure and exploration games are recommended, as they facilitate the student's understanding of a subject without requiring extensive practice.
Apply	Apply knowledge to something	Cooperation, Competition, movement, tasks, time pressure, progression, Feedback	Simulation games are more recommended because they give practical actions to the student.
Analyze	Explain how concepts are related by breaking them down into parts	Meta-game, Realism, observation, Experimentation, infinity game play, Feedback	Puzzle, RPG and strategy games are more appropriate because they make the student think about different possibilities.
Evaluate	Create a critical basis and understand patterns about what was learned	Action points, game turns, rewards, Collaboration, Feedback	RPG, adventure and strategy games are recommended because they make the student think about a certain subject.
Create	Reorganize the learnt data to form something new	Design, create, infinity game play, Feedback	Simulation games are recommended because they allow the student to create something.

It is important to understand that these types of game and mechanics have several purposes; for example, a storytelling-type game could be used to motivate the learner to remember something. However, it could also be used to present material for those who have no previous knowledge, that is, there are several ways to use these types of game and mechanics, however, they have certain uses that are more recommended.

2.3   Education in Software Engineering

The quality and method of education determine the quality of learning. Teaching method has a significant impact on students learning [39]. Educators have traditionally utilized lectures and slides to transmit information throughout the years. The conventional method of teaching is called passive because students receive knowledge verbally and are not actively engaged, which could interfere with students learning. On the other hand, active teaching tends to engage students more by having them participate in discussions, flipped classrooms, videos, and projects, among other approaches [40]. Because of this, educators are increasingly looking for forms of active teaching, innovative learning strategies that combine pleasure with education [41].

STEM refers to Science, Technology, Engineering, and Mathematics, as well as interdisciplinary combinations of these subjects. In general, the study of these subjects has been seen as having various obstacles and challenges due to the subject's complex, abstract, and multifaceted nature, requiring methods that may provide students with practical exercises [42].

SE is an interdisciplinary combination found within STEM and, as a result, shares the same issue, with courses that are heavily teacher-centered and contain a great deal of theoretical material to be taught. Although essential, research indicates that theoretical knowledge alone is not enough for a student's preparation for the employment market, which requires practical content [43]. As a result, numerous academics are already working on developing educational games for SE teaching [44].

3   Related Work

As stated previously, the use of SR for game development is not new. In fact, there are already visible features of SPL in certain games produced by famous companies. Furthermore, current engines offer an extensive number of resources that are specifically intended for the demands of assets and components.

Based on the research conducted by Neto et al. [45], it can be inferred that games can be incorporated into two distinct categories of product lines. The first category refers to the game domain, covering the development of functionalities and rules. The second category refers to the game's execution console, which may include platforms such as mobile devices or video game consoles. This study also presented several models that concentrated on the development of SPLs for games. These models showcased how the characteristics of games could be organized, although at a conceptual level. They also demonstrated the potential for organizing the characteristics of games in a conceptual level and were predominantly adapted to specific domains, rather than specifically addressing the particular characteristics of educational games.

The works by Furtado and Santos [46] and Furtado et al. [18] also aimed at using SPL for game development, but without an educational focus. The demonstrated application was basically divided into two parts: a first one where game models can be created and a second one where developers can specify game characteristics. The tools demonstrated were focused on a domain of adventure games, which can be described as a genre that encompasses games that take place in a "world" usually composed of multiple rooms or connected screens and in this way the developer can create game rooms and connect them through connection actions.

The research carried out by González García et al. [12] has a shared objective with the present study, as the authors aims to construct an SPL for educational games that facilitates the efficient and practical creation of games for teachers. However, the approach taken in the aforementioned article diverges from the strategy suggested in this study, as it specifically emphasizes Quiz-type games. Furthermore, it does not provide a platform that allows teachers to visualize the SPL and the corresponding characteristics that they can choose for their game.

The work of Chimalakonda and Nori [47] shows slight variations from the approach proposed in this research; however, it shares a common goal of developing an SPL with a specific emphasis on educational applications. The primary concept of this approach involves the utilization of patterns to model various aspects of instructional design. These patterns are then represented by ontologies and transmitted to the development of an SPL via mapped characteristics. This SPL is intended to facilitate the development of eLearning systems for diverse instructional initiatives that may involve multiple languages. The project uses the featureIDE plugin that aims to organize the project by the characteristics of the SPL, thus facilitating the creation of the tree of line characteristics, however, in this way the teacher still needs to understand certain programming concepts to work with the tool, differentiating itself from the proposal of this work that is something focused for the teacher to create quickly, practically and without knowledge in programming, looking like a NoCode platform [48].

As previously stated, there exist various methods for utilizing SPL, ranging from altering the console for usage purposes to modifying the attributes of the game. However, the application of SPL extends beyond its use in the entirety of the game. It can be employed in more granular aspects such as the creation of diverse maps or distinct characters within the game. This exemplifies the efforts of Trasobares et al. [49], who used SPL to generate a number of variations for the game's boss.

4   Preliminary Investigations

This section aims to demonstrate some initiatives that have already been carried out in order to combine the concepts of educational games and SPL. The first initiative was a prototype of a basic quiz with questions about SR. This game is very similar to an SPL for quiz-style games, where certain characteristics can be selected by the game's creator, giving the possibility for the teacher to be able to create his/her own quiz. Among the most prominent characteristics are: the ability to alter the game's questions, the display of the correct answer, the response time for each phase, the score, and the progress bar. From this product line, various variants of quiz games can be created. Although some game academics do not consider quiz-type games to be true games due to their simplicity, the concept behind beginning the development with this type of game was to demonstrate in a straightforward manner how this product line could be created, demonstrating how characteristics could be modified, added, or removed. Figure 1 demonstrates a product line that represents the possible games that can be created.

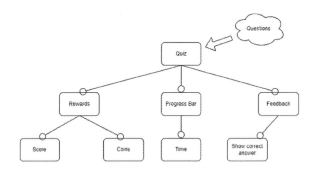

Fig. 1. SPL Game Quiz.

The second initiative was a modification of the game Lightbot [50], which is used to teach fundamental concepts of programming logic. This game aims to concatenate actions that make the character move from the beginning of the game to their destination in the phase. As stated previously, a mod created from an existing game is very similar to opportunistic SR, which uses something previously created to create something new in response to a need. Taking into account the concept of SPL, it is possible to believe that every mod is nothing more than a modified version of the original game, in which certain features of the original game have been altered. Using this as a starting point, Fig. 2 illustrates a general product line for this game. For ease of understanding, some minor variation points have been omitted and only large variations are shown.

From Fig. 2, it is possible to see that some points of variation were created along the SPL, which will be described in more detail below. To make it easier, each point of variation is shown with a letter from A to D.

- **A**: Original game called LightBot, the purpose of which is to teach programming concepts.
- **B**: Variation point that modified the game sprites.
- **C**: At this point of variation three modifications were made
  - **1**: Exchange of educational purpose, game with Software Reuse teaching purpose.
  - **2**: Addition of the concept of product line modeling. With the addition of the FODA tree [51], the game now has two objectives: the primary objective, represented by the right side of the tree, and an optional objective, represented by the left side of the tree.
  - **3**: Added reuse/recursion concept, where the player can create a function and call it N times. The function can be created by adding actions in the bottom square demonstrated in the game.
- **D**: Added reuse/recursion concept, where the player can create a function and call it N times. The function can be created by adding actions in the bottom square demonstrated in the game.

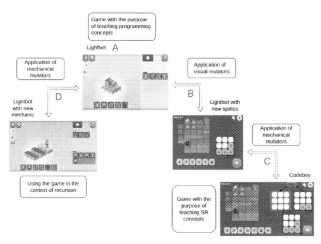

Fig. 2. SPL Game Mod.

The two prototypes presented in this section were preliminary examples of the potential for creating product lines for game development. Even though they are basic prototypes, the concept of creating the line could be observed and demonstrated. The first demonstrates that it is possible to create quiz games with various characteristics, while the second demonstrates that an educational game can be derived from the construction of a mod, thereby demonstrating two distinct ways in which a product line can develop.

5   Proposal

There are several types of games and mechanics, and when considering a product line, from the highest point to the final node of the line, it is possible to see that the first definition that must be made is the game's typing, which is the highest point. It was clear to see, from Table 1, that some games have extremely similar characteristics, despite the fact that they are distinct games. Because of this, it is easy to understand that in order to produce a generic product line for the development of educational games, it will be essential to conduct research on a greater variety of game types and, as a result, a greater variety of game mechanics. As a result, the Educational SPL (ESPL) would be an SPL with underlines inside it, and the underline features may cross. For the early development of ESPL, four categories of games were defined: quiz, match, puzzle, and adventure games. As previously mentioned, each of these games may or may not have similar features, hence the first definition would be the traits that each game may or may not have. Table 2 shows the main characteristics of each of these four game types, dividing them between educational and gaming characteristics.

Table 2. Games and their features

Game type	Game features	Educational features
Quiz	Rewards, Progress Bar, Score, Coins, Time pressure, Select, Game turns	Cascading information, Feedback
Match	Find, Drag and drop, Select, Score, Coins, Game turns	Feedback, Cascading information, Compare
Puzzle	Find, Drag and drop, Select, Score, Coins, Game turns	Feedback, Cascading information, Compare
Adventure games	Action points, Game turns, Score, Coins, Movement, Jump, Rewards	Collaboration, Feedback

From the definition of the characteristics of these four game types, it is possible to think of an SPL with all of them, resulting in a meta SPL, i.e. an SPL with other SPLs within it, in which the characteristics of the four types are shared. Figures 3 and 4 show examples of how these SPL could be created through educational and game mechanics. Although these two images depict completely different games, with sprites and different ways of playing, and provide a completely different experience for the final player, when looking at the game and educational mechanics, it is possible to see that they share many similarities, enabling the use of the concept of SR and, consequently, SPL.

From Figs. 4 and 5, it is evident that various games end up sharing many mechanics, prompting the need for different game types with different mechanics in a generic ESPL. With this, the goal is to develop an application that makes this ESPL available, allowing the teacher to select the game's characteristics and then have a game created for his/her class. However, there are two issues that must be addressed in order to create a generic SPL with this direct interface with the teacher. First, while the mechanics are recommended for learning, they do not play the role of teaching; it is necessary that this mechanics be elaborated in some way to provide teaching, and second, because it is a generic SPL, it can end up serving math games as well as history games, which means that any discipline can be the context of the new game.

As previously stated, only quiz, match, puzzle, and adventure game types were chosen for this initial version of the SPL. Following that, each of these games will be assessed in light of the issues outlined above, seeking to explain how these two problems will be solved.

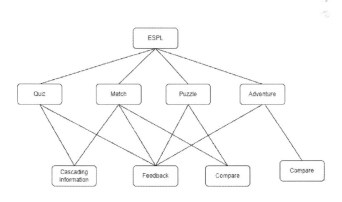

Fig. 3. ESPL - Educational mechanics

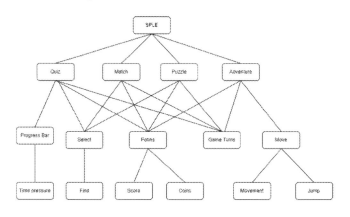

Fig. 4. ESPL - Games mechanics

– Quiz-style games, being the simplest, already have the capacity to retain knowledge; all that require a modification of the mechanisms selected to alter the learning experience and the instructional context defined by the questions inserted. Consequently, no specific adjustment is required for this form of game;
– The vast majority of match-type games aims to correlate information; therefore, to solve the problem of teaching it will be necessary to create predetermined mechanics for this type of game. For instance, just as in the quiz game the teacher could enter a list of questions to ask, so also in the match-type game the teacher could enter a list of objects to be correlated and the SPL would visually assemble this relationship;
– Puzzle-type games may be made in a variety of ways, ranging from basic mechanics in which blocks must be combined to form an image to more complex mechanics in which the puzzle must be completed by linking things obtained in games via challenges;
– As a result, it will be required to consider how to make this sort of game general for teaching and for any subject. The idea was to build a game in which the player must determine the potential sequence to overcome the task, with the problems being supplied by the instructor and the SPL creating a game in which this sequence must be informed;
– It is believed that adventure games are the most difficult to make generic for educational purposes, so it will be necessary to restrict certain features. For this game type, it was considered to develop a platform game in which the player must navigate obstacles to reach the stage's. Aiming to utilize the SPL meta concept, this game will utilize the characteristics of the three categories of games previously demonstrated, so that the adventure game will be a meta game type containing quiz, match, and puzzle games as obstacles for the player to surpass.

It is worth remembering that an SPL will always be limited to its domain; therefore, even though the line has been thought in a generic manner and it is possible to create numerous games from it, it will never be possible to create any type of game from it, as it will always be limited by the application's domain. However, using the SPL idea, it is possible to make the tree structure shown in Figs. 3 and 4 real and make it accessible to professors so they may choose the game's characteristics.

Roblox gaming platform began as a basic game, but it has now evolved to allow users to build their own games using the platform's blocks. With this in mind, they may be seen as a metagame that allows for the creation of N games inside them [52]. However, this platform has evolved so much that it can now be likened to an engine and relies on the developer's skills to produce games inside the platform. This metagame idea will be utilized to make the SPL accessible, where the instructor will join the game and the game will enable the construction of an educational metagame inside it, functioning as a platform for generating educational games. In the game creation area, the SPL with the characteristics of the games illustrated in Figs. 3 and 4 will be displayed as a standard SPL containing the four games.

In front of the SPL tree, it is possible to observe a variety of game characteristics, with each node representing a different attribute. Thus, the concept of the utility proposed in this work consists of two major components, the first of which is this tree of previously created characteristics from which the user can select all of the game's attributes. After selecting all of the game's attributes, it is possible to adjust each one individually by clicking on the nodes that correspond to the attributes, allowing for the micro-editing of these attributes and the modification of the SPL. From this edition on, it will be possible to modify sprites, colors, and add actions and events, among other features, allowing the construction of N games. Finally, it is still possible to construct brand-new game features directly in the SPL.

For editing these characteristics, prefabricated objects such as cards, pop-ups, and triggers will be made available. These objects will be responsible for activating game actions such as awarding the player with points, playing music, restarting the game, and harming another player, among others. In other words, every game created on the platform can be viewed as a junction of SPL nodes, each of which is comprised of player-editable prefabricated objects. For further illustration, consider a quiz game with a progress gauge, score, and feedback that shows the player the correct and incorrect answers; therefore, these three characteristics must be selected from the characteristics tree. By pressing, for instance, on the progress bar characteristic, there will be a trigger that specifies

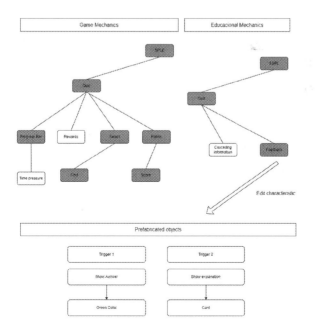

Fig. 5. Example of a quiz created with SPL

that when advancing in a phase, the bar must be increased by one more tally, a similar action to that of rating. In the feedback feature, for instance, there will be a trigger indicating that the game must display the correct answer for the player; however, it could be modified by adding an additional trigger to display an explanation for the player in the event that he/she makes a mistake, thereby creating a card with the corresponding description. The following image demonstrates an example of the idea of prefabricated objects within the SPL characteristics.

6   Final Remarks and Limitations

The purpose of this work was to demonstrate the concept of combining educational games and SR, more specifically SPL, with the main objective of constructing an SPL for the development of educational games, where the domain of the application and code of the SPL would be developed, and a tool would be made available to teachers so that they could use the SPL to develop their own games, enabling the creation of N games and N versions of games.

To begin the validation of the construction of this product line, two small prototypes were developed to demonstrate the initial concept of the work. Using these prototypes, it was possible to demonstrate that it would be possible to develop an SPL to which game mechanics could be added or removed, proving that the concept of developing the ESPL is a sound one.

As mentioned in the beginning of this piece of writing, it is feasible to make the observation that the games that are produced by huge corporations have a lot of similarities with one another, where the concept of SPL can be applied. On the other hand, formal texts that indicate these product lines being utilized in the labor market could not be discovered anywhere in the available literature. As a result of this, it is planned to conduct a survey among these businesses in order to get an understanding of how the SPL approach is being used in the labor market, and to comprehend how these strategies might aid in the development of the SPL of educational games.

It is also intended to perform a literature study on the use of SPL for game development, without restricting the search for educational purposes, in order to have additional results about the usage of SPL. The goal of this inquiry is to find new inputs for the development of ESPL.

Finally, it is important to note that this is a preliminary suggestion of an ESPL, where the number of game types and mechanics are reduced. From the literature survey and research, it is expected that this SPL will be investigated and new games and mechanics will be incorporated.

References

1. Bonwell, C.C., Eison, J.A.: Active learning: creating excitement in the classroom. ASHE-ERIC Higher Education Report No. 1. The George Washington University, School of Education and Human Development, Washington, D.C. (1991)

2. Larmer, J., Mergendoller, J.R., Boss, S.: Setting the Standard for Project Based Learning: A Proven Approach to Rigorous Classroom Instruction. Association for Supervision and Curriculum Development (ASCD) (2015)
3. Bergmann, J., Sams, A.: Flip Your Classroom: Reach Every Student in Every Class Every Day. International Society for Technology in Education (2012)
4. Freeman, S., et al.: Active learning increases student performance in science, engineering, and mathematics. Proc. Natl. Acad. Sci. **111**(23), 8410–8415 (2014)
5. Pivec, M., Dziabenko, O., Schinnerl, I.: Aspects of game-based learning. In: 3rd International Conference on Knowledge Management, Graz, Austria, vol. 304 (2003)
6. Gee, J.P.: What video games have to teach us about learning and literacy. Comput. Entertainment **1**(1), 20–20 (2003)
7. Prensky, M.: The Digital Game-Based Learning Revolution, ch. 1. McGraw-Hill (2001). http://www.marcprensky.com/writing/Prensky
8. Kalmpourtzis, G.: Educational Game Design Fundamentals: Journey to Creating Intrinsically Motivating Learning Experiences. CRC Press (2019)
9. Boyle, E.A., et al: An update to the systematic literature review of empirical evidence of the impacts and outcomes of computer games and serious games. Comput. Educ. **94**, 178–192 (2016). https://www.sciencedirect.com/science/article/pii/S0360131515300750
10. Bellotti, F., Kapralos, B., Lee, K., Moreno-Ger, P., Berta, R.: Assessment in and of serious games: an overview. Adv. Hum. comput. Interact. **2013**, 1–1 (2013)
11. Jenkins, H., Squire, K., Tan, P.: You can't bring that game to school! Designing supercharged. Design Res. 244–252 (2004)
12. González García, C., Núñez-Valdez, E.R., Moreno-Ger, P., González Crespo, R., Pelayo G-Bustelo, B.C., Cueva Lovelle, J.M.: Agile development of multiplatform educational video games using a domain-specific language. Univ. Access Inf. Soc. **18**(3), 599–614 (2019)
13. Abbott, D.: Modding tabletop games for education. In: Gentile, M., Allegra, M., Söbke, H. (eds.) GALA 2018. LNCS, vol. 11385, pp. 318–329. Springer, Cham (2019). https://doi.org/10.1007/978-3-030-11548-7_30
14. Ncube, C., Oberndorf, P., Kark, A.W.: Opportunistic software systems development: making systems from what's available. IEEE Softw. **25**(6), 38–41 (2008)
15. Krueger, C.W.: Software reuse. ACM Comput. Surv. **24**(2), 131–183 (1992)
16. Meftah, C., Retbi, A., Bennani, S., Idrissi, M.K.: Mobile serious game design using user experience: modeling of software product line variability. Int. J. Emerg. Technol. Learn. **14**(23), 55–66 (2019). https://online-journals.org/index.php/i-jet/article/view/10899
17. Garcia, L.A., OliveiraJr, E., Morandini, M.: Tailoring the scrum framework for software development: literature mapping and feature-based support. Inf. Softw. Technol. **146**, 106814 (2022)
18. Furtado, A.W., Santos, A.L., Ramalho, G.L., de Almeida, E.S.: Improving digital game development with software product lines. IEEE Softw. **28**(5), 30–37 (2011)
19. Bourque, P., Fairley, R.E.: Guide to the Software Engineering Body of Knowledge SWEBOK, 3rd ed. IEEE Computer Society (2014)
20. Washizaki, H.: Building software process line architectures from bottom up. In: Münch, J., Vierimaa, M. (eds.) PROFES 2006. LNCS, vol. 4034, pp. 415–421. Springer, Heidelberg (2006). https://doi.org/10.1007/11767718_37
21. Salen, K., Zimmerman, E.: Rules of Play: Game Design Fundamentals. MIT Press (2004)

22. Xexéo, G., et al.: What are Games: An Introduction to Ludes Object of Study. Universidade Federal do Rio de Janeiro, Rio de Janeiro, Brasil (2017). (In Portuguese)
23. Huizinga, J.: Homo Ludens: A Study of the Play-Element in Culture. Routlegde (1999)
24. Costikyan, G.: Uncertainty in Games. MIT Press (2013)
25. Juul, J.: Half-real: Video Games Between Real Rules and Fictional Worlds. MIT Press (2005)
26. Brown, D.: Games and the Magic Circle, pp. 1–4. Springer, Cham (2015). https://doi.org/10.1007/978-3-319-08234-9_32-1
27. Flanagan, M., Nissenbaum, H.: Values at Play in Digital Games. MIT Press (2014)
28. Adams, E., Dormans, J.: Game Mechanics: Advanced Game Design. New Riders (2012)
29. Bau, D.: Droplet, a blocks-based editor for text code. J. Comput. Sci. Coll. **30**(6), 138–144 (2015)
30. Unger, A.: Modding as part of game culture. In: Fromme, J., Unger, A. (eds.) Computer Games and New Media Cultures, pp. 509–523. Springer, Dordrecht (2012). https://doi.org/10.1007/978-94-007-2777-9_32
31. Moreira, R.A.F., Assunção, W.K., Martinez, J., Figueiredo, E.: Open-source software product line extraction processes: the ArgoUML-SPL and phaser cases. Empir. Softw. Eng. **27**(4), 85 (2022)
32. LeBlanc, M., Hunicke, R., Zubek, R.: A formal approach to game design and game research. In: Proceedings of the AAAI-04 Workshop on Challenges in Game AI, pp. 1–5 (2004)
33. Arnab, S., et al.: Mapping learning and game mechanics for serious games analysis. Br. J. Edu. Technol. **46**(2), 391–411 (2015)
34. Boller, S., Kapp, K.: Play to Learn: Everything You Need to Know About Designing Effective Learning Games. Association for talent development (2017)
35. de Araujo, G.G., da Silva Aranha, E.H.: Formative assessment of skills and abilities: instrumentation for digital games. RENOTE, vol. 11, no. 3, (2013). (In Portuguese)
36. Anderson, L.W., Krathwohl, D.R.: A Taxonomy for Learning, Teaching, and Assessing: A Revision of Bloom's Taxonomy of Educational Objectives. Addison Wesley Longman Inc., New York (2001)
37. Ahmad, T., Hussin, A.A.: Application of the bloom's taxonomy in online instructional games. Int. J. Acad. Res. Bus. Soc. Sci. **7**(4), 1009–1020 (2017)
38. Louchart, S., Lim, T., Westera, W.: In persuit of a 'serious games mechanics' a theoretical framework to analyse relationships between 'game' and. Procedia Comput. Sci. **15**, 314–315 (2012)
39. Diepreye, F.F., Odukoya, J.A.: The impact of passive and active teaching methods on students' learning among secondary school students in Yenagoa, Bayelsa state. In: Journal of Physics: Conference Series, vol. 1378, no. 2, p. 022099. IOP Publishing (2019)
40. Baker, A., Navarro, E.O., Van Der Hoek, A.: An experimental card game for teaching software engineering processes. J. Syst. Softw. **75**(1–2), 3–16 (2005)
41. Ritterfeld, U., Cody, M., Vorderer, P.: Serious Games: Mechanisms and Effects. Routledge (2009)
42. Wang, L.-H., Chen, B., Hwang, G.-J., Guan, J.-Q., Wang, Y.-Q.: Effects of digital game-based stem education on students' learning achievement: a meta-analysis. Int. J. Stem Educ. **9**(1), 1–13 (2022)
43. Dicheva, D., Dichev, C., Agre, G., Angelova, G.: Gamification in education: a systematic mapping study. J. Educ. Technol. Soc. **18**(3), 75–88 (2015)

44. Udeozor, C., Toyoda, R., Russo Abegão, F., Glassey, J.: Digital games in engineering education: systematic review and future trends. Eur. J. Eng. Educ. **48**(2), 321–339 (2023)
45. Neto, B., Fernandes, L., Werner, C., de Souza, J.M.: Reuse in digital game development. In: Proceedings of the 4th International Conference on Ubiquitous Information Technologies & Applications, pp. 1–6. IEEE (2009)
46. Furtado, A.W., Santos, A.L.: Using domain-specific modeling towards computer games development industrialization. In: The 6th OOPSLA Workshop on Domain-Specific Modeling (DSM06) (2006)
47. Chimalakonda, S., Nori, K.V.: A family of software product lines in educational technologies. Computing **102**(8), 1765–1792 (2020)
48. Silva, J.X., Lopes, M., Avelino, G., Santos, P.: Low-code and no-code technologies adoption: a gray literature review. In: Proceedings of the XIX Brazilian Symposium on Information Systems, pp. 388–395 (2023)
49. Trasobares, J.I., Domingo, Á., Arcega, L., Cetina, C.: Evaluating the benefits of software product lines in game software engineering. In: Proceedings of the 26th ACM International Systems and Software Product Line Conference-Volume A, pp. 120–130 (2022)
50. Gouws, L.A., Bradshaw, K., Wentworth, P.: Computational thinking in educational activities: an evaluation of the educational game light-bot. In: Proceedings of the 18th ACM Conference on Innovation and Technology in Computer Science Education, pp. 10–15 (2013)
51. Kang, K.C.: FODA: Twenty years of perspective on feature models. SPLC (2009)
52. Rospigliosi, Pa.: Metaverse or simulacra? roblox, minecraft, meta and the turn to virtual reality for education, socialisation and work. Interact. Learn. Environ. **30**, 1–3 (2022)

A Videogame for Architectural Design? Minecraft for Young People to Imagine Desirable Climate Futures

Bruno Andrade[1,3]([✉]) [iD], Saul Crowley[2] [iD], Chiara Cocco[2] [iD], and Brenda McNally[2] [iD]

[1] REMIT – Research on Economics, Management and Information Technologies, Portucalense University, Porto, Portugal
brunoandrade@upt.pt
[2] School of Architecture, Planning and Environmental Policy, University College Dublin, Dublin, Ireland
[3] Centre for Climate and Society, Dublin City University, Dublin, Ireland

Abstract. Cultural heritage has been under pressure from impacts of climate change, yet its conservation and rehabilitation seldom play a role in coastal sustainable development. Two-thirds of the world's population will live in cities until 2050, and more than one billion will live in coastal areas. New digitalization methods and tools have been applied in architectural, urban and landscape design to raise awareness of coastal communities about climate change adaptation and to protect their cultural heritage. Still, younger people have seldom been involved in the planning process, such as the review of master plans. Geogames, location-based games for public engagement, such as Minecraft, have been applied as an active educational tool for young people. Thus, how can Minecraft support youth engagement in co-designing climate adaptation scenarios for heritage-sensitive sites? We applied Minecraft as a geogame to engage 10–12 years old children to co-design climate adaptation scenarios for the Rogerstown Estuary area in North Dublin, Ireland. Parents also got involved, supporting their children's design process and reflections on climate change impacts and risks to their local/cultural heritage. Young people showed awareness of environmental issues and community needs. New questions emerged about using Minecraft and other geogames for capacity-building in wider consultation processes, as well as informing urban policy-making for greater conservation and sustainability of heritage-sensitive sites.

Keywords: Geogames · Co-Design · Youth Engagement · Climate Adaptation · Cultural Heritage

1 Introduction

Cultural, built and natural heritage has been under pressure from climate change [1, 2], yet its conservation and rehabilitation seldom plays a role in sustainable development [3, 4]. According to the World Urbanization Prospects published by the United Nations in 2018, two-thirds of the world's population will live in cities until 2050, and more

© The Author(s), under exclusive license to Springer Nature Switzerland AG 2024
L. Vale Costa et al. (Eds.): VJ 2023, CCIS 1984, pp. 150–165, 2024.
https://doi.org/10.1007/978-3-031-51452-4_11

than one billion will live in coastal areas. Despite the urgency of such impacts, public policy and stakeholders' responses have yet to satisfactorily respond to this 'wicked problem'. Climate change is an adaptive challenge with practical, political and personal dimensions [5]. This requires systematic changes to climate action dependent upon a value system change.

Cultural values play an important part in value system change. They are the ones influencing the conservation of cultural heritage [6–8]. There is great risk for cultural heritage to be destroyed when the public is unaware of its significance or when it is unlisted, which is often the case of heritage only valued by citizens. Better informed architectural and urban rehabilitation can capitalize on the significance of cultural heritage to make coastal cities and communities more inclusive, resilient, safe, and sustainable. Hence, the main challenge concerning the relation of climate change with cultural heritage is whether and how, in particular, coastal communities will be able to conserve their cultural values in decades to come while facing climate threats.

New digitalization methods and tools have been applied in climate change adaptation planning for the co-design of conservation and sustainability scenarios. Digital and non-digital games got serious about climate change [9–11], acting as a form of interactive education, knowledge exchange and policy-making. Research being done in the last decade by online platforms such as "Games for Change"[1], "Games4Sustainability"[2], and "Climate Centre"[3] revealed that games are a fun and yet educational method for citizens to tackle complexities and uncertainties of the global and local climate. For instance, Minecraft, a block-building game, has been used in architectural, urban and landscape design all over the world. Block by Block, a joint initiative by Mojang, Microsoft and UN-Habitat has been successfully using Minecraft to redesign and rebuild public spaces in the Global South with the local community.

Though potentialities of these tools have been revealed as methods for active learning and engagement, the simplification of complex problems, decision-making and feedback exchange, systemic and scenario thinking, generative design, still younger people have seldom been involved in planning processes e.g., public consultation about the review of master plans, and assessment and monitoring of heritage under threats [12–15]. Younger generations are and will be key transformation actors in the development of a possible climate-proof future. Such involvement is crucial for awareness raising and capacity building of coastal communities to better equip them to face present and future adaptation scenarios.

This is why we applied Minecraft, a 3D block-building geogame, for young people to co-design climate adaptation scenarios [16–19]. Minecraft is categorised as a geogame when there is a 3D representation of a real socio-spatial context, and a design goal for public engagement [20, 21]. It allows players to 'mine' resources and use them to build a variety of 3D blocks following the brick-building logic of Lego. As a result, the game can reproduce real life building challenges by using geospatial data of the built and ecological environments. It fosters players' creativity to build structures such as buildings, public spaces as well as trees, animals, and rocks. In these cases, the game

---

[1] Available at https://www.gamesforchange.org/games.

[2] Available at https://games4sustainability.org/.

[3] Available at https://www.climatecentre.org/priority_areas/innovation/climate-games/.

simulates a real socio-spatial context to allow players to visualize and make changes in a fun and easy way.

1.1 Theoretical Framework

The theoretical framework brings together the "Three Spheres Framework" [5, 22] (personal, political and practical), and the cultural significance framework (values and attributes) of cultural heritage [6]. The "Three Spheres Framework" underlines the cor-related domains where transformations to sustainability may occur, referred to as prac-tical, political and personal. These spheres represent objective and subjective aspects of transformation. Objective refers to technical aspects of knowledge. Subjective refers to individual and collective aspects related to beliefs, values, interests, and emotions.

Specifically, the subjective aspect of transformation will be assessed through the categories of values (social, economic, ecological, age, political, historic, scientific, and aesthetical) according to the framework of heritage values [23]. The objective dimension of transformation will be assessed through the categories of tangible attributes (e.g., built element, building, urban element, natural element) and intangible attributes (e.g., character, relation, use and knowledge) according to the framework of heritage attributes [24].

The level of transformation will be analysed according to the objective (attributes) and subjective (values) dimensions. This will point out to new perspectives about aware-ness raising and behavioral change related to the conservation and sustainability of heritage sensitive sites.

Only the personal sphere was considered due to the youth engagement process struc-ture. Assumptions were made in other spheres due to the participation of parents and of local authorities. The levels of transformation were identified and discussed when com-paring the future design scenarios with the current problems e.g., coastal erosion and flooding putting cultural and natural heritage under threat as well as coastal communities' ways of living.

2   Methodology

This research was part of the Coastal Communities Adapting Together (CCAT)[4] project which sought to explore the use of digital technologies to engage communities on the Irish Sea (Ireland and Wales) about climate adaptation. Our methodology adapted the US National Park Service (NPS) four-pillar approach to climate-change threats to cultural heritage: science, mitigation, adaptation, and communication [4]. Due to the potential of Minecraft as a visual research tool of inquiry, time and online engagement constraints, we focused on two of these aspects, adaptation (designs), and communication (images analysed). Ethical dilemmas were addressed and followed according to principles of justice, consent, and confidentiality. We got a full ethical approval by the University College Dublin's Research Ethics Committee.

We proposed a series of Minecraft online workshops between May and October of 2021 with young people ranging 10–12 years old, taking the Rogerstown Estuary

---

[4] Available at https://www.ccatproject.eu/category/resources/.

area in Fingal, North Dublin, Ireland, as case study. Young people were recruited by Fingal County Council's Library team. They had a contact list for having already run Minecraft workshops before. They advertised it more widely to the local community using a "Minecraft Building Competition" slogan. In May there were 4 boys and 8 girls, 12 in total. In July there were 7 boys and 4 girls, 11 in total. In October there were 8 boys and 7 girls, 15 in total. Participants could choose one of the three towns, Rush, Donabate or Portrane. These workshops sought to include them in climate adaptation planning as part of a pilot consultation of Fingal County Council's local development review. Traditionally, this is an activity restricted to adults using conventional methods such as focus groups, questionnaires, and interviews.

Thus, how can Minecraft support youth engagement in co-designing climate adaptation scenarios for heritage sensitive sites? Particularly, we applied the "Geogames for Geodesign" methodology [25]. Such methodology brings together aspects from A) overlaying thematic layers of geographic information systems from Geodesign [26], and B) location-based games as a multi-player simulation for collaborative design from Geogames [20, 27, 28]. The model was built using FME (Feature Manipulation Engine), a geospatial extract, transformation and load (ETL) software, with geodata collected from Ordnance Survey Ireland.

A clear design goal was set for young people to design improvements in the estuary area for climate adaptation, which could encompass adding, removing and/or changing architectural structures such as buildings, coastal defenses, urban furniture, mobility, and greenery. Though it is a complex issue, the authors only gave general design options for the participants to follow their own ideas. This way their designs would reveal the current state of their knowledge and creativity.

Before the workshops, participants were asked to access learning resources about coastal climate change adaptation produced by the CCAT research team. Then, they were asked to complete an online questionnaire, and geolocation survey to foster their imagination for improving the local area. Finally, each online Minecraft workshop was structured and held sequentially over a strict time on a weekend:

1) Introduction session with explanation of the topic, design goal and workshop structure, 1-h duration.
2) Design session where each child worked remotely with the supervision of at least one guardian, 2-h duration, remotely.
3) Presentation session where children presented the visual representation of their design process accompanied by at least one guardian, 1-h duration.

Some of the 3D architectural designs were then selected as images for a research project aimed at understanding young people's visual representations of desirable climate actions and spatial changes [19]. The images provided insights on how Minecraft could also be used to shed light on young people's climate imaginaries. Imaginaires offer a way of understanding collective visions and therefore these images were also powerful indicators of young people's desirable climate futures. The study showed that young people's climate imaginaries offered an alternative vision to mainstream news and entertainment media preoccupation with dystopian constructions of the climate crisis. They also showed the power of Minecraft as a visual medium to open up new ways of seeing nature and envisioning nature-society relations. The images were analysed using the theoretical framework to identify and reflect on the attributes and values (cultural significance), respectively, objective and subjective spheres of transformation. This helped assess the cultural significance which young people address to the new climate scenario. Understanding the cultural significance of heritage assets is crucial to review and/or develop more effective heritage policies that promote higher conservation and sustainability of these areas.

These images were also exhibited as part of the CLIMATE LOOK Lab 2022 held at the Open Eye Gallery, Liverpool. The gallery invited researchers, community groups and artists to use their space as a lab to engage visitors with reflections about the changing climate and to explore how different types of images can change the visual narrative on climate change.

3   Results

The first step was to analyse the online geolocation survey called "Map my Area", which was undertaken before the workshops on the Geodesignhub platform. The geo-survey focused on three assignments: 1) Design new bike path in Donabate, 2) Improve Rogerstown park, and 3) Improve Portrane's peninsula. Within these assignments, the young people were also encouraged to share what they liked about these places. Through a qualitative content analysis method, the data was clustered to identify and interpret patterns related to meanings, contexts, and intentions about the three assignments above mentioned.

Most proposals focused on the relation of greenery and the beachside, for instance, the path to connect Donabate and Portrane, the park and the beachside, e.g., "*It would be good if there was a path to the beach through here and if people in wheelchairs were able to get down to the beach and if there was somewhere for people to change for swimming and if there was a shower beside the beach*". There were mentions also to building a "*playground or play equipment on the green*" with "*charging points and WiFi*". Sports and active play was mentioned regarding "*football*", "*skip stones on the water*", and "*walks along the coast*". Young people's concerns centred on health aspects such as cleanness of the estuary and sea waters. Table 1 presents the results from the geo-survey and their respective existing or suggested design category.

There were also pre- (Table 2) and post-workshop (Table 3) questionnaires. However, the response rate was very low, only two participants overall responded. Tables 2 and 3 are, therefore, illustrative about reflections of children and their guardians/parents. This is not a generalization of the pool of participants.

The second step was to analyse the images (Minecraft screenshots), which were selected from the 3 online workshops held with 38 young people (10–12 years-old) in the Rogerstown Estuary area according to gathering a diverse range of climate adaptation designs. Participants proposed their designs to respond mostly to risks of coastal erosion and flooding due to climate change. They were also encouraged to propose improvements to at least one of the towns (Portrane, Rush and Donabate). First, we selected emblematic images on how young people are changing the visual narrative about climate change and climate futures. Then, we clustered these images by architectural design types: coastal defenses (see Fig. 1), new architecture and infrastructure (see Fig. 2), public spaces (see Fig. 3), and biodiversity (see Fig. 4).

Table 1. "Map my Area" online geo-survey results

Response	Category
"Telescopes with Bird information board- App information or the QR codes for bird sounds so people can scan, listen to the sounds, Small wooden walks hill walks or mazes or theme areas for kids like Slieve Gullion Forest Park".	Your own idea
"Skate park on the top and picnic area"	Skatepark
"...telescopes, benches, outdoor exercise equipment and information boards and maps on the landscape and animals"	Your own idea
"A cafe beside a playground so after you go to the playground you can buy something to eat or drink"	Your own idea
"I'd put a seawater pool here, which would make it safe to swim in and any dirt and pollution would be filtered out"	Your own idea
"I would put the pitch here because the solar/ panels could power the lights on the pitches"	Pitches
"A park to go on walks and to play ,put loads of trees in for the birds and animals. I think there should be an outdoor pool linked to the sea"	Wind mills and solar farm
"Bee hives & wildflower field & fruit trees"	Your own idea
"Multi-sport court or/and café because it will create a good atmosphere"	Your own idea
"I would put the pitch here because the solar/ panels could power the lights on the pitches"	Pitches
"A park to go on walks and to play ,put loads of trees in for the birds and animals. I think there should be an outdoor pool linked to the sea"	Wind mills and solar farm
"Multi-sport court or/and café because it will create a good atmosphere"	Your own idea
"Enclosed dog play/ off lead area"	Your own idea
"Because you don't have to walk too far from the car park to the playground"	Playground
"Because it would have a nice nature feel about it and possibly fish or pond dip"	Lakes/ponds
"I'd say a small pitch, something about the area and a few trees you can climb"	Pitches
"People will see it coming by so more people will visit"	Skatepark
"Bike trail"	Tree planting
"I would like to have an outdoor gym and obstacle course beside a playground"	Your own idea
"I think there should be a wind mill and solar farm because there is a power generator right beside. (...) should be a tree planting area because there would be plenty of fresh air for the entire area. (...) should have a skatepark as it is a small area and skateparks don't need a whole field of space. (...) should be a playground as it is right beside the skatepark and tree planting area, it shouldn't be beside the windmills because it might be quite windy (on windy days it may be more windy because of the wind mill). (...) will be where I make my own design which will be a café beside a ice-cream stand".	Your own idea

(continued)

Table 1. *(continued)*

"...this would be great for the environment, and you could put a little mountain biking trail in between the trees connecting to the skatepark"	Tree planting
"...this would be good here because the street lamps could feed off the wind and solar electricity. You would also not have that many people going there because it used to be a gas generator"	Wind mills and solar farm
"...away from the main road and a bit of a walk from the entrance. the ramps I will build in Minecraft"	Skatepark
"I think there should be a playground here because its a big area and there is a skatepark right next to it"	Playground
"...this would make this area better because there is a lot of space for a few pitches for different sports"	Pitches
"The power generator would be a good place for the wind mills and solar farm"	Wind mills and solar farm
"With the landfill and generator here, its a good spot for the windmill"	Wind mills and solar farm
"An enclosed area for dogs off lead with a pond for them to splash in. families with dogs would use the park much more if their dog can get some running exercise too. You could also plant trees so that later in time you may be able to use a fully grown forest"	Your own idea
"For younger kids this could be lots of fun because they might not be able for a very long walk"	Playground
"A hedge maze. This could be lots of fun for the family all year round but especially at Halloween. Native hedgerow plants could be used as a habitat"	Your own idea
"A pump track, this is for bmx and mountain bikes, kids of all ages can practice biking without any extreme hills. there is no track like this in north county Dublin"	Your own idea
"...cafe on a boardwalk, so you can see all the wildlife in the estuary, like birds on the wetlands and fish in the water, people walking won't damage the habitat. The cafe could be a pop-up coffee truck or a building"	Your own idea
"I would like to put a few small lakes, some trees and maybe some picnic benches and a few swings or see-saws. It would provide entertainment for children and would be a nice place to have a picnic. There would also be lots of wildlife habitats and nature"	Your own idea

The coastal defenses cluster revealed visual constructs of climate futures related to reimagining coastal defenses strategies solely to protect from sea level rise and erosion. Since this is a conceptual phase of the design process, it did not mean to dive into the complex adaptive system behaviors of such structures. Young people envisioned structures which serve both protective and infrastructural functions (see Fig. 1): a concrete wall that doubles as a passage/bridge, a green wall that also functions as a contemplative space, and a floating coastal viewpoint which monitors the sea level while also serving as a contemplative and socialization space.

Table 2. Pre-workshop questionnaire

Question	Response 1	Response 2
What do you know about environmental problems and the need to protect the environment	*Problem with environment is known for Years and it's evolving to some extraordinary level during the last couple of years. CO2 emission has been growing incredibly, amount of pollution globally especially in the 3rd world countries, where people don't really have enough awareness about environment had become a serious problem. There is a global need to reduce CO2 emission, take care about natural resources and create more awareness*	*I know about Climate Change and environmental problems because of things I have learnt in school eg. Fossil fuels, oil spills, farming, the dyeing of clothes, polluting of rivers especially ammonia. I watch David Attenborough documentaries. His last documentary was about how the planet has changed since he started work making documentaries. I know about recycling and biodegradable things. I am quite concerned about the environment*
Are there any actions you currently take to help protect your local environment? If yes, please tell us what actions you take or what actions your family take	*Currently we are segregating our bins, always switching off electricity when not needed, walking to the nearest store instead of using a car. Also always using reusable bags instead of buying plastic ones. Never leaving running tap during the cold weather (this actually became a serious problem locally) and cycle if possible. Also planning to get more into Hybrid/Electrical Vehicles (still a plan for my dad)* 😊	*I recycle things. I tell my parents to buy products that are recyclable and biodegradable. I know about Fair Trade and I lok for the sign on things in supermarkets. I pick up litter in the field/park near where I live*

(*continued*)

Table 2. (*continued*)

Question	Response 1	Response 2
How important is taking care of the environment to you	*This is something we must take extremely seriously if we want to care about our future generations. We are putting ourselves in extreme risk pollution, Extreme weather (which are a result of a CO2 Emission levels). Environmental awareness is something we are trying to engage regularly with our family. Trying to explain why we should all separate our rubbish or switch off electricity*	*Very, very, very important*
Do you take part in any activities (with your family or school) that involve taking care of the environment or talking about protecting it? Which ones?	*I'm a member of Scouts in Rush and we have regular programme for environmental awareness where I'm heavily involved. At school we have regular environmental awareness classes*	*We learn about climate change. We are raising money for people in India whose river is polluted with ammonia. We pick up litter in school*

The new buildings and infrastructure cluster revealed visual constructs of climate futures related to reimagining how to add new architecture for the use of the whole community. All designs below (see Fig. 2) encompassed public functions such as expanding the train station to better connect the towns to Dublin, new pathways for pedestrians and bikes, renewable energy (wind turbines), restoring old windmills, and an intriguing and innovative Café for both bees and humans. No buildings were demolished, green areas were kept, and new architecture added was mainly one-storey buildings in harmony relation with built heritage through form, materials, colors and textures.

The public spaces cluster revealed visual constructs of climate futures related to reimagining the use and appropriation of outdoor and open spaces. The images below (see Fig. 3) show that young people envision not a fearful future about climate impacts, but an outdoor life structured by design which can take advantage of the need to protect with the need to play (maze, aquatic play structures), learn (recycling plastic), contemplate (benches, pathways) and socialize (community picnic area). This changes the aesthetic from fear (of sea level rise to damage and destroy buildings) to the possibility of enjoyment in the waterfront. The focus on food-sharing and creating spaces for food-sharing in this area exemplifies visually a counter-narrative to mainstream consumerist relation to food.

Table 3. Post-workshop questionnaire

Question	Response 1	Response 2
How often do you think about environmental problems as you go about your day?	*"Actually on a daily basis. Always trying to have in mind some things which can help to improve our environment"*	*"Very often"*
Has the Minecraft workshop increased your understanding of the need to protect your local environment and help stop climate change? If yes, tell us about what you have learnt	*"I've learnt about good planning and need for some facilities for people which will lead to make our environment better (more bins, more places where we can exercise) but also create more awareness"*	*"Yes, I learnt that there are park designers. I learnt that it is important to make family nature reserves so we can realise what is happening to the environment and how to stop it"*
Has the Minecraft workshop inspired you to do more to protect the local environment and stop climate change? If yes, can you tell us more about what it has inspired you to do	*"Definitely inspired me to be more aware and creative but also talk to the others about this so there is a chance that by spreading proper message – more people became more environmentally aware just like myself"*	*"Yes, because I learnt about parks. It has inspired me to buy less plastic and to recycle more"*
Do you think this game experience will lead to you working/connecting with others to tackle climate change issues or raise awareness of these issues? If yes, please explain why and in what ways you think you might work with others? If no, can you tell us why not	*"As mentioned it actually made me more to spread more awareness between my friends to speak about environment and climate change and think more about what we are doing in our day to day life for to tackle climate change with success"*	*"No, not really. I think playing the game more often would help and also talking about it. Suggest to show people the controls. Do the project over more than 2 days"*

The biodiversity cluster revealed visual constructs of climate futures that attempt to imagine human-nature relations by focussing on co-existence, such as bird watching, beehives, vegetable garden, wildflowers, farm animals. The designs below (see Fig. 4) show the co-existence possibilities of human and non-human as resources for a climate future. This is an attempt to associate heritage restoration, preservation and development. Such planning and management direction of heritage sensitive sites has been most appreciated and defended in the heritage field in the last decades [3, 29].

The results revealed that the young people involved understood better the educational purpose of the game mission, including their parents. By anecdotal evidence, parents shared in the final presentations they supported their children's design process and reflections over climate change adaptation and the risk to their cultural heritage, without interfering in their choices. Interestingly, one representative of Fingal County

(a)   (b)

(c)   (d)

Fig. 1. Coastal defenses

(a)   (b)

(c)   (d)

Fig. 2. New buildings and infrastructure

Council (FCC), present in the final online session of the first workshop in May 2021, shared there were similarities between young people's design ideas and FCC's master plan review e.g., renewable energy; grey, blue, and green infrastructure; biodiversity

(a)
(b)

(c)
(d)

(e)
(f)

Fig. 3. Public spaces.

parks; recreation areas; and coastal defenses. This was evidence to FCC of the value of engaging young people in town planning consultation processes.

While there was a balance in the number of boys (18) and girls (20) participating overall, it was noted that boys designs were more active whereas girls produced more contemplative designs. Both boys and girls included similar environmental solutions: focussing on green areas, and prioritising biodiversity and wildlife through design solutions involving reforestation, bird watching, bees and beehives.

Most designs had signs which revealed the proposed function or acted as orientation for the use of the space, such as "Bird watching: keep quiet", "Bee town", "Bee Café for pollen", "Toss a coin, make a wish!", "In case of lost children, please call the number 5551743", "Welcome to the path of Rogerstown, enjoy!", "Here is water, you don't need plastic bottles", "Over here there be a playground". This showed how young people value a clear design with information about how to use such spaces. Designs showed that only a few participants focused only on recreation designs, whilst most of them showed climate

(a)   (b)

(c)   (d)

(e)   (f)

Fig. 4. Biodiversity

adaptation awareness and tried to propose solutions related to coastal defenses, greenery and biodiversity, and renewable energy.

Potential barriers revealed by this study on youth engagement with Minecraft may be related to 1) access and resources, 2) technical skills, 3) time and commitment, 4) safety and privacy, and 5) feedback integration. Not all young people may have access to the technology to play the game. It can be challenging for them to learn how to use the game on a desktop computer (instead of mobile phones and videogame console) to better understand and propose solutions to issues related to urban planning processes. Though it is not time-consuming it is hard to engage young people in Minecraft workshops apart from partnering with schools and libraries to include in their present curricular or extra-curricular activities. Ensuring their online safety and privacy adds another layer of difficulty, since the presence of a guardian is required to monitor their interactions with other players. Lastly, gathering feedback about the design process can be difficult, because to take place in-game adds more complexity and can break the flow.

Potential strengths revealed by this study were 1) digital literacy, 2) environmental and heritage engagement and motivation, 3) creativity and collaboration, 4) visualization and immersion, and 5) youth empowerment. Young people can develop and enhance digital literacy skills by using Minecraft to materialize their design ideas. The game is popular among young people and can attract and hold their attention in a diverse range of activities. It is a creative, friendly and immersive platform for visualizing and designing architectural and urban spaces, in which young people can bring imaginative and innovative solutions and test the impact of their choices in a real-world context. The game allows for collaborative design, enabling young people to work together, and learn to negotiate and reach consensus about heritage-sensitive sites. Hence, the process can empower young people to foster a sense of ownership in the future of their cities and communities, creating a culture of participation. Lastly, the outcomes of such a process can inform local authorities about the needs and values of the youths, who have an unique perspective and positioning about architectural, urban and landscape issues.

4   Conclusion

The Minecraft workshops were a valuable opportunity to include young people's visions on climate adaptation as part of a local development consultation (a process which is traditionally restricted to adults). We explored Minecraft as a participatory visual method of inquiry to simulate climate adaptation design with/for young people. Strengths of the game encompassed active learning through playing, socialization and engagement, comprehension of complex problems via scenario thinking, and knowledge exchange and peer-review. Limitations were mainly technical about learning to play Minecraft on a computer, acquiring a license, and joining the online session. Another one related to the abstract aesthetics of the block-logic representations, which did not allow detailing less than 1 m^3.

The Minecraft geogame tool, with colored bulky blocks and cumbersome pixels, enabled young people to express their climate agency, the subsequent, and unexpected interest of parents in the exercise fostered intergenerational conversations about climate change adaptation in the local area. This online youth engagement process was also used as a space to provide recommendations for 1) local authorities on the uses of Minecraft as a co-creation design tool for the review of master plans through the lenses of climate adaptation, and 2) educational institutions on the extracurricular learning opportunities of Minecraft as an awareness raising tool for alternative and counter-narrative climate futures and cultural heritage conservation and sustainability.

Both recommendations call for strengthened policy integration and change in Irish and other coastal and water-front areas over climate change adaptation and public participation. Moreover, actively involving young people in decision-making and policy implementation is key to realize the benefits of their contributions. New questions emerged about how to up-scale, capitalize and give feedback to young people about their inputs. Also, which is the best option to include Minecraft as an educational and capacity-building tool for schools and libraries, in present curricular or extracurricular activities. Further research is needed to investigate Minecraft as a gaming-simulation resource to raise awareness about intergenerational exchange, assessing behavioral issues, as well as quickly responding to emergencies and problematic climate change scenarios impacting heritage-sensitive sites and communities.

Acknowledgements. This work was supported by the UIDB/05105/2020 Program Contract, funded by national funds through the FCT I.P. This work is also supported by the project 2022.08215.CEECIND, being undertaken at REMIT – Research on Economics, Management and Information Technologies (https://remit.upt.pt/en/), Portucalense University.

Special acknowledgment to the Coastal Communities Adapting Together (CCAT) research team (https://www.ccatproject.eu), who collaborated with organizing, engaging young people, and running the Minecraft workshop in Ireland. Many thanks to Hrishikesh Ballal, founder of the Geodesignhub company, who was a partner on this project responsible for the geo-survey application for youth engagement in climate change adaptation design.

References

1. Orr, S.A., Richards, J., Fatorić, S.: Climate change and cultural heritage: a systematic literature review (2016–2020). Policy Pract. **12**, 434–477 (2021). https://doi.org/10.1080/17567505. 2021.1957264
2. Sesana, E., Gagnon, A.S., Ciantelli, C., Cassar, J., Hughes, J.J.: Climate change impacts on cultural heritage: a literature review assessing impacts of climate change. Eval. Future Impacts of Climate Change (2021). https://doi.org/10.1002/wcc.710
3. Pereira Roders, A., Van Oers, R.: Wedding cultural heritage and sustainable development: three years after. J. Cult. Herit. Manage. Sustain. Dev. **4**, 2–15 (2014)
4. Rockman, M., Morgan, M., Ziaja, S., Hambrecht, G., Meadow, A.: Cultural Resources Climate Change Strategy (2016)
5. O'Brien, K.: Is the 1.5° C target possible? Exploring the three spheres of transformation. Curr. Opin. Environ. Sustain. **31**, 153–160 (2018). https://doi.org/10.1016/j.cosust.2018.04.010
6. Pereira Roders, A., Post, J.M., Aguiar, J.M., Erkelens, P.A.D.: Architectural, and Engineering, 'Re-architecture: lifespan rehabilitation of built heritage - scapus' (2007). urn:nbn:nl:ui:25-d21f479c-1d0e-409e-a3ee-30aba18fb962
7. De la Torre, M.: Assessing the Values of Cultural Heritage: Research Report (2002). http://www.getty.edu/gci. Accessed 19 Sept 2023
8. Mason, R.: Assessing values in conservation planning: methodological issues and choices. Assess. Values Cult. Herit. **1**, 5–30 (2002)
9. Flood, S., Cradock-Henry, N.A., Blackett, P., Edwards, P.: Adaptive and interactive climate futures: systematic review of "serious games" for engagement and decision-making. Environ. Res. Lett. **13**(6), 63005 (2018)
10. Khoury, M., et al.: A Serious Game Designed to Explore and Understand the Complexities of Flood Mitigation Options in Urban-Rural Catchments (2018). https://doi.org/10.3390/w10 121885
11. Wu, J.S., Lee, J.J.: Climate change games as tools for education and engagement. Nat. Clim. Chang. **5**(5), 413–418 (2015). https://doi.org/10.1038/nclimate2566
12. Bridgman, R.: Criteria for best practices in building child-friendly cities: involving young people in urban planning and design. Can. J. Urban Res. **13**(2), 337–346 (2004)
13. Dodig, M.B., Groat, L.N.: The Routledge Companion to Games in Architecture and Urban Planning: Tools for Design, Teaching, and Research. Routledge, Abingdon (2019)
14. Mansfield, R.G., Batagol, B., Raven, R.: "Critical agents of change?": Opportunities and limits to children's participation in urban planning. J. Plan. Lit. **36**(2), 170–186 (2021)
15. Simpson, B.: Towards the participation of children and young people in urban planning and design. Urban Stud. **34**(5–6), 907–925 (1997). https://doi.org/10.1080/0042098975880

16. Andrade, B., Poplin, A., Sousa de Sena, Í.: Minecraft as a tool for engaging children in urban planning: a case study in Tirol Town, Brazil. ISPRS Int. J. Geoinf. **9**(3) (2020). https://doi.org/10.3390/ijgi9030170
17. Camuñas-García, D., Cáceres-Reche, M.P., de la E. Cambil-Hernández, M.: Maximizing engagement with cultural heritage through video games. Sustainability **15**(3), 2350 (2023)
18. McDaniel, T.: Block by Block: The Use of the Video Game "Minecraft" as a Tool to Increase Public Participation (2018). https://hdl.handle.net/10877/7214. Accessed 19 Sept 2023
19. McNally, B., Andrade, B.: Altered spaces: new ways of seeing and envisioning nature with Minecraft. Vis. Stud. **37**(3), 175–182 (2022). https://doi.org/10.1080/1472586X.2022.2090121
20. Poplin, A., Kerkhove, T., Reasoner, M., Roy, A., Brown, N.: Serious Geogames for Civic Engagement in Urban Planning: Discussion based on four game prototypes. In: The Virtual and the Real in Planning and Urban Design, Routledge, pp. 189–213 (2017)
21. Andrade, B.: O conceito de geogames em ambientes inovadores de aprendizagem / Developing the concept of geogames for innovative learning environments. *V!RUS*, vol. 17, no. parti.cipate+col.laborate (2018)
22. Sharma, M.: Radical Transformational Leadership: Strategic Action for Change Agents. North Atlantic Books, Berkeley (2017)
23. Tarrafa, A.S., Pereira Roders, A.: Cultural heritage management and heritage (impact) assessments. In: Proceedings of the Joint CIB W070, W092 & TG72 International Conference on Facilities Management, Procurement Systems and Public Private Partnership, Cape Town, South Africa, 23–25 January 2012, pp. 23–25 (2012)
24. Sobhani Sanjbod, H., Hermans, L., Reijnders, D., Veldpaus, L.: Captain, Where can we Find the Attributes?. Historic Environ. Policy Pract. **7**(2–3), 177–188 (2016). https://doi.org/10.1080/17567505.2016.1172786
25. Andrade, B.: O Planejamento, a Criança e o Jogo: O Geodesign na Identificação de Valores Cotidianos e Simbólicos do Território, Belo Horizonte (2019). https://repositorio.ufmg.br/handle/1843/31034
26. Steinitz, C.: A Framework for Geodesign: Changing Geography by Design. Esri Press, Redlands (2012)
27. Ahlqvist, O., Schlieder, C.: Geogames and Geoplay: Game-Based Approaches to the Analysis of Geo-Information. Advances in Geographic Information Science. Springer, Cham (2018). https://doi.org/10.1007/978-3-319-22774-0
28. Schlieder, C., Kiefer, P., Matyas, S.: Geogames: designing location-based games from classic board games. IEEE Intell. Syst. **21**(5), 40–46 (2006)
29. Albert, M.-T., Bandarin, F., Roders, A.P.: Going Beyond: Perceptions of Sustainability in Heritage Studies No. 2. Springer, Cham (2017). https://doi.org/10.1007/978-3-319-57165-2

Math-Masters: An Educational Game to Practice the Mathematical Operations

João A. B. T. Marques[1], João L. A. P. Ferreira[1],
and Frutuoso G. M. Silva[1,2]([☒]) (iD)

[1] University of Beira Interior, Covilhã, Portugal
fsilva@di.ubi.pt
[2] Instituto de Telecomunicações, Covilhã, Portugal
http://regain.it.ubi.pt

Abstract. Educational games have gained significant popularity in recent years as an innovative and engaging means of enhancing learning. These games use technology and game design principles to create a fun learning environment. Educational games have changed how we learn by combining fun and learning goals. They offer an engaging, interactive, and personalized learning experience, promoting critical thinking, problem-solving, and collaboration. However, the design of educational games must combine the fun factor with the learning goals, which sometimes does not happen, creating the impression that educational games are not fun.

In this paper, we describe an educational game to learn multiplication operations in a fun way. The game is a point-and-click deck-building and partially rogue-lite third-person educational game with the purpose of teaching multiplication operations in mathematics. It is themed around medieval fantasy, with monsters on one hand and magic spells on the other. The player has a card deck that he can use to solve the mathematical questions and defeat the monsters.

Some preliminary tests were carried out with fifty-eight students, which showed the potential of this kind of tool. Most of the students agreed that the game helped them with the multiplication operation and that they would like to play more levels of the game.

Keywords: Educational Game · Math Game · Serious Game · Adventure Game

1 Introduction

One of the primary advantages of educational games is their capacity to make learning engaging and enjoyable. By providing a fun and entertaining experience, these games can motivate learners, increase their level of interest, and promote a positive attitude towards the subject [6,20]. This engagement factor can improve knowledge retention and deeper understanding of the concepts being taught [13,17].

© The Author(s), under exclusive license to Springer Nature Switzerland AG 2024
L. Vale Costa et al. (Eds.): VJ 2023, CCIS 1984, pp. 166–173, 2024.
https://doi.org/10.1007/978-3-031-51452-4_12

There is no one way to make learning games because they depend on many factors, such as the target audience, the game genre, and the content to be taught. However, several methodologies for designing educational games are available. For example, Barbosa et al. [5] presented a methodology based on the concept of learning mechanisms that must be included in the game, either in mechanics, gameplay, storytelling or mini-games. Also Ke [11] identified the need to situate learning activities within the game story, making games pleasantly challenging.

Most of the educational math games that are developed add only a layer of learning content to the game, which breaks the gameplay. Furthermore, the majority cannot be considered a game because they are more similar to a digital exercise book illustrated [1, 12].

The main idea is to effectively engage the player by creating an enjoyable experience while keeping learning [18, 19, 22]. For example, Aparício and Silva [4] developed an educational math game that followed this strategy, i.e., the learning contents were included in the game mechanics, which means that the player/student does not lose focus on the gameplay and keeps the fun. Thus, he will be motivated to play again, and each time he plays, he also learns the contents. Most of the learning in games is due to the repetition option that the games allow the player, at their pace and without real penalties, on the contrary to the traditional learning system [15].

There are several studies about the use of games for learning mathematics that show the positive effect on learning and students' memory, attention, and cognitive skills [3, 9, 16, 21]. Recently, Draganoiu et al. [8] presented a teaching method designed to present mathematics, programming, and 3D modelling concepts in a multidisciplinary approach, combining theory and practice in a game-like 3D virtual environment. The results were positive because of its ability to teach theoretical concepts through practice, which is aligned with the cone of experience of Dale [7]. In the same way, in the games, the player learns by doing, i.e., with experience.

The next section describes in detail the features of the math game developed.

2   Math-Masters Development

The educational math game developed is a point-and-click type since the target audience is primary school students. It is themed around medieval fantasy, with monsters on one hand and magic spells on the other. Through a card deck available to the player, he can answer the math questions and, at the same time, defeat the monsters. Thus, he can practice mathematical exercises while defeating enemies. This genre of the game was chosen to prove that it is possible to develop an educational game from any genre of the game if the learning content is part of the gameplay, as it happens in reference math games (e.g., [2]). However, the genre of the game must be adequate for the target audience.

The game is played in Samos Town (see Fig. 1), where the player can explore and have access to shops to change their appearance or upgrade their stats. This location is a safe zone, and the exit gate from this town will take the player to several levels to face the monsters and gain gold as a reward.

Player attacks against said monsters are represented by cards, which can be an answer to a mathematical exercise or a spell card that gives an advantage to the player. This way, the learning contents are incorporated into the game mechanics, and then the gameplay is not broken by the mathematical exercises.

Fig. 1. Screenshot of the Samos Town.

In order to progress through the game and gain rewards, the player must solve the mathematical questions that appear on the screen. In order to answer, the player must click on one of the cards that appear in their hand on the bottom side of the screen (see Fig. 2). Answering correctly will allow the player to strike the monster; answering incorrectly will be met with retaliation from the monster. Each attempt will reshuffle the deck of cards.

In each level, the player runs from left to right, and each time he faces a monster, it will stop the movement and the combat will begin. A turn begins with a new deck of cards and a mathematical exercise to solve and defeat the monster.

The player has two types of cards available: attack cards and spell cards. The attack cards have the answer to mathematical exercises, while the spell cards can give an advantage to the player, such as, for example, blocking the monster attack if the player's answer is incorrect, restoring one point of the player's health, or doubling the damage to the health of the monster if the answer is correct. Both the player and the monsters have health points represented by hearts in the upper corners of the window. Normally, each attack well done removes one health point (i.e., one heart). When the monster's health reaches

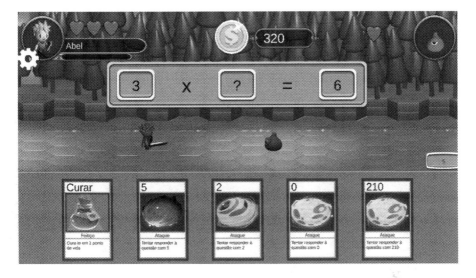

Fig. 2. Screenshot of the gameplay combat.

zero, he dies, and the player starts moving to reach the next monster. On the contrary, if the player's health reaches zero, he dies, and the level ends.

The game contains three separate types of object data that shape the gameplay: attack cards, spell cards, and questions. All three types of data objects are saved like objects in three separate files, one for each type, containing all variables and their information. For example, each question has a unique tier, and each enemy has a minimum tier and a maximum tier. Thus, for each combat, randomly pick a question between the minimum and maximum tiers of the enemy. The use of these three files allows the designer to describe the data to be used in the game with the minimum intervention of the programmer.

Figure 3 shows the several modules of the game, where the first one refers to the login. This module will be described in more detail in the next Sect. 2.1.

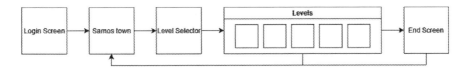

Fig. 3. Diagram of the modules of the game.

The current version of the game has only five levels, as shown in Fig. 3, and what differs for each one is the tier of the questions. The levels available have a blue background color, while the levels blocked have a gray background color, as shown in Fig. 4. Every time the player finishes a level, the next level becomes available. The version of the game for Windows is available to be tested at https://thejokelion.itch.io/math-masters.

Fig. 4. Screenshot of the level selector scene.

2.1 Login Module

In our game, we decide to create a login for the players as a way to collect some information about their performance in the game. For that, we need an online database service, and the most popular today are Google Firebase [10] and Microsoft Azure PlayFab [14].

In this case, we chose PlayFab which has an API for Unity and allows the free use of databases on up to ten games, each with fewer than one hundred thousand players. Thus, the player needs to register with a name, email, and password. This task requires the use of the Internet, which is a requirement of the game. But the database is also used to store the player's progress, such as the level completed and the points earned.

The idea behind saving a player's performance is to give teachers, who will use this game as a complementary activity in the classroom, an overview of the student's performance in the game (see Fig. 5). Note that other information can be added about the player's performance if needed, such as the number of times he plays, the time he plays, etc.

Player data

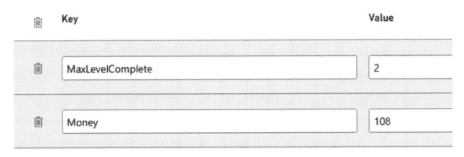

	Key	Value
	MaxLevelComplete	2
	Money	108

Fig. 5. Example of the player data in the PlayerFab website.

2.2 Preliminary Evaluation

In this preliminary evaluation, two questionnaires were filled out, one to evaluate the habits of the players and the other to evaluate their experience with the game. The number of students who tested the game was fifty-eight, with ages between seven and nine years old, with 57.2% of men and 42.5% women. The majority of them have the habit of playing games daily: 28.8% less than an hour a day, 42.5% between one and two hours a day, 12.3% between two and three hours a day, 5.5% between three and four hours a day, and 6.8% more than four hours a day. Only three said that they only play occasionally.

The questionnaire to evaluate their experience with the game used a 5-point Likert scale. When asked if the game is simple and intuitive, around 95% of the players agreed (i.e., totally agree + agree), and if they enjoyed the game and didn't feel bored or anxious about it, more than 84% agreed. When asked if the game helps them improve their results in multiplication, more than 87% agreed. More than 85% considered that the exercises that appear in the game are similar to those that appear in the lessons. And more than 89% said that they make an effort to obtain a good result in the game, which means that using educational games has good results for the learning process. Additionally, more than 81% considered that their interest in math improved due to the game. Finally, when asked if they wanted to have more game levels, more than 97% agreed.

3   Conclusion and Future Work

A prototype of an educational math game was developed, which was well received by the students that tested it. It is a simple point-and-click game because the target audience is primary school students. The player has a deck of cards to use to solve math questions, but also some magic cards that give him an advantage over enemies.

The tests done showed that the majority of the students play games regularly, and they appreciate this kind of tool to support the learning process. However, the development of educational games requires an appropriate methodology, i.e., introducing the learning content into the gameplay without breaking it, which was done in this case with success. Thus, the genre of the game is not the most important thing, but rather, placing learning content in the game without breaking gameplay is a way to keep the player's engagement.

In the future, more levels can be introduced, namely for the other mathematical operations (i.e., addition, subtraction, and division). Note that the structure of the game is already prepared to have other operations through the JSON files.

The creation of a teacher and class account where the players/students can join will be very useful. Thus, the teacher could have access to the progress of their students, for example, by seeing other types of information like the time played, the level reached, the score for each level, etc.

An evaluation of the student's performance through a pre-test and a post-test with a control group will be another task in the future essential to validating the use of this tool.

Acknowledgements. This work is funded by FCT/MCTES through national funds and when applicable co-funded EU funds under the project UIDB/50008/2020.

References

1. AdaptedMind: Learn K-6 math and reading (2023). https://www.adaptedmind.com
2. Adventure, K.: Math blaster premium (2015). https://apps.apple.com/us/app/math-blaster-premium/id811704280
3. All, A., nez Castellar, E.P.N., Looy, J.V.: Assessing the effectiveness of digital game-based learning: best practices. Comput. Educ. **92–93**, 90–103 (2016). https://doi.org/10.1016/j.compedu.2015.10.007
4. Aparício, A.F.C., Silva, F.G.M.: Arithmetic bird: a game for training mathematical operations. EAI Endorsed Trans. Seri. Games **5**(17) (2019). https://doi.org/10.4108/eai.11-7-2019.159526
5. Barbosa, A., Pereira, P., Dias, J., Silva, F.: A new methodology of design and development of serious games. Int. J. Comput. Games Technol. **2014**, 1–8 (2014). https://doi.org/10.1155/2014/817167
6. Boyle, E., et al.: An update to the systematic literature review of empirical evidence of the impacts and outcomes of computer games and serious games. Comput. Educ. **94**, 178–192 (2016). https://doi.org/10.1016/j.compedu.2015.11.003
7. Dale, E.: Audiovisual Methods in Teaching. Dryden Press, New York (1946)
8. Draganoiu, R., Moldoveanu, F., Morar, A., Moldoveanu, A.: DigiMathArt: a game-based approach to learning mathematics and programming. Interact. Learn. Environ., 1–26 (2023). https://doi.org/10.1080/10494820.2023.2205903
9. Drigas, A., Pappas, M.: On line and other game-based learning for mathematics. Int. J. Online Eng. (iJOE) **11**, 62–67 (2015). https://doi.org/10.3991/ijoe.v11i4.4742
10. Google: Firebase (2023). https://firebase.google.com
11. Ke, F.: A case study of computer gaming for math: engaged learning from gameplay? Comput. Educ. **51**(4), 1609–1620 (2008). https://doi.org/10.1016/j.compedu.2008.03.003

12. Laato, S., et al.: Evaluation of the pedagogical quality of mobile math games in app marketplaces. In: 2020 IEEE International Conference on Engineering, Technology and Innovation (ICE/ITMC), pp. 1–8 (2020). https://doi.org/10.1109/ICE/ITMC49519.2020.9198621

13. Michael, D., Chen, S.: Serious Games: Games That Educate, Train, and Inform. Course Technology PTR (2005)

14. Microsoft: Azure PlayFab (2023). https://playfab.com

15. Moyer-Packenham, P.S., et al.: How design features in digital math games support learning and mathematics connections. Comput. Hum. Behav. **91**, 316–332 (2019). https://doi.org/10.1016/j.chb.2018.09.036

16. Núñez Castellar, E., All, A., de Marez, L., Van Looy, J.: Cognitive abilities, digital games and arithmetic performance enhancement: a study comparing the effects of a math game and paper exercises. Comput. Educ. **85**, 123–133 (2015). https://doi.org/10.1016/j.compedu.2014.12.021

17. Prensky, M.: Computer games and learning: digital game-based learning. In: Raessens, J., Goldstein, J. (eds.) Handbook of Computer Game Studies. The MIT Press, Cambridge (2005)

18. Shi, Y.R., Shih, J.L.: Game factors and game-based learning design model. Int. J. Comput. Games Technol. **2015**, 1–11 (2015). https://doi.org/10.1155/2015/549684

19. Silva, F.G.M.: Practical methodology for the design of educational serious games. Information **11**(1) (2020). https://doi.org/10.3390/info11010014. https://www.mdpi.com/2078-2489/11/1/14

20. Wu, B., Wang, A.: A guideline for game development-based learning: a literature review. Int. J. Comput. Games Technol. **2012** (2012). https://doi.org/10.1155/2012/103710

21. Yong, S.T., Gates, P., Harrison, I.: Digital games and learning mathematics: student, teacher and parent perspectives. Int. J. Ser. Games **3** (2016). https://doi.org/10.17083/ijsg.v3i4.112

22. Zemliansky, P., Wilcox, D.: Design and Implementation of Educational Games: Theoretical and Practical Perspectives. Information Science Reference. 1st edn. (2010). https://doi.org/10.4018/978-1-61520-781-7

A Framework for the Creation of a Reading Video Game for Children

Hakim Boussejra[(✉)]

Université de Bourgogne, Esplanade Erasme, 21000 Dijon, France
hakim.boussejra@u-bourgogne.fr

Abstract. When children start to learn how to read in primary school, they are given children's books, collections of tales, to read in class or at home, but not all children enjoy books to the fullest, and worse, many do not like reading at all. The aim of this paper is to propose a method to adapt such books into video games, hence giving the possibility to read the same stories in a different, interactive medium. Children being familiar with video games, and being avid players, they may more easily enjoy a story through this medium rather than another. But as we work on the matter at hand, two main issues arise, which we will discuss further below. How to adapt from text, often illustrated, to video game? Considering the target audience of this effort, how are we going to make it understandable, legible, and accessible to young children? Said questions are meant to help developers and researchers understand better how to work with children's literature and children's games having always their audience in mind.

Keywords: Children's Video Games · Children's Literature · Video Game Adaptation · Video Game Accessibility

1 Introduction

What makes children better at reading and manipulating words is frequent engagement with written text. Lété has explained that the more they read, the more they unconsciously learn the implicit rules of language [1]. It does not matter which type of text they read. However, in primary schools, where the formal teaching of reading happens, children are more likely to encounter written text in the form of manuals, textbooks and short tales, often coming with illustrations. In other words, they will mostly read through a diverse range of books. Before my current work in research, between 2017 and 2020 I used to teach French and English to primary school and middle school children, and experience has shown me that it is getting harder to find children willing to read a book, sometimes, even a comic book. That experience is shared by a lot of teachers and researchers in education. Cunningham reports such testimonies, adding that forcing reading unto children does not help making them good readers, as it lacks motivation, a key attitude to enjoy reading [2]. Love and motivation are aspects shared by many others, such as Leland et al. [3] and Powell-Brown [4].

Powell-Brown has published in 2006 an article whose title is "Why Can't I Just See the Movie? Fostering Motivation in Children Who Struggle with Reading" [4], using

© The Author(s), under exclusive license to Springer Nature Switzerland AG 2024
L. Vale Costa et al. (Eds.): VJ 2023, CCIS 1984, pp. 174–183, 2024.
https://doi.org/10.1007/978-3-031-51452-4_13

on purpose a sentence many may have heard coming from children and teenagers who would rather see a movie version of any story rather than its written form. Reading does not imply only reading books, and knowing that a part of our target audience does not enjoy reading books so much, why not give them an alternative? Enjoying a popular story in another form still means enjoying that same classic tale, and if the children Powell-Brown had to face preferred movies, maybe some others may prefer other media as well. Hence comes the main topic of this paper: turning classic tales for children into video games. Going back to Aarseth's definition of cybertexts as "ergodic literature", meaning "nontrivial effort is required to traverse the text" [5], or in other words, in the case of games, greater involvement from the player is necessary to play. Hodent describes games as "intrinsically gratifying" [6] Then, if games need a lot of effort to be played and at the same time are so popular and gratifying, it means that players feel genuinely motivated to play.

Several famous characters of children's literature have appeared in video games such as Cinderella in *Cinders* [7], the Big Bad Wolf in *The Wolf Among Us* [8] or Alice in *Alice: Madness Returns* [9]. However, these three games share a common point: they expand on the universes from the tales into their own thing, and are not adaptations of the written tales, and worse, the games are not designed for children, but rather for a n adult audience, in the case of the latter two. Adaptations of children's literature into video games are nearly nonexistent. One could mention *Never Alone*, based on the traditional Inupiat tale "Kunuuksaayuka" [10], to which we may add a few games with a structure akin to a fairy tale like *Child of Light* [11] and *The Cruel King and the Great Hero* [12], but the examples are only a few.

The 2023 statistics from the Entertainment Software Association state that 76% of American children under the age of 18 play video games [13]. Since the majority of children plays games, adaptations of classics of children's literature into video games is a relevant idea. In the following sections, we will propose a set of design methods that need be applied to make such games a reality. The first questions that must be wrestled with are related to the needed transformations from the source text, and next, several issues of accessibility for children. The existing literature on such matters is scarce, Bernal-Merino mentioned a few issues on children's texts in games in relation to questions of video game translation and localization [14, 15] and Fisher wrote a book on important general guidelines for game design for children, but its contents lack specificity regarding the literary material we suggest using as a source [16].

2   Dealing with the Source Text

2.1   Issues of Length, Complexity and Violence

Some classic tales can be long, have complex syntax and vocabulary, and may involve gruesome events that would not fit well with the teachings we want to provide children with in 2023. Hence, the source text needs to be transformed into a controlled form adapted to children. Of course, depending on the age of your target audience, the level of transformation will change. The older the children, the more independent they are in their reading practice. Consequently, the focus of this work will stay within the scope of primary school children, aged 6–10, who have greater needs in terms of making text and game accessible. Depending on the source text used, there may need more or less work. There can be as many games as there are tales, and it would be humanely impossible to count the number of folk and fairy tales that have been passed down through human history. Some are shorter, simpler and less violent than others. But in general, classic tales, as Hintz, Zipes or Bernal-Merino have shown, were not necessarily initially intended for children [15], they are socially backwards to modern audiences [17], children today may have a hard time relating to them [18]. To illustrate my words, we will use "Sinbad the Sailor" from *The Arabian Nights* as an example. As there are several versions of it available to us today, for the remainder of this article, we will use the the classic 1885 version by Sir Richard F. Burton [19].

"Sinbad the Sailor" is a series of seven adventures collected in the sixth volume of *The Arabian Nights*. They portray Sinbad, a young man from Baghdad who dilapidated his family inheritance, seeking adventure in faraway lands. He reaches the port city of Bassorah and embarks on a voyage. In each of the seven tales, he ends up shipwrecked and stranded on an unknown land. Through his wit, sheer luck and a bit of magic, he always manages to get back to Baghdad richer than he was before. The origins of the Sinbad stories are unclear, but may date back to the 9th or 10th century [20]. Henceforth, the set of morals and ethics therein differs from those of today, and will need to be adapted to better fit our current society. To deal with all the problems mentioned above, the text will have to be adapted through three main means: reduction, deletion and gameplay.

Reduction. Reduction is the process of making the text shorter while keeping its meaning intact. Sentence length, syntax and vocabulary may become an obstacle for the comfortable reading of young children. The first of the seven adventures of "Sinbad the Sailor" amounts to 3500 words. Turning such a tale into a video game would make it, given the different sets of signs making up a video game, an interactive illustrated story. Since there's a dominant visual element to video game stories, we will compare them with picture books, which are often given as reading items to children, facilitating reading and comprehension thanks to rich, beautiful and detailed illustrations. However, since their audience are children in the process of learning to read, the amount of words is precisely calculated depending on the age of the intended readers, with a standard amount of words being between 500 and 600 words [21]. The initial amount of words should strive to be reduced to make it closer to the amount found in picture books (Table 1).

Table 1. Reduction example taken from the first adventure of "Sinbad the Sailor".

Source text extract	Suggested reduction
"My father was a merchant, one of the notables of my native place, a monied man and ample of means, who died whilst I was yet a child, leaving me much wealth in money and lands and farmhouses."	My father was very rich, and left me with all his wealth after he died

Deletion. Deletion is the process of deleting entirely a part of the text, which implies a loss of meaning. As mentioned earlier, a lot of stories can be gruesome, violent, and inadequate for a young audience in the 21st century [15, 17, 18], and because of that, excerpts from the source text may need to be deleted. In the seven adventures of "Sinbad the Sailor", the main character is at times murderer, owner of slaves or concubines, or the husband in a forced marriage. It is part of the continuous life of folk and fairy tales to be retold in a new manner befitting of their new context [22]. Such elements must then be deleted. Sentences or paragraphs containing such events can need both reworking through reduction and deletion, as shown in the example below (Table 2).

Table 2. Reduction and deletion example taken from the 1st adventure of "Sinbad the Sailor".

Source text extract	Suggested combined reduction and deletion
"Reaching the city in due time, I went straight to my own quarter and entered my house where all my friends and kinsfolk came to greet me. **Then I bought me eunuchs and concubines, servants and negro slaves till I had a large establishment**"	I got home and all my friends and family came to greet me

For both processes, the choice of words is important, it is required that the vocabulary be as understandable as possible for children. To that effort, I recommend using frequency dictionaries as the one published by Davies and Gardner [23], which is based on the Corpus of Contemporary American English Davis designed, or the frequency list developed by Snauwaert which can be found online [24], based on a corpus of 6 million words taken from 12 popular American TV shows including *The Simpsons, Friends, The Office* and more.

2.2 Gameplay

A video game is a narrative construct made of different signs including not only text, but also visuals, sound and different kinds of interactions. While a great deal of the source text will be adapted through reduction and deletion, a big part of the text will have to be adapted into gameplay and interactions with the audiovisual environment of the game. The choice of interaction will vary depending on the genre of game being designed. In the case of "Sinbad the Sailor", the story follows the motifs of the fantasy adventure, traveling being one of the main elements of the tales [20], so a game adapted from this very tale could be an adventure/RPG hybrid in the vein of the *Legend of Zelda* series, which is what I am currently developing as part of my research project.

The following example is drawn from Sinbad's fourth adventure, in which he becomes stranded in a faraway kingdom that welcomes him with open arms. He befriends the local king, who gifts him in marriage the nicest woman in town. She eventually falls ill and dies, after which Sinbad learns of a local tradition: when someone in a couple dies, the other is buried alive with them in a giant cave below the city where all couples are eventually buried. Each person buried alive is given a few pieces of bread and a bit of water, allowing them to survive for a while before their inevitable death. Sinbad eventually finds his way out through a crack in the cave and escapes, but before he does, to survive, he kills every living person that gets thrown in the cave to steal their bread and water. In this tale, we have two big issues that need to be solved, first the issues of forced marriage and then the issue of murder. Some of this will require the use of deletion, but the events there are central to the plot of the tale and cannot be entirely erased, which means that something needs to happen, albeit in a different manner. The adaptation has to be multimodal, transforming the source text at the same time in regards to words, visuals, interaction and gameplay which implies recreation and rewriting. Find below a possible solution taken from the murder scene in the cave (Table 3).

Table 3. Deletion of violence and rewriting into new gameplay elements in "Sinbad the Sailor"

Source text extract
"Then I took the leg-bone of a dead man and, going up to the woman, smote her on the crown of the head; and she cried one cry and fell down in a swoon. I smote her a second and a third time, till she was dead, when I laid hands on her bread and water […]. I carried the vivers to my sleeping place in the cavern-side and ate and drank of them sparingly, no more than sufficed to keep the life in me"

Issue	Solution
Violence	Deleted
Means of survival: Food	Sinbad finds mushrooms growing in the cave as well as nuts left by animals from the outside
Means of survival: Water	Sinbad finds a small stream of clean water in the cave

In this new version of the tale, Sinbad meets a woman in this faraway kingdom, they eventually fall in love and marry, but she dies of illness. Sinbad learns of the ritual in which they bury alive the spouses of the deceased and is thrown into the cave with some bread and water. That being not enough, he looks for sustenance elsewhere. In the source text, he eventually finds his way out through a crack, which means there is an opening to the outside world, so small mammals could store seeds, fruit and nuts in the cave that he could eat. Within the cave could grow edible mosses and mushrooms that the player would have to collect to stay alive. While searching for food, the player would eventually find a small stream of drinkable water, which will lead him to the exit of the cave as well. To sum up, the player will have to explore the cave, and to delete any violence from the source text, we have added to the scenery a few edible elements and a stream of water, allowing us to keep the central plot point of the burial and consistency of the story.

Up to now, we have mainly focused on textual matters and how to adapt the text using reduction, deletion and recreation into gameplay. However, that is not sufficient to create a video game for children. The processes the text have gone through are already a first step towards accessibility for children, but there are many other design issues that must be taken into account when designing a game for children.

3 Video Game Accessibility for Children

3.1 Accessibility Issues

According to Grammenos, video game accessibility is "used to describe a situation in which a person is able to play a game even whilst having "diversified needs", or whilst playing under "limiting conditions" which may include permanent and temporary physical, sensory and mental disabilities" [25]. This includes as well the limitations of children, which vary depending on their age, among which we find motor skills, that develop and grow more and improve throughout childhood [16], as well as the lack of experience with games, since while most children play video games, a very young child could be playing a video game for the first time or could be playing a specific genre of game for the first time and not know its conventions. Also, when it comes to reading, while theory wants children at any given age to have received the same instruction and thus have the same level of literacy, in practice, that is not the case, as some children will learn faster and others slower, depending on many social, economic, cognitive and family factors that go beyond the scope of this article. One very frequent reading impairment that needs to be taken into account, however, is dyslexia, which according to the Yale Center for Dyslexia & Creativity, "affects 20% of the population and represents 80–90% of all those with learning disabilities" [26]. The following subsections will focus on three main accessibility points: fonts, visuals and sounds.

Fonts. Dyslexia potentially affects a fifth of the population, and causes difficulties in learning how to read associated with a developmental delay and difficulties in the automatization of language skills [27, 28]. Rello and Baeza-Yates have studied the impact of fonts on reading performance for dyslexic people. Different fonts have different shapes and some, like Helvetica, Courier, Arial or Verdana, their findings show also that writing for a dyslexic audience should favor sans serif, roman and monospaced fonts [29]. Aside from a specific type of font, the British Dyslexia Association also recommends using a bigger font size, at least 12–14 point, or possibly more depending on the reader [30]. Bigger letters also makes reading more comfortable for young readers and adults alike, so this is an improvement for everyone, especially on text-heavy digital media [31]. The International Game Developers Association and Game Accessibility Guidelines both recommend using bigger fonts to improve readability with enough contrast in the background of the text box [32, 33].

Visuals. Video games allow for beautiful, complex and detailed graphics, whether in 2D or 3D. While graphics improve immersion, the have to keep a sense of purpose. Part of this is representing the universe of the game, its nature, animals, people, as well as a wide range of elements the player can interact with. Kress and van Leeuwen, in their *Grammar of Visual Design*, explain that in any visual medium, what is important stands out [34], drawing from Gibson's "Theory of Affordances" [35]. In a video game, it means, as Hodent said, that "form follows function" [6]. Sharp explains this concept further as "qualities of an object or being that suggest its use or abilities" [36]. Just the same as we all know that on computer software the floppy disk is synonymous with saving, we are made to understand in video games that elements that stand out might do so for a reason. The vines growing on the walls of the *Legend of Zelda* games invite you to climb on them to progress to new areas, a crack on a wall can imply that said wall can be broken, and luckily, our avatar earlier found bombs, which means they must be usable to tear down that wall. While such mechanics will seem obvious for seasoned players, they might be less natural for children who would not know as well the conventions of the games they are playing. As such, visual cues can be bigger, strong contrasting colors can help make elements stand out better, and other visual cues can be added to important elements that can be interacted with, such as the sparkling lights above the grass in *Pokémon* games that tell the player there is a rare shiny Pokémon to be found there. All these visual cues must be associated with clear tutorials to explain the player how they can interact with items and elements in the landscape of the game.

Sounds. Music, voice acting and sound effects also play a big part in the immersion of players in video games in any subgenre, as have discussed Bessel and Burke on action-adventure, FPS, horror, sports games and RPGs [37, 38]. Music and sound effects, apart from ambience, can serve as cues in the same way as visual clues. A specific music plays on a boss battle, which means the player knows they are in for a rough time. When the player picks up an important item, a special tune plays for a few seconds, or when they press a switch, a sound effects hints at the unlocking of a door somewhere. A combination of sound effects and vocal and textual cues can help make sure the information was properly given in different sets of signs. When the player hears the sound of the door unlocking, a text should appear saying so, reflecting the thoughts of the in-game character, which should also be dubbed to allow for the player to hear and read the words of the character at the same time. Dubbing is extremely important for children. While good voice acting is expensive [15], games for children should strive to be entirely voiced, especially when the game is associated with reading practice. Video games present a story that makes children readers of this specific type of interactive text. One way children first experience stories at school or at home, through professors and family, is when they are read to. Leland et al. confirm that reading aloud to children helps them progress in their mastery of literacy [3], which is why video games for children should be wholly voiced, as the game will provide written words on screen but also will vocalize this text to help with comprehension and the association of graphemes, syllables and words with their pronunciation.

3.2 Testing with Children

Any game has to be player tested during its development, and time should be given to the testing of accessibility issues, with enough iterations to adjust any accessibility issues arising during and after the collection of testing data until a final product ready for release is obtained [39]. If a game's target audience is children in a specific age range, it has to be tested with children of the corresponding age group. Testing with children can be more complex for various ethical reasons, but is however mandatory as they are at the heart of the design process of the game. The data collected from children can be subject to several biases, such as wanting to please the adult they are with and thus telling them what they want to hear rather than what they really think. Knoll adds that researchers should avoid leading questions and keep their language neutral, as well as inviting the children to talk aloud about what they experience [40]. He also mentions that children, especially the younger they are, can have spontaneous, unexpected behaviors compared to adults [40]. Adult playtesters are doing their job and getting paid for it, whereas children testing games are just playing and having fun, so it is best, as Fisher explains, to set short test sessions of an average of 30 min to avoid boredom, give power to the children in their practice by making them feel at home and in charge of their playing, and also allocating time for them to simply play the game, and possibly play around with something else and rest if needed [16]. They are children and it is in their nature, especially when they are very young, to be very energetic and require different activities to stay stimulated. Keep in mind that they need time to simply be children.

4 Conclusion

Making video games for children is a complicated process that requires the application of numerous accessibility rules in many design aspects, whether it is text, visuals and sounds. Such rules already exist, to some extent, but were not necessarily designed to be applied for children, and further work is needed to properly establish an accessibility guide for game design for children that could be used in the video game industry. It is an even greater challenge when working with literary material to find exactly how to adapt the text into a video game for a younger and modern audience, but the processes described in this article, reduction, deletion and transformation into gameplay, are already a solid basis to continue working in that direction. More work needs to be done in adaptation studies, which have left video games out of its spectrum for too long a time, with only brief mentions of video game adaptation in the works of Hutcheon [41], Stobbart [42] or Martin [43]. Video games can be an entertaining new way of reading classic stories on an engaging medium that can motivate children to get involved in their reading practice. Children's classics are only waiting to be retold in video game form, as they have been in movies before. The more classic stories will be available as video games, the more children will have opportunities to experience them in different ways. Such games do not intend to replace books, of course, but to be an adjacent medium that some will enjoy more, or at least differently, than the text. We can only hope that if they enjoy the story they read through a game, they might want to move to the original book or tale. The objective of these games is, just like storybooks, to nurture the love for reading.

Acknowledgements. This paper presents a work in progress that is part of a PhD funded by the French region Bourgogne-Franche-Comté. The theory explained here is being applied to the creation of video game prototypes which are part of the same project.

References

1. Lété, B.: Quel est le rôle des apprentissages implicites dans la lecture. Presented at the Conférence de Consensus: Lire, Comprendre, Apprendre (2016)
2. Cunningham, P.: If they don't read much, how they ever gonna get good? Read. Teach. **59**, 88–90 (2005). https://doi.org/10.1598/RT.59.1.10
3. Leland, C., Lewison, M., Harste, J.C.: Teaching Children's Literature: It's Critical! Routledge, Taylor & Francis Group, New York; Abingdon (2023)

4. Powell-Brown, A.: Why can't I just see the movie? Fostering motivation in children who struggle with reading. Interv. Sch. Clin. **42**, 84–90 (2006). https://doi.org/10.1177/105345 12060420020701
5. Aarseth, E.J.: Cybertext: Perspectives on Ergodic Literature. Johns Hopkins University Press, Baltimore (1997)
6. Hodent, C.: Dans le cerveau du gamer: neurosciences et UX dans la conception de jeux vidéo. Dunod, Malakoff (2020)
7. Cinders I MoaCube. http://moacube.com/games/cinders/. Accessed 25 July 2023
8. The Wolf Among Us – Telltale Games. https://telltale.com/the-wolf-among-us/. Accessed 25 July 2023
9. Arts, E.: Acheter Alice: Madness Returns^{TM} – PC – EA. https://www.ea.com/fr-fr/games/alice/alice-madness-returns. Accessed 25 July 2023
10. Never Alone – Homepage. http://neveralonegame.com/. Accessed 25 July 2023
11. Child of Light I Ubisoft (EU / UK). https://www.ubisoft.com/en-gb/game/child-of-light. Accessed 25 July 2023
12. The Cruel King and the Great Hero I Coming Early 2022. http://nisamerica.com/cruel-king/. Accessed 25 July 2023
13. ESA: Essential Facts. https://www.theesa.com/2023-essential-facts/. Accessed 25 July 2023
14. Bernal-Merino, M.A.: Video games and children's books in translation REF. J. Specialised Transl. **11**, 234–247 (2009)
15. Bernal-Merino, M.Á.: Translation and Localisation in Video Games: Making Entertainment Software Global. Routledge, Taylor & Francis Group, London New York (2017)
16. Fisher, C.: Designing Games for Children: Developmental, Usability, and Design Considerations for Making Games for Kids. Focal Press/Taylor & Francis Group, Burlington (2015)
17. Zipes, J.: Fairy Tales and the Art of Subversion: The Classical Genre for Children and the Process of Civilization. Routledge, Milton Park (2012)
18. Hintz, C.: Children's Literature. Routledge, Taylor & Francis Group, London; New York (2020)
19. Burton, R.F.: The Arabian Nights. Barnes & Noble (2016)
20. van Leeuwen, R.: The Thousand and One Nights: Space, Travel and Transformation. Routledge, London (2010)
21. Basu, B.: Children's picture books and illustrations. In: The Routledge Companion to Media and Fairy-Tale Cultures, pp. 443–450. Routledge, New York (2018)
22. Zipes, J.: Why Fairy Tales Stick: The Evolution and Relevance of a Genre. Routledge, New York (2006)
23. Davies, M., Gardner, D.: A Frequency Dictionary of Contemporary American English: Word Sketches, Collocates, and Thematic Lists. Routledge, London (2010)
24. Snauwaert, F.: Frequency List. https://frequencylist.com. Accessed 26 July 2023
25. Grammenos, D.: From game accessibility to universally accessible games. In: Fun for All: Translation and Accessibility Practices in Video Games, pp. 21–43. Peter Lang, Bern (2014)
26. The Yale Center for Dyslexia & Creativity: Dyslexia FAQ. https://dyslexia.yale.edu/dyslexia/dyslexia-faq/. Accessed 26 July 2023
27. Nicolson, R.I., Fawcett, A.J., Brookes, R.L., Needle, J.: Procedural learning and dyslexia. Dyslexia **16**, 194–212 (2010). https://doi.org/10.1002/dys.408
28. Fawcett, A.: Procedural learning, dyslexia and delayed neural commitment. Int. J. Psychophysiol. **168**, S20 (2021). https://doi.org/10.1016/j.ijpsycho.2021.07.059
29. Rello, L., Baeza-Yates, R.: Good fonts for dyslexia. In: Proceedings of the 15th International ACM SIGACCESS Conference on Computers and Accessibility, pp. 1–8. ACM, Bellevue (2013). https://doi.org/10.1145/2513383.2513447

30. British Dyslexia Association: Dyslexia friendly style guide. https://www.bdadyslexia.org.uk/advice/employers/creating-a-dyslexia-friendly-workplace/dyslexia-friendly-style-guide. Accessed 27 July 2023
31. Rello, L., Pielot, M., Marcos, M.-C.: Make it big! The effect of font size and line spacing on online readability. In: Proceedings of the 2016 CHI Conference on Human Factors in Computing Systems, pp. 3637–3648. ACM, San Jose (2016). https://doi.org/10.1145/2858036.2858204
32. IGDA: SIG guidelines. http://igda-gasig.org/get-involved/sig-initiatives/resources-for-game-developers/sig-guidelines/. Accessed 27 July 2023
33. Game accessibility guidelines | A straightforward reference for inclusive game design. https://gameaccessibilityguidelines.com/. Accessed 27 July 2023
34. Kress, G.R., Van Leeuwen, T.: Reading Images: The Grammar of Visual Design. Routledge, London (2021)
35. Gibson, J.J.: The Theory of Affordances. Perceiving, Acting and Knowing: Toward an Ecological Psychology, pp. 67–82 (1977)
36. Sharp, J.: Dimensionality. In: The Routledge Companion to Video Game Studies, pp. 91–98. Routledge (2016)
37. Bessel, D.: What's that funny noise? An examination of the role of music in cool boarders 2, alien trilogy and Medievil 2. In: King, G. (ed.) Screenplay: Cinema/Videogames/Interfaces, pp. 136–144. Wallflower Press, London (2002)
38. Burke, K.R.: Alien waves: sonic reverberations of the RPG interface in Lagrange Point. In: Gibbons, W., Reale, S. (eds.) Music in the Role-Playing Game: Heroes & Harmonies, pp. 57–75. Routledge, New York (2020)
39. Chandler, H.: The Game Production Toolbox. CRC Press, Boca Raton (2020)
40. Knoll, T.: The think-aloud protocol. In: Games User Research, pp. 189–202. Oxford University Press, Oxford (2018)
41. Hutcheon, L., O'Flynn, S.: A Theory of Adaptation. Routledge, London (2013)
42. Stobbart, D.: Adaptation and New Media: Establishing the video game as an adaptative medium. In: The Routledge Companion to Adaptation, pp. 382–389. Routledge, London (2018)
43. Martin, C.: "Wonderland's become quite strange": From Lewis Caroll's Alice to American McGee's Alice. In: Frus, P., Williams, C. (eds.) Beyond Adaptation: Essays on Radical Transformations of Original Works, pp. 133–143. McFarland & Co, Jefferson (2010)

Games and Culture

Video Games and Adaptation: An Introduction

Tatjana Ristić[1]([✉]) [iD] and Darjan Kubik[2] [iD]

[1] Faculty of Philology, University of Belgrade, Studentski trg 3, Belgrade, Serbia
tanja1326d@gmail.com
[2] Pancevo, Serbia

Abstract. The main idea of the paper is to analyse the relation of video games and adaptation both synchronically and diachronically. The synchronic aspect of the paper builds on contemporary academic insights while the diachronic one is founded in the gaming industry itself. In the first part, we outline a theoretical framework which is mainly derived from Linda Hutcheon's idea of adaptation as re-mediation between three modes of engagement: the telling, showing and participatory mode. Her insights are then compounded with contemporary video game studies in order to shed a light on the unique features of video games as a medium and how other media are transcoded into and from the semiotic sign system constituted in these features. In the second part, we analyse examples from crucial periods of video game history. These include the badly received *E.T.* and *Cyberpunk 2077*, and influential video game series such as *Warcraft*, *The Witcher* and *Halo*. By looking into video games that chart all possible relations the participatory mode has with those of showing and telling, we wish to open up case-study examinations into the field of video game adaptation. The goal of the paper is therefore not to offer a comprehensive guide to the theory or history of video game adaptation but rather an overview meant to direct researchers toward possible and highly required further work in the field.

Keywords: Video Games · Adaptation · Transmediality · Media Convergence

1 Introduction

An important question arose with the emergence of new media: will it produce new narratives? Looking at Disney's numerous live-action remakes of animated movies, which have become emblematic of contemporary creative production, we can almost univocally answer: no. The era of mass production of content has also become the era of retelling old stories instead of starting new ones. Due to the fact that adaptive practices are establishing themselves as the dominant form of mainstream culture, adaptation studies are now a more important research area than ever.

Such practices are, of course, a direct result of what Henry Jenkins calls "economic convergence" – the restructuring of cultural production for transmedia exploitation of

Darjan Kubik—Independent researcher.

© The Author(s), under exclusive license to Springer Nature Switzerland AG 2024
L. Vale Costa et al. (Eds.): VJ 2023, CCIS 1984, pp. 187–201, 2024.
https://doi.org/10.1007/978-3-031-51452-4_14

branded properties, such as *Pokemon*, *Harry Potter*, *Tomb Raider* and *Star Wars* (Jenkins 2001). Simply put, old stories, especially those with a loyal fanbase, sell well.

Video games hold an important place in media franchising given the fact that the video game industry annually makes more profit than the movie and music industries combined (Patience 2022). This is just one of the reasons to analyze video game adaptation. Another is the very nature of the medium: video games are a "bastardisation of forms" (Keogh 2014: 10). Jenkins sees them as a part of a bigger complex he famously named transmedia storytelling, the result of yet another aspect of media convergence – cultural convergence (Jenkins 2001; 2007). Due to the transmedial nature of video game adaptation, the relationship of adaptation and video games is theoretically a fertile ground as much as it is financially.

We hope to provide theoretical and historical insights derived both from academic research and the video game industry. The paper is thus divided into two segments: we offer a synchronic scope of the problem, and then we diachronically pinpoint significant examples. The first segment connects Jenkins' idea of media convergence to adaptation, especially that of video games. Moving from Linda Hutcheon's incremental insights into the theory of adaptation, we consider what makes video game adaptation specific in comparison to other adaptive re-mediations. Apart from providing a top-down model, in the second section, we offer a descriptive, bottom-up analysis that considers particular adaptations (*E.T.*, *Warcraft/DotA*, *The Witcher*, *Halo*, and *Cyberpunk 2077*). Our contribution examines not only the adaptations themselves but the social and economic structures that have shaped them and their being in the cultural world.

Even in 2001, Jenkins noticed that media convergence is sparking a range of disputes because of the conflicting goals of consumers and producers (Jenkins 2001). With the consumers being most often enraged with the adaptations they get, it is important to consider the theoretical thought and historic practices that have brought us here.

2   Theory of Video Game Adaptation: The Synchronic Perspective

At the beginning of the new millennium, when the talk of media convergence escalated, Jenkins stated that real media convergence is on the verge of transforming our culture as profoundly as the Renaissance did, creating a digital renaissance – a period of transition and transformation that will affect all aspects of our lives (Jenkins 2001). Before going deeper into the issue, we must understand that by media convergence he meant "the flow of content across multiple media platforms, the cooperation between multiple media industries, and the migratory behavior of media audiences who will go almost anywhere in search of the kinds of entertainment experiences they want" (Jenkins 2006: 2). The condition for this "cultural shift" [ibid., 3] was set by digitization, but it is corporate conglomerates that made it imperative [ibid., 11]. Franchising, in which adaptation plays a key role, pushes media industries to embrace convergence [ibid., 19]. This is the reason why it is essential to talk about adaptation in the context of convergence culture – a culture, as Jenkins has put it in his book's very title, where old and new media collide.

As some video game scholars have already pointed out, Jenkins has excluded adaptations from transmedia storytelling, insisting on a "narrow" definition of adaptations as mere movement of content from one medium to another (Fehrle 2019: 12). In our transmediatised postmillennial era, however, most efficient adaptations are strategically related across a variety of media, with each medium contributing in unique ways (Kérchy and McAra 2017: 225). Jenkins' concept challenges adaptation studies to approach not only texts but the contexts of their creation, distribution, and reception (Fehrle 2019: 15). Literary and film studies, the disciplines that have traditionally informed adaptation studies, only offer limited tools to describe and conceptualize changes that media convergence has brought to adaptation [ibid., 21]. More interactive media necessitate a rethinking of adaptation studies, and the new direction requires critical perspectives from other disciplines, such as video game studies [ibid., 17].

Prior to looking into the novelties interactive media has bestowed upon adaptation studies, it is of utmost importance to chart their "traditional" beginnings. Critics unequivocally name Linda Hutcheon's book A Theory of Adaptation (2006) the cradle of adaptation studies. The importance of studying adaptation Hutcheon finds in the fact that adaptations are so much a part of Western culture that they appear to affirm Walter Benjamin's insight that "storytelling is always the art of repeating stories" (Hutcheon 2006: 2). Adaptation is repetition, but repetition without replication [ibid., 7] – repetition with variation. The experience of adaptation is, therefore, twofold: on the one hand, it invites recognition and remembrance, and on the other, it also leads to change [ibid., 4]. Adaptations are inherently "palimpsestuous" works, haunted at all times by their adapted texts, but are also aesthetic objects in their own right [ibid., 6].

Hutcheon finds adaptation to constitute three things simultaneously [ibid., 8]:

1. the product: an acknowledged transposition of a recognizable other work or works;
2. the process of creation: the act of (re-)interpretation and (re-)creation[1] through "appropriation" (criticism of the source) or "salvaging" (preservation of the source);
3. the process of reception: an intertextual engagement with the adapted work, which is only possible if the receiver is acquainted with the prototext [ibid., 21].

We will be mostly concerned with the first meaning of adaptation. In this context, adaptation is an announced and extensive transposition of a particular work or works. This "transcoding" can involve a shift of medium or genre, or a change of frame and therefore context. Transposition can also mean a shift in ontology from the real to the fictional [ibid., 7–8]. Adaptations to a different medium are re-mediations, that is, translations in the form of intersemiotic transpositions from one sign system to another. This is a translation in a very specific sense: as transmutation or transcoding into a new set of conventions as well as signs [ibid., 16].

Hutcheon nonetheless suggests that focusing on the change of medium in an adaptation inevitably invokes the long history of debate about the formal specificity of the arts and thus of media [ibid., 34]. She, therefore, offers a different approach, one that focuses on modes of engagement that can be shared among plural media. Starting from Wayne Booth's distinction of telling (e.g. novels) versus showing (e.g. films),[2] she adds a third mode that corresponds to new digital media and calls it the participatory mode (e.g. video games). The telling mode immerses us through imagination in a fictional

---

[1] Where "adapters are first interpreters and then creators" [ibid., 18].

[2] Analyzed in his famous book The Rhetoric of Fiction [1961].

world, the showing does so through the perception of the aural and the visual, and the participatory mode immerses us physically and kinesthetically [ibid., 22–23]. Hutcheon thinks that keeping these three modes of engagement in the forefront can allow for certain precisions and distinctions that a focus on medium alone cannot [ibid., 27].

For our purpose, however, the focus on the medium is inevitable. In the next part of the paper, we will use Hutcheon's modes of engagement to outline possible relations between video games and other media, but now we have to consider the specificities of the medium of video game and adaptation from and into it. Even though Hutcheon recognizes video games as a medium and often analyzes them in her study, she does not offer an in-depth approach to the issue. As with other digital media, she acknowledges "deliberate user action",[3] as their fundamental and "truly distinctive" feature [ibid., 50]. She also points to a close relationship video games have to film: they draw on televisual, photographic, and cinematic devices, tropes, and associations, but they always have their own logic [ibid., 51].[4] Most importantly, citing Oliver Grau,[5] she distinguishes that what gets adapted in video games is the heterocosm, an "other world", or more precisely, in Descartes' terminology, the "res extensa" of that world: its material, physical dimension, which is transposed and then experienced through multisensorial interactivity [ibid., 14].[6]

The interactive, physical nature of this kind of engagement entails changes in the story and even in the importance of the story itself [ibid., 13]. More recent studies have thus proposed a new term: storyworld. Many instances of transmedia storytelling are not adaptations in the narrow sense of the word – an attempt to recreate existing stories in a new medium. Rather, they expand on the original instantiation of a storyworld, expanding its hyperdiegesis as they adapt, transform, and add to a fictional world. (Fehrle 2019: 11–12). Some game elements which are not even of narrative nature are incorporated in adaptations of video games' storyworlds. Hutcheon did accentuate that stories might not be of the biggest importance to games but, as a narratologist, she never put emphasis on non-narrative elements. When a video game gets adapted into a film, for example, the film does not have to solely transpose its plot, characters and other traditional story elements. It can also adopt mechanics of digital storytelling and gameplay, such as clear-the-level plot structures and try-die-try-again movement through the story (Papazian et al. 2013: 10–11).

As Kevin M. Flanagan remarks, video game adaptation hence presents a unique set of design and discursive challenges (Flanagan, 2017: 443). Even when it comes to their most narratological aspects, a game must translate linear narratives or stable fictitious properties into quasi-ludic, player-controlled experiences [ibid., 444]. Flanagan's biggest contribution to adaptation studies of video games is his classification of four types of relationships that exist between video games and adaptation [ibid., 444–445]:

---

[3] Term coined by Marie-Laure Ryan. See: Ryan 2001: 338.

[4] The reasons for the similarity of video games and film/television are listed in more detail in: Picard 2008: 293–294.

[5] Grau 2002: 3.

[6] She also states that video games cannot easily adapt that which novels can portray so well: the "res cogitans", the space of the mind [ibid., 14]. In our opinion, this can, however, be disputed, which we will show through our analysis of morality in *The Witcher*.

- adaptation as creation: representative transmedia properties adapt source materials;
- adaptation as porting: porting a game from one console/operating system to another;
- adaptation as localization: the linguistic and cultural translation of games;
- adaptation as "modding": player-generated adaptation.

In further analysis, we will be mostly concerned with the first relationship between video games and adaptation but we will also touch on the last one. Modding stands for "modifying" and refers to adapting, adding to, or altering game content by players [ibid., 453]. Even though we will mainly talk about re-mediated adaptations, adaptations can happen within the same medium, too. Such is the case with adaptation as modding. In the next section, we will discuss examples of adaptation that move from the telling/showing to the participatory mode and vice versa, but we will also offer cases of interactive-to-interactive adaptations: one being the modding of video games, and the other adaptation of board and card games. In this aspect, we will diverge from Juul's distinction between game adaptations and what he calls "game implementations". In his opinion, card and board games on computers should be considered implementations since it is possible to unambiguously map one-to-one correspondences between all possible game states in the computer version and in the physical game, while sports games on computers are adaptations because much detail is lost in the physics model of the computer program. As an example of this, Juul states that the video game player's body is not part of the game state in sports game adaptations (Juul 2005: 49). We want to rethink this due to the fact that in many board and card game computer versions, especially the instances of video games' precursor, the electro-mechanic games, what was once essentially a multiplayer form is now transcoded into a singleplayer game. In addition to this, the other player – the opponent – is interpreted by becoming an AI. The opponent's mind is not part of the game state either then, which makes for a "selective adaptation" [ibid., 49] and not a simple implementation.

As Linda Hutcheon herself stated, theory is futile if it is not derived from practice – as wide a cultural practice as possible (Hutcheon 2006: XII). When we started researching the examples themselves, it proved simply unfeasible to talk about any of them without discussing the then state of the video game market and the perceived objective of adapting a title which always lead to market value. Therefore, we propose that adaptation in the field of video games cannot be disconnected from the market itself, so much so, that it even becomes a question whether adaption in video games would exist if the market were not a factor.

3   Case Study Examination: The Diachronic Perspective

Before delving into the analysis of concrete video games, we wish to suggest that the history of video games can be seen as a history of adaptation in a certain sense. Tristan Donovan calls the 1940s and 1950s a time when scientists were teaching computers to play board games (Donovan 2010). The precursor of video games, the early electro-mechanic and electronic games, were the continuance of Turing's goal to develop artificial intelligence. It is the complexity and interestingness of (board) games as a problem that makes them desirable for AI (Yannakakis 2018: 15). As Juul said, these interactive-to-interactive adaptations bring nothing new to the table from the aspect of game mechanics, but their very aim was to interpret, or in other words, adapt the player's mind, creating an "electronic brain" (Donovan 2010). The history of video games thus starts as scientific experimentation in the field of AI, but experimentation in adaptation nonetheless.

Even with the first games that were acknowledged as video games, researchers have recognized their history as history of adaptation. Since the early days of Tennis for Two (Higinbotham 1958) and Spacewar (Russell 1962), video games have looked to other textual forms and media histories for their inspiration (Flanagan 2017: 442). With the first video game console Odyssey 100 appearing in the early 1970s, the partnership between literature and video games grew more intense. In this period, games such as Space Invaders (Taito 1978) were produced inspired by H. G. Wells' literary works (Araújo 2017: 228). Not long after, in the early 1980s, video games became well known for their adaptations of television series and American films, especially on the Atari 2600 console (Picard 2008: 2).

3.1 Showing-to-Interactive: *E.T. The Extra-Terrestrial*

Wolf lists 33 game cartridges for the Atari 2600 based on movies and 23 based on television shows (Wolf 2003: 9). Among them is the infamous *E.T. the Extra-Terrestrial* (Atari 1982). The very first point that comes to mind is the fact that *E.T.* the movie (1982) and *E.T.* the video game were published in the same year, with the game coming out nine months after the Cannes premiere of the film. For modern standards of AAA development, this timeframe is comical. However, Howard Scott Warshaw says six to seven months would have been a fair amount of time for the development of such a game but the team, in fact, had a little over five weeks to make it.[7] The pressure to have the game on the shelves by Christmas season resulted in it becoming a disappointment, so much so, that it was dubbed "the worst game in history" (Eklund 2022: 1).

The player controls the titular E.T. in order to help him go back home by collecting three pieces of an interplanetary telephone, thus mirroring plot points from the movie. In order to do this, E.T. moves, teleports, falls into a pit and levitates back from said pit in six different terrains, all inspired by the movie. The character loses energy by taking actions and that energy can be replenished by eating Reese's Pieces (mimicking the movie), a famous candy in the 80s, making it one of the earliest examples of product placement in video games. Once E.T. has the three telephone pieces, he needs to go to a specifically designated location where he can call home and once he gets picked up, the game is over. The player then gets the option to play it all again on the same difficulty, with the phone pieces placed in different locations, which left the gameplay design lacking even for the era.

While sales of Reese's Pieces went up by 300% at the time, *E.T.* the video game had dismal reception both commercially and critically. Kent (2001: 238–239) called its graphics primitive even for Atari and the game was criticized for failing to convey any of the emotional notes of the movie. Its poor commercial success along with a group of other factors caused the "video game crash" of 1983, with several thousand Atari unsold cartridges ending up buried under cement and video games getting a rating system due to scores of unhappy customers. As a closing remark on the subject of *E.T.*

---

[7] See: http://www.digitpress.com/library/interviews/interview_howard_scott_warshaw.html.

the video game and its importance, we want to highlight that a cartridge recovered from the cement mass grave was added to The Smithsonian in 2014, clearly pointing to the landmark character of the game. In a blogpost by the museum regarding this addition, it is said that The Smithsonian is no hall of fame – it is their job to share the complicated technological, cultural, and social history of any innovation, including video games.[8] This example shows that an adaptation can be a disappointment in the eyes of the public and the critics but can in spite of that have a significant impact. However, only retroactively can an adaptation which is unsuccesfull from a market standpoint earn its right to memorialization.

3.2 Interactive-to-Interactive: *Warcraft 3* and *DotA*

Our second example, *DotA* or *Defence of the Ancients*, inspired by *StarCraft's* custom campaign *Aeon of Strife*, came to be as a mod scenario in the multiplayer mode of *Warcraft 3* (Blizzard 2002). It is credited as the sole originator of a subgenre – the Multiplayer Online Battle Arena or MOBA.

What is fascinating about this mod is the fact that it adapted some of the elements of *Warcraft 3* which were not present in the final version of the game. *Warcraft 3* had numerous iterations, with the team wanting to create something they called a "role-playing strategy" rather than a real-time strategy (RTS).[9] The role-playing strategy, which never came to be, was innovative in two respects: 1. it introduced hero units who could gain experience, fight and equip items, like in RPGs; 2. the hero could recruit only a handful of non-hero units, in contrast to Blizzard's previous RTS, *StarCraft* (Blizzard 1998), which had whole swarms of them. The idea was to choose non-hero units based on their special skills and to create synergies by carefully timing the use of skills, which was to be a core gameplay focus and an innovative step away from the standard RTS formula. This concept was abandoned and the final version of *Warcraft 3* includes the innovative hero units but the player only has control over moderately sized armies with more special skills than units had in *StarCraft*. Therefore, the final version of the game is an RTS with role-playing strategy elements, a middle of the road compromise between innovative tendencies and the cornerstone of the genre.

DotA, on the other hand, consists of two teams of up to five players trying to destroy the Ancient located in the base of the other team, with the players controlling *only* hero units (or later termed "heroes"), which radicalized the game's focus. While the mod did build upon elements freely provided by Blizzard Entertainment's campaign editor, it was created by avid fans of *Warcraft 3*, and its multiplayer resources (such as servers, matchmaking and ban lists) were maintained entirely by the same fans. The success of the mod radicalizing a half-abandoned innovative focus of *Warcraft 3* makes for an interesting conclusion in hindsight – the potential for a new approach to strategy games was not unrecognized, but was unrealized by the developers. It was the player base that fulfilled its own need for it through adaptation as modding.

---

[8] See: https://americanhistory.si.edu/blog/landfill-smithsonian-collections-et-extra-terrestrial-atari-2600-game.

[9] See: http://web.archive.org/web/20000831114421/blizzard.com/war3/description.shtml#rps.

The final version of the mod was *DOTA All-stars*,[10] with over 100 unique heroes. They were inspired by hero units in the original game but other hero tropes were adapted from various sources as well. To name just a few, Kunka can be seen as the swashbuckling pirate archetype, Void's appearance points to Lovecraftian tendencies and Ezalor is habitually compared to *Lord of the Rings'* Gandalf both in terms of game mechanics and in appearance.

In 2021 *Dota 2*, the most obvious descendant of *DotA*, took the road many other franchises did by offering its heroes for further adaptation into a Netflix animated series *DOTA: Dragon's Blood*. While the lore of *Dota* deals with a general cosmogony of its in-game universe, the animated series focuses on building relationships between characters who had no connection to begin with, allowing the animated series autonomy in characterization. With each new step along the way, the adaptation becomes increasingly character-driven. What started as an innovative gameplay concept, gave life to more and more narrative elements in the adapted versions of this storyworld. Therefore, even though Flanagan talked about modding itself as adaptation, considering it the process of creation in Hutcheon's terms, the example of *DotA* shows that it is also an adaptation as a product, being important in a twofold sense for our research.

3.3   Interactive-to-Telling: *Halo: Combat Evolved*

If it is true that the game industry has benefited from literature as an inspiration source, it is also true that games have been inspiring writers from around the world to construct their narratives, such as *Assassin's Creed, Diablo, Battlefield: the Russian, God of War, World of Warcraft, StarCraft, Uncharted* and *Mass Effect* (Araújo 2017: 229–230). Our third example brings to the fore one such media convergence in tandem with overlapping commercial efforts on an unprecedented scale for the time. With the first Xbox console and the first *Halo* game, *Halo: Combat Evolved* (Bungie 2001), being released on November 15, 2001, and the book *Halo: The Fall of Reach* (Eric Nylund 2001) around two weeks earlier, it quickly becomes a challenge to view the entire initiative as anything other than a unified attempt to tackle several media and the market at once, rather than trying to establish substantial relations between the products. We deem they were all meant to bring commercial success to each other by emerging simultaneously in the public. These very relations are in our focus since they question what can even be called an adaptation.

Halo: Fall of Reach is a self-sustained novel[11] whose narrative leans heavily on the game even though the game was its chronological successor in terms of their publication dates. The novel was written in only seven weeks, the author's shortest deadline, and

---

[10] *DOTA All-stars* gained popular acclaim and became a fixture in e-sports and Blizzcon in 2005. By 2008, MOBA as a genre gained mainstream popularity, as several other MOBAs came out (e.g. *League of Legends, Heroes of Newerth*), and in 2013 *Dota 2* was released by Valve.

[11] By 2001, manuals containing gameplay instructions and bits of the story accompanying video games were no surprise and were provided with the purchase of the game. Such manuals soon grew into novels based on video games, with *Resident Evil: The Umbrella Conspiracy* (S. D. Perry 1998) paving the way. However, it was unprecedented for the novel to be published alongside the game it was based on, as was the case with *Halo: Fall of Reach*.

was clearly intended to supplement the game and give depth to its story. It was based on *Halo's* story bible (a part of the narrative design document), which gave the author material regarding the game's future canon and boundaries to write within. Despite being published earlier than the game, it adapted *Halo: Combat Evolved's* key story points. It cannot in earnest be called anything but an adaptation of a body of media work that was yet to see the light of day at the time of the novel's publication.

The novel was critically and commercially successful, with the first part of that success being a rarity for books which adapt video games. While we can argue that the future popularity of the game contributed to the success of the book, it remains clear that the novel did the narrative heavy lifting for the game and had an even wider impact. Jolley describes how she used the popularity of *Halo: Combat Evolved* to turn otherwise reluctant students to reading *Halo: The Fall of Reach*. In her own words, "their [the students'] experience with games and game-based texts allowed them to establish a purpose for their reading of texts they wouldn't have considered reading otherwise" (Jolley 2008: 7). The game provided all the fun of playing while the book did the background work of enriching the canon of *Halo* with historic influences.[12]

If distinguishing between the success of the book and that of the game seems to be a blurry line, much the same can be said of the success of Xbox as a console and its flagship game. In TV commercials from 2001,[13] they are almost never advertised separately. But Microsoft's use of the *Halo* franchise for promotion of its assets did not end there. Microsoft's AI assistant for Windows 10, Cortana, mirrors an AI character from the franchise. Originally, Cortana was only the project's code name but when the fans enthusiastically accepted the idea that the virtual assistant will be named after *Halo's* Cortana, the decision stuck, with actress Jen Taylor providing the voice for both the in-game AI and the Windows 10's virtual assistant. More than any of the other examples discussed in this paper, the adaptation of *Halo* highlights the economic nature of its convergence. However, this by no means implies that it is less interesting or important to analyze it from the perspective of cultural convergence.

3.4 Telling-to-Interactive-to-Showing: *The Witcher*

Our fourth example delves into re-mediation the most: *The Witcher* (CD Projekt Red 2007). This section will focus on two key elements prevalent in its adaptive journey: a lack of structural narrative constraints and a devotion to ethical realism in a fantasy setting. These are found to be key in adaptive focus and commercial success for both the books and the games. What is interesting to comment on is that only after the games were released, the novels saw a gradual translation into 37 languages – the commercial success of the video games caused the belated success of the novels. This is thus a rare instance where the creators chose to adapt a material which was not (yet) popular.

---

[12] For example, similar to Spartan rigorous military training and education of children, in the canon of *Halo*, there exists a "SPARTAN" program that identifies humans genetically suitable for special combat training and abducts them as children, while supplanting them with clones genetically modified to die of natural causes. The abducted children are given a first name and a number, and their sole purpose in life is combat. The player character is one of those children, named Master Chief Petty Officer John-117.

[13] See: https://www.youtube.com/watch?v=LmSHCO1LFAA.

It behooves us to remark on the seemingly unending adaptive trail of *The Witcher*: firstly, Slavic folklore is adapted into novellas known mainly in Poland, which get adapted into *The Witcher* novels, following their adaptation into *The Witcher* video games, then a Netflix live-action series and an animated series, and lastly, a number of board games and a digital collectible card game inspired by both the books and the video games. The nature of media convergence surrounding the franchise and the impact it has on popular culture can perhaps be best underlined by the lead actor, Henry Cavill, who has now departed from the series, calling himself a fan of the games.[14] The likely reason for his departure was attributed to his feelings that the third season would not do the source material justice. This demonstrates an approach Hutcheon tried so strongly to fight: "fidelity criticism", as it came to be known, once the critical orthodoxy in adaptation studies, especially when dealing with canonical works such as those of Pushkin or Dante (Hutcheon 2006: 6–7). From the actor's standpoint, which many fans of the franchise today share, *The Witcher* can, therefore, be added to such a canon.

The novel' author (Sapkowski 2017) mentions a version of the Polish folk tale, in which the protagonist, the shoemaker, is his primary source of inspiration, though not in terms of "salvaging" but rather of "appropriation", as Hutcheon would put it. Slavic mythology survived mainly in the form of folk tales, which is the reason for its lack of structure. Sapkowski freely adapted the folk tale by exchanging the shoemaker with a professional monster slayer. He was dedicated to adapt the protagonist with ethical realism as his main focus: Geralt of Rivia was no knight in shining armour off to save the world but a professional out to turn a profit.

The very same freedom in narrative structure was given to the game designers: Sapkowski agreed to let them write entirely original stories using the elements of his tales and he parted ways with his rights to the narrative direction of the games, which would have included a percentage of the profits, and instead accepted a one-time upfront payment. A percentage would have been much to the author's financial benefit but, while his income has no bearing on the focus of this paper, we cannot resist to quote him: "What I expect from an adaptation: a big bag of money. That is all" [ibid.].

With narrative freedom in hand, the first *Witcher* game was a fresh take on what seemed like a tired setting by 2007. Fantasy had been used in role-playing games more often than not, mostly in a naïve manner soon to be done away with in both video games and other media. Racial[15] tensions in the game's story were abundant (in later instalments even central) and sexism was running rampant. This spells out a clear tendency – fantasy settings were leaving the fairytale-like waters of *The Lord of the Rings*, where good and evil were absolute, for a world of morally grey heroes.

Similar to Sapkowski's freedom in adapting his prototexts, the game designers had free reign to make a game about Geralt of Rivia as a space pirate were they so inclined but they built upon the existing storyworld. Even though there are significant narrative divergences between the source and the adapted work, this example confirms what we have mention before – that video games adapt the storyworld rather than narrative particularities of their source. However, keeping key narrative elements, such as the morally grey characters of the books, and transposing such approach to ethics to the

---

[14] For example, see: https://ew.com/comic-con/2019/07/19/the-witcher-henry-cavill/

[15] Here we term humans, dwarves and elves as races, as does the game.

players themselves (often offering no absolutely morally good choices), or in other words, converting this aspect of the novels into a gameplay mechanic, resulted in great critical and commercial success of the adaptation.

3.5 Interactive-to-Interactive-to-Showing: *Cyberpunk 2077*

Our final example, *Cyberpunk 2077* (CD Projekt Red 2020), takes the field of adaptation in video games even further. While the choice of two games by the same studio may seem like researchers' personal preference, we will now outline why *Cyberpunk 2077* offers truly unique points for a discussion about adaptation.

It is a lesser-known fact that *Cyberpunk 2077* is itself an adaptation of the *Cyberpunk* pen-and-paper role-playing system written by Mike Pondsmith in 1988. This system is notably absent from adaptation into other interactive media which points to its prover-bial difficulty to adapt. Companies have, over the years, announced and then cancelled titles based on it, which makes specific news articles about those titles very difficult to find.[16] Adapting something which has not yet been adapted successfully, as was Slavic mythology in *The Witcher*, gave CD Projekt Red the confidence to take a leap of faith and take on the *Cyberpunk* role-playing system.

Cyberpunk 2077 has a complicated but not a strained relationship with Pondsmith's system. Departures have been made in terms of the game mechanics, while the themes and locations were familiar to the pen-and-paper enthusiasts. Elements such as corporations, corporate wars, body modification, Night City and cyberpshychosis were all successfully adapted into the game. The most important aspect of the game for our research is the NPC Johnny Silverhand, the cyber ghost and main provider of quests for the player. The character is not only voice-acted but rather digitally embodied by Keanu Reeves, a universally loved Hollywood actor. The character of Johnny Silverhand is an exact digital replica of the actor, save the eponymous silver hand. In this, we may find hints that the choice to have the actor replicated almost entirely was an attempt to adapt his image for marketing purposes. Some authors even call the actor himself a palimpsest (Middlemost and Thomas 2022). While they focus on Reeves's film career, this video game appearance further reinforced their thesis.

What makes the matter more interesting is the fact that Reeves was not the only well-liked person who got adapted in the game. Nina Kraviz, a Russian-born Berlin-based DJ, has too been adapted both in likeness and professionally. Her character in the game, also called Nina Kraviz, is an underground medical professional (a "ripperdoc" in Cyberpunk slang). It is not confirmed whether Bara Nova, a DJ in the setting of *Cyberpunk 2077*, and the character Nina Kraviz are the same person in the game. Should that be the case, it would add another layer of adaptation to the character, mirroring a phase in Kraviz's life when she worked as a dentist by day and as a DJ by night.

Another celebrity joining the roster is Idris Elba, once again a generally beloved actor, stated to appear in *Cyberpunk 2077: Phantom Liberty*. While we cannot know

---

[16] In contrast, *Dungeons & Dragons* received several adaptations – *Baldur's Gate 1* and *2* (BioWare 1999, 2000) – and *Vampire the Masquerade* had its day in the video game adaption sun with the cult classic *Vampire the Masquerade: Bloodlines* (Activision 2004).

how much of the actor's life will be adapted, if anything at all, it is certain that his likeness will be digitally included into the additional game content.[17]

Much has been said about the critical and commercial performance of *Cyberpunk 2077*, which concerns this paper only tangentially but to sum it up: the game underperformed, perhaps mostly due to the extreme success of the marketing campaign accompanying it that created expectations among the public the game did not meet, and also because of the bugs it had on release. It came as a surprise that the world of *Cyberpunk* would be adapted into *Cyberpunk: Edgerunners* (Netflix 2022).[18] All previous instances of adaptations into Netflix animated series were based on well-loved games, which was not the case with *Cyberpunk 2077*.

It is interesting to compare the case of *Cyberpunk: 2077* to what happened in the 1980s. Apart from the video game crash of 1983, primarily caused by *E.T.*, another reason for the movie industry to stop showing interest in video games may have been the commercial failure of Steven Lisberger's film *Tron* (1982), the first movie based on a video game world. Its lack of success helped push Hollywood away from CGI technology and the whole video game industry for a decade (Picard 2008: 294). Today, however, we are witnessing commercial failures being given a second chance. This poses the following question: is it possible that the aim of some contemporary adaptations is to revitalize IPs in the making of which a significant amount of money has already been invested? And if so, does adaptation as a process even focus on the love of the general public for a certain material or rather on its attention, be it positive or negative?

3.6 Discussion

Since this part of the paper focused on specific video game adaptations, it is necessary to comment on the criteria we chose the examples upon. We are certain that a different pair of researchers might have made both entirely different choices and much the same conclusion. Given the fact that video game adaptions and video games which adapt other media easily number in the thousands by 2020s, it would be a nigh impossible task to go through all of them, which is why we settled on two points as the main criteria for our choices. The first is re-mediation: showcasing all possible relations between Hutcheon's modes of engagement and especially distinguishing those examples that manage to interconnect plural media (*Halo*, *The Witcher*, and *Cyberpunk 2077*). The second point was the "milestone" character of the examples: most are taken from different generations of video games, and some were considered "game changers" of popular culture and the gaming industry (*E.T.*, *DotA*).

Every game we have analysed points to important research topics. In the case of a commercially unsuccessful adaptation such as *E.T.*, we have shown that even though there was no market value, the video game gained substantial worth over time as cultural heritage, and the presence of archeologists at the burial site testified to its historic and

---

[17] For the trailer, see: https://www.youtube.com/watch?v=gdvPG4sUbr8.

[18] The development of *Cyberpunk: Edgerunners* caused a rare instance of media convergence coming full circle – a tabletop role-playing game is being developed by R. Talsorian Games based on the setting of the animated series. See: https://www.polygon.com/tabletop-games/234 45746/cyberpunk-edgerunners-2077-starter-set-announcement.

scientific meaning. We, therefore, used this example to challenge one of our starting points: that the success of an adaptation must be connected to its market value. However, we still believe this is the reason why most adaptations are being made today.

In our second example, we indicated how the player base fulfilled its own need through modding when the industry did not dare to. The case of *DotA* shows how unwilling the creators were to break new ground, and how adaptation can also be a result of fandom. Only after the fans delved into it, the adaptive trail could start enfolding both creatively and, eventually, financially.

Unveiling the economic convergence as the true reason for almost any media convergence was proposed through our discussion of *Halo*: the video game was made to ensure the success of the console, and the book was written to induce the favourable outcome of the game. The economic convergence was, however, only possible due to a successful cultural convergence, with elements of the game outgrowing the entertainment business and becoming part of the Microsoft brand.

The case of *The Witcher* demonstrates how it is even possible to bring fame to the source through the process of creatively unrestricted adaptation instead of using the source to gain fame. This title reveals how unnecessary it is for a video game adaptation to comply with standards of fidelity, but how at the same time the fandom expects faithful adaptations when the video game is the source.

Lastly, through the example of *Cyberpunk 2077*, we analysed how contemporary creators are utilizing all resources at their disposal, both financially and creatively, to assure the return of their investment into an IP. Hutcheon suggested that adaptation often implies a shift in ontology from the real to the fictional, and even though the creators made such a step by casting celebrities to play fictive characters, they have also brought the shift full circle by ensuring the characters resembled their actors in every way, thus making significant effort in the expansion of possible audiences for the game.

These are but a few topics to explore in adaptation studies of video games and our examples only serve as evidence of how broad and hermeneutically fruitful the field is.

4   Conclusion

We have introduced Henry Jenkins' ideas regarding media convergence to our analysis of adaptation from and into video games, as some other scholars have also done before us, to supplement Linda Hutcheon's focus on cultural rather than on economic convergence. The theoretical part of this paper is thus a sum of contemporary insights both explicitly and implicitly regarding video games and/or adaptation. Through it we establish a framework for our diachronic analysis. Our approach was simultaneously based on Jenkins' ideas of economic convergence and Hutcheon's distinction of three modes of engagement – the showing, telling and participatory modes. We strongly believe that future researchers should bear in mind both the cultural and the economic convergence of adaptation from and into video games. By combining our efforts in case study examinations, we will shed a brighter light on a practice which seems to be taking over the creative production of our time.

Video game and adaptation studies are interrelated fields that can mutually benefit and inform one another. Today it is impossible to delve into adaptation studies without consideration for video games given that they are becoming a staple of most franchising efforts, as it is painstaking to discuss a wide range of video games without at least acknowledging some of them as adaptations. Both of these disciplines are rather young, like the very medium of video games, but it is crucial to establish their methodologies as interconnected as possible so as not to think about the phenomena that define our age after it has passed and already defined us as audiences, and as people as well.

References

Araújo, N.S.: Literature and videogames: adaptation and reciprocity. Revista Letras Raras **6**(3), 222–323 (2017). https://doi.org/10.35572/rlr.v6i3.872

Donovan, T.: Replay - The History of Video Games. Yellow Ant, Lewes (2010)

Eklund, L.: From Trash to Treasure: exploring how video games are moving from popular culture to cultural heritage. In: Proceedings of DiGRA 2022, pp. 1–16 (2022). https://doi.org/10.5040/9781350960374

Fehrle, J.: Introduction: adaptation in a convergence environment. In: Fehrle, J., Schäfke-Zell, W. (eds.) Adaptation in the Age of Media Convergence, pp. 7–30. Amsterdam University Press, Amsterdam (2019). https://doi.org/10.2307/j.ctvpbnqd0.3

Flanagan, K.M.: Videogame adaptation. In: Leitch, T. (ed.) The Oxford Handbook of Adaptation Studies, pp. 442–457. Oxford University Press, Oxford (2017). https://doi.org/10.1093/oxfordhb/9780199331000.013.25

Grau, O.: Virtual Art: From Illusion to Immersion. Custance G. (trans.) MIT Press, Cambridge (2002). https://doi.org/10.7551/mitpress/7104.001.0001

Hutcheon, L.: A Theory of Adaptation. Routledge, New York (2006). https://doi.org/10.4324/9780203957721

Jenkins, H.: Convergence? I diverge. MIT Technol. Rev. (2001). https://www.technologyreview.com/2001/06/01/235791/convergence-i-diverge/. Accessed 05 Nov 2023

Jenkins, H.: Convergence Culture: Where Old and New Media Collide. New York University Press, New York (2006). https://doi.org/10.18574/nyu/9780814743683.001.0001

Jenkins, H.: Transmedia Storytelling 101. Confessions of an Aca-Fan (2007). http://henryjenkins.org/blog/2007/03/transmedia_storytelling_101.html. Accessed 05 Nov 2023

Jolley, K.: Video games to reading: reaching out to reluctant readers. Engl. J. **97**(4), 81–86 (2008)

Juul, J.: Half-Real: Video Games between Real Rules and Fictional Worlds. The MIT Press, Cambridge (2005)

Keogh, B.: Across worlds and bodies: criticism in the age of video games. J. Games Crit. **1**(1), 1–26 (2014)

Kent, S.L.: The Ultimate History of Video Games: From Pong to Pokemon and Beyond – The Story Behind the Craze That Touched Our Lives and Changed the World. Three Rivers Press, New York (2001)

Kérchy, A., McAra, C.: Introduction. Eur. J. Engl. Stud. **21**(3), 217–230 (2017). https://doi.org/10.1080/13825577.2017.1369270

Middlemost, R., Thomas, S.: Introduction to the special issue: Keanu Reeves as palimpsest. Celebr. Stud. **13**(2), 137–142 (2022). https://doi.org/10.1080/19392397.2022.2063394

Papazian, G., Sommers, J.M.: Introduction: manifest narrativity – video games, movies, and art and adaptation. In: Papazian, G., Sommers, J.M. (eds.) Game on, Hollywood!: Essays on the Intersection of Video Games and Cinema, pp. 8–18. McFarland & Company, Jefferson (2013)

Patience S.: When did the video game industry overtake Hollywood and the music industry? Driverless Crocodile (2022). https://www.driverlesscrocodile.com/sustainability-and-change/when-did-the-video-game-industry-overtake-hollywood-and-the-music-industry/. Accessed 05 Nov 2023

Picard, M.: Video games and their relationship with other media. In: Wolf, M.J.P. (ed.) The Video Game Explosion: A History from PONG to PlayStation® and Beyond, pp. 293–300. Greenwood Press, London (2008)

Ryan, M.: Will new media produce new narratives? In: Ryan, M. (ed.) Narrative Across Media: The Languages of Storytelling, pp. 337–359. University of Nebraska Press, Lincoln (2001)

Sapkowski, A.: Meeting Andrzej Sapkowski, the writer who created The Witcher – Does he really hate games? Eurogamer. Interviewed by Purchese, R. (2017). https://www.eurogamer.net/mee ting-andrzej-sapkowski-the-writer-who-created-the-witcher. Accessed 05 Nov 2023

Wolf, M.J.P.: The Medium of the Video Game. University of Texas, Austin (2003). https://doi. org/10.7560/791480

Yannakakis, G.N., Togelius, J.: Artificial Intelligence and Games. Springer, Cham (2018). https:// doi.org/10.1007/978-3-319-63519-4

A Lantern Called Desire: Time Travel, Space Nostalgia, and Desiring-Machines in *The Great Perhaps*

Diego A. Mejía-Alandia(✉) ⓘ

University of Seville Américo Vespucio s/n, 41092 Sevilla, Spain
dmejia@us.es

Abstract. Articulated through time travel mechanics and post-Communist aesthetics, the indie game *The Great Perhaps* (Caligari Games 2019) is an example of the trend known as *space nostalgia*. The game portrays representations of past, contemporary, and future Russian societies using narrative strategies that substitute the context of a perpetual—yet unstartable—cycle for the context of origin and the worldbuilding of its representations—as both socialist societies and the real world. This fact turns the time of the game from history into an impossible, private nostalgic time of its own making. Following the deleuzian concepts of *desiring-machines* and the *body without organs* this paper argues that, through the use of desire, nostalgia, and the protagonist's imperative need to save his family as narrative and worldbuilding strategies, the game presents a ludic argument about nostalgia and the impossibility to live in the past by means of a time paradox that turns its hero into a *desiring-machine* whose by-products are a *miraculating-machine*, that projects the hero's desire into reality, and a *body without organs,* embodied in a *monster* destined to haunt the protagonist. The paper concludes that the representations portrayed by the game and its *miraculating-machine* carry a post-Soviet retro-futuristic nostalgia and aesthetics as well as a prospective nostalgia that looks to the future of the current generation rather than its Soviet past.

Keywords: Post-Communist Representations · Space Nostalgia Video Games · Time Travel · Desiring-Machines

1 Introduction

By the end of the twentieth century, modern nostalgic phenomena presented a vast array of mnemonic narratives. While they used to be "a longing for a home that no longer or has never existed. [...] a sentiment of loss and displacement, but [...] also a romance with one's own fantasy" [6], these phenomena evolved into a *modernist nostalgia*—"a *mode* of longing [for a nostalgia] that is no longer possible" [4]. At the same time, popular culture representations gave birth to a *nostalgia of style* [17] that emphasized the reification of the past and—thanks to its commodification—the fabrication of a *free-floating* version of a past that could be reused over and over again, like a film or TV set.

© The Author(s), under exclusive license to Springer Nature Switzerland AG 2024
L. Vale Costa et al. (Eds.): VJ 2023, CCIS 1984, pp. 202–216, 2024.
https://doi.org/10.1007/978-3-031-51452-4_15

In the past thirty years, a variety of manifestations of post-communist nostalgia have emerged that employ a mix of these mnemonic narratives in the form of a *postmodern pastiche* [18] which shows a certain fascination with the end of the Cold War era and a nostalgia for its *lost futures* [13], producing cultural objects that portray an ironic celebration of retro-authenticity based on Cold War material and popular cultures. One of these manifestations is the trend known as *space nostalgia* [2, 24, 30], a postmodern pastiche framed by the nostalgia and cultural memory of the Soviet space program's ethos and aesthetics, the commodified memory of the "Great Patriotic War"[1] and—as I have particularly observed in the case of video games—by the globalized popular culture of the Cold War period that includes, but is not limited to, western music, cinema, and literature.

In line with current trends in science fiction, however, contemporary video game representations of post-communist nostalgia, such as the *Metro* [1] and *S.T.A.L.K.E.R.* series [16], tend to replace the celebratory aspects of nostalgia with a darker and more melancholic scenario. This replacement represents a symptom of a derridian *hauntology*[2] that can also be used to understand how phenomena and ideas that seem to belong to the past and are supposedly long gone are, in fact, still present in a variety of sociocultural and political discourses since, like *spectres,* they "still actively influence the current state of affairs, and also taint the future" [14]. Video game examples of the capitalization of space nostalgia such as *Lifeless Planet* [31], *Little Orpheus* [33], *The Great Perhaps* [7], *Golf Club Nostalgia* [10], or the VR series *Red Matter* [35, 36], also involve dystopian and post-apocalyptic-like settings[3] "trapping the player within a virtual embodiment of their own utopian desire, to provoke them to escape it, or seek alternatives to it" [23]. They thus make a point not only about the nostalgic human desire to return to the origin but also about the impossibility of continuing to live in the past. All these games, however, are in essence hopeful for the future, while also certain of an imminent collapse of the environment and human civilization. A fact which, in the face of the latest developments of SpaceX—among other [inter]national and private endeavors—, together with the nostalgic notion that "Ukraine is not a country"[4] [3], makes the fatalistic perspective of these games more relevant than ever.

This paper presents a close reading of the game *The Great Perhaps* (henceforth abbreviated as *TGP*) that considers the role of the protagonist's nostalgic utopian memories and desires—instead of his lived experience or the nation's historic memory—in shaping the design of the game's mechanics and, consequently, the aesthetic and discursive worldbuilding of its post-communist nostalgic representations of past, contemporary, and future Russian societies. For this purpose, I have carried out an aesthetic and narratological analysis of a direct play of the game, drawing from literature on the aesthetics of

---

[1] The Soviet term for the Second World War.

[2] The concept of hauntology problematizes the *ghost*—a liminal figure that "is neither living nor dead, present nor absent" [11]—and Jacques Derrida uses it to show how Karl Marx's philosophy persist in contemporary politics even after the demise of communism.

[3] These games offer scenarios that range from mythical and pasts realities to distant futures and that depict various sociocultural and technological stages of socialist societies.

[4] This discourse, claiming that Ukraine is not a country but a historical part of Russia, appeared long before the start of the ongoing conflict (2005-present).

nostalgia and the deleuzian concepts of *desiring-machines* and the *body without organs* [9] also derived from the notion of *hauntology*.

2 The Great Perhaps

Developed by the Moscow-based studio Caligari Games, *TGP* uses narrative strategies that substitute the context of a perpetual—yet unstartable—cycle for the context of origin and the worldbuilding of its representations—as both a socialist society and the actual world. This fact turns the time of the game from history into an impossible, private nostalgic time of its own making.

As a space nostalgia narrative, *TGP* looks into the future by re-imagining tropes found in Soviet SF and updating them to current technological advances and environmental challenges. As such, the game neither adapts nor reenacts any actual historical events or national narratives. On the one hand, from what we can gather from its cartoon-like "wistful hand-drawn 2D art style"[5] and environmental narrative, *TGP*'s worldbuilding is based on the legacies of the Soviet space program, and the Eastern bloc's cultural memory—including its aesthetics, sci-fi literature scene, and material culture—as well as a mix of popular culture references to Western music and cinema. On the other hand, *TGP*'s design is aimed at an international audience and most of its environmental narrative and worldbuilding information are written in English—plus subtitles available in eight languages. Nevertheless, *TGP* also features a native Russian language dubbing besides the English one.

2.1 Kosmos's Context

The unique story of "Kosmos", the cosmonaut protagonist of *TGP*, starts with him aboard a space station as what looks like an atomic explosion on Earth is followed by a series of cataclysmic storms that prevent all communication with HQ as well as the possibility of his safe return. In order to conserve resources, Kosmos enters a cryo chamber where he will wait for the right time to communicate again with or go back home. When he wakes up, however, a hundred years have passed, leaving no trace of his family or human civilization. Accompanied solely by his spaceship's AI called "L9", Kosmos returns to Earth and his hometown, a post-apocalyptic version of Moscow that is now barren, heavily polluted, and inhabited by deadly mutant beasts. There, once L9's scanner shows him only "one signature of a living human being found" [7] in a thousand-kilometer radius, Kosmos goes in search of it.

Among the ruins, Kosmos finds an unusual artifact: an *old lantern* (see Fig. 1) in the *light* of which (i) he can see glimpses of another time (*apparently past*) at will and (ii) he is able to travel to said time momentarily and in *real-time*[6]. Further along in his adventure, these mechanics will help Kosmos avoid dangers as well as interact

---

[5] As described on *The Great Perhaps* official website: http://drageusgames.com/tcportfolio/the-great-perhaps/

[6] Nevertheless, Kosmos is unable to *reset* or *rewind time* to change the outcome of his actions—unlike in *Prince of Persia: The Sands of Time* [34], *Braid* [25], or *Life is Strange* [12]—and the game's realities/timelines run parallel to each other.

with certain humans in the past and carry key objects back and forth through time in order to solve environmental and mini-game-like puzzles. Nevertheless, since *TGP* is more focused on storytelling and environmental exploration, besides time traveling, the game includes minor 2D side-scrolling mechanics and a design more akin to a *walking simulator* than a *puzzle platform*—like Playdead's *Limbo* [27] or *Inside* [26]. For instance, dying entails no penalty for the player.

Fig. 1. The finding of the lantern and the first encounter with the Monster.

Furthermore, following the example of the non-militaristic approach of Soviet SF, the protagonist remains unnamed and designated solely by his professional role[7] as a *Kosmonaut*, hence *Kosmos*—as happens with characters in the novels of Stanislaw Lem or the Strugatsky brothers. The fact of him being faceless also emphasizes the non-individualistic nature of the Soviet hero [15]. Kosmos is thus unable to carry any weapons, harm any living being, or use violence—features also shared by other space nostalgia games [10, 31, 33, 35]. Even though, as a cultural nostalgic object, *TGP* incorporates ideological mechanisms—namely the Repressive State Apparatus (army, police, and militia) and Ideological State Apparatuses[8]—to convey various systems of beliefs and values, it is critical of all of them. As neither a *war-themed game* nor one played from an *American perspective*[9] [29], it does not incorporate *modes* of either anti- or pro-Soviet or Russian propaganda.

Right after discovering the lantern, Kosmos encounters a black voiceless Monster, twice his size, that L9's scanner mistakes as a human survivor (see Fig. 1). Although the hero manages to escape the creature with the help of the newly found artifact, this monster will haunt him throughout the game. After this encounter, Kosmos decides to

---

[7] The same applies to the non-player characters (NPCs) such as *Colonel, Scientist,* or the game's version of a Russian *Suicidal Writer* in one of its side stories.

[8] Mainly associated with Cold War styles and stereotypes as well as ideas of progress, unbridled capitalism, and of scientific advances with no consideration for human or environmental impacts.

[9] In fact, it is completely absent besides the popular culture references.

return to the apartment where he used to live with his wife and daughter before the explosion. In order to navigate across the city's post-apocalyptic landscape, he will need to constantly travel back and forth through time.

2.2 Timeline and Fictional Times

As happens with hauntology's time perspective, *TGP*'s time is not linear and seemingly also unstable. Accordingly, for the purpose of my analysis, I have divided the game's timeline into three *fictional times*:[10] (i) an *original present*, (ii) an *absolute future*, and (iii) a series of—*unmappable*[11]—*possible pasts*.

Original Present. This is the game's *original starting point*—i.e. when the first explosion happens—and is set in an undefined future not far from the year of the game's release (2019). This period starts with the intro cutscene and ends with Kosmos entering the cryo chamber after the explosion. This period is therefore non-playable and can only be seen in the game's intro, once the game is launched for the first time.

Absolute Future. This is the game's post-apocalyptic future which I call *absolute* in the sense that it is the furthest fictional time in the future depicted in the game from its starting point, set a hundred years after its *original present*. This future presents the image of a Moscow in ruins, still heavily polluted, and seemingly inhabited solely by deadly mutant beasts. This fictional time starts when Kosmos wakes up from the cryo chamber and ends when he encounters the lantern together with the black monster, and travels to the past for the first time.

Possible Pasts. I call *possible pasts* all the instances after the first use of the lantern to where/when the protagonist jumps back and forth, since they are never absolute—even Kosmos is unsure whether he remembers them in the way he encounters them—neither physically nor temporally. These possible pasts are portrayed *between* and *before* the game's *original present* and *absolute future*—even *after*—and, accordingly, it is not possible to *map* or *fix*[12] their place in the game's timeline, with one exception that I will discuss in Sect. 2.3.

When Kosmos navigates the city, he encounters graphic evidence showing that part of human society survived the cataclysm, at least for a while in a less distant future's past (see Fig. 2), and later he finds the ruins of an underground city. The latter's walls, however, are covered with graffiti calling for resilience and survival, not with propaganda or messages of militarism,[13] but with symbolic resistance in the form of quotes from songs.

---

[10] Using Jesper Juul's lexicon, *fictional time* is "the time of the events in the game world" [19].

[11] *Mapping* refers to the process of claiming that whatever the player does is *also* something in *fictional time*; namely, a projection of the play time onto *fictional time* [20].

[12] *Fixation* refers to the *historical time* of the *fictional time*, if applicable [20].

[13] Although it is not made completely clear, part of human civilization survived the explosions and storms, afterwards living in an undefined period of post-apocalyptic dystopification of society. Haunted by the past, mankind apparently repeated it, by experiencing a new series of revolutions and social turmoil, but ultimately died out in the middle of a power struggle (see **Fig. 2**).

Fig. 2. Representations of the dawn and rise of a post-apocalyptic mankind.

Fig. 3. Environmental narrative. Top: "Imagine there's no Heaven". Bottom left: Film and popular culture references and influences. Bottom right: "Can you hear me, Major Tom?"

These diegetic texts take the Beatles or David Bowie as an environmental [para]textual discourse—along with the ruins themselves as a form of post-apocalyptic environmental narrative (see Fig. 3)—and as subliminal messages of *ecocriticism,* calling for action to present—past and future—human practices. In this sense, the environment metaphorically works as a palimpsest that remembers and keeps a record of history and human actions.

Furthermore, these time travels create an aesthetic convergence between Kosmos's *past* and *future,* with settings that project a reality in which the Soviet *style* and his memories of popular culture, and not the country's—past or present—*ideologies,* bind together the actual Russian past and future representations. This way, the time before the explosion is portrayed as the actual nostalgic modern Russia, one that still carries the Soviet *space culture*—reflected in the games' *Socialist Realist* monumental architecture and *public art*—and plays with *space politics* [28], but also as a representation that has a place for humor, meta-nostalgia, and nods to archetypes of popular history and culture in its physical and discursive environments.

For instance, while Kosmos's AI companion "L9" is a clear reference to "HAL 9000" from the film *2001: A Space Odyssey* [22], there is also a poster of the film *Back to the Future* [37] in his space station. These are both a meta-reference to nostalgia and a nod to its sci-fi paradox influences and aesthetics, since all of these references come from a time when the USSR was still in existence. In addition, the subway graffiti quotes such as "Can you hear me, Major Tom?" [5], though apparently completely out of context, allude to a rich meta-mythology based on David Bowie's character's space misadventures that adds gravitas to the hero's feeling of disorientation throughout his journey (see Fig. 3).

2.3 The Return to the Origin

Time jumping between the ruins of his present and what he believes is the past right before the storms started, Kosmos reaches his home in search for his family, long after his first failed search for another human survivor. Running again from the monster, he ultimately finds the apartment where his family used to live but, in a non-paradoxical and yet ironic outcome, Kosmos makes a complete circle that takes him back not just to his family but to his actual *origin*: the ultimate reason for his existence and survival. When Kosmos opens the door of what—in *a* past—should have been his daughter's room, he finds *himself* as a *nameless child* (see Fig. 4). "This... This is the wrong time" Kosmos tells himself. Despite a calendar confirming that the year is 1999, the apartment is furnished in a typical Eastern Bloc's '80s style, on the wall a poster of the mythical 1972's John Lennon's concert *One to One*[14]. The Child, who must be 6 or 7 years old[15], greets Kosmos:

- – Child: Wow! A real astronaut!
- – Kosmos: This... This is the wrong time...
- – Child: Mister, mister! Have you been to space?
- – Kosmos: Yes, little one. I have.
- – Child: Can you take me with you? Please, I did all my homework!
- – Kosmos: I'm afraid I can't take you with me. [7]

The Child vanishes, "It was me. All this time it was me" Kosmos laments. "They're not here. Maybe they survived that storm...". In this scene, the relation between Lennon's poster (see Fig. 4) and the nostalgic memory of Kosmos is not arbitrary, for the poster's referent is the generalized desire that is "the signified [not only] of all commodity relations in late capitalism" [32] but also of aesthetic pleasure and ideology. Even though it remains partial (*in the background*), Kosmos's nostalgic memory is supplemented by the environmental narrative design which articulates the play of desire on various levels. This environmental narrative not only gives Kosmos direction but also provides an anchor for his own identity, and the music is crucial to understanding it.

Moreover, with this jump, Kosmos returns not only to his primordial origin—his childhood home—but to the moment where his career as a cosmonaut begun: with a young Kosmos daydreaming as an astronaut suddenly appeared in the middle of his bedroom. We are thus taken back to the first scene of the game's intro in which a spacewalking Kosmos is having a casual conversation with a Crew Member on Earth: "So, how did you end up in space?" asks the woman on the radio. "Me? Well, I met an

---

[14] Could Lennon still be alive in this reality?

[15] Meaning that all the potential nostalgic and experienced memory of Kosmos is by default *post-communist* since he has no personal memory of the USSR.

Fig. 4. "Mister, mister! Have you been to space?"

astronaut when I was a kid. It really impressed me back then" [7] Kosmos replies. Then the explosion happens, and the story begins.

3   A Lantern Called Desire

Although we can assume that the game's *original present* and—*absolute*—*future* return to an apocalyptic Earth both follow the same timeline, it is hard to establish the rules of time once Kosmos encounters the lantern. Besides its basic mechanics, in fact, the lantern's rules are never disclosed and it is never made clear: (i) how to *map when* or *how far in time* Kosmos travels back—or forth—exactly, (ii) whether this time distance *changes* as a result of his use and misuse of the lantern, (iii) whether these travels *follow the same timeline* or *create new ones* or, finally, (iv) whether the *time distance* remains *constant* every time he advances in his journey. Following the same time logic, the game's storytelling makes it hard to establish *when*—in *human* or *game time*—the game develops or, for instance, whether the game *is unique* or *creates an alternative version* of its own universe.

Nevertheless, as an object, the lantern is not just a magical device, such as Aladdin's lamp in the *Arabian Nights,* that grants wishes to its owner but a *nostalgic device* that turns the romantic autofiction of its owner into *reality.* Immanuel Kant defined the faculty of desire as "[…] the faculty of being, through its representations, the cause of the reality of the objects of these representations" [21]. As Deleuze and Guattari point out, however, Kant chooses *superstitious beliefs, hallucinations,* and *fantasies* as illustrations of this definition of desire. Nevertheless, they also understand that the real object can only be produced by an *external causality* and *external mechanisms*; they indeed believe in the intrinsic power of desire to create its own object, "if only in an unreal, hallucinatory, or delirious form—or from representing this causality as stemming from within desire itself" [9].

Accordingly, the lantern I describe here occupies the place of this *external mechanism,* while Kosmos's actions form part of the consequent *external causality.* This way, "if desire is the lack of the real object" [9], the lantern in fact *renders the desire of the bearer* as a form of phantasmatic compensation of what Kosmos is *missing/lacking.* Although the lantern is able to show *a past,* and to transport its bearer to *said past,* paradoxically, as occurs with non-official *individual memory*[16] and especially with nostalgia, the fact that this device allows us to travel back to it does not necessarily mean

---

[16] Memory not based on *verifiable facts, fabricated, written,* or *fixed* as a *national narrative.*

that *that past existed* at all or that the time distance between said present, past, and future times has a fixed travel or that there is a precise way to measure it. Moreover, since this reality can only exist *in the light of the lantern*, "[t]he reality of the object, insofar as it is produced by desire, is thus a *psychic reality*[17]" [9].

Therefore, when Kosmos inadvertently projects his longing for home, it is not the home that he built beside his wife and daughter he travels back to, but to the quintessential *parental home* of his childhood, where his romantic dreams of becoming a cosmonaut started. In the same vein, and following the Kantian logic of desire, it could be argued that most of the graffiti, popular culture references, and even part of the architecture that can be seen among the ruins, are none other than a projection of the internal states of Kosmos as he navigates his adventure[18]. As an "autoproduction of the unconscious" [9], these are in fact the result of a passive syntheses of desire that ultimately shapes the game's environmental narrative and worldbuilding. Meanwhile, the history of mankind visually depicted by the environment could be working both as proper history—or an *intuition* of it—and as symbol in the form of self-inflicted punishment for Kosmos[19], turning the environment into a character itself.

Furthermore, as Susan Stewart identifies in the case of souvenirs as cultural objects, the lantern both distinguishes and offers a measurement for the past while authenticating the player's experience by anchoring it in the *actual* present [32]. At the same time, however, the lantern works in itself as an *object of desire*, namely in the capacity of *souvenir from the past* that exists because it marks the transference of origin to trace, *moving from event to memory and desire*[20].

As a narrative strategy, the use of an object like the lantern substitutes a context of a perpetual —yet unstartable—cycle for its context of origin, thus represents not the lived experience of its maker but the nostalgic secondhand memory of its bearer. The lantern is an object transformed into its own impossibility, able to reduce and [re]produce the space—i.e., the public, monumental socialist (common) spaces of Moscow—into a 2D post-communist representation appropriated by the view of Kosmos as an individual[21], a fact that turns the time from (shared) *historical time* into *private time*. As symbolic spaces, the environments rendered *in the light of the lantern*—granting wishes and demanding sacrifices—thus reconcile "the utopian promise and dystopian horror apparent in them" [23].

---

[17] Nevertheless, the realities produced by the lantern are filled with dangers and do not offer any kind of utopian pleasure beyond the aesthetics and discourses of the lyrics.

[18] We could read this only from the melancholic setting of the game, but the lantern as a render of desire enhances this fact and, in the process, makes it even more relatable.

[19] As Fousek Krobová, Janik & Švelch recognize happens in *Someday You'll Return* [14].

[20] As Stewart points out, through the use of these strategies, "the narrative process of nostalgic reconstruction of the present is denied and the past takes on an authenticity of being, an authenticity which, ironically, it can achieve only through narrative" [32], one that Kosmos projects into the world and completes with the dialogue, and not the other way around.

[21] Charged with Kosmos's nostalgic memories, these spaces tend to be simultaneously familiar and yet different from the actual Moscow, or from Kosmos's recollections of it.

4 The Resetting of the Possible Pasts

After Kosmos's encounter with his younger self, L9 suggests looking for records regarding the cataclysm in a nearby *military science center*, so that they can "take them back to the past to warn everyone of what's coming" [7]. However, *as if the past realizes that Kosmos wants to alter it*, a series of anomalies are produced and time starts to *fluctuate*. Firstly, the fictional times start mixing, causing hidden clues, key elements, and later NPC's, to appear to be *stuck, trapped between pasts* or, present *in both fictional times,* while sometimes they can be seen in the light of the lantern but do not appear to exist in any of the fictional times. Later, these anomalies get more complex by forming *waves of time* that seem to fluctuate across the space. Vertical waves force Kosmos to jump back and forth between the dangers of each reality as they move across the screen, deconstructing and changing the space in real-time (see Fig. 5) or horizontal waves undo Kosmos's progress when he tries to solve some mini-game-like puzzles.

The information Kosmos gathers between travels seems to indicate that all the damage was caused by a secret Russian experiment gone wrong. When Kosmos finally manages to get the black box—from the *military science center*[22] where the experiment was carried out—containing the records necessary to prevent the cataclysm in the past, the monster comes back into the scene and tries to take the lantern from him. Kosmos tries to fight back for it but, as the monster ultimately touches the lantern, time and space collapse at the origin of the cataclysm. Suddenly, Kosmos appears on a white screen, running while the space is *drawn* in front of him. His nostalgia transports him again and he is allowed to see his wife and daughter, alive and holding hands while looking at the horizon right before the explosion reaches the city and destroys everything (see Fig. 6).

Kosmos: I need to be careful. When I'm in this wave, I may be noticed in the past.

Fig. 5. A *wave of time* crossing Kosmos's reality. On the left side the post-apocalyptic future, on the right the possible—future's—past.

Time and space collapse again and the screen returns to white, with only a voice, the inner monologue of Kosmos, filling the void:

---

[22] Paradoxically, it is also the place where L9 was created.

Fig. 6. Kosmos's desire draws reality before the explosion.

I... I failed? I failed to save you... But it's only for now... I won't stop. Never. I won't abandon you. I will return, no matter the cost! I will walk this crazy path a thousand times more, but I will save you. I will not stop as long as I still have this great "perhaps". [7]

4.1 The Conjuration

Here is where the game works its actual magic, and the lantern turns itself into an Aladdin's lamp kind of paradoxical wish-granting device. Stranded in time and space before his consciousness vanishes, with his monologue Kosmos not only reaffirms his love for his family and his nostalgic love relationship with the reconstruction of his lost past but also, inadvertently, he makes the *conjuration*[23]. He makes a wish, and the lantern complies. However, as happens with this kind of devices, in fairy tales wishes do not come cheap, but there are a *caveat* and a *cost*.

The Caveat. The lantern creates a *loop,* a *logical impossibility* that produces a *time paradox,* in the sense that Kosmos is ultimately trying to fix a chain of events that he himself started—in a different primordial past that we do not witness or that probably did not even occur—in the hope of saving his family and the world with/for them[24]. There-fore, right after Kosmos makes the conjuration, "everything stops dead for a moment, everything freezes in place—and then the whole process will begin all over again" [9]. Time space rearranges itself, Kosmos's spaceship enters the atmosphere once more, L9 repeats the phrase "One signature of a living human being found" [7]. From the barren

---

[23] I use the word "conjuration" with the same semantic values as Derrida: (i) the act or process of *conjuring,* or an *incantation* [that creates the time loop]; (ii) a solemn appeal [to his family]; and, (iii) the exorcising of the spirits [the monster] convoked by said invocation [11].

[24] Similar to a *predestination* or *ontological paradox,* which arises when the protagonist brings about an event by trying to prevent it or by bringing information from the future to the past in order to alter it, the information in this scenario ends up having no origin/maker since the events that produced the information will not happen [8].

surface we see the monster watching the ship's landing. The story starts over, the *caveat* is that Kosmos will have to suffer the whole process again and again.

The Cost. Unable to let Kosmos go through a process of mourning—since the cataclysmic event that destroys Earth represents for Kosmos a disappearance of his present, past, and future—, *TGP* makes a ludic argument about nostalgia, splitting Kosmos's self into two beings:

A desiring-machine. The game turns the natural embodiment of the protagonist's lack into a *desiring-machine* that ends up not only projecting new fictional times for him to travel but, in order to save Earth, also building new representations of the past and future by the means of a second machine to which it is connected: the lantern, a d*esiring-production machine*. The game thus turns Kosmos into a *desiring-machine* in search for his family, a task from which he cannot escape. The playable game ends, and the credits roll.

A Body Without Organs. As the representations that these fictional times depict take the shape of Kosmos's desires and nostalgic memories, this process has as a by-product what Deleuze and Guattari called a *body without organs.* This splitting of Kosmos presents him as a schizophrenic subject who feels so haunted, by both the reconstruction of the past and his desire to reunite with his family, that he *decides* to renounce desire altogether in order to fulfill his mission. However, rather than becoming a body without organs himself, the desire itself seems to issue from this body as a *miraculate*[25] in the shape of the monster. As the antagonist and virtual embodiment of Kosmos's utopian nostalgic desire, the *monster* is a body without organs destined to haunt him not only by trying to thwart his impossible task but by also being connected to the time anomalies.

Whereas for the players it must have been the first time playing the game, for Kosmos it is a cursed Sisyphean task that he will have to repeat till the end of times and that paradoxically, because of his own actions, will never happen. At least not in the universe his desires have created because, as Deleuze and Guattari argue, "Desiring-machines work only when they break down, and by continually breaking down" [9].

4.2 The AI Machine

Kosmos's AI companion L9 is designed to learn and while it maintains a *logical approach* to the events the hero goes through; it also shows some sensibility, for instance, L9 asks Kosmos to take it with him at the beginning of the game because it *does not want to be alone.* Later, in one short cut-scene just halfway of the total *play time*[26], Kosmos finds a mural painting depicting nature in a socialist realism fashion. Nostalgically he reflects:

– Kosmos: How ironic... Men tried to take over the flora and fauna, but in the end there are no people left on Earth, yet nature remains. If not for this storm... How would it all be? Or maybe in the grand scheme of things humanity itself was a devastating

---

[25] A force or agent that comes to represent a miraculous form of its own power, since they appear to be *miraculated* by it [9]. Accordingly, it is not arbitrary that every place in which the monster appears is, visually, heavily charged by either shared or individual memory.

[26] The time used by the player to play the game [20].

storm, and now everything is exactly as it should be? Then is there any meaning to life at all?
- L9: The most terrifying fact about the universe is not that it is hostile but that it is indifferent. Everything you say has no meaning at all. What's done is done. You need to learn how to accept it and even love it. Only then life shall acquire meaning.
- Kosmos: Yeah, you're probably right. [7]

Although there is logic in L9's response, the answer is both encouraging and fatalistic towards Kosmos's objectives. As the game progresses, L9 will start to feel compassion and even *wonder whether it has a soul*. When the game is about to reach its conclusion, L9's speech will get more articulated as it appears to *learn,* and later *project,* its own sentiment of nostalgia. Once the AI sees its creator dead in the past, it starts to understand Kosmos's feelings of loss and sadness.

5 Conclusions

The aesthetic and material desire-production of the lantern and the splitting of Kosmos's self—into a desiring-machine and a body without organs—make a ludic argument about nostalgia and the impossibility to keep living in the past. These same results, as a metaphor, challenge the notion of a national homogeneous nostalgia based on official historical narratives or political ideologies. Similarly, the aesthetics and narrative strategies of other ludic representations of space nostalgia, like the ones found in *Lifeless Planet*, *Little Orpheus*, *Golf Club Nostalgia,* or *Red Matter,* suggest a strong relationship between the significance of popular culture and everyday life memories of the Soviet period and its growth as both an identity marker and an important aesthetic catalyst rather than as a reactionary nostalgic revival of past ideological systems—or of the political agendas some commentators read in recent post-communist ludic representations.

Nevertheless, this ludic argument also makes evident that the post-Soviet retro-futuristic nostalgic aesthetics of the representations portrayed by these games have the function of a prospective nostalgia that in fact looks to the future of the current generation—and the state of the current space race—rather than into the past. Likewise, this argument works more as an environmental cautionary tale rather than just as an ideological one. The latter is especially true in *TGP*, since the hero himself does not have a first-hand memory of the USSR and the projections of the Soviet nostalgia that can be found in the future died long ago with the demise of the Soviet Union and the decay of its space exploration program and promises.

Lastly, while these games display an inherent tendency towards fatalism, the next step of this research will investigate how their desiring-production also turns them into *survival manuals* which intend to prepare the players to meet the needs of the upcoming apocalypse.

Acknowledgments. This research is funded by the Spanish Ministry of Universities and the European Union (NextGenerationEU) through a Margarita Salas grant and is part of an individual postdoctoral research project on representations of post-communist nostalgia in video games, VR, and digital experiences. This project started in collaboration with Tampere University's Centre of Excellence in Game Culture Studies (Finland) and the University of Seville.

References

1. 4A Games: Metro (Series). Deep Silver, Kiev, Ukraine (2010)
2. Andrews, J.T., Siddiqi, A.A.: Into the cosmos: space exploration and Soviet culture. University of Pittsburgh Press, Pittsburg (2011)
3. Apt, C.: Russia's Eliminationist Rhetoric Against Ukraine: A Collection. https://www.justsecurity.org/81789/russias-eliminationist-rhetoric-against-ukraine-a-collection/
4. Bach, J.: What remains: everyday encounters with the socialist past in Germany. Columbia University Press, New York (2017)
5. Bowie, D.: Space Oddity. Philips, UK (1969)
6. Boym, S.: The Future of Nostalgia. Basic Books, New York (2001)
7. Caligari Games: The Great Perhaps. Daedalic Entertainment, Moscow, Russia (2019)
8. Callender, C.: The Oxford Handbook of Philosophy of Time. Oxford University Press, Oxford (2011)
9. Deleuze, G., Guattari, F.: Anti-Oedipus: Capitalism and Schizophrenia. University of Minnesota Press, Minneapolis (1983)
10. Demagog Studio: Golf Club Nostalgia. Untod Tales, Belgrade (2021)
11. Derrida, J.: Specters of Marx: the state of the debt, the work of mourning and the new international. Routledge Classics, New York (1994)
12. Dontnod Entertainment: Life is Strange. Square Enix, Paris, France (2015)
13. Fisher, M.: Ghosts of my life: writings on depression, hauntology and lost futures. Zero Books, Winchester (2014)
14. Fousek Krobová, T., et al.: Summoning Ghosts of Post-Soviet Spaces: A Comparative Study of the Horror Games Someday You'll Return and the Medium. Stud. East. Eur. Cine., 1–14 (2022). https://doi.org/10.1080/2040350X.2022.2071520
15. Gomel, E.: Idylls of the Same: Soviet SF, Cosmic Humanism, and Escape from History. In: Gomel, E. (ed.) Science Fiction, Alien Encounters, and the Ethics of Posthumanism: Beyond the Golden Rule. pp. 69–92 Palgrave Macmillan UK, London (2014). https://doi.org/10.1057/9781137367631_3
16. GSC Game World: S.T.A.L.K.E.R. (Series). GSC Game World, Prague, Czech Republic (2007)
17. Ivy, M.: Discourses of the Vanishing: modernity, phantasm. Japan. University of Chicago Press, Chicago (1995)
18. Jameson, F.: Postmodernism, or. The cultural logic of late capitalism. Duke University Press, Durham (1991)
19. Juul, J.: Half-Real: Video Games Between Real Rules and Fictional Worlds. The MIT Press, Cambridge (2005)
20. Juul, J.: Introduction to Game Time. In: Wardrip-Fruin, N., Harrigan, P. (eds.) First Person: New Media as Story, Performance, and Game, pp. 131–142. MIT Press, Cambridge (2004)
21. Kant, I.: Critique of the Power of Judgment. Cambridge University Press, Cambridge (2000)
22. Kubrick, S.: 2001: A Space Odyssey. Metro-Goldwyn-Mayer, UK, USA (1968)
23. Leiderman, D.: The landscape of durance: utopianism and eastern europe in video games. Russ. Lit. **129**, 47–71 (2022). https://doi.org/10.1016/j.ruslit.2022.02.001
24. Maurer, E., et al.: Soviet Space Culture: Cosmic Enthusiasm in Socialist Societies. Palgrave Macmillan, Basingstoke (2011)
25. Number None: Braid. Number None, San Francisco, USA
26. Playdead: Inside. Playdead, Copenhagen, Denmark (2016)
27. Playdead: Limbo. Playdead, Copenhagen, Denmark (2010)
28. Privalov, R.: Space nostalgia: the future that is only possible in the past. Balt. Worlds. **15**(1–2), 52–56 (2022)

29. Seiwald, R.: Down with the Commies: Anti-Communist Propaganda in American Cold War Video Games. Paid. – Zeitschrift für Comput. (2021)
30. Siddiqi, A.A.: The red rockets' glare: spaceflight and the Soviet imagination, 1857–1957. Cambridge University Press, New York (2010)
31. Stage 2 Studios: Lifeless Planet: Premier Edition. Serenity Forge, Seattle, USA (2014)
32. Stewart, S.: On longing: Narratives of the Miniature, the Gigantic, the Souvenir, the Collection. Duke University Press, Durham (1993)
33. The Chinese Room: Little Orpheus. Secret Mode, Brighton, UK (2022)
34. Ubisoft Montreal: Prince of Persia: The Sands of Time. Ubisoft, Montreal, Canada (2003)
35. Vertical Robot: Red Matter. Vertical Robot, Madrid, Spain (2018)
36. Vertical Robot: Red Matter 2. Vertical Robot, Madrid, Spain (2022)
37. Zemeckis, R.: Back to the Future. Universal Pictures, USA (1985)

Adolescent Masculinity and the Geek Aesthetic: A Study of Gaming Magazine Imagery 1982 to 1993

Robin Bootes[✉]

Newcastle, UK
bobbootes@outlook.com

Abstract. This paper presents a study of the early UK specialist gaming press and charts how these vanguard texts helped initiate, and articulate, an emergent gamer culture, specifically in terms of producing a distinctly adolescent gaming aesthetic from pre-existing Fantasy and Sci-Fi tropes. Textually orientated discourse analysis is combined with content analysis to examine the illustrations used in over 100 magazines, both in terms of their cover pages and advertising content, in order to establish and examine their dominant tropes. Findings show the imagery used on the magazines prioritised certain themes and identities whilst excluding others. As such these texts acted as sites of masculine role-play, with idealised bodies and minds set within a network of fetishistic Fantasy and hi-tech environs. Crucially, these images would provide gamers with a diegetic bridge into the new game worlds they represented.

Keywords: gaming magazines · masculinity · geek culture · Fantasy art · Sci-Fi art

1 Introduction – The Gaming Magazine as Cultural Industry

As media texts the gaming magazine resists seriousness. They are juvenile, playful, consumerist guides, arguably little more than advertorials for software companies. Furthermore, they are guides for games that very few people play anymore. The magazines are ostensibly throwaway items, made obsolescent and superseded a few months after they went to print. Yet, increasingly these magazines are now being recognised within academia as an invaluable resource for the cultural-historical analysis of digital gaming. Whilst this study, and the research it forms part of (Bootes 2016) is focused on the UK, there is a growing body of work that is attempting to map gaming's cultural evolution through the local specialist press that supported it (Kirkpatrick 2015; Pasanen and Suominen 2019; Lima Pinto and Gouveia 2022). This new cartography of digital gaming could help address prior US-centric tendencies within games study, and provide a localized, yet international, understanding of the similarities and divergencies that exist across different gaming cultures (Swalwell 2021).

Before examining the magazines' contents, it would be useful to ask what relevance do old videogame magazines still have today, and indeed what level of significance

© The Author(s), under exclusive license to Springer Nature Switzerland AG 2024
L. Vale Costa et al. (Eds.): VJ 2023, CCIS 1984, pp. 217–237, 2024.
https://doi.org/10.1007/978-3-031-51452-4_16

did they have originally. To answer the last part first, the question of what gives them historical significance, part of what makes early UK videogaming magazines interesting as texts, invaluable as an archive, and a distinct category of media production, is their innovation and popularity. As publications designed specifically for the gaming sector they are globally the first of their type, and whilst initially niche they quickly grew into a strong specialist industry. By 1983 combined totals of home computer magazines were outselling women's magazines (Haddon 1988, p. 5), with some brand circulations passing 100,000 copies (Kirkpatrick 2015). To provide some context this is in a market where computer ownership was itself only at around 1 million. The chances are if you had a micro-computer you bought one of these magazines.

This level of popularity matters because it enabled them to inform many of the debates around computer usage, and gaming identity, that attended the expansion of videogames as an entertainment industry in the 1980s. Furthermore, whilst the niche character of videogame magazines might reduce what can be termed their 'scale' (the amount of the world they generate representations about), they do hold high degrees of 'repetition', 'commonality' and 'stability' (Fairclough 2003). As a result they do show a notably cohesive sense of identity.

The significance of the videogame magazine is connected to their role as record and agent of societal change, in that they both reflect, and construct, the tastes of their producers and consumers. They 'provide us with an invaluable archive through which we can chart the development of a culture and a way of speaking about computers and software that elevates games to a position of prominence.' (Kirkpatrick 2015, p. 13) As the Kirkpatrick quote emphasises, by understanding the gaming magazine we can gain a clearer awareness of how gaming as a culture emerged. The agency of these texts enables them to operate as elements of social events, they 'have causal effects – i.e. they bring about changes.' (Fairclough 2003, p. 8). Furthermore, from such a discourse analysis perspective, 'it is vital to understand these consequences and effects if we are to raise moral and political questions about contemporary societies,' (Fairclough 2003, p. 14).

In terms of who these magazines were significant to, whilst the early gaming magazine (in terms of readership) was the province of teenage boys in general (Haddon 1988; Kirkpatrick 2015), sub-culturally it was arguably geeks that engaged most fully with the texts as high-end users. As such the videogame magazine connects with a certain form of adolescent masculine subjectivity, one that Burill has termed 'Digital Boyhood' (Burrill 2008) – these postmodern characters are often defined by their intimate relationship to technology. Whilst they seem (due to their technological affiliations) to be inherently contemporary, these digital boys, or geeks/nerds, have been an identifiable cultural set in popular media since the early 1950s. As such the rise of the geek can be mapped on to the rise of a techno-scientific ideology in the post-war period.

To understand the appeal of early gaming magazines, and their choice of aesthetics, it is useful to briefly summarise the geek culture it both articulates and constructs. Traditional nerd or geek interests stereotypically include computers, Science Fiction and Fantasy (Kendall 2011), whilst their media image is 'asexual, intellectual, wimpy, uncool' (Kendall 2011, p. 515). Regarding computing, traditional physical prowess is supplanted by the promised potency of these new technologies, 'of an almost superhuman ability to control the inner workings of technology' (Lane 2017, p. 11).

The concept and territory of geek culture is not an uncontested one, and is more mainstream & nebulous now than in the 1980s/90s timeframe of this study. However, the content analysis performed in this study did find the dominant imagery of the sample clearly centred on such geek associated themes of action-adventure, Fantasy, and Sci-Fi, in what could be termed a thematic consonance with geek culture. Also, geek culture is posited to exist outside hegemonic masculinity, whilst retaining a 'hyperwhite' identity (Bucholtz 2001), where 'women and men of color are excluded entirely … protecting the superior economic and technological status of white men.' (Kendall 2011, p. 519). My content analysis also supports this hyperwhite/masculine theorem, as the magazines systematically exclude representations of both women and non-whites, with the exception of occasional fetishised imagery.

This paper will continue by examining the rest of the findings from the content analysis, and then go on to look at specific magazine covers from the sample, in relation to the dominant thematic categories of Fantasy and Sci-Fi and how they constituted a masculine geek aesthetic.

2 Sample and Methodology

The selection of the 6 magazine brands examined in this study was directed by a desire to be as inclusive and representative as possible - within the limits of the project. I have been extremely fortunate in that the gaming community are very active in their online preservation of these retro-gaming texts.

The content analysis sample for cover illustrations and advertising imagery comprised of 100 covers and 100 advertisements. The date range for the sample was 1982 to 1993, with the April and October issues for each of the 6 magazine titles being utilised. The 6 titles examined were *Sinclair User, Your Sinclair, CRASH, CVG, Computer Gamer, ACE*. The magazines chosen are representative of the two key formats of videogame magazine, that of platform specific and the multi-platform magazine. These magazines were all initially produced by different publishing companies – though several of them would be acquired by their rivals in the 'mergers' that occurred in the consolidation phase of videogame publishing during the mid-1980s.

This sampling approach seeks to add synchronic and diachronic value to the research. It is an approach which ensures not only the high profile 'successes' (e.g. *CVG, CRASH*) receive attention, but also the lesser-known 'failures' (*Computer Gamer*). It is a sample that looks to examine both those texts traditionally included and excluded from the gaming historical narrative.

After initial research into the available archive of gaming magazines it was decided that the mixed-genre format of the magazine medium would fit favourably with a mixed-methodological approach of content analysis and discourse anlaysis. My selection of such a methodology was informed by a variety of sources and factors: including the magazines themselves; the kinds of questions I wished to ask of them; and the existing literature on magazines regarding identity, consumerism, and representation.

Content analysis was chosen in order to produce valid inferences from the data, for a broad sample formed by different magazine brands, effectively and transparently over a substancial period of time (1981 to 1993). The use of textually orientated discourse analysis, informed by the work of Fairclough, would enable such inferences to be then further examined via a fine grain examination of the various visual genres that populate the gaming magazine.

This combination of methods can be seen as responding to the demand for pluralism made by the texts under examination, specifically by the hybrid nature of the texts. A textually orientated form of discourse analysis has been utilised for the fine detail of the analysis. It is an approach that encourages a consideration of the texts as being socially embedded, within an interlinked set of societal and institutional procedures and processes, which are both discursive and material. Within the CDA framework discourses are perspectives on the world. They are ways of seeing, which are related to the subject's position in the world, their identity, and their relationships to others. Through acts of mediation these discourses come to represent 'aspects of the world – the processes, relations and structures of the material world, the 'mental world' of thoughts, feelings, beliefs and so forth, and the social world.' (Fairclough 2003, p. 124).

Furthermore, through such representations 'Discourses not only represent the world as it is (or rather is seen to be), they are also projective, imaginaries, representing possible worlds which are different from the actual world, and tied in to projects to change the world in certain directions.' (Fairclough 2003, p. 124) For example, 'gaming as a male hobby' would be a discourse that is realized in its mediation by the gaming specialist press, either via the language of the reviews (Kirkpatrick 2015) or the hyper-masculine representations used on front covers. The importance of placing gaming discourse, as Lima et al. argue in their analysis of the gaming press in Portugal, within the broader societal one 'is because they are also a part of the dominant culture … provide a window to visualize how video games were typified, the profile of the public who integrated this niche, and the main social tensions of the time in which they appeared.' (Lima, Pinto and Gouveia 2022, p. 2) As such each of the discourses constructed by the gaming press work to include, exclude, prioritise, and subordinate the potentiality of what gaming culture might become.

3   Content Analysis Findings

The content analysis enacted for this study had 2 key propositions, these centre on visual themes and demographics. The first proposition is that the dominant visual themes within the sample would match the areas of interest conventionally marked as geeky (Kendall 2011). Initial examination of the archive led to the coding of twelve thematic categories (including other). The five dominant themes, comprising over 80% of the combined sample, did show a very high level of thematic correlation between the areas of publishing self-promotion and software marketing (see Table 1) – ie. Between the covers of the magazines and the adverts that heavily populated their interior. Specifically, they showed a prioritisation of Sci-Fi and Fantasy motifs, alongside a broader reliance upon the competition/combat centric discourse of sports, military conflict, and action adventure. It is significant that these themes are ones traditionally considered as masculine territories.

The second proposition was that the choice of representational subjects in the sample would mirror the male demographic of the publications (surveys performed by the magazines themselves consistently listed around 95% male readership, with an average age of 16), and favour images of white youthful males, representing women only

Table 1. Aesthetic thematic dominance.

Theme	Covers	Adverts
Sci-Fi	36%	30%
Fantasy	14%	14%
Military	9%	11%
Sports/Racing	9%	17%
Adventure	9%	13%

in secondary and supplementary roles. The archival sample did show, unsurprisingly, a substantial masculine bias in its choice of participants. Of those images where the participants were clearly gendered 89% featured a male only cast. The participants are also overwhelmingly white (96% of magazine covers showed white only participants). While a higher level of non-white participants (22%) were present in the advertising sample these exceptions mainly consisted of black athletes and highly mythical images of Oriental warriors. The content analyses would allow it to be argued that whites are presented as the representational norm, and non-whites are only present as physical and ideological fetish (in this case primarily a fantastical martial east). The whiteness of the participants in the sample can be seen as corresponding to a wider hyper-whiteness within geek culture.

Notably this study did find a key region of disconnect between the readership and the imagery being used to identify with them. The imagery may be, like the readership, white and masculine but the participants are overwhelmingly (90%) portrayed as adult (not as children or teens). Indeed, the represented participant is more likely to be elderly than child-like, due in part to the popularity of the wise Sage or Wizard figure. Therefore, whilst the idealised user is ostensibly being presented as an adult white male, the absence of the child, even of the teenager, reveals a central desire, and fear, within videogame culture. On one level play acts for the child as a drama of adulthood, a means of acting out the potency of the adult realm. Yet, there is also a fear of being seen as child-like, both within the spheres of production (the computer as low value toy) and consumption (play as infantile), which leads to an imagined world without children, where the only representation of childhood allowed is a parodic one. Accordingly, the few children that appear in the sample are rebellious icons Bart Simpson, and Jack the Nipper, both sub-cultural characters that connect to a key promise of the computer – adventure.

4   Action and Adventure – The Promises of Computing

'Try to think of something more exciting than a computer. What did you come up with: A trip up the Amazon, scoring a goal for England, landing on Mars or, maybe, beating the bank at Monte Carlo? A computer will give you the chance to do any of these in your own living room.' CVG1:3 (1981).

This extract from the 1981 launch issue of *CVG* serves as a useful introduction to the dominant discourse of gaming, that of adventure. When hailing the gamer, as a new type of entertainment user, the gaming magazine is presenting the core promise of the computer as fun and excitement, as adventure. This salesman's pitch contains the a priori that a computer *is* exciting in itself, rather than being a functional device per se (unless that function is to excite). The computer is presented as a gateway to extraordinary experiences, as an experiential interface. Access to these experiences (previously marginal to unattainable) are now presented as immediate and domesticated via the power of technology. Adventure will also act as the core conceptual metaphor that links the seemingly disparate themes and tropes that populate the covers of the 1980s videogame magazine, and the advertisements therein. Adventure is the conceptual node of the wider gaming aesthetic. It is what the images are about.

The content analysis carried out on these magazines, as previously outlined, revealed a reliance upon images of sports, action/adventure, Sci-Fi, and Fantasy. These broad genres are represented via established tropes and characters which shift and slide from the relatively every-day to the bizarre and exotic, from the concrete to the imaginary. These tropes include the racing driver, the footballer, the fighter, the cop, the soldier, the mercenary, the spy, the fighter pilot, the astronaut, the spaceship, a plethora of mythological creatures, wizards, knights, barbarians, princesses, sorceresses, and amazons. From sports cars to spaceships these images comprise an early gaming aesthetic, one that connects intertextually with pre-existing representational fields (Fantasy Art posters, album covers, illustration for pulp fiction novels, etc.). The connection between these various texts is both an aesthetic and a relationship, one where texts 'set up dialogical or polemical relations between their 'own' discourses and the discourses of others.' (Fairclough 2003, p. 128) This notion of relations is significant in that it acts as a reminder to consider the themes of gaming culture both alongside each other, and in connection to the wider cultural landscape.

Whilst artistic styles and technical execution varied from illustrator to illustrator, the subject matter on the magazine covers was notably consistent with that wider landscape. Perhaps most pertinently the themes evidenced across the sample are concurrent with contemporaneous comic book literature. Similar hypermasculine warrior /hypersexualized female tropes can be seen in strips such as Slaine from 2000AD (published by IPC Magazines), alongside its predecessor the Conan series by Marvel. Likewise, the science fiction spaceman has roots in comic art and the pulp fiction covers of the 1950s, with imagery owing much to publications such as Weird Science, Strange Worlds, et al. An evolution of this is the cinematic external spaceship composition, which is influenced by the book cover art of artists such as Chris Foss, and which in turn will be appropriated (and elevated in terms of cultural capital) by the British painter Glenn Brown in the 1990s. In terms of cross-pollination between mediums, Sci-Fi and Fantasy both owe much to the products of the film industry, whether it be the Rebel fighters of *Star Wars* or the lurking *Alien* of Rildey Scott. All these fields find a new site of coalescence on the covers of early gaming magazines.

In the remainder of this paper I shall focus on two areas that come to dominate the gaming cultural landscape, specifically Fantasy and Sci-Fi. Whilst these were already well established, albeit fringe areas of media interest in the 1980s, thirty years later they have obtained mainstream acceptance, and increased cultural capital, in both modern film, television, and videogames. Yet, notably, in the 8-bit era of limited computing verisimilitude it was the artwork for videogames, magazine covers, adverts, and software packaging that helped develop and disseminate this new gaming aesthetic, rather than any diegetic gaming content. It is my contention that whilst developing an aesthetic these representations maintained and challenged established notions of boyhood masculinity and technology. As such they form masculine murals of desire and aspiration.

In terms of conceptualising masculinity I have utilised several influential film theorists (Neale 1993; Tasker 1993; Jeffords 1994) that are contemporaneous to the magazines under examination. These pieces of early 1990s film theory have been chosen as they asked pertinent questions of gendered identity with regards to the genre of action cinema – a genre which contains many of the same action/adventure tropes as videogame magazines. This is not an attempt to map one academic field upon another, as has often been done with videogames, but to recognise that certain representations, desires, and identities traverse from one medium to another - though they may well change upon doing so. The key concepts that emerge from their academic work, with regards to my own, centre on processes of identification, the idea of the spectacular hard-body, narcissism, fetishism and female musculinity (or 'flex appeal').

To begin applying the theory to the sample I shall move to examine the theme of Fantasy, a land of Might & Muscle.

5   Drawing on the Past – The Use of Fantasy Tropes

The key male tropes from the magazine sample fall into a binary of might/magic, they are Warriors & Wizards. It should be noted that whilst that the Fantasy pantheon, as an aesthetic tradition, contains a large array of other related tropes (Knights, Elves, Dwarves, Bards, etc.), the Warrior and the Wizard were found to be most pervasive within the archive studied. What follows is firstly a brief summation of the tropes, followed by examples from the sample.

Wizards: are wielders of Magic, physically slight, possessing esoteric knowledge of the occult, able to command & subjugate, morally ambiguous, manipulative/controlling, and intellectual (See Fig. 1.1).

Warriors: possess strength, power/potency, muscularity, sexuality, wild - bound to nature (furs/long hair), tribal, aggressive, driven by base desires, lone warriors (See Fig. 1.2).

It should be noted these are highly condensed readings, and historically contingent to the era of the sample. Each of the tropes mentioned has a long and varied history outside the sphere of gaming, some going back millennia (as is the case with the classical mythic warrior). Yet, what this highly partial reading does begin to evoke is a certain segmentation within the modern Fantasy tradition. It is a Cartesian quantification of the subject into binaries of might/mind, chaos/order. Where the Barbarian is strong & chaotic, the Wizard has a controlling intellect, he is a form of proto-scientist – a technologist who orders the elements around him, subjugating matter to his sometimes malevolent will.

This division of the self into a quantifiable set of characteristics is an instrumental process, where attributes become abilities, which then allow certain actions to be performed. This is a process most clearly enunciated by the role-playing tradition that coalesced into *Dungeons & Dragons* (1974), a phenomenon that was a primary influence over early videogaming in general, and Fantasy illustration in particular. In *D&D*

the balance of the role-play, its rules and structure, rely upon an agreed set of skill specialisations, with each player choosing their abilities in terms of Strength, Intelligence, Wisdom, Constitution, Dexterity, and Charisma.

These qualities become testable quantities, ones that can succeed or fail within the dice-based realm of the gaming narrative. The Fantasy images under examination in this study contain those very same qualities, the same binaries. They can be seen to offer the male readership a fluid set of selectable identities, and constitute the parts of the psyche that are on parade for the gaming user to appropriate. Such an identification is not a simple mapping process, where the viewer sees and desires themselves as being reflected in the image, but is rather one where 'desire itself is mobile, fluid, constantly transgressing identities, positions, and roles.' (Neale 1993, p. 10) This conception of the identification process contains elements of narcissism and narrative play. In the case of the Wizard and the Warrior they talk of Order and Power, the power to protect the self, to change the body, and to order the world around to you.

Just as many action movies of the early 1980s performed as 'spectacular narratives about characters who stand for individualism, liberty, militarism, and a mythic heroism.' (Jeffords 1994, p. 16), so too the male Fantasy figures that populate many of the videogame magazine covers contain within them an idealised sense of masculinity. The body of the Warrior, which Jeffords describes as 'Hard Bodies', and their ever-ready phallic weaponry, is the key to their potency, their heroism. For 'what determines a hero is the possession of a hard body.' (Jeffords 1994, p. 53). In the case of the conventional Knight figure it is hardened with metal, but for the Barbarian it is a body-suit of hyperreal muscularity, one where 'The muscular male body functions as a sort of armour – it is sculpted and worked on' (Tasker 1993, p. 18). For Lane, in her work on geek culture, hypermasculinity 'has its roots in the exaggeration of masculine cultural stereotypes, usually with a corresponding hostility towards the feminine' (Lane 2017, p. 3). As this study can confirm, when women are present in the sample, the depictions of them are indeed often highly ambivalent and sexualized.

The Wizard, represents a different type of power to the Warrior, one that is less overtly militaristic. It is a soft form of power, one which is centred on persuasion and control. The Wizard's defining feature is their capacity for transmutation: the ability to transform one substance into another, convert thought into action, to conjure the ethereal, and adapt the elements to their bidding. They promise mastery, the power of the will over nature, mind over matter.

Both these male Fantasy figures, the Wizard and Warrior, and their popularity within the gaming imaginary, can be viewed as part of a response to the evolving expectations of manhood in the 1980s, specifically those often termed as the New Man - the need to be seen as emotionally engaged, and sensitive, whilst retaining vestiges of hegemonic masculinity. The Fantasy male figure enables two responses to this new set of responsibilities, firstly by eliding them, and secondly by deconstructing them.

Fantasy as a genre is highly capable of escaping questions of social responsibility due to its inherently fantastical nature in that it provides a parallel space to reality. A space where the usual conventions and social norms can be re-framed; a space where an alternate set of discourses can be established and explored. Whilst the Fantasy figure always has one foot in the reality that they exist outside of, they are nevertheless able to stand 'to one side of the conventional standards of social behaviour.' (Neale 1993, p. 30) Simply put, they offer the male reader an escape from the pressures and limitations of reality, a place where they can be both strong & wise, virtuous and barbaric. Ostensibly this reading would support Burrill's notion of an escapist digital imaginary (Burrill 2008).

Yet, if these Fantasy heroes do act as a form of idealised surrogate self for the reader then that heroic imago could still be a source of anxiety to the reader, as the 'ideal is something to which the subject is never adequate.' (Neale 1993, p. 13). In escaping the contradictions of the 1980s New Man they have potentially returned to an older, yet still unattainable ideal, a classical form of masculinity. A form of manhood that emanates from the revitalisation of the Fantasy literary genre between the 1930s and 1950s, via the work of such writers as Robert E. Howard (with his popular *Conan* series of stories).

However, a deconstruction of such idealised heroic masculinity is enabled (for the reader) via a process of fluid alternations - the identification with one trope after another, each one with a specific skill set. By having various moulds, or tropes, to enter/identify with, the reader can enact the various types of manhood that are expected of him, and do so without facing the inherent contradictions that exist within the concept of masculinity as a whole. In this context Fantasy imagery is not so much retrograde & escapist, but a strategic process of fluid gendered identifications. A mobile reconnaissance of the self, at one moment wise and caring, in another moment fierce and merciless. However, it could be argued that such recognition is always already misplaced, and is instead a form of meconnaissance. That these Fantasy figures are only ever part of a narcissistic illusion, representing 'phantasies of power, omnipotence, mastery and control.' (Neale 1993, p. 11).

Whether narcissistic or strategic, the male Fantasy tropes utilised by the videogame magazines are quintessentially about power, and provide a sliding scale of identifications. The Wizard represents technological power, centred on intellectual specialisation and the ability to control and convert nature into instrumental power. The Barbarian is pre-technological, raw elemental power. In Freudian terms these two figures would respectively relate to ego and id. These Fantasy tropes together form an adolescent narrative, a 'dramatization of the struggle to become powerful in difficult circumstance.' (Tasker 1993, p. 31). Therefore, Fantasy becomes a rational response to reality.

6 Princess, Amazon, and Sorceress – 'Welding Brass Tits on the Armour' (Altmann 1992)

The Fantasy female is a peripheral, and highly ambivalent, figure within the sample. As the content analysis revealed the participants represented on the covers, and in the adverts, of gaming magazines are overwhelmingly (89%) male. However, notable exceptions are the Fantasy figures of the Princess, Amazon, and Sorceress. Together they illustrate a turbulent set of contradictions that speak to exaggerated, sometimes bizarre, notions of femininity within the male gaming culture of the 1980s and early 1990s. Highly sexualised, they offer the readership processes of objectification and identification that involve both sadism and masochism, what has been termed 'the have me/be me axes of desire' (O'Day 2004, p. 204).

The scantily clad voluptuous female is a mainstay within 1970s & 1980s Fantasy illustration, with the work of artists, including Frank Frazetta and Boris Vallejo, often veering towards the pornographic in their idealisations. This element of voyeurism is clearly present within the sample. The imagery associated with the *Barbarian* (Fig. 1.4) and *Vixen* (Fig. 1.3) games were notorious within 80s gaming culture (Sci-Fi examples would include the art for *Game Over*). These images perform as comic Fantasy hyperboles, as 'parodic exaggerated characteristics of gendered identity.' (Tasker 1993, p. 14). Such exaggerations, whilst demeaning, are also innately comical, where the 'Humour is derived from the juxtaposition of the barely clad heroes and heroines (so clearly offered as sexual spectacle) with the intense earnestness of the mock mythologies constructed for these fantasy worlds.' (Tasker 1993, p. 28) As such Princess Marianna (*Barbarian*) is typical of the sexualised Fantasy Princess, alluring and passive, she enables the male to act out his heroic role as saviour and receive his voluptuous reward.

The *Vixen* photoshoot, used as both advertising image and magazine cover, is a highly standardised trope of the Amazonian style. The emphasis here is on an exaggerated and raw sexuality, an animal nature which is connoted via the faux-fur bikini costume. Athletic, rather than muscular, the Amazon represents a dichotomy: they are an active subject, whilst remaining the erotic object of visual spectacle. Such active subjects potentially disrupt the classic active/passive division, where narrative & spectacle exist separately. The male driving the story, and the female there to be seen. Yet, primarily the Amazonian *Vixen* represents a savage challenge to the male warrior, she is there to be subdued. She is the natural realm that must be conquered and made orderly.

A more ambiguous image is that of *Athena* (Fig. 2.1), as illustrated by Bob Wakelin. Athena can be seen as a female warrior figure that embodies 'a contradictory set of images of female desirability, a sexualised female image which emphasises physical strength and stature.' (Tasker 1993, p. 14) Such embodiments are arguably very much about the mapping of masculine traits on to the feminine body. These images can therefore be viewed as the de-othering of the female, where via the addition of musculature the feminine is made masculine, a process of 'welding brass tits on the armour' (Altmann 1992) – this quote from one of Altmann's female students perfectly captures the rather shallow feminising of essentially masculine tropes. Such a process thereby allows the male reader to convert threatening difference into the already known and comfortable.

Whilst these sexualised images of women may be provided to the reader for purely voyeuristic pleasures, active images like *Athena* may be performing other roles for that readership. Are these female figures instead part of the parade of the self mentioned earlier, one more role for the teenage reader to play out? These Fantasy females are clearly defined in part by their strength: 'these heroines have physical prowess, in swordplay or marksmanship, a strength that marks them as transgressive, as perverse.' (Tasker 1993, p. 30) They can also be seen as controlling figures, offering the male reader fantasies of masochistic domination. Such transgression is key to understanding the final female trope, that of the Sorceress.

The front cover of *CRASH18* (Fig. 2.2) from 1985 explicitly depicts the Sorceress as a dominatrix. Here she forces the male figure to kneel chained at her feet, subjected to her will, in the same manner that the reader is subjected to her gaze. Like the Sirens in Homer's *Odyssey* these magical figures traditionally overwhelm the hero by means of manipulation and seduction. They offer a masochistic scenario for the male reader, but their power is soft, rather than hard muscularity. It is their hyper-femininity that makes them lead roles in a castration tale of loss, 'a dramatizing of the pleasures of empowerment and the fear of powerlessness.' (Tasker 1993, p. 18).

Yet, whilst such complex processes are potentially at play, and are certainly available to the male reader, the reality is arguably more straightforward. The provision of the *Athena* image in poster form by many of the gaming magazines suggests a more overtly erotic function for these images. They are acceptable soft-porn bedroom decoration. As the men of Fantasy exist on a scale of Order and Power so the women of Fantasy literature exist on a sliding scale, one that moves between the classic binary of object/subject, and passive/active. They are male fantasy sites of heroism and domination, victory and subjugation. The further along the scale you go, the more powerful the Fantasy female, the more potentially transgressive and masochistic the identification. The next section will explore the most dominant of the genres in this sample, one that was over twice as recurrent as the Fantasy realm, that of Sci-Fi.

7 Science Fiction as a Genre of Illustration

The genre of Sci-Fi illustration is one with a diverse and rich history. This study wishes to locate the aesthetic of videogame magazines within that history, especially with regards to Sci-Fi illustration, and the dominant tropes that populate those illustrations.

The videogame magazine, as an aesthetic space for Sci-Fi illustration, is part of a publishing lineage that goes back to the 1920s, where such American titles as *Weird Tales* (1923), and *Amazing Stories* (1926) provided an outlet for Fantasy and Sci-Fi illustration via their covers. These were later joined by such British magazines as *New Worlds* (originally *Novae Terrae* 1936). Whilst *Weird Tales* focused mainly on gothic horror and the occult, a distinct Sci-Fi pulp fiction scene can be said to have emerged in the inter-war and post-war eras. For a history of the medium, the informed, exhaustive, and comprehensive work of Mike Ashley (Ashley 2000) is an invaluable source. Sci-fi and Fantasy art illustration as a genre would flourish via these magazines, and it is my contention that the videogame magazine cover offered an additional supplementary outlet in the 1980s. One that shared a key demographic, and a certain set of discourses, as it coalesced around gaming culture.

The central common ground between the Sci-Fi illustrations utilised by videogame magazines and gaming culture is a shared fascination with the relationship between the individual, the social, and the technological. It is perhaps an obvious point, but one that it is important to re-iterate, that Sci-Fi is not about the future, or possible futures, but rather it uses those future scenarios as a backdrop to explore present anxieties and desires. As such it is 'a time machine that goes nowhere, for wherever it goes it materialises the same conjunctions of the space-time continuum: the conundrums of Western civilisation.' (Sardar and Cubitt 2002, p. 1) Furthermore, with regards to this scientistic worldview, 'Science fiction is both afraid of science and in love with science.' (Sardar and Cubitt 2002, p. 5).

This notion of ambivalence (to the imagined referent of an idealised 'science') is a useful starting point in understanding the images within the sample. For in this section

I shall ask if this ambivalence does exist, then what types of fears and desires are being constructed in the texts, and how do they relate to their users. It is not a question of whether those fears or aspirations are 'real' or not, fact or fiction, but why do they come to dominate this particular social imaginary.

Indeed from a constructivist perspective Sci-Fi is a fiction that produces reality, and can be said to operate both as a 'normative genre' (Sardar and Cubitt 2002), and as a 'genre of governance' (Fairclough 2003), in that it is part of the discourse that determines what is allowed and what is excluded. It's not just little green men and spaceships (though there are a lot of them too).

The genre of Sci-Fi is one that grounds itself in the formulaic, in that formulaic conventions provide the readership with purchase upon often otherwise unwieldy and esoteric narratives. In his introduction to the subject Roberts (Roberts 2000) isolates 6 categories, or conventions, by which the standard Sci-Fi narrative operates:

1. Spaceships, interplanetary or interstellar travel.
2. Aliens and encounters with aliens.
3. Mechanical robots, genetic engineering, biological robots.
4. Computers, advanced technology, virtual reality.
5. Time travel, alternative history.
6. Futuristic utopias and dystopias.

Of these 6 categories only the first two (spaceships/aliens) appear with any regularity in the sample, whilst the third (robots) appear surprisingly rarely. The fourth (computers) could be said to be implicit within all the others, whilst the final 2 categories receive no explicit engagement by the texts. Therefore, it can be said that these magazines prioritise what is often termed hard sci-fi, as opposed to the softer, more cerebral variety. This study will take the first two categories and examine them in terms of the metaphors they draw upon and in turn reproduce; the types of identity that they enable and encourage.

It is significant that several of the magazine titles in the sample (*CVG*, *CRASH*, *Computer Gamer*) use the trope of the Alien on the covers of their all-important launch issues - so close is the association between Sci-Fi & videogaming. This suggests that for the new sector of 1980s videogame magazine publishing the established tropes of Sci-Fi are a natural discursive fit. The ideal language in which to speak to their potential readership. This bond between Sci-Fi and videogaming was in part constructed in the 1970s via such arcade successes as *Space Invaders* (1978), *Galaxian* (1979), and the innumerable clones of them that emerged in the early 1980s.

In terms of them & us, of determining those individuals and ideas who are included and excluded by social discourse, the Alien stands at the edges. As such these 'Monsters have always defined the limits of community in Western imaginations.' (Haraway, 1990, p. 56). The role of the Alien as monstrous, and its prevalence in the sample, offers a means of questioning the limits of the gaming community's social imaginary, of what is acceptable and what is not, and of interrogating the kinds of identity on offer.

Fig. 1. From top left in clockwise order: Fig. 1.1 *CVG cover* April 1985 Wizard as soft power; Fig. 1.2 *Computer Gamer* cover April 1986 – hypermasculine warriors; Fig. 1.3 *Vixen* (1988) image used as both advertisement/poster and cover image. Figure 1.4 *Barbarian* (1987) advert, released as advert & free poster.

Fig. 2. From top left in clockwise order: Fig. 2.1 *Athena* (1987) image by Bob Wakelin was released as both advert image and free poster in several magazines; Fig. 2.2 *CRASH* cover July 1985 – the lure of the Sorceress; Fig. 2.3 *CVG* launch issue cover November 1981, little green men search out their readers; *CRASH* cover October 1984 - the Spaceman as frontier hero.

Fig. 3. From top left in clockwise order: Fig. 3.1 *Computer Gamer* cover April 1985 benign alien observer; Fig. 3.2 *CVG* cover October 1986 – the capital ship of empire; Fig. 3.3 *CRASH* magazine cover October 1986 - the gamer re-imagined as jubilant alien pilot; Fig. 3.4 *CRASH* cover October 1985 raiders or defenders?

8   Beasts, Invaders, and the Benign

There are three essential Alien tropes within the magazine sample, which exist on a scale of sophistication, ranging from the bestial to the benign. Similar to the Warriors and Wizards of the Fantasy realm they present a conceptual range, from monsters of the id to masters of the ego. The Alien-Beast is the basest type (Fig. 2.4), the primal allegory of the Alien as unthinking animal (cunning creatures perhaps, but without civilization). Whether they have tentacles or claws they operate as targets for man's technological prowess. These Beasts serve to highlight man's progress and are closest to the 'monstrous mothers' of feminist film theory. These others must meet their nemesis in the imago of the classic spaceman (Fig. 2.4). The spaceman here represents the noble explorer-hunter, a civilising force, bound to technology, encased in a fragile shell of control. He is a recycled version of the Victorian adventurer, akin to Haggard's Allan Quatermain (*King Solomon's Mines*). Therefore, the classic spaceman can be regarded as emblematic of hegemonic Western masculinity, and the Alien Beast's role is to populate a space safari, one that enables the performance of his masculinity and prowess, his frontier heroism.

The mid-range of Alien sophistication can be termed the Space Invader (or Little Green Man), and these Aliens have much in common with the classic Aliens of HG Well's *War of the Worlds*, in that they are 'unknowable, fanatic, equipped with superior technology, bloodthirsty, merciless and cruel.' (Sardar and Cubitt 2002, p. 6) This trope, as epitomised by the 1981 launch cover of *CVG* (Fig. 2.3) is the one most distinctly identified with the medium of videogaming, due to the success of the arcade original *Space Invaders*. Of the three Alien types these Invaders are arguably presented as the greatest threat, due to their possession and control of technology. They are dark reflections of our heroic spaceman, where we explore they Invade, and represent a subverting of the Western heroic-vision of science.

Whilst the Alien is generally presented as violent, aggressive, and antagonistic, there is an alternate trope – the cerebral, physically slight, benign E.T. explorer (Fig. 3.1). These are binary opposites to the savage beast, and represent an idealised image of Western civilisation projected into the future, a future that then returns to view us from without. They are not monsters of the id, but mimetic creatures of the ego. In this regard Sci-Fi literature can be viewed as a modern version of 19th Century anthropology (Sardar and Cubitt 2002), which sees itself in the lives of the other. Through such an empirical lens planetary types and entire civilisations are classified and categorised.

These three Alien tropes, Beast, Invader, Benign, represent a certain type of Western technological Imaginary, a scale of sophistication that ranges from the primordial savage to cerebral detachment. Where the Fantasy realm reflects upon issues of order and power, here the emphasis is on technological mastery and the unknown, the seductions of a scientistic and instrumental ideology, and the promises of empire building. Furthermore, 'For the political imagination, sf created tools with which audiences could imagine the steady consolidation of technoscientific hegemony, defined by the drive to construct a universal regime of technoscience … a technoscientific empire.' (Bould et al. 2009, p. 362) This hegemony of science and technology is an idea best typified by the trope of the Spaceship.

9   The Medium of Technology - the Spaceship

'Wherever we look, the colonising, imperial mission of science fiction is hard to miss.' (Sardar and Cubitt 2002, p. 16).

The image of the spaceship, and a broad section of the Sci-Fi genre (as typified by *Star Trek*), has been connected in academic discourse with issues of empire and hegemony. The colonising spaceship becoming a metaphor for scientific triumphalism, where new frontiers replace those of the Wild West, and where science replaces the sheriffs badge as the 'warrant to colonise and control.' (Sardar and Cubitt 2002, p. 9) In this section I shall utilise the magazine sample to question and expand upon this perspective. Whilst the Sci-Fi novel offers great scope for a nuanced discussion of, and elaboration upon, such issues as hegemony (Ian M. Banks *Culture* series often centres itself on such a debate), the distilled medium of illustration must instead rely upon pre-existing tropes. The key question here is what kind of reality does the spaceship enable? As imagined evocative objects (Turkle 2011) what do they make us think about.

Upon examining the sample it became evident that there are two main types of ship being portrayed: firstly the big capital ships of empire already referred to (Fig. 3.2). These ships of state are the explorers and colonisers of the sci-fi genre. The notion of progress as a journey, specifically a maritime journey, has particular entailments – movement, hierarchical order (crew), the crossing of borders, direction/purpose, discovery and conquest. Such a metaphor of the trade/war ship connects smoothly to previous conceptions of empire and imperial trade. In the Sci-Fi milieu the zero-g of deep space can be seen as connecting to the monetarist ideals of friction-free capitalism, and to the attendant neoliberalist discourse of post-industrial digital utopias (Dyer-Witheford 1999).

Therefore, the exploring grand spaceship represents a metaphor for such technological determinism and a neo-liberal conception of economic order. They are the digital capitalists who are constructing 'a new world of low-friction, low-overhead capitalism, in which market information will be plentiful and transaction costs low.' (Gates et al. 1995, p. 171). These notions of technologically determined free enterprise have historically served as both theory, rationale, and policy legitimization. By the mid-1980s this ideology had become a material force, shaping modern reality. It can be viewed as a partisan prophecy of a future without ideology and without end, where there is only eternal progress. As such these vast ships work to present such progress as inevitable, but it is a progress that must still be steered; there must be captains for this industry. One promise to the readers of the videogame magazine is that they can be those very captains, masters and commanders of the Information revolution. Yet, there is a second, arguably more dominant (certainly more recurrent) image of the spaceship in the illustrations examined; a second type of metaphor and promise.

Numerous illustrations of small and agile fighter ships populate the sample. If the large ships can be said to represent hegemony, and neo-liberal authority, then these small ships would seem to be images of rebellion and individuality - always portrayed in action they are inherently combative and resistant. However, whilst they may appeal to a youthful and rebellious demographic, are these representations opposing or supporting the existing order; are these raiders or defenders?

The prevalence of images where small craft attack larger ships (Fig. 3.4) does suggest a level of opposition to the hegemonic metaphor. Brought into a collective by a common enemy the fighter ships operate as sub-cultural pirate squadrons that dodge and weave around the powerful state-ships. This resonates with a concurrent wider debate within technological circles concerning the popularity of PC vs mainframes during the early 1980s. In both cases there is a level of ambivalence and a critique towards technology, where the grand narrative of progress is deconstructed by the individual users. Whereas the large ships represent the use of technology to control society and produce social change, the nimble fighter ships connect with an individualistic desire to control the direction of technology itself, and to be immersed within it.

However, these images are still inherently about power and control; the potency of technology itself is never in question. Instead, the space fighter-pilot becomes a metaphor for the interface between man and machine, and it is only a question of where you point the technology. It should be noted that where women were under-represented and objectified within the realm of Fantasy, they are entirely absent when it comes to Sci-Fi representations in this sample. Spacemen are very much men, reinforcing the notion that 'technologies are associated with values that Western culture identifies as masculine symbols, which allows a greater approximation of the technological artefact to the male gender.' (Lima, Pinto and Gouveia 2022, p. 6).

The illustrations used by videogame magazines on their covers reveal a nuanced engagement with pre-existing Sci-Fi tropes that goes beyond their original remit of boosting retail magazine sales. Furthermore, they do work to advance one trope in particular, and in doing so help develop a new metaphor: that of the active-user. Where 'You' become the space-pilot (see Fig. 3.3), and are built into the very interface itself. This is achieved via devices of opacity and disembodiment, which in turn produce what Lupton terms a technosocial subject (Lupton 1995). A subject that is idealised and impervious, the apotheosis of a post-Enlightenment separation of body and mind. This is an aspect that joins the seemingly disparate fields of Fantasy and Sci-Fi imagery, a Cartesian segmentation of the subject into might/mind (the Warrior vs the Wizard), and flesh/circuitry. Furthermore, the spaceships illustrated in the sample are not objects for passive reflection, but empty vessels awaiting active engagement; they require a controller in order to function.

This interactive quality is conveyed by obscuring the presence, or identity, of any on-board active agents. The ships generally either have no visible pilot (especially with the large ships), the pilot's face is obscured via an opaque helmet visor, or the angle of the depiction (commonly from above and behind, in gaming parlance 3rd person view) hides their face from view. In doing so the ships becomes trapped in stasis, and in order for the image to function the reader must occupy a position within the cybernetic network of the cockpit. Similar to the cyborg being an idealised form of masculinity, or superman (Halacy 1965), the fighter pilot has a long history as an emblem of individualised heroic masculinity. As such these new 'Knights of the Sky' offer a potent source of fantasy, and an imaginary means of escape from the dilemmas of daily life.

This escape is not just from the user's own reality, but from the body in general, and as such it forms part of that 'central utopian discourse around computer technology … the potential offered by computers for humans to escape the body.'(Lupton 1995). By entering into the cybernetic interface of the cockpit the reader-user can obtain the 'control and communication' (Wiener 1965) between self and technology that is the central promise of cybernetics and Sci-Fi discourse. This is a shoring up of the masculine subject by the always already masculine gendered resource of technology. These fantasies of disembodiment are common across cyberculture, be it the fiction of Gibson, or the theory of Haraway (Haraway 1990). The physical body is always secondary and must be transcended. It is 'meat' a hindrance to total immersion in the cyberscape. The Empty Cockpits of Sci-Fi provide one means of such imagined immersion.

10 Conclusion

The tendency to prioritise the white male in gaming has been clearly noted in other areas of contemporary videogaming culture, with extensive research carried out regarding the hyper-sexualisation of videogame characters (Williams et al. 2009; Downs and Smith 2010; Martins et al. 2011). My findings expand on these studies in two ways. Firstly, by examining gaming magazines rather than games – the non-diegetic rather than the diegetic – and secondly by putting the participants into their wider thematic framework (in this case the genres of Fantasy and Sci-Fi). Thereby asking not only what kind of imagery dominates, but how do those images relate to wider conceptions of technology and masculinity.

To conclude, I would like to raise the spectre of escapism and regression. A recurrent moral panic around videogaming, gamer culture, and fan based cultures more generally, is that they encourage a disconnection from reality, and are escapist, obsessive and juvenile (Jenkins 2012). The Fantasy imagery discussed here, with its hyper-masculine and hyper-feminine fetishes, and the fascination Sci-Fi has with escaping the body and voyaging into the unknown would ostensibly support such 'technonostalgic' criticism. However, it needs to be recognised that this question of regression and escapism is itself partly one of demographics, in citing Erikson, Sherry Turkle notes, 'the playing adult steps sideward into another reality; the playing child advances forward into new stages of mastery.' (Turkle 1995, p. 204) This highlights the difficulty when discussing the cultural practices of a group whose core demographic exists on the borders between the child and the adult. Their liminal status raises the problematic of which direction the subject is stepping, forwards or to the side. Rather than regressive I would argue that the imagery analysed in this chapter acted in an enabling role for its readership, providing a cast of characters, and a range of settings, for the users to playfully experiment with. A means of dramatizing their own experiences of change and loss. Over time the young geeks who imagined themselves in these images would have the potential to become more inclusive and diverse, rather than exclusive and homogeneous. A collection of stranger things rather than a clique of vengeful Nerds.

What can be stated with confidence is that the use of such vibrant and creative illustrations on the covers of videogame magazines did fulfil an important function, which was to enable the reader to step more easily into the coarsely pixelated games on offer. These images smoothed out the transition from the real into the simulation, and the pluralistic identities that formed on those cover pages helped connect the inner game world with the expectations and desires of the user. In her cyborg manifesto Haraway writes that 'By the late twentieth century, our time, a mythic time, we are all chimeras, theorized and fabricated hybrids of machine and organism.' (Haraway 1990, p. 35)

In the 1980s it was the distinctly non-digital realm of Fantasy and Sci-Fi magazine illustration that enabled such a fusion for the videogame entertainment industry. The chimeric characters it helped create continue to exist, both on and off the screen, in the contemporary cultural imaginary.

Bibliography

Altmann, A.E.: Welding brass tits on the armor: an examination of the quest metaphor in Robin McKinley'sThe Hero and the Crown. Children's Literat. Educ. **23**(3), 143–156 (1992)

Ashley, M.: The time machines: The story of the science-fiction pulp magazines from the beginning to 1950. Liverpool University Press Liverpool (2000)

Bootes, R.: The emergence of gamer culture and the gaming press: the UK videogame magazine as cultural and consumer guide, 1981–1993. Newcastle University (2016)

Bould, M., et al.: The Routledge companion to science fiction. Routledge (2009)

Bucholtz, M.: 'The whiteness of nerds: Superstandard English and racial markedness'. J. Linguistic Anthropol. Wiley Online Library **11**(1), 84–100 (2001)

Burrill, D.A.: Die tryin': Videogames, masculinity, culture. Peter Lang (2008)

Downs, E., Smith, S.L.: Keeping abreast of hypersexuality: a video game character content analysis. Sex Roles **62**(11–12), 721–733 (2010)

Dyer-Witheford, N.: Cyber-Marx: Cycles and circuits of struggle in high-technology capitalism. University of Illinois Press (1999)

Fairclough, N.: Analysing discourse: Textual analysis for social research. Psychology Press (2003)

Gates, B., et al.: 'The road ahead'. Viking New York (1995)

Haddon, L.G.: The roots and early history of the British home computer market: Origins of the masculine micro. Imperial College London (University of London) (1988)

Halacy, D.S.: Cyborg: Evolution of the superman. Harper & Row (1965)

Haraway, D.: A manifesto for cyborgs: Science, technology, and socialist feminism in the 1980s'. Feminism/postmodernism. New York, pp. 190–233

Jeffords, S.: Hard bodies: Hollywood masculinity in the Reagan era. Rutgers University Press (1994)

Jenkins, H.: Textual poachers: Television fans and participatory culture. Routledge (2012)

Kendall, L.: '"White and nerdy": Computers, race, and the nerd stereotype', J. Popular Culture. Wiley Online Library **44**(3), 505–524 (2011)

Kirkpatrick, G.: The formation of gaming culture: UK gaming magazines, 1981–1995. Springer (2015)

Lane, K.E.: Age of the geek: Depictions of nerds and geeks in popular media. Springer (2017)

Lima, L., Pinto, C. and Gouveia, P.: 'Genesis of a Gaming Culture: a Historical Analysis Based on the Computer Press in Portugal' (2022)

Lupton, D.: The embodied computer/user. Body & Society. SAGE publications **1**(3–4), 97–112 (1995)

Martins, N., et al.: Virtual muscularity: a content analysis of male video game characters. Body Image. Elsevier **8**(1), 43–51 (2011)

Neale, S.: Reflections on men and mainstream cinema. Screening the male: Exploring masculinities in Hollywood cinema, p. 9 (1993)

O'Day, M.: Beauty in motion: Gender, spectacle and action babe cinema. Action and adventure cinema. Routledge London and New York, pp. 201–218 (2004)

Pasanen, T., Suominen, J.: Examining the Gaming Subcultures through the Lens of Finnish Game Journalism: From the 1980s to the 2010s. EasyChair (2019)

Roberts, A.C.: The History of Science Fiction: Page 48 in', Science Fiction (2000)

Sardar, Z. and Cubitt, S.: Aliens r us: The other in science fiction cinema. Pluto Press London

Swalwell, M.: Game history and the local. Springer Nature (2021)

Tasker, Y.: Spectacular bodies: Gender, genre and the action cinema. Routledge (1993)

Turkle, S.: Life on the Screen: Identity in the Age of the Internet London. Weidenfeld and Nicolson (1995)

Turkle, S.: Evocative objects: Things we think with. MIT press (2011)

Wiener, N.: Cybernetics or Control and Communication in the Animal and the Machine. MIT press (1965)

Williams, D., et al.: 'The virtual census: Representations of gender, race and age in video games. New Media & Society. Sage Publications Sage UK: London, England 11(5), 815–834 (2009)

For a Pragmatic Study of the Generic Categorization of Video Games: The Case of Survival Horror

François-Xavier Surinx$^{(\boxtimes)}$ (iD)

University of Liege, 4000 Liege, Belgium
fxsurinx@uliege.be

Abstract. The study of video game genres has been largely inspired by theories from other media, notably literature and film. In doing so, it has also taken up the aporias of these other theories, the question of genres never having found truly satisfactory answers. I will focus here on the case of survival horror in order to explore three types of generic theory (formalist, emotional and semio-pragmatic) and to expose their strengths, their weaknesses, in particular by pointing out the relative artificiality of certain approaches. Then, on the basis of the comments made, I will set out the criteria that should be considered as part of a generic classification close to the actual use of gamers, who remain the main people interested in the use of genres. However, the exact methodology for taking such criteria into account has yet to be defined.

Keywords: Generic classification · Survival Horror · Reception · Formalism · Pragmatics · Emotions

1 Generic Classification: An Age-Old Problem

As far back as antiquity, human beings were already thinking about how to classify cultural works. With his *Poetics* [1], Aristotle was probably the first to propose a classification model that we represent today in the form of a double-entry table [2]: on the abscissa, the modes of representation (dramatic or narrative); on the ordinate, the nature of the objects (superior or inferior). This gives us four genres: tragedy (superior dramatic), epic (superior narrative), comedy (inferior dramatic) and parody (inferior narrative) (Fig. 1).

Despite the ingenuity of this theory, it remains fallible in certain respects. A structuralist before his time, Aristotle drew up a rigid table that did not allow for the inclusion of hybrid works. Today, it would be hard to place most literary works within this framework, given their tendency to evolve rapidly, seeking out new and original paths[1].

---

[1] Unfortunately, very few texts have survived from antiquity compared to the authors' actual output, and those that have reached us are probably among the most exemplary in terms of the aesthetic criteria recommended for each genre, the concept being highly prescriptive at the origin [3]. So, it is possible that many of the works that have come down to us may have introduced significant variations in the classic generic schemes, without poeticians even taking note of these evolutions.

© The Author(s), under exclusive license to Springer Nature Switzerland AG 2024
L. Vale Costa et al. (Eds.): VJ 2023, CCIS 1984, pp. 238–253, 2024.
https://doi.org/10.1007/978-3-031-51452-4_17

MODE OBJET	DRAMATIQUE	NARRATIF
SUPÉRIEUR	tragédie	épopée
INFÉRIEUR	comédie	parodie

Fig. 1. Double-entry table based on Aristotle's generic classification in *Poetics* [2, p. 19]

Since then, many scholars have set out to find new ways of classifying works, especially literary works, with always relative success. Whether it is Aristotle's followers who use multi-entry tables (with the problem of creating numerous empty cells) or researchers attempting to establish biological trees (with the problem that works do not act like living beings), the many methods of classification, even when they work at the outset, never seem able to stand up to the passage of time and the appearance of new works, in addition to being confronted with the gaze of critics interpreting works in cultural contexts that vary both in time and space [4] (Fig. 2).

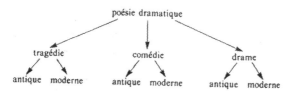

Fig. 2. Tree diagram of the subdivisions of dramatic poetry according to Georg Wilhelm Friedrich Hegel. Jean-Marie Schaeffer points out that modern forms have evolved in ways that bring them closer to other forms. For example, ancient tragedy, which depicts the opposition of certain social forces (city and family for example), has no modern descendants, and, in fact, modern tragedy is more similar to modern drama. However, biologically, such a transfer raises a few difficulties [4, p. 44].

Like literature, video games have also quickly come to grips with the phenomenon of generic classification, often echoing the aporias of theories developed in literature and cinema. In this article, I will focus on some of the generic theories developed specifically for video games, to highlight some of the classification issues facing this medium. Indeed, just as cinema and literature (but also all the other cultural objects I will not be dealing with here, such as painting, music and comics) benefit from their own semiotic frameworks, video games have a number of particularities specific to their genericity and their classification into genres. I will use the survival horror genre as a case study, since it has a few specificities that make its circumscription complex, and it has already been the subject of study by several researchers. In order, I will analyse a historical and formal approach to the genre, followed by a cluster of theories based on the psychology of emotions and, finally, a semio-pragmatic theory.

Next, I will consider a way of overcoming the aporias highlighted, at least from the point of view of generic logic and, above all, of the authority to be considered in establishing a generic classification, which will lead to a new vision of the genre.

Indeed, it would seem both vain and arrogant to attempt to establish a rigorous method of classification for an object as polymorphous and fluid as genres. However, without renouncing all classification (which would be just as futile, since genres exist whether we like it or not), I think it would be useful to rethink the criteria governing genericity today.[2]

2 Survival Horror: Questions Surrounding a Mutating and Polymorphous Genre

There are several reasons why survival horror is an ideal subject for a study of the specific features of video game genres. First, Mark J. P. Wolf [5] has pointed out that genres in this medium tend to fall into two categories: on the one hand, those with a thematic, iconographic or narrative dimension; on the other, those that describe gameplay or the nature of interactivity. Taking up this distinction, Dominic Arsenault and Martin Picard [6] distinguish between thematic genres and strictly video game genres (which I prefer to call mechanical genres, to avoid confusion with a broader category that encompasses all genres that may belong to video games, including thematic genres).[3] So, survival horror belongs to both categories, which makes its classification complex. Indeed, if classification is based solely on the genre name, games belonging to survival horror should offer both a horrific experience (thematic component) and, on the other hand, an experience centred on survival (mechanical component, or game principle). I will be showing the difficulties of such a definition shortly.

Furthermore, survival horror is regularly cited as the genre par excellence for inducing fear in the player [8]. Compared with other genres, this definition is of considerable interest, since the emphasis here is not on the game's thematics or mechanics, but directly on the player's feelings. However, as we shall see, such a definition is not without its difficulties.

2.1 Defining a Genre by Its History and Formal Features?

According to Dominic Arsenault's thesis [9] (which draws on the theories of Alastair Fowler [10] and Eric Zimmerman [11]), the evolution of a genre goes through three phases. First, an innovative work emerges, defining a new paradigm by introducing significant innovations. However, this first work is not recognised as being of exceptional quality: on the one hand, we can imagine that the creation of innovations goes through a testing phase during which it is observed that certain novelties work, while others have to be modified or abandoned; on the other hand, the audience of this first work is often

---

[2] In the interests of honesty, I warn the reader that this article is an update on the progress of my doctoral thesis about video game genres. Despite some of the wording, which may seem assertive or prescriptive, I would also like to stress that some of the ideas developed in the following lines are to be understood as research proposals that I believe will help improve our understanding of the complex phenomenon of genres.

[3] It should be noted that this bipartition is based on the most common and recognisable generic labels, which is useful for my purpose. However, other researchers distinguish more generic categories (based, for example, on the game support or the number of players). [7]

not the most receptive, as it has to adapt to new thematics or mechanisms that appear curious at first sight. Secondly, a paradigmatic work is born. It refines the proposals of the innovative work and erases its major flaws to deliver a more accomplished product. Such a work then sees its model taken up by various creators who attempt to restore the successful formula while adding enough innovations to make their production stand out. Thirdly, by dint of iterations on a proven basic model, an ultimate work is born. Acknowledged by a vast community, the ultimate work is deemed too mature to benefit from significant improvements, forcing creators to find relevant innovations and, in the process, relaunch a new cycle of creation.

If we follow this theory, the origins of survival horror can probably be traced back to the early 1990s. According to Bernard Perron [12], the first game to adopt survival horror mechanics and thematics (an innovative work) was *Alone in the Dark* [13] in 1992, a French game developed by Frédérick Raynal. The game features a number of landmark characteristics: a horrific bestiary inspired by gothic and Lovecraftian thematics, a fragile avatar, limited resources that are difficult to access, controls that the player has to struggle with, fixed camera angles [14]. Four years later, Shinji Mikami drew inspiration (unofficially[4]) from *Alone in the Dark* to create the paradigmatic work *Resident Evil* [15]. While the bestiary shifts from fantastic creatures to the undead, the atmosphere remains similar, and the gameplay echoes the inventions of *Alone in the Dark*. A noteworthy fact is that it was also Capcom who introduced the survival horror label and used it to better promote its subsequent games. After the release of *Resident Evil*, several years followed in which development studios repeated the formula perfected by Capcom, introducing new thematics (allegorical monsters and a sticky town in *Silent Hill* [18], spectres and a haunted mansion in *Fatal Frame* [19]) and variations in gameplay (moving camera in *Silent Hill*, first-person view in *Fatal Frame*). In 2005, Capcom closed the cycle initiated with *Resident Evil* by releasing *Resident Evil 4* [20], which brought the saga, and indeed the whole survival horror genre, to a new level of gaming experience: the camera switched to TPS view, confrontations became more brutal, the avatar became less fragile and the bestiary, despite the ever-present horrific theme, now inspired less anguish.

According to Perron's theory, survival horror came to an end with the release of *Resident Evil 4*. From this pivotal event onwards, the researcher thinks that the genre has evolved too much for future games to still carry the survival horror label, a label intended for games applying a formula close to that proposed by the first *Resident Evil*. In fact, Perron points out that even Capcom seems to want to break away from this label on the back of the *Resident Evil 4* game box: "FORGET EVERYTHING YOU KNOW ABOUT RESIDENT EVIL. Forget Survival Horror. This is the most epic and horrific action game ever." [12, p. 221].

Perron notes a dichotomy post-*Resident Evil 4*: Fight or fly. On the one hand, many studios followed in Capcom's footsteps and sought to follow in the new formula proposed by the Japanese studio. Faced with technical innovations and considering that classic survival horror seemed to be running out of steam, several studios turned to what Perron calls action-horror, which includes games such as *Dead Space* [21], *Condemned:*

---

[4] Mikami would not admit to having been inspired by the French game until twenty years after the release of the first *Resident Evil* [16;17].

Criminal Origins [22] and *Resident Evil 5* [23] and *6* [24]. This formula includes more means of defence and more brutal sequences, while inheriting certain mechanics such as the avatar's vulnerability supported by slow movements and an aiming system that prevents all movement [25].

On the other hand, a few years later, a few studios (often smaller ones) attempted to return to a more primal conception of fear by creating what Perron calls "terror games". Instead of making the genre more accessible through an action/FPS orientation better known to the public (as it was quite present in the games of the time), some developers reinforced the avatar's vulnerability, to the point where it simply became incapable of defending itself and had no option but to flee. As Thomas Grip, one of the founders of the Frictional games studio (behind, among others, the *Penumbra* trilogy [26] and *Amnesia: The Dark Descent* [27]) points out, "it turns out, when the player has an opportunity to kill something, they will. " [...] "not only were enemy encounters changed, but it changed how they looked at the game" [28]. In addition to weapons, the limited inventory disappears and the only resources to manage are often linked to the visibility of the action (oil, batteries). The general consequence of such gameplay choices is to increase the tension felt by the player, who must carefully weigh up each of his decisions to avoid being seen or to be able to escape.

From the outset, it should be stressed that such a theory proves very useful in demonstrating the evolution of a certain video game experience. Indeed, Survival Horror is a label used to catalogue such different productions that it comes to conglomerate works radically opposed in their vision of survival [29]. What do the first and sixth *Resident Evil* have in common, apart from their titles and references to the universe of the series? In fact, just as most generic labels in literature no longer refer to the same concept as their origin, the term "survival horror" is no longer in phase with the object it originally designated. It therefore seems useful to divide the whole into smaller categories that are better able to reflect the genre's internal divergences.

However, such a model is not without its flaws. One of the first is probably the varying degree of abstraction in Perron's descriptions. His definition of survival horror is focused on the first productions belonging to the genre, while action-horror and terror game are reduced to a post-*Resident Evil 4* dichotomy focusing primarily on the mechanical aspects of the games studied (the corpus of Perron's study comprises some 300 works). This raises two problems. On the one hand, such categories, which are intended to be stricter, struggle to take hybrid games into account, particularly in the post-*Resident Evil 4* period. Where to classify *Alien: Isolation* [30], since the protagonist can acquire efficient weaponry against most enemies but remains powerless against the xenomorph that stalks her relentlessly. On the other hand, some games appear to be anachronisms. Released in 1995, *Clock Tower* [31], in which the protagonist must flee from a killer armed with a huge pair of scissors, appeared more than ten years before the golden age of the terror game. Added to this is Perron's attempt to better frame the gaming experience, notably through formal elements. However, it is difficult to compare the experience of two games in the same category. For example, a game like *The Evil Within* [32], also developed by Shinji Mikami, is renowned for its frightening experience. Nevertheless, it is in the same category as *Resident Evil 6*, considered one of the most action-oriented (and least frightening) episodes of the saga. More fundamentally, we can also question the legitimacy of these labels. While the term action-horror has become relatively common in gamers' discourse (though much less so than survival horror), the term terror game is a scholarly label that does not refer to a categorisation that exists outside academia. I will come back to this point in the second part of this article.

2.2 Through Emotions?

Aside from purely formal definitions, it is generally accepted that survival horror can be recognised by the fear it naturally inspires in the player. In fact, this is often one of the buying criteria for such a game. But is such a statement self-evident?

As mentioned earlier, a survival horror is normally composed of a horrific thematic part, which must find an echo in a mechanical part designed to put the player in a survival situation. The meaning of this horrific component is already open to question. Tanya Krzywinska [33] and Bernard Perron [12] rightly point out that the horror genre, in the broadest sense of the term, can include games that have no real propensity to induce fear, disgust or horror[5], but which possess thematic elements specific to the genre (occultism, bestiary and locations drawn from a gothic imaginary, gory effects). Thus, we could also include in the horror thematic genre games such as *Mortal Kombat X* [35], known for its bloody fatalities, *MediEvil* [36], though more humorous than frankly frightening, or even *Cthulhu Saves the World* [37], which parodies the cosmic horrors created by writer Howard Phillips Lovecraft. However, such a classification proves unsatisfactory in certain ways. If horror were to include everything that comes under the heading of stereotyped sociocultural imagery, the number of productions belonging to this genre would become so immense that it would lose its usefulness. On the one hand, it risks incorporating works that few would intuitively classify as part of the horrific genre. To take my previous example, even if it is necessary to perceive the reference to the Lovecraftian universe to fully appreciate the content of *Cthulhu Saves the World*, most players would still classify this game parodic or, possibly, fantastic[6]. On the other hand, a thematic definition runs the risk of not including horrific works with few or no supernatural elements. How, for example, can we include a game like *Doki Doki Literature Club!* [38], whose horrific purpose lies above all in transgressing the boundaries of fiction? [39] In short, a definition of horror on a purely thematic level remains sterile.

---

[5] For the purpose of this article, I prefer to remain vague on the precise definition of these emotions, which themselves require precise circumscription using a theoretical framework derived from psychology. For an example of a model for analysing the emotions surrounding fear and horror, I refer the reader to my master's thesis [34].

[6] The case of parody and satire (in fact, the "second degree" genres) is probably the main obstacle facing many generic classifications, particularly the formal ones. To determine that *Cthulhu Saves the World* is a parodic game, the player must be aware of the existence of the Lovecraftian genre and how it works. Only then will he be able to determine that the game is parodying a pre-existing genre. However, the Lovecraftian genre does not disappear when he plays. It remains present in a latent state, without which the humour of the game could not be understood. This double label is complex to demonstrate, since it depends on the perception of the public, who sometimes have completely opposite opinions.

A second understanding of the genre is suggested by Noël Carroll [40], who defines what he calls art-horror as a particular emotion experienced by the audience of a work. By extension, the term designates a genre of works capable of provoking such a feeling.

"Assuming that 'I-as-audience-member' am in an analogous emotional state to that which fictional characters beset by monsters are described to be in, then: I am occurrently art-horrified by some monster X, say Dracula, if and only if 1) I am in some state of abnormal, physically felt agitation (shuddering, tingling, screaming, etc.) which 2) has been caused by a) the thought: that Dracula is a possible being; and by the evaluative thoughts: that b) said Dracula has the property of being physically (and perhaps morally and socially) threatening in the ways portrayed in the fiction and that c) said Dracula has the property of being impure, where 3) such thoughts are usually accompanied by the desire to avoid the touch of things like Dracula." [40, p. 27].

It is worth noting that Carroll originally suggested that the entity capable of art-horrifying the public should be threatening and impure. He defined impurity as the biological impossibility of a being in our present world, which turns out to be too restrictive a criterion. Indeed, it becomes impossible to incorporate works featuring sick or insane individuals, such as *Psycho* [41] or *American Psycho* [42]. However, following a commentary by Georges Ochoa [43], Carroll revised his theory, envisaging a two-headed impurity, either physical or psychological. Nevertheless, such a vision of horror still overlooks certain specific cases that nonetheless belong to the register of horrific experience. Hugo Clémot [44] points out that works featuring epidemics without monsters, such as *28 Days Later* [45] and *Carriers* [46], should be added to Carroll's definition. In his view, an element is horrific when it "constitutes a threat to an anthropocentric teleology [my translation]" [44, p. 4]. Such a definition is less open to criticism, insofar as it seems effectively capable of incorporating all existing horrific works, at least on a symbolic level. However, I would like to point out another flaw in such a line of reasoning, which I believe is hard to overcome.

When we talk about emotions and feelings in the game, we are no longer interested in the developers' intentions or formal elements, but rather in what players feel. It seems complex to claim the existence of a standard player, responsible for representing the emotional state of all empirical players. Horrific games present a particularly complex case study from this point of view, as the elements they employ to arouse emotions can lead to variable effects, not least because of their frequent use of an aesthetic of monstration and hyperbole, also found in comic works. In fact, depending on their state of mind and previous experiences, audiences may tend to find hyperbole frightening or, on the contrary, hilarious. In the cinema, for example, films such as *Braindead* [47] or *The Evil Dead* [48] show great respect for horror codes, but can at the same time provoke laughter by employing overly gory elements (endless sprays of blood, grandiloquent execution, display of overly deformed monstrosities). A similar observation applies to video games: *Mortal Kombat X* probably shocks an unprepared audience, while the deluge of shattered bones and exposed guts provokes laughter from some haemoglobin-loving gamers. All this is without going back to the obvious fact that public sensitivity has evolved over time and space.

In short, a thematic definition of horror seems both too broad (the category seems to expand without reasonable limits) and too narrow (it does not directly allow for the incorporation of certain works that the public instinctively classifies in this genre). As for the emotional definition of this genre, the deep subjectivity of human experience prevents its stabilisation, even in a synchronic state. But what is left to define the survival horror genre?

2.3   A Semio-Pragmatic Theory?

The theory I am synthesising here stems mainly from Dominic Arsenault's PhD thesis [9], the final demonstration of which is to define survival horror in terms of the experience it is supposed to provide. However, the theoretical model he establishes differs markedly from emotional approaches in its insistence on the role of the producer pole in determining the genre.

Regarding the horrific component of survival horror, Arsenault uses a highly thematic definition, the limitations of which I have already discussed.

"The ranks of video game horror thus include just about any game that uses occult or satanic imagery, creatures drawn from the traditional bestiary (zombies, ghosts, vampires, werewolves, demons…) and/or typical settings (gothic mansion, place of worship, cemetery, dark lighting). In short, horror is used in the same way as fantasy or science fiction genres in video games: the player confronts the undead in a cemetery rather than barbarians in a field or robots in a spaceship. [my translation]" [9, p. 293].

Meanwhile, his approach to the survival component (which is intimately linked to the horrific component) differs from the classic definitions of the genres, since it relies on what he calls "generic effects". Arsenault postulates the existence of a model player (modelled on Umberto Eco's model reader [49]) who, as he progresses and fails, will learn to master and make the best use of all the affordances included in a game in order to get the most out of his experience. According to him, someone who does not use all the affordances of the game is in a different relationship to the game, since instead of playing the game, he plays with the game or makes fun of the game, which rules out the possibility of being a model player. Based on this theory, Arsenault determines that the survival genre is not defined by formal criteria or by the emotions felt, but by the fact that developers have consciously introduced certain mechanical or thematic elements (whose form is not fixed) into the game in order to provoke a standard reaction in the player – in this case, the desire for absolute preservation of the avatar. The researcher defines three conditions that must simultaneously be found in a survival game (and therefore in survival horror): firstly, the avatar must be put in a vulnerable position and seeks above all to ensure his survival and re-establish the status quo; secondly, the balance of power between the protagonist and his enemies must be to the latter's advantage; thirdly, direct confrontation is to be avoided due to the permanent rationing of resources.

In a way, Arsenault's classification method is certainly one of the most accomplished in the world of video games. Compared with primarily formal studies or methods based on players' emotions, his theory overcomes diachronic difficulties: a survival horror cannot be anything other than a survival horror if the developers have decided so. In this way, he also reduces the hybridity of most games, since most of them follow in the footsteps of their predecessors (although in some cases they do break new ground). Furthermore, he succeeds in ensuring that the highly variable experiences of players do not encroach on the generic categories formulated in a given time and place. In short, if we assume that the intention of the producer pole is invariable, Arsenault provides a model that is sufficiently padlocked to classify games in perennial categories.

However, while his method suffers from no inconsistencies as such, some of his basic postulates remain questionable. First, the theory of the model player appears questionable in its attempt to freeze the player's experience[7]. Indeed, a player who does not use the affordances necessary to appreciate the game experience is not necessarily playing with the game or playing the game. For example, it is easy to imagine a user who does not use all the affordances because he is unaware of the existence of some of them, without making his experience frustrating. In the same way, he may unintentionally resort to an unfair technique that makes the game so much easier, without directly realising that it has not been designed by the developers.

In the light of this first observation, we can also question the criteria used by Arsenault to define survival, for although developers may think of a game experience of a certain type, the individual game experience is extremely variable, even within the same game. For example, one of the most representative survival horror games of its generation, *Silent Hill 2* [51], features, at least in its early stages, a relatively fragile protagonist, with few weapons, facing powerful (and in some cases invincible) enemies. Such elements are indeed likely to provoke a sense of survival and fear. However, a meticulous player, even a novice, who takes the time to scour every element of the setting and masters the combat system, will soon find himself with such a large arsenal that he will no longer have any significant difficulty in triumphing in the combat phases. So, by following the game's affordances as closely as possible, the player will finally have succeeded in deviating his experience from what seemed expected by the designers.

Furthermore, the developers' intention appears to be a relatively imprecise, vague and equally complex criterion to determine. Indeed, in an economic context where communication has an enormous influence on the way a work is received, considering the speeches made by the pole producer as gospel truth presents a significant bias. In addition, even if certain studios have a figurehead who can take responsibility for certain development choices (I have mentioned Shinji Mikami, for example), a huge proportion of those involved in game design remain in the shadows, and often have no means of expression. As a result, the apparent discourse of producers is biased and incomplete, calibrated for the purposes of communication and sales rather than exegesis.

Additionally, the survival criteria defined by Arsenault allow for the inclusion of games that are not traditionally considered to belong to this genre, which brings us back to the issue of the invalidity of formal criteria. For example, *Dark Souls 2* [52] incorporates all the elements defined by the researcher. The protagonist is initially presented as a weak undead, highly vulnerable to waves of enemies that can quickly overwhelm him. In the early stages of the game, at least, avoiding or fleeing certain powerful enemies is also recommended. What is more, regular deaths hinder progress, as the character's life gauge decreases with each death. The only way to regain full life is then to purchase a resource available in limited supply. Scenaristically, death also has a storyline implication, since the protagonist is supposed to regress and progressively lose his humanity each time he

---

[7] Ewan Kirkland [50] casts doubt on the realism and pragmatism of concepts close to the model player, namely Rune Klevjer's "implied designer" and Jesper Juul's "ideal sequence".

is killed. Yet most gamers will be far more likely to class *Dark Souls 2* as an action RPG, hack and slash or die and retry.

In addition, the games Arsenault has lumped together under the survival horror label may seem curious. Indeed, in his desire to create a survival horror category bringing together similar experiences, he likens the experience provided by *Resident Evil* to that of *Diablo* [53][8]. However, few gamers will make the connection between the two game experiences, as *Diablo*'s survival mechanics are far less frightening and punishing than those of *Resident Evil*. For example, the limited number of saves in Capcom's game necessarily brings a tension that *Diablo* does not, since it is possible to save at any time.

Finally, this theory works particularly well with "good games", such as *Resident Evil* and *Diablo*, often cited as masterpieces. In such cases, producers have every reason to emphasise the game's qualities. But we must not forget that, for every few exceptional games that find their way onto gamers' shelves, many other passable or even downright bad games are not retained by history. For example, in 2016, the developers of a new studio, Madmind, successfully completed a crowdfunding for a project called *Agony* [54], to be released in 2018. The game promised by the studio is intended to be an intense horrific experience, a more than Dantesque journey through a nightmarish representation of Hell. However, the finished product turns out to be excessively bad: numerous bugs make the experience tedious, the gameplay and difficulty are poorly calibrated, and several reviewers also point out the game's lack of subtlety in its direction (consisting of a disjointed story and scenes of massacres and rape where, more than bodies, it is the textures that constantly overlap), resulting in a feeling more dismayed or amused than the traumatic experience promised by Madmind. All the generic effects fail miserably, and it is hard to feel any fear other than that of seeing the game crash. Yet few would question that *Agony* belongs to the survival horror genre. So how can we approach the generic question?

3 Study the Categories Formulated by Players and Give the Genre a Chance to Evolve

3.1 Synthesis of Previous Comments

While each of these approaches has its merits, it is also some of their assumptions that stand in the way of a unified, enduring theory of video game genres (even if many examples apply to the genres of most media). Let's look at the main comments I have made in order to determine which angles of research should be favoured in order to better understand the logic that governs video game genres today.

First, I would like to return to the lack of pragmatism in formalist approaches. It is possible for such theories to work on a certain scale, but their intrinsically artificial

---

[8] Arsenault insists on a passage in *Diablo* that he considers symptomatic of survival horror, namely the encounter with the butcher, a boss too powerful for neophyte players and likely to generate a vivid sense of fear for the rest of the adventure. However, this boss is totally optional, and it is possible for a player to miss out. In doing so, he will not necessarily be affected by the emotion of constant anguish described by Arsenault as part of the *Diablo* experience, as the encounter with the butcher is part of the preferred route for the model player.

nature must be acknowledged. Formalism makes no real attempt to find some logic in the existing categories used by the public. On the contrary, the aim of these purely academic approaches is to find a way of linking works that sometimes have little in common, sometimes via the creation of artificial labels that are generally only used by researchers, condemning them to rapid obsolescence [55][9]. Yet it is striking to observe that such models have prevailed from the earliest generic theories (regardless of the media targeted) right up to the present day. This desire to find new ways of classifying (via tables, trees, diagrams) is even more curious in that it rarely results in fully functional, let alone perennial, theories. To take a literary case in point, Vladimir Propp, with his *Morphology of the Folktale* [56], was long held to be the proponent of a large-scale structuralist theory that could be replicated in other cases. However, this great success is now disputed in more ways than one. Propp seems to have deliberately left out certain variants of the tales he was studying to enable his model to work, and even if we consider only the tales he retained, it is not difficult to find a few contradictions in some of his analyses. Despite his interesting idea of considering the mutation of a genre through different major evolutionary phases, Perron faces a similar problem, especially as his corpus has certain limitations that make it not very representative, notably the omission of the indie scene, which is nevertheless very active in the horror genre. Thus, in a formal theory of genres, exhaustiveness will forever remain a problem, since the theoretical model must accept neither counterexamples nor exceptions (which, in this case, do not confirm the rule, but nullify it). In short, empiricism remains the greatest enemy of formalism or, as the epistemologist Karl Popper says:

"It is far from obvious, from a logical point of view, that we are justified in inferring universal statements from singular statements however numerous they may be; any conclusion drawn in this way can always, in fact, be found to be false: no matter how many white swans we may have observed, it does not justify the conclusion that all swans are white. The question of whether inductive inferences are justified, or under what conditions they are justified, is known as constituting the problem of induction. [my translation]" [57, pp. 23–24].

Formal theories, which often involve a thematic or mechanical analysis of the works, are therefore not particularly conducive to generic studies, especially as the criteria considered for classification are multiple, and some labels amalgamate indissociable components. This is especially true of survival horror, which is mechanically a survival game and thematically a horror game. However, the experience provided by this genre is not the simple addition of the effects of two genres, but a particular combination that each game actualises in its own way.

Attempting to classify games and genres on the basis of the feelings players are likely to experience is also proving to be a dead end. Where formal theories had a form of objectivity in the forms observed (despite a certain subjectivity in the interpretation of these forms), theories based on emotions fail to standardise players' feelings, which

---

[9] I am critical of the use of formalism in purely generic theories. In my view, such theories should seek to match the forms transmitted and accepted by the public in a certain spatiotemporal context, or even in a specific social context. However, I do not question the value of formalism in other types of approach, especially when it comes to creating interpretative categories, notably for the exegesis of certain works.

logically leads to undesirable hybrid classifications. Besides, the validity of generic labels derived in this way is questionable, even in the case of survival horror, since it appears that this is not a game genre that systematically provokes fear. Conversely, to erect the category of "games that scare" would be artificial, since such a classification does not exist in the eyes of the gaming community (in addition to being, once again, subjective).

On the opposite, using the producer's intention to obtain a generic classification proves fallible for a variety of reasons: difficulty in discerning an enunciator for the game, influence of the economic context, or variability of discourse depending on the reception of the game. However, it is interesting to consider the role of the industry (and its relay, the video game press) in the creation of certain generic labels [9]. For example, even if the survival horror label has seen its referent vary in time and space, let's remind that it was Capcom that popularised it to facilitate communication around its flagship series [12]. Today, however, it is hard to see how the categories that producers sometimes assign to their games can still have absolute legitimacy.

3.2   Another Way of Thinking About Gender

Among the criticisms I addressed to the models analysed, the most recurrent concerns the criterion of artificiality. Indeed, rather than understanding the logic behind the use of genres by gamers – who remain the main people concerned with these generic issues – most research has focused on scholarly classifications whose interest is above all heuristic. Without denying the interest of these approaches, I postulate that the objective of a true theory of genres should be to understand, in practice, the way in which real players (and the communities they belong to) understand genres and manage to operate generic classifications.

Of course, such an approach to generic logic is not without its problems, not least because it reshapes the notion of genre. First, considering the notion of genre from the point of view of reception is not self-evident, since, as we have seen, most theories are based on the production pole or on the work itself. In play studies, we need to make a shift similar to that proposed by Roland Barthes in literature in his famous article "The Death of the Author"[58]. Interpreting a work in terms of its author denies the audience's ability to act on the work, its capacity to reshape it to give it a personal meaning. And yet, the genre of a work intimately depends on its interpretation. Gamers therefore seem entirely legitimate in their quest to confer meaning on video games.

It may be objected that considering the players' discourse necessarily leads to a certain subjectivity. However, I do not propose to analyse each player's discourse independently, which would only lead to further confusion. At present, video games play an active part in many community phenomena, such as participatory culture [59, 60], fan cultures [61, 62] and folksonomy [63, 64]. Generic categories and labels are not the work of isolated individuals, but the result of the collective activity of many individuals. We need only think of sites like the wikis, which are based entirely on the collaboration of several people, or systems like tags, which enable direct and democratic categorisation of games. Today, gamers are able to determine the generic labels for their video games and, what is more, legitimise their choice in the eyes of the rest of the community.

However, even if we can get around the problem of excessive subjectivity by focusing on communities of players (rather than isolated individuals), we still need to understand how to respond to two other issues highlighted above. Firstly, the hybridity of games is not really a problem in absolute terms. The failure of formalism leads me to believe that games should be considered as an amalgam of various trends from different genres. Attempting to reduce a game to one or two categories is ultimately of no particular interest. On the contrary, it deprives it of part of its richness, and in a computerised system, there is a good chance that many games will remain untraceable for certain players who refer to the wrong encoded categories, even though these categories make sense to them. In this respect, a venture like Steam's tagging system shows a truly exciting way of understanding video game genres. While not allowing an unreasonable multiplication of genres (and, consequently, interpretations), the system makes available the genres accepted by most of the community (even if, when a game is released, it is the producers who determine which categories appear).

Secondly, spatiotemporal variability remains the major concern of any categorisation. After all, as Benedetto Croce noted as long ago as 1902: "Every true masterpiece has violated the law of an established genre, thus sowing confusion in the minds of critics, who were obliged to broaden the genre [my translation]" [quoted in 65, p. 41]. If the world of video games is a river churned by new, innovative works, then there is no point in fighting the current. In fact, a resolutely pragmatic theory of video game genres (but this is probably also the case for genres in other media) is only conceivable if we renounce one of the defining criteria of the genre, namely its stability, often associated with its prescriptive feature. There is no such thing as a permanent categorisation, and there never will be. Each new attempt at categorisation at time X and place Y is condemned to a more or less rapid obsolescence, depending on the ingenuity of its creator.

But let's not let this disappointment mask a perhaps promising future. If categorisation cannot be detached from the human being – who is a better judge than the player – the analysis of categorisations may no longer be directly in our hands in the future. Given that the communities of players are in the best position to determine the genre of a work and that these communities are extremely active online, there is reason to believe that the future of categorisation will involve automated procedures enabling the update of institutional databases in real time.[10]

By the time such a project is completed, the generic categories of play will probably have mutated (yet again). Questions surrounding generic theories will still have had the opportunity to be revised (probably more than once). Given such a renewal, it remains to be seen if this article will not itself soon be obsolete in what it says about the logic of creating and legitimising generic video game labels. In the meantime, I hope to have contributed to the reflection on generic issues which, thanks to certain practical applications, will make it possible to facilitate access to video game works and a better preservation of them.

---

[10] As part of my thesis, this is what I plan to achieve with the AUREJ project (unified access to playability resources) supported by the Bibliothèque nationale de France, which is responsible for the legal deposit of all works published or produced in France.

References

1. Aristote: Poétique. Les Belles Lettres, Paris (1990)
2. Genette, G.: Introduction à l'architexte. Seuil, Paris (1979)
3. Genette, G.: Seuils. Seuil, Paris (1987)
4. Schaeffer, J.-M.: Qu'est-ce qu'un genre littéraire? Seuil, Paris (1989)
5. Wolf, M.J.P.: Genre and the video game. In: Wolf, M.J.P. (ed.) The Medium of Video Game, pp. 113–134. University of Texas Press, Austin (2001)
6. Arsenault, D., Picard, M.: Le Jeu vidéo entre dépendance et plaisir immersif: les trois formes d'immersion vidéoludique. In: Le Jeu vidéo : un phénomène social massivement pratiqué. University of Quebec at Trois Rivières (2007). https://ludicine.ca/sites/ludicine.ca/files/arsenault,-picard---le-jeu-video-entre-dependance-et-plaisir-immersif_0.pdf. Accessed 29 July 2023
7. Burn, A., Carr, D.: Defining Game Genre. In: Carr, D., et al. (eds.) Computer games: text, narrative and play, pp. 14–29. Polity press, Cambridge (2006)
8. Baychelier, G.: Jeux vidéo horrifiques et artialisation des émotions extrêmes. In: Nouvelle revue d'esthétique 2(14), pp. 81–92 (2014)
9. Arsenault, D.: Des Typologies mécaniques à l'expérience esthétique. Fonctions et mutations du genre dans le jeu video. Ph.D. thesis in art history and film studies, University of Montreal (2011)
10. Fowler, A.: Kinds of Literature. Harvard University Press, Cambridge, An Introduction to the Theory of Genres and Modes (1982)
11. Zimmerman, E.: Play as Research: The Iterative Design Process. In: Laurel, B. (ed.) Design Research: Methods and Perspectives, pp. 176–184. MIT press, Cambridge (2003)
12. Perron, B.: The World of Scary Video Games. A Study in Videoludic Horror. Bloomsbury Academic, New York (2018)
13. Infogrames: Alone in the Dark (1992)
14. Fahs T: *Alone in the dark* retrospective. In: IGN (2012). https://www.ign.com/articles/2008/06/23/alone-in-the-dark-restrospective. Accessed 26 July 2023
15. Capcom: Resident Evil (1996)
16. Perron B: Le Survival Horror: marquer la culture vidéoludique avec un écran de chargement. In: Penser (avec) la culture vidéoludique, Université de Lausanne (2017). https://www.youtube.com/watch?v=kgPS-38a_HA, last accessed 2023/07/29
17. Roux-Girard, G.: Plunged Alone into Darkness: Evolution in the Staging of Fear in The *Alone in the Dark* Series. In: Perron B (eds.) Horror Video Games: Essays on the Fusion of Fear and Play, pp. 145–167. McFarland & company, Jefferson (2009)
18. Konami: Silent Hill (1999)
19. Tecmo: Fatal Frame (2001)
20. Capcom: Resident Evil 4 (2005)
21. Redwood Shore: Dead Space (2008)
22. Monolith: Condemned: Criminal Origins (2005)
23. Capcom: Resident Evil 5 (2008)
24. Capcom: Resident Evil 6 (2012)
25. Niedenthal, S.: Patterns of Obscurity: Gothic Setting and Light in *Resident evil 4* and *Silent Hill 2*. In: Perron, B. (eds.) Horror Video Games: Essays on the Fusion of Fear and Play, pp. 168–180. McFarland & company, Jefferson (2009)
26. Frictional Games: Penumbra [trilogy] (2007–2008)
27. Frictional Games: Amnesia: The Dark Descent (2010)
28. Douglas, J.: Amnesia Designer: Removing Combat Opens up "New Horizons". In: Gamespot (2011). https://www.gamespot.com/articles/amnesia-designer-removing-combat-opens-upnew-horizons/1100-6328973/. Accessed 29 July 2023

29. Weise, M.: The Rules of Horror: Procedural Adaptation in *Clock Tower*, *Resident Evil* and *Dead Rising*. In: Perron, B. (eds.) Horror Video Games: Essays on the Fusion of Fear and Play, pp. 238–266. McFarland & company, Jefferson (2009)
30. Creative Assembly: Alien: Isolation (2014)
31. Human Entertainment: Clock Tower (1995)
32. Tango Gameworks: The Evil Within (2014)
33. Krzywinska, T.: Reanimating Lovecraft: the ludic paradox of *Call of Cthulhu: Dark Corners of the Earth*, In: Perron, B. (eds.) Horror Video Games: Essays on the Fusion of Fear and Play, pp. 267–287. McFarland & company, Jefferson (2009)
34. Surinx, F.-X.: Lire la peur dans leur jeu. Exploration du potentiel effrayant du texte dans le jeu video. Master thesis in French and Romance languages and literature, University of Liege (2020)
35. NetherRealm: Mortal Kombat X (2015)
36. Sony Computer Entertainment: MediEvil (1998)
37. Zeboyd: Cthlhu Saves the World (2010)
38. Team Salvato: Doki Doki Literature Club! (2017)
39. Alan, M: Doki Doki Subversion Club! Gothic Ghosts, Uncanny Glitches, and Abject Boundaries. In: Press Start 9(1), pp. 39–57 (2023)
40. Carroll, N.: The Philosophy of horror or paradoxes of the heart. Routledge, New York (1990)
41. Hitchcock, A.: Psycho (1960)
42. Ellis BE: American Psycho (1991)
43. Ochoa, G.: Deformed and Destructive Beings. The Purpose of Horror Films. McFarland & company, Jefferson (2011)
44. Clémot, H.: Le Monstre dans la philosophie contemporaine de l'horreur cinématographique. In: Amerika 11 (2014). https://journals.openedition.org/amerika/5192#ftn14. Accessed 29 July 2023
45. Boyle, D.: 28 Days Later (2002)
46. Pastor, A., Pastor, D.: Carriers (2009)
47. Jackson, P.: Braindead (1992)
48. Raimi, S.: The Evil Dead (1981)
49. Eco, U.: Lector in fabula: le rôle du lecteur ou la Coopération interprétative dans les textes narratifs. Librairie Générale Française, Paris (1985)
50. Kirkland, E.: Storytelling in Survival Horror Video Games. In: Perron B (eds.) Horror Video Games: Essays on the Fusion of Fear and Play, pp. 62–78. McFarland & company, Jefferson (2009)
51. Konami: Silent Hill 2 (2001)
52. FromSoftware: Dark Souls 2 (2014)
53. Blizzard: Diablo (1996)
54. Madmind: Agony (2018)
55. Dozo, B.-O.: Pour une histoire polyphonique du jeu video. In: Liège Game Lab (eds.) Culture vidéoludique!, pp. 21–35. Presses universitaires de Liège, Liège (2019)
56. Propp, V.: Morphologie du conte. Gallimard, Paris (1970)
57. Popper, K.R.: La Logique de la découverte scientifique. Payot, Paris (1973)
58. Barthes: The Death of the Author. In: Aspen 5–6 (1967)
59. Jenkins, H.: Textual Poachers: Television Fans and Participatory Culture. Routledge, London (1992)
60. Raessens, J.: Computer games as participatory media culture. In: Raessens, J., Goldstein, J. (eds.) The Handbook of Computer Game Studies, pp. 373–388. MIT Press, Cambridge (2005)
61. Jenkins, H.: Fans, Bloggers, and Gamers: Exploring Participatory Culture. New York University Press, New York (2006)

62. Le Guern, P. (ed.): Les Cultes médiatiques. Culture fan et œuvres cultes. Presses Universitaires de Rennes, Rennes (2002)
63. Petrucco, C.: "Folksonomie" nella Rete : costruire categorie alternative, creative ed interculturali. In: TD: tecnologie didattiche 1, pp. 38–50 (2006)
64. Le Deuff, O.: Folksonomies : les usagers indexent le Web. In: Bulletin des bibliothèques de France 4, pp. 66–70 (2006)
65. Jauss, H.R.: Littérature médiévale et théorie des genres. In: Genette, G., et al. (eds.) Théorie des genres, pp. 37–76. Seuil, Paris (1986)

Game Design and Development

Cities: Skylines: The Digital and Analog Game Design Lessons for Learning About Collaborative Urban Planning

Micael Sousa$^{(\boxtimes)}$ (iD)

School of Architecture, Planning and Environmental Policy, University College Dublin, Dublin, Ireland
micaelssousa@gmail.com

Abstract. City-building games (CBGs) are a popular type of game. Researchers and teachers have been exploring the potential of CBCs for learning and support planning systems. Cities: Skylines (C:S) is one of the contemporary games showing more potential for these purposes, but the analog version of the game has been ignored. The digital and analog versions of C:S were adapted and tested with undergraduate and master students (n = 17) of urban and regional planning courses from two different polytechnic institutes in Portugal. Participants considered the analog version more fun and collaborative (decision-making), but the digital version was better for testing creative solutions and simulating realistic cities. Analyzing the players' perspectives and game design elements of each game allowed us to address the potential and limitations of each game platform for teaching and use as a planning support system. Our findings also contribute to developing future collaborative playable experiences in general.

Keywords: Board games · Cities: Skylines · Game-based Learning · Game Design · Urban Planning

1 Introduction

City-building Games (CBG) have been around for decades. Zagal & Cox [1] define CBG as "…*these are generally open-ended games where players manage resources in the process of creating and developing a simulated human settlement.*".

Since the dawn of SimCity (1989), the game has been the most influential CBG in the history of video games. Many other games then addressed the human fascination to build, manage, develop, and interact with urban simulation games. SimCity became a series of games, with each new release trying to simulate the complexity of urban realities. Despite the effort to generate more realistic simulations, urban scholars argue that the game has many limitations when using it for other purposes beyond entertainment. Other CBGs appeared in the following years. The one that seems to be the most popular one, constantly updated, is Cities: Skylines (C:S). The game was released in 2015 and continues to engage contemporary players. C:S is also studied as an interactive simulation tool for teaching and participatory planning.

© The Author(s), under exclusive license to Springer Nature Switzerland AG 2024
L. Vale Costa et al. (Eds.): VJ 2023, CCIS 1984, pp. 257–271, 2024.
https://doi.org/10.1007/978-3-031-51452-4_18

City: Skylines the board game (C:SBG) was released in (2019), proposing an analog alternative way to build a city inspired by C:S. This multiplayer game, which allows solo play, is a collaborative game. C:SBG is directly inspired by the digital version (C:S) but follows the design trends of modern board games. Although the C:S video game has been getting some attention in academia, its analog version has been ignored. The analog C:SBG simplifies the urban simulation and, instead of aiming for detail, fosters collaboration. These two features relate to the application of games for urban planning. And specifically for participatory and collaborative planning [2]. Identifying the design elements in each platform (analog/digital) provides tips and guidelines for gamification and serious game approaches inspired by C:S games [3]. Addressing the specific game mechanisms that foster collaboration can be a way to build game-based collaborative planning processes. This way, we aim to contribute to testing the games as possible planning support tools (games serious purpose): auxiliary learning activities about urban concepts and urban systems and supporting decision-making (e.g., collaborative decision-making).

In this paper, we propose to analyze the digital and analog (board game) design elements, defining the similarities and differences between each platform that tries to deliver similar playable experiences. The games were played by undergraduate and master students of urban planning courses in two different polytechnic institutes in Portugal. Each class played the two versions of the same game, supported by a game facilitator, and answered a survey after playing the games. The gameplay was filmed.

In the first sections of the paper, we introduce CBGs and address the C:S. After, we present the modern boardgame revival movement and how C:SBG is played, simplifying C:S. The two games supported a game-based learning methodology to facilitate the games and collect data. Data collection allowed us to conclude that the analog version was less fit for simulation but easier to play, more fun, and collaborative, according to the students' perceptions. These conclusions show that choosing commercial CBGs for game-based activities depends on the purpose of play. Digital and analog versions of the same game can provide different play experiences, and simple game mechanisms can simulate urban dynamics without entering detailed simulations.

2   Cities: Skylines as the Dominant CBG

For many years, SimCity was the reference when talking about CBG. This rule changed when the SimCity series stopped producing new games and when City: Skylines (C:S) was released by Paradox. We are not saying that other CBGs are not relevant or played today, but C:S dominates as the most played and recognizable CBG of today, with more than 700.000 followers on Steam (https://steamdb.info/tag/4328/). No other realistic urban simulator has similar scores and followers on Steam. This reputation has drawn researchers and game enthusiasts to explore the game as a tool to address urban planning issues.

2.1   The Planning Fascination Towards C:S

Besides the direct relationship between CBG and urban planning, these games address sustainability concepts like the management of water, land use, energy, clean air, social well-being, population density, and trade [1]. In the case of C:S, the ability to simulate time, the ongoing development of a city, and a prospective reality in a game context that approaches simulation [4].

Several researchers tested and evaluated CBGs' potential as support planning tools or teaching dynamics, all finding several limitations [5–8]. Oversimplification, starting cities from zero, and unlimited power to act and manage the city are some of the problems of using these games, making them enjoyable but poor tools to simulate the complexity of urban realities. Bereitschaft [9] compiled the limitations of C:S. Although we might argue that C:S is one of the most sophisticated and complex CBG available, these games cannot deal with the complexity of political power under democratic systems, the mixed land used that is essential to address sustainable urban models, the overfocus on cars as the transport system, the heritage, and historic preservation claims. The oversimplification of the political systems follows the simplification of societies depicted in the game. However, the game publisher (Paradox) has been releasing new game modules to address some of these dimensions and provide payers with new game experiences. Researchers like Minnery and Searle [6] identified as a problem the difficulty to access and modify digital CBGs due to requirements to dominate programming but also because of the "black boxes" and intellectual property rights. These have been partly solved since we can access the C:S code and modify it. It is possible to convert from GIS and the game and vice-versa [10, 11]. Regardless of these new possibilities, teachers or planners who wish to use C:S still need considerable programming skills to change the game for educative or project purposes.

Bereitschaft [12] summarized a list of recommendations for using digital CBG for education purposes (having C:S as the guiding tool). The author recommends that educators define specific purposes for game usage, like one specific urban dimension. Students should be taught the key concepts before using the game, as well as to help the users learn the controllers and game mechanics. The play experience should deliver experimental exercises to apply the concepts in a virtual practice. These exercises produce more impact on the students through repetition and mastery. Bereitschaft [12] recommends working in groups, although using only a computer limits the multiplayer experience.

In the cases where the C:S was tested with students, the finding shows that students were engaged and able to train skills like critical thinking, problem-solving, and creative thinking [13], which are considered essential skills for planners but also fit the concept of essential skills for the XXI century jobs [14]. Khan and Zhao [13] recommend the C:S be adapted to fit learning purposes and highlight the need to provide multiplayer experiences to share and foster a collaborative learning process.

2.2 The Modern Board Game Implementation of C:S

Board games seem to be thriving despite the massification of digital games. Some authors describe this movement as the golden age of board games [15], others say we are living in an age of modern board game renaissance [16, 17]. Despite the terms we use to describe the modern board game phenomenon [18], people are looking for these new analog games, engaged by the type of play experiences they offer based on innovative game systems [19]. New board game releases show an exponential tendency, with thousands of new games released in the last twenty years [20]. Several authors argued, based on surveying the modern board game communities, that despite the new game design elements the games include, it is the social interactions that motivate more players to enter the board game hobby [16, 17, 21–23].

There are modern board games of all different types, complexity, themes, time duration, thematic, and mechanical systems. One of them is analog versions of digital games. Mechs vs. Minions [24] from Riot Games was inspired by League of Legends. The most recent (2023) winner of the prestigious prize Spiel des Jahres (game of the year in Germany, since 1979) was Dorfromantik: the board game [25], which is a reimplementation of a popular videogame. This War of Mine: the board game [26] appear is the 169 best boardgame of all time, according to BoardGameGeek (BGG)) (www.boardgamegeek. com), which is the place to find information about modern board game movement [27, 28]. Among these video game implementations is C: S. Cities: Skylines: The board game (C:SBG) [29] was released in 2019 and is considered the 3.160 best board game by BGG. All these previous board games allow solo play. Playing them with several players simultaneously is possible only through collaborative play. The game designers have implemented solitaire versions for cooperative versions by allowing a single player to assume the roles and actions all players could do, using uncertainty mechanisms like card drawing or dice rolling to generate the game challenge [30].

C:SBG is a cooperative game, playable solo, allowing a maximum of four players simultaneously. It is considered a medium-light game, with a complexity of 2.36 (from 1 to 5, according to BGG). In C:SBG, players try to grow the city and score the most points. They play cards to add cardboard tiles with polyominos (Tetris 2D pieces) shapes that represent housing, commercial and industry zones, and public facilities. Players spend money to play cards and manage the limits of crime, traffic, and pollution. Players control the employment levels and resources like water, energy, and waste collection (Fig. 3). The balance of all these dimensions allows players to grow the city by placing tiles and acquiring new land for the city to expand. Players can lose the game if they run out of resources.

2.3   Comparing the Digital and Analogue Version of C:S

The digital and analog versions of C:S provide different play experiences. The games use similar concepts, dimensions, and iconography and enforce spatial expansion. Players manage resources to keep the cities growing, addressing the residents' demands related to generic urban planning and sustainability requirements. The simulation detail is much deeper in the digital version, while the ability to generate a collaborative decision-making process is a key element of the analog versions. The digital version seems to deal with the complexity of urban planning identified by Bereitschaft [12], while the analogue version simulates the complexity of political decision-making and the collaborative learning experiences Khan and Zhao [13] prescribe. The following summary table describes the similarities and differences between the two games (Table 1).

We must explain some details of Table 1 more deeply. C:S is a single-player but allows multiplayer through a network of computers. But if several players discuss the decisions, it can be played collaboratively. C:SBG, when played by multiple players, requires actions from all players to achieve a collective goal. All players play cards and spend/produce resources for the group to continue managing the city's growth.

Table 1. Features and characteristics of C:S and C:SBG.

Dimensions	Digital (C:S)	Analogue (C:SBG)
Player count	Single-player	Single-player and Multiplayer
Interactions	Competitive solo play	Collaborative play
Simulation level	High	Low
Duration	Infinite	70 min (average)
Requirements to play	Computer and the game license	One copy of the game and a table

We consider C:S to deliver a higher level of simulation. It represents the topography and urban morphology in detail. Traffic effects emerge from the road capacities and surrounding urban activities. The scarcity and needs of the population are represented in the game world, precisely located and identified in the city. C:SBG represents the population's needs by using track bars. The urban morphology is predefined by the roads in the land tiles players can buy to expand the city. Players do not decide how to build the road system and the urban zones that deliver a realistic urban morphology. Players place cardboard tiles to fill spaces. C:SBG only simulates the zoning and adjacency effects of the land uses and public facilities. A board game can simulate more detailed urban dimensions and allow players to build more freely. Games like Small City [31], Suburbia [32], and Antiquity [33] do this better, but the game duration can be increased by several hours. The complexity of learning these games approaches the maximum of 5, according to BGG.

3   Building a Learning Experiment with C:S Versions

The literature about CBG, and specifically about C:S, argues that these games have educative potential. However, researchers have highlighted the game's limitations. We pretend to test C:S and C:SBG with the same group of users. In our case study, with undergraduate and master students from the urban planning field (learning the same contents). We set an experience where users played to digital and analogue versions of C:S, asking them to build the best city as possible. After this, the facilitator challenged the players to think about the learning insights and purposes of playing the games, connecting the experience to the course content about urban planning. The experiment was set as decided in the following sub-section.

3.1   Methodology for the Experiment

Students participated in a two-hour session where they played each game for approximately one hour. The class was divided into groups, simultaneously playing each version of the game, and switching between games. This process allowed us to play the games with 5 to 12 (n = 17) students with only two licenses of C:S and two copies of C:SBG.

We filmed the gameplay of all games without identifying the players during play, following personal data protection and ethical requirements. The participants did the pre-test and post-test surveys without sharing personal and identifiable data. The surveys followed Mayer [34] recommendations to evaluate serious games, considering the previous game experiences, the playability, enjoyment, and changes after playing the games related to urban planning issues and collaborative processes. The purpose of the experience was to analyze how students perceived the use of games as tools for teaching urban planning concepts and the experiences of collaborative decision-making processes. The surveys collected students' perceptions through Likert scales (1 to 7), using the same dimensions to compare before and after playing the games (Table 2). In the post-test, students chose which game (analog/digital) provided a more intense experience according to several dimensions (Table 3). The post-test also included a comment section where students could describe possible advantages of using game-based planning approaches. Data were analyzed according to the grounded theory [35], forming two hierarchical cluster levels associated with urban planning content and playability.

Because C:S and C:SBG provide different playable interactions, some changes were necessary for the games to be comparable. C:S (digital version) was played in teams. One player had the controller but could only build after asking other players their opinions. The analog version had no modification because the game was designed to be a multiplayer collaborative experience. Limiting the time each group would play each version of the game allowed us to compare how each group progressed in the game ($\pm$ 45 min), which allowed each group to play both games during a standard two-hour lecture. In both versions, players played the standard version of the game. In the C:S (digital), players would unlock more money if they reached the thresholds of residents (400, 800, etc.). This way of progressing is similar to what the analog version provides. C:SBG uses three types of decks (I, II, and III), requiring more resources and having a higher impact on the game (Fig. 3). As players exhaust each deck, they can advance to the next one (we enforced this rule). This way, we tried to provide similar play experiences for the players while they played each of the game versions.

3.2 Results of Play C:S and C:SBG

In the first session 1 (S1) with ESEC-IPCoimbra students, 5 participants played the games. In session 2 (S2) ESTG-IPLeiria, 12 students played the games. We formed two groups per session. Students admitted having average game habits of 4 (1 to 7) and an SD of 1.2 (S1) and 1.6 (S2). None of the players played any version of C:S. The ages in each session were very different. S1 was participated by master students with a median age of 30 years old. In S2, the median age of the undergraduate student was 21. The majority of participants were male in both sessions (more than 70%).

Table 2 shows the quantitative results for the survey questions. Due to the low number of participants, applying statistical sophisticated tests was unfeasible. To analyze the data, we show the median results for the groups of players in each session and identify the change comparing (C) between the pretest (B) with the posttest (A).

The questions presented in Table 2 tried to provoke the students to think about the experience. The median values did not reveal a high degree of change (D) from the perceptions before and after playing the games. In S1, the change in values (D) shows that the perception of games as something related to fun seemed to increase, but the educative potential decreased. Players' perception of the quality of analog games, when

Table 2. Players' perceptions before (B) and after (A) play, including the difference (D).

Players' perceptions	S1			S2		
	B	A	D	B	A	D
Are games fun?	4	5	+1	4	4	0
Are games educative?	7	6	−1	6	6	0
Would you like to have games in your classes?	5	6	−1	6	6	0
Are games childish?	3	3	0	3	3	0
Are analogue games as good as digital ones?	6	6	0	5	6	+1
Formal lectures can be replaced by games?	5	4	−1	4	5	+1
Can games improve relationships?	6	6	0	6	6	0

compared to digital ones, increased in S2. The possibility of replacing lectures with games increased as well.

In the post-test, we asked the participants to classify the games they played directly. In all sessions (S1 and S2), the median value was 6 for all the following perceptions after the experience: fun, learning, social relationships, creativity, and test urban solutions. The same overall median result (6) when asked if the game made them think about the urban contents and if it fostered their curiosity to play more different games. Regarding the desire to play the same games again, the median classification was less (5). This median result of 5 was high (near the maximum of 7). We also asked the students to say which version of the games were the best game to address dimensions related to playability, simulation of urban realities, and the interactions between players (Table 3). To strengthen the critical analysis and deal with the limitations of the quantitative data, we compared these results with the gameplay visualization and players' commentaries from the post-test (see next sub-section).

Table 3 reveals that participants considered the analog game (C:SBG) more fun, interactive, and collaborative. Participants considered the digital game (C:S) harder to start playing and more complex to play overall because of the detailed simulation. A higher quantity of choices and options generates complexity. However, players can generate more creative solutions.

Recording the gameplay of each session allowed us to compare the progression in each game. Table 4 shows the time each group needed to achieve a game threshold and related score for C:S digital game.

G1 and G3 had difficulty mastering the game controllers, while G2 was just in the initial minutes. In G4, no difficulty was recorded. In G2, there was a trackable debate between players. But in G3, it was intense, and players debated before expanding the city, discussing every option. G3 followed the planning process of defining the road system and urban blocks, only then defining land uses and public facilities. All other groups adopted an ongoing process of building a road and defining the land uses. G1 adopted a linear urban model (segregated land uses and less defined urban blocks) (Fig. 1).

Table 5 presents the progression results for the four groups playing C:SBG.

Table 3. Players' preferences between C:S and C:SBG according to experiences.

Perceptions and experiences	S1		S2	
	C:SBG	C:S	C:SBG	C:S
Difficult to start playing	40%	60%	17%	83%
More complex simulation and playability	40%	60%	33%	63%
More fun experience	75%	25%	75%	25%
Allows more creative choices	40%	60%	25%	75%
More interactive and dynamic	80%	20%	100%	0%
Foster collaboration	80%	20%	100%	0%

Table 4. General progression in C:S

Groups	Total Duration	Delivering roads, water, and energy to population	Reach 400 population	Reach 800 population
G1 (S1)	45 min	13min10s	31min 15s	-
G2 (S1)	51 min	29min 41s	39min 43s	46min 30s
G3 (S2)	50 min	24min 20s	36min 48s	-
G4 (S2)	32 min	11min 28s	15min 21s	22min 09s

Fig. 1. G1 planning a linear city with separated land uses, not adjacent (housing distant from commercial and industrial zones, reducing walkability).

The record play showed that the difficulties in understanding the rules were insignificant after the facilitator explained C:SBG a second time. There were no controllers to activate. Players played the cards, moving the track system and adding the polyominos to the territorial boards directly and through the team players' support. Players passed the cards and helped others to place the game components in the correct space.

Table 5 shows that G3 ended the game in the worst game situation because they were near the maximum thresholds of 5 for pollution, traffic, and crime. Although they had

Table 5. General progression in C:SBG

Groups	Total Duration	New urban territorial expansion	Money	Happiness	Energy	Water	Waste se vices	Employment	Pollution	Traffic	Crime
G1 (S1)	43 min	19 min 01s	8	9	0	5	0	−1	1	3	2
G2(S1)	42 min	27min 50s	8	13	0	2	−2	3	4	1	0
G3 (S2)	39 min	32 min 05s	7	3	3	−1	1	−1	0	1	0
G4 (S2)	42 min	16 min 00s	7	9	3	0	4	−1	2	4	4

Fig. 2. Videorecording a play session of C:SBG. Players discussing their options.

similar money and a good happiness score, it would be difficult for them to progress more. G4 had more resources to manage. G2 had more happiness (scoring) and overall resources to keep expanding the city. G4 had a higher and faster expansion, which explains why it had fewer resources than G2.

Exploring Additional Qualitative Results.

In the post-test, players could write what they perceived to be the possible advantages of using game-based approaches (analog/digital) to support urban planning. Table 6 shows the process and examples of participants' comments to form the first and second-order clusters. Table 7 shows the total number of comments per cluster.

Table 6. First and second order clusters

Example of comments from participants (Px)	1st order	Sustainability		Participation/ Collaboration	Urbanism	Playability
	2nd order	Sustainable growth limits	Address all requirements	Discuss solutions	Importance of public facilities	Interactive and visual simulation
"*Difficulty of managing a city and all its aspects; sharing information and identifying problems can be an asset; solutions to these problems can be varied but consensus can be reached*" (P1)		●	●	●		
"*Mark problems on maps. Easy visualization*" (P4)						●
"*I learned that to create a city you have to take into account several aspects from different points of view, so it was important in the game to dialogue with others to find solutions, since each thing also has its consequence.*" (P7)		●		●		●
"*Importance of urban facilities for the city*" (P14)					●	

Table 7. Table captions should be placed above the tables.

1st order clusters	2nd order clusters	Number of related comments
Sustainability	Sustainable growth limits	4
	Address all requirements	10
Participation/ Collaboration	Discuss solutions	3
Urbanism	Playful interactive and visual simulation	2
Playability	Importance of public facilities	2

4   Discussion

When analyzing the results from Tables 2 and 3, it seems that students considered all games had high potential for learning but less as fun activities. This perception did not change after playing the games, even though they were entertainment games. Maybe playing the games during a lecture affected this perception. Despite the absence of sophisticated statistical analysis, the changes from the pre-tests and post-tests show some cases that can be related to the demographics of each session. We see an increase of + 1 in S1 students about games being fun. The reduced number of participants and the higher age average might influence this (30 years old), like the reduced game habits (S1 and S2 had the same median value of 4, but SD was higher in S2, meaning more experienced gamers were present). The perception that analog games can be better than digital games increased in S2 as the possibility to replace classes with games. This effect might result from less exposure to analog games by younger participants. Board game hobbyists tend to be older than 25 years (Booth 2021). All participants perceived games not to be childish and saw some benefits of using them as tools, but replacing traditional classes with games only got the students' enthusiasm in S2.

Table 3 revealed that students considered the analog (C:SBG) game to be more fun and fit for collaboration. The digital version is a single-player game. Players can discuss the moves when adapted for cooperative play but not control the game directly. The digital game had no specific controllers or mechanisms to foster collaborative play. Also, C:S is a real-time game, while C:SBG is turn-based. These game structures and mechanisms of C:SBG deliver collaborative experiences (e.g., sharing the game resources and building the same urban space). We could argue that the position of the players around the table, sharing the game components, moving, and handling them together helped this sense of collaboration (Fig. 2). In C:S, players were side by side facing the screen. Table 7 shows that three players highlighted the collaborative dimensions of the experience with the games. Being more active in the game could affect the sense of fun because players were unanimous, considering the C.SBG as more fun (Table 3). Other popular board game versions of digital games tend to be cooperative (Mechs vs. Minions, This War of Mine, and Dorfromantik).

The game progression in C:S was different from C:SBG. Groups 1 and 3 struggled more with the game, not achieving the threshold of 800 population in the given time (Table 4). In these groups, the game had many downtime moments. Players struggled with the controllers and the game menus. This effect was not present in C:SBG. Groups progressed differently but never stalled (Table 5). Despite this limitation, C:S was considered more suited for simulating a city and testing creative solutions for urban development, which relates to its higher game complexity (Table 3). What seems surprising is that the analog game that demanded the players to know all the rules before playing (Calleja 2022) seems simpler to play than the digital game with specific UI/UX techniques to help the game progress and master the controls [36].

We observed that students who progressed more in a game had similar progress in the other game (S2/G4), revealing a possible relationship to the heuristics of playing games and spatial and economic planning regardless of being analog or digital (Tables 4 and 5). In S2, more gamers were participating (Higher SD variation).

The qualitative analysis of the comments revealed clusters related to sustainability, urban planning, and urban decision-making. Students had no previous lectures about using game-based methods applied for urban and regional planning. Clusters about sustainability and the need for balance in growth, including collective decision-making, fit urban panning contemporary principles of social justice and environmental concerns [37–39]. Highlighting the participatory and collaborative decision-making approaches in the face of conflict, scarcity, and complexity fits the collaborative planning approaches [2, 40]. Addressing complexity and doing it through collaborative decision-making was identified by Sousa [41] as a way to profit from game-based planning.

Going into game design, it was clear that the detailed simulation of C:S has high potential to represent realistic urban models, but a simplification like C:SBG, that ignores detailed urban morphology, the transport system, and flows, representing them by track bars is viable to invoke urban issues (3 in Fig. 3). The polyominos provide the urban shapes and managing the track bars for resources and problems seems enough (2 in Fig. 3). C:SBG also deals with progression by using different decks of cards (1 in Fig. 3). This simplification has the potential for serious game and gamification purposes when addressing nonexperts or users learning urban concepts and the complexity of urban systems. Using simple analog to prototype complex digital CBG follows the literature game development [42, 43].

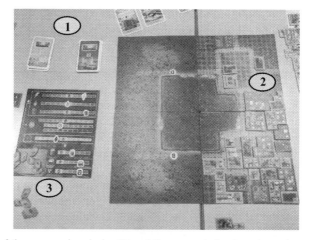

Fig. 3. View of the progression decks (1) and the connected polyominos pieces forming urban patterns (2), table to track urban indicators and resources (3).

5 Conclusion

The experiment addressed the use of entertainment games in urban and regional planning lectures. The games had minimum adaptation, played as the original Cities: Skylines digital (C:S) and analog version (C:SBG). Adapting the games is necessary when teachers have limited time and resources (computers, game copies, etc.) and balance the number of players to the attending students.

The two-hour sessions required two copies of each game to use in a standard class of a maximum of 16 students and only one facilitator. Four groups (four students each) can play the games simultaneously (two computers with the game installed and two board games). In the digital game, players must share the controllers, turn by turn (defining a timeframe or other metric per turn), discussing the options before playing them. These requirements are feasible to include introductory game-based learning and explore what could be game-based planning possibilities for future urban planning professionals. Proposing these fast experiences can be an introduction to games as support planning tools, addressing the possibilities and limitations of analog and digital game-based approaches for planning. From a game design perspective, the analog game revealed that addressing complex systems can be simplified by placing tiles over an orthogonal board and managing multiple urban indicators and resources through tack bars.

Students enjoyed the games moderately but were able to express their knowledge about the course topics, like the sustainable and decision-making issues involved in planning. Playing during a class might affect the fun dimension. Future research could assess the impact of suggested play if the students would play C:S freely and if they could identify learning advantages of using the game for urban planning.

Despite their different ages and backgrounds, urban planning students who participated in the experiment perceived the digital games as a more complex simulation while classifying the analog game as an engaging group activity that helped to implement collaborative decision-making. Future research could explore new hybrid games that include both dimensions, having the simulation detail of digital games and the social dimension of analog games. Another limitation affecting the case study outcomes is that C:S and C:SBG are different. They propose a similar progression but use different game mechanisms, progression, and feedback loops. The complexity is not equivalent (C:SBG is considered a median-light game). These differences forced us to adapt the games, and, regardless of our efforts, the games were not exact replicas. Despite this, the case study reveals that an analog reimplementation (using alternative game mechanisms) of a specific digital game can provide similar but not exact play experiences. Besides this, understanding why analog implementations of video games tend to be collaborative is yet to be explained. Is it that playing as a team tries to emulate the single-play aspect of digital games?

In C:SBG, the combination of game elements and mechanisms simulates a collective entity playing the game that resulted from the individual and coordinated decisions of all players involved. We have seen that, to transform C:S into an engaging playable collaborative dynamic, there is a need to introduce specific rules and game mechanics. We argue that collaborative playable behaviors tend to emerge only when the game design intentionally fosters it. Testing more game examples can contribute to new game design frameworks for collaborative game development.

References

1. Cox, M., Zagal, J.P.: Sustainability in City-Building Games (2022)
2. Innes, J.E., Booher, D.E.: Planning with complexity: an introduction to collaborative rationality for public policy. Routledge (2018). https://doi.org/10.4324/9781315147949

3. Deterding, S., Dixon, D., Khaled, R., Nacke, L.: From game design elements to gameful-ness: defining gamification. In: Proceedings of the 15th International Academic MindTrek Conference: Envisioning Future Media Environments, pp. 9–15 (2011)

4. Gandolfi, E.: Subjective temporalities at play: Temporality, subjectivity and gaming affor-dances in cities: skylines, Europa Universalis IV and Pillars of Eternity. Simulation Gaming **47**, 720–750 (2016)

5. Adams, P.C.: Teaching and learning with SimCity 2000. J. Geog. **97**, 47–55 (1998)

6. Minnery, J., Searle, G.: Toying with the city? Using the computer game SimCity^{TM} 4 in planning education. Plan. Pract. Res. **29**, 41–55 (2014)

7. Arnold, U., Söbke, H., Reichelt, M.: SimCity in infrastructure management education. Educ. Sci. **9**, 209 (2019)

8. Gaber, J.: Simulating planning: SimCity as a pedagogical tool. J. Plan. Educ. Res. **27**, 113–121 (2007)

9. Bereitschaft, B.: Gods of the city? Reflecting on city building games as an early introduction to urban systems. J. Geog. **115**, 51–60 (2016)

10. Pinos, J., Vozenilek, V., Pavlis, O.: Automatic geodata processing methods for real-world city visualizations in cities: skylines. ISPRS Int. J. Geo-Inf. **9**, 17 (2020)

11. Olszewski, R., Cegiełka, M., Szczepankowska, U., Wesołowski, J.: Developing a serious game that supports the resolution of social and ecological problems in the toolset environment of cities: Skylines. ISPRS Int. J. Geo-Inf. **9**, 118 (2020)

12. Bereitschaft, B.: Commercial city building games as pedagogical tools: what have we learned? J. Geogr. High. Educ. **47**, 161–187 (2023)

13. Khan, T.A., Zhao, X.: Perceptions of students for a gamification approach: cities skylines as a pedagogical tool in urban planning education. In: Responsible AI and Analytics for an Ethical and Inclusive Digitized Society: 20th IFIP WG 6.11 Conference on e-Business, e-Services and e-Society, I3E 2021, Galway, Ireland, September 1--3, 2021, Proceedings 20, pp. 763–773 (2021)

14. Rotherham, A.J., Willingham, D.T.: 21st-century" skills. Am. Educ. **17**, 17–20 (2010)

15. Konieczny, P.: Golden age of tabletop gaming: creation of the social capital and rise of third spaces for tabletop gaming in the 21st Century. Polish Sociol. Rev. **2019**, 199–215 (2019). https://doi.org/10.26412/psr206.05

16. Booth, P.: Board Games as Media. Bloomsbury Publishing USA (2021)

17. Calleja, G.: Unboxed: Board Game Experience and Design. MIT Press (2022)

18. Sousa, M., Bernardo, E.: Back in the Game. In: Zagalo, N., Veloso, A.I., Costa, L., Mealha, Ó. (eds.) VJ 2019. CCIS, vol. 1164, pp. 72–85. Springer, Cham (2019). https://doi.org/10.1007/978-3-030-37983-4_6

19. Martinho, C., Sousa, M.: CSSII : a player motivation model for tabletop games. Found. Digit. Games 2023 (FDG 2023), April 12 to 14, 2023, Lisbon, Port. 1 (2023). https://doi.org/10.1145/3582437.3582477

20. Nand, A.: 110,000 games in a chart. https://boardgamegeek.com/blogpost/116720/110000-games-chart

21. Kosa, M., Spronck, P.: Towards a tabletop gaming motivations inventory (TGMI). In: Zagalo, N., Veloso, A.I., Costa, L., Mealha, Ó. (eds.) VJ 2019. CCIS, vol. 1164, pp. 59–71. Springer, Cham (2019). https://doi.org/10.1007/978-3-030-37983-4_5

22. Woods, S.: Eurogames: The Design, Culture and Play of Modern European Board Games. McFarland, Incorporated, Publishers (2012)

23. Rogerson, M.J., Gibbs, M.: Finding time for tabletop: board game play and parenting. Games Cult. **13**, 280–300 (2018). https://doi.org/10.1177/1555412016656324

24. Cantrell, C., Ernst, R., Librande, S., Saraswat, P., Tiras, N.: Mechs vs. Minions (2016)

25. Palm, M., Zach, L.: Dorfromantik: the board game (2022)

26. Oracz, M., Wiśniewski, J.: This War of Mine: the board game (2017)
27. Samarasinghe, D., et al.: A data driven review of board game design and interactions of their mechanics. IEEE Access 1 (2021). https://doi.org/10.1109/ACCESS.2021.3103198
28. Kritz, J., Mangeli, E., Xexéo, G.: Building an Ontology of Boardgame Mechanics based on the BoardGameGeek Database and the MDA Framework. In: XVI Brazilian Symposium on Computer Games and Digital Entertainment, pp. 182–191. Curitiba (2017)
29. Håkansson, R.: Cities: Skylines – The Board Game (2019)
30. Sousa, M., Silva, M.: Solitaire paper automation: when solitaire modern board game modes approach artificial intelligence. In: 22nd International Conference on Intelligent Games and Simulation, GAME-ON 2021, pp. 35–42 (2021)
31. Viard, A.: Small City: Deluxe Edition (2023)
32. Alspach, T.: Suburbia (2012)
33. Doumen, J., Wiersinga, J.: Antiquity (2004)
34. Mayer, I., et al.: The research and evaluation of serious games: toward a comprehensive methodology. Br. J. Educ. Technol. **45**, 502–527 (2014). https://doi.org/10.1111/bjet.12067
35. Charmaz, K.: Constructing grounded theory. SAGE (2014)
36. Hodent, C.: The gamer's brain: how neuroscience and UX can impact video game design. CRC Press (2017)
37. Fainstein, S.S.: New directions in planning theory. Urban Aff. Rev. **35**, 451–478 (2000)
38. Taylor, N.: Urban Planning. Theory Since 1945, pp. 1–192 (1998)
39. Allmendinger, P.: Planning theory. Bloomsbury Publishing (2017)
40. Portugali, J.: What makes cities complex? In: Portugali, J., Stolk, E. (eds.) Complexity, Cognition, Urban Planning and Design. SPC, pp. 3–19. Springer, Cham (2016). https://doi.org/10.1007/978-3-319-32653-5_1
41. Sousa, M., Antunes, A.P., Pinto, N., Zagalo, N.: Serious games in spatial planning: strengths, limitations and support frameworks. Int. J. Serious Games. **9**, 115–133 (2022). https://doi.org/10.17083/ijsg.v9i2.510
42. Ham, E.: Tabletop game design for video game designers. CRC Press (2015)
43. Brathwaite, B., Schreiber, I.: Challenges for game designers. Nelson Education (2009)

Humans vs AI: An Exploratory Study with Online and Offline Learners

João Inácio[1] , Nuno Fachada[1,2]([⊠]) , João P. Matos-Carvalho[1,2] ,
and Carlos M. Fernandes[1,2]

[1] Lusófona University, ECATI, Campo Grande, 376, Lisbon, Portugal
a22202654@alunos.ulht.pt,
{joao.matos.carvalho,carlos.fernandes}@ulusofona.pt,
nuno.fachada@ulusofona.pt
[2] Lusófona University, COPELABS, Campo Grande, 376, Lisbon, Portugal

Abstract. We present an exploratory study comparing human player performance against online and offline AI learning techniques—the Naive Bayes Classifier and Genetic Algorithms, respectively—using a simple turn-based game. Human player performance is also assessed according to gender, age, experience playing games, and boredom level during game sessions. Human players and AI techniques are shown to obtain statistically equivalent score distributions. No gender performance differences were found, although performance seems to decrease with age. To a lesser extent, performance appears to improve with self-assessed experience and boredom levels. This study offers a base for more comprehensive experiments, suggesting various directions for future research.

Keywords: Computer games · Naive Bayes Classifier · Genetic Algorithms

1 Introduction

Artificial Intelligence (AI) has revolutionized the gaming industry, enhancing player experiences and creating more immersive, challenging, and realistic virtual worlds [21,36]. One important aspect of AI in games consists of simulating intelligent behavior within the game environment, making non-player characters (NPCs) and opponents more lifelike and responsive [29,37]. This technology has come a long way since the early days of computer games, progressing from simple rule-based systems to complex deep reinforcement learning models [38].

This paper presents an exploratory study with the aim of evaluating human player performance against AI techniques in a simple turn-based game, originally proposed by Melanie Mitchell [22]. It also offers a comparison of human performance based on gender, age, experience playing games, and motivation playing this particular game—attributes collected through a post-game survey.

Supported by Fundação para a Ciência e a Tecnologia (Portugal) under Grant UIDB/04111/2020 (COPELABS).

© The Author(s), under exclusive license to Springer Nature Switzerland AG 2024
L. Vale Costa et al. (Eds.): VJ 2023, CCIS 1984, pp. 272–286, 2024.
https://doi.org/10.1007/978-3-031-51452-4_19

This study is a proof of concept, providing a foundation for more comprehensive studies with more complex games and AI techniques, and a more detailed evaluation of how the attributes of human participants impact their performance.

Two AI techniques are experimented with: the Naive Bayes Classifier (NBC) [14,21] and Genetic Algorithms (GA) [13,22], used in online and offline learning contexts, respectively. In online learning, the AI is trained as the game is being actively played by a human, the decisions and actions of which inform the algorithm, which is later (hopefully) able to mimic the human player and play the game. In offline learning, the AI is trained during the game's development process, without immediate player input. The NBC was selected as the online learning technique due to its simplicity and capability of offering a solid baseline for experimenting with more complex algorithms [21]. In turn, GAs were showcased with the original formulation of the turn-based game tested here [22], which together with their common use in academic game AI research [37], makes them an appropriate choice as an offline learning technique. However, given the preliminary nature of this work, GAs are mainly used to validate the performance of the NBC, and were not thoroughly experimented with.

This paper is organized as follows. In Sect. 2, related work on using NBC and GAs in game-related AI is discussed and the present study is contextualized. Section 3 describes the used methods, namely the rules and implementation of the turn-based game, the experimental procedure (including data collection), setup of both AI algorithms, as well as the employed data analysis techniques. Results are presented in Sect. 4 and discussed in Sect. 5. Finally, Sect. 6 sums up the study, highlighting various interesting areas of future work.

2   Background

Developing AI that can play games in a human-like manner serves three primary purposes [24]. Firstly, it enhances the gaming experience by creating believable non-player characters (NPCs), making the game more engaging. Secondly, it can be used to demonstrate how to play the game effectively, offering guidance to players who are stuck on a particular level. Finally, it aids in understanding how a specific player would approach and play through game content, which is valuable for tasks like procedural content generation and content selection to improve gameplay and content evaluation processes.

The NBC is a simple and efficient algorithm appropriate for various classification tasks, particularly as an initial step in machine learning projects [14,21]. Its simplicity, ability to handle large datasets, and suitability for online training make it a valuable tool for the purpose of developing artificial players which play in a human-like manner [10]. On the other hand, GAs, which simulate evolution for optimizing game mechanics or character behaviors, offer substantial potential for creating more engaging and unpredictable gameplay experiences [1,11,35], and have also been used for imitating human-like player behavior [33].

One of the works using NBC in game environments is reported by Fernandéz and Salmerón [10] where they devised an heuristic for playing chess based on a minimax algorithm with alpha-beta pruning and then refined the parameters of the playing engine with an NBC. Their objective was not only to improve the search heuristic, but also to adapt the engine playing style to the user's style. Thus, they developed another NBC with a set of features that described some characteristics of the opponent's game. They demonstrate that the engine is able to learn and that behavior improves quickly as the size of the learning set increases.

In [9], the authors resorted to a game-playing environment to infer students' learning style. For that purpose, a set of students was asked to solve a puzzle called Equilibrium, while relevant information from their interaction with the game was being extracted. Once the students' profiles were built from their interaction with the game, they trained and tested an NBC classifier. The proposed model's accuracy demonstrates that it is possible to infer the learning style from a non-educational environment and with little information.

Wang and Shang [34] used an NBC to predict the outcome of the DOTA2 multiplayer online game. The accuracy of the classifier on the training set was 85.33%. However, that value decreased significantly when classifying the test set. Similarly, Chan et al. [3] used an NBC to predict the outcome of a Massive Online Battle Arena game based on the roles of heroes chosen by the players.

Saini et al. [27] combined an NBC and a data-driven Finite State Machine (FSM) to implement an AI fighting video game player that is capable of mimicking real players' tactics and strategies. Using a proof-of-concept game, the model first collects data from human vs. human playing and then uses an NBC that has been trained to classify the collected data to assign the moves to three different pre-determined states. Then, an FSM, based on the health of the AI player and combining the previous, current, and next state for a given transition, is created. The presented results demonstrated the engine's ability to mimic real players' strategies and tactics.

This work further explores these topics, using a simple turn-based game for evaluating the performance of NBC and GAs in online and offline learning scenarios, respectively, comparing the collected results with those obtained by human players—whose game sessions were used to train the NBC online.

3   Methods

3.1   The Trash Picker Game

The *Trash Picker* game used in this work was developed in the context of the AI course [5] at Lusófona University's Videogames BA [6,8], and was implemented in the Unity engine [32] using the MVC architectural pattern, and leveraging the *libGameAI* library of AI algorithms for games [7].

In this game, the player—a human or an AI algorithm—controls a robot tasked with picking litter from the ground. The robot is placed on a 10×10 toroidal grid of square tiles. Each tile can be empty or have trash on it, as shown in Fig. 1. A map configuration is generated randomly for each game session, where each tile has a 50% probability of spawning trash. The robot can perform

Fig. 1. The *Trash Picker* game during play. The robot, in orange, is located in a tile without trash, and is able to see (and potentially move to) his Von Neumann neighborhood, which in turn contains trash (in red) in the tiles left, right, and below the robot. (Color figure online)

Table 1. Points per action in the *Trash Picker* game.

Action	Points
Explicit movement in one direction	-2
Random movement	-1
No action (spends turn)	0
Pick up trash successfully	$+10$
Pick up trash with no trash present in tile	-5

seven different actions: move north, move east, move south, move west, move in a random direction, do nothing (which spends an action), and collect trash. Movement can be performed a single tile per turn, and since the grid is toroidal, the robot can move into a boundary of the grid and appear at the opposite boundary on the same axis of movement. At any moment, only the tiles in the Von Neumann neighborhood of the robot's position are visible to the player, as highlighted in Fig. 1.

The goal of the game is to obtain the highest score possible by executing one of the seven available actions, which modify the score as detailed in Table 1, over a pre-specified number of turns. The t number of turns (and therefore of actions that can be performed) in a single game session is given by Eq. 1:

$$t = L^2 - (L/2)^2 \tag{1}$$

where L is the side of the grid (assuming it is a square grid, which we do in this game). With a 10×10 grid, this equates to 75 turns.

The *Trash Picker* game is overtly inspired by Mitchell's *Robby's World* [22], although adapted to be played by humans. For example, *Robby's World* contains walls, which the AI player can bump into and be penalized for it. With this knowledge, a human player would never bump into a wall other than by mistake. Therefore, the *Trash Picker* game is toroidal, i.e., it has no walls. To consider human mistakes, we kept the rule that penalizes the player for picking up trash in an empty tile. Additionally, the fact that random movement is less penalized than explicit movement, as well as that performing no action (skipping a turn) has no penalty, provides an additional strategic layer for both AI and human players to exploit.

3.2 Experimental Procedure

The experimental procedure for each participant consisted of playing a minimum of ten *Trash Picker* game sessions. The rules, controls, and score system were explained to participants beforehand, and the authors assisted the participants as they played, answering questions and clarifying doubts, if necessary. Afterwards, participants filled out a fully anonymous survey following the required legal data protection regulations, answering four questions:

Q1 *(gender)* "What is your gender?"
 – Possible answers: *male, female, other.*
Q2 *(age)* "How old are you?"
 – Possible answer: positive integer value.
Q3 *(experience)* "How often do you play video games?"
 – Possible answer: five-point Likert scale, from 1 (*"Never"*) to 5 (*"Whenever I'm able to"*).
Q4 *(boring)* Did you found the game and the experience boring?
 – Possible answer: five-point Likert scale, from 1 (*"Not boring at all"*) to 5 (*"Extremely boring"*).

3.3 Naive Bayes Classifier Learning

An NBC was trained during the ten game sessions of each human subject. After each human game session, the updated NBC would automatically play a game in the background and log its score. The human and NBC scores were saved to a file when exiting the game. At the end of an experiment, this file was associated with the survey replies given by the human subject.

3.4 Genetic Algorithm Learning

To use GAs for learning how to play *Trash Picker*, we followed Mitchell's approach [22] in terms of representing individuals in the GA's population. Specifically, individuals are represented as a list of possible game states (from the perspective of the individual), to which one of the seven actions described in the previous subsection is associated with. Given the set of five tiles in a Von Neumann neighborhood, where each tile can be either empty or containing trash, there are a total of 2^5 possible game situations from the robot's perspective.

The algorithm was configured to create a population of 200 individuals with randomly selected actions associated to the possible game states. For the next generation, parents are first selected using tournament selection, with two individuals chosen at random and the one with the best fitness selected for crossover. The population is then fully replaced by new individuals, created through one-point crossover with a randomly selected split point. Lastly, mutation is applied to individuals, where there is a small probability that an action in each game state-action pair is replaced by a random action. An individual's fitness is evaluated by running 100 games with its strategy and taking the average of scores obtained in those games. Tests were done with mutation probability between 0.5% and 2%, as further described in Subsect. 4.2.

3.5   Data Analysis

Statistical tests were used in combination with box plots to assess possible differences and trends between scores, for example, between human subjects and AI techniques, or between human subjects with different characteristics (e.g., gender or age). For the null hypothesis H_0 of groups having the same underlying distribution, two non-parameteric tests were used, namely the Mann-Whitney test [19] when comparing two groups (i.e., *male* or *female* in the case of gender[1]), and the Kruskal-Wallis test when considering more than two groups [18] (such as the case of Likert scale replies). When significant differences were found and an upwards or downwards trend was visually observed, the Jonckheere-Terpstra trend test was used [12,30] assuming the null hypothesis that the empirically noted trend does not exist.

Kendall's rank correlation coefficient [15,16], a measure of correspondence between two rankings, was used for assessing the correlation between "experience" and "boredom". As is common in correlation measures, values near 1 (or -1) indicate strong positive (or negative) correlation, while values close to zero indicate that the two rankings are independent (i.e., there is no correlation between them). This non-parametric coefficient is appropriate when data consists of categories with a clear rank order but unknown intervals between them, and when multiple data points have the same value (i.e., there are ties), and therefore a robust choice for comparing Likert scale-type data. An associated hypothesis test, whose null hypothesis is the absence of correlation, is also performed.

Since this work is essentially exploratory, we do not establish a pre-defined significance level α, evaluating the significance of test result p-values in context of the overall data analysis [2], while considering commonly employed thresholds for α if appropriate.

---

[1] No participant identified as *other* in the survey.

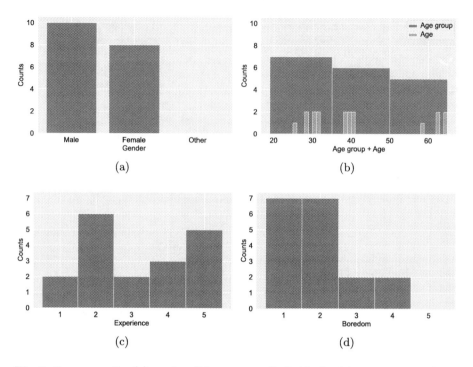

Fig. 2. Survey results: (a) gender; (b) age group (individual subject age counts shown in orange); (c) experience playing videogames; and, (d) boredom playing this particular game/performing this experience. (Color figure online)

4   Results

4.1   Survey

A total of 18 human players participated in the experiment. Survey results for these participants are presented in Fig. 2. In terms of *gender*, Fig. 2a, 10 participants identified as male, 8 as female, while none identified as other. The age distribution is shown in orange in Fig. 2b, forming the three clusters shown in blue in the same figure. Therefore, we consider these three *age groups* rather than individual ages for the remainder or this work. Most participants stated that their *experience* playing video games was either at level 2 or level 5 of the employed Likert scale (Fig. 2c). Finally, participants did not seem to find the game and the experiment *boring* at all, with most answering at level 1 or 2, while none specified level 5 (*"extremely boring"*).

4.2   Genetic Algorithms

The genetic algorithm was parameterized as described in Subsect. 3.4, with mutation set between 0.5% and 2.0%. Figure 3 shows the evolution of fitness (i.e., the average game score over 100 played games for the best individual) over 500 generations under these conditions. It is possible to observe that fitness plateaus after approximately 400 generations. With 0.5% and 1.0% mutation rate, the genetic algorithm reached a high score of 242 points, limited to 240 points when mutation was set to 2.0%.

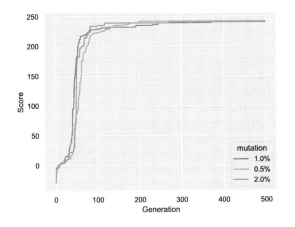

Fig. 3. Evolution of score over 500 generations of a genetic algorithm with a population size of 200, tournament selection, 100% crossover probability, and mutation rate set to 0.5%, 1.0%, and 2.0%.

The individual with higher fitness from the GA with 1% mutation rate was then selected to play 20 games, the performance of which was compared with human players and NBC-trained players, as discussed in the next subsection.

4.3 Comparing the Performance of Human Players Versus AI Techniques

The 18 participants played a total of 10 game sessions each. Data from each game session was fed into an NBC, which therefore learned to play by example. The NBC played a game session after each human-played game, and we kept track of its score. In total, there were 180 human-played game sessions, and correspondingly, 180 NBC-played game sessions. For this analysis, we also considered 20 GA-played games, with the GA trained separately as discussed in the previous subsection. Results for the human participants and both AI techniques are shown in Fig. 4.

Observing Fig. 4a, it becomes clear that human players quickly understand the rules of the game, and start playing at a good level from the offset. Even though there is an apparent slight increase in score from session 1 to 10, the overall improvement is not as noticeable as in the case of the NBC. After one learning session, the NBC is already capable of playing at an interesting level, although variance is very high. After 10 training sessions, the NBC is able to play at a human level. At session 10, score distributions between human players

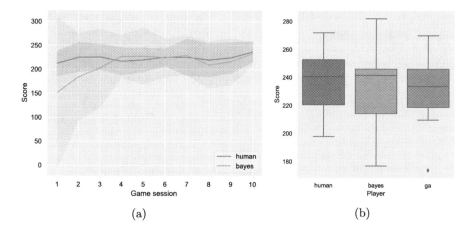

Fig. 4. Performance of human players versus AI techniques: (a) mean score of human players and NBC after a given number of game sessions (NBC always plays after the human player); shaded regions show the standard deviation; (b) performance of human players and NBC after 10 sessions compared with the performance of "best" GA.

and the NBC (Fig. 4b) is statistically indistinguishable, with a p-value of 0.8239 for the Mann-Whitney test.

The best GA solution (obtained with 1% mutation rate) plays at a similar level to the human and NBC players (Fig. 4b). Applying the Kruskal-Wallis statistical test to the three score distributions (human, NBC, and GA) yields a non-significant p-value of 0.7118, meaning that the null hypothesis that these three score groups are derived from the same distribution cannot be rejected.

4.4   Human Player Performance

Considering the results presented in Fig. 4a, which shows that human improvement over game sessions is limited, we consider all 180 human-played games (18 players × 10 game sessions) when comparing human-player scores based on *gender*, *age group*, *experience* playing video games, and *boredom* level during the ten game sessions. Figure 5 shows the performance of humans over these dimensions, while Table 2 presents the p-values denoting the respective differences and trends (or lack thereof).

Regarding *gender*, scores were very similar, as highlighted by Fig. 5a and a non-significant p-value of 0.1918. However, the same cannot be said for *age group*, as well as *experience* playing games and *boredom* levels. With respect to the *age group*, scores appear to decrease for older subjects (Fig. 5b). Detectable differences between age groups were confirmed by a significant p-value of 0.0016, which led us to apply the Jonckheere-Terpstra trend test assuming the alternative hypothesis that score decreases with age. This test yielded a significant p-value of 0.0002, confirming that the scores do seem to display a downwards trend with increasing age.

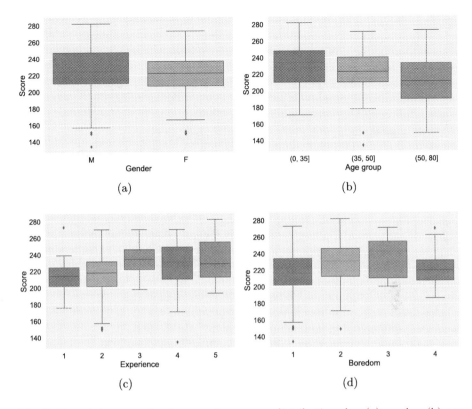

Fig. 5. Box plots comparing human player score distributions by: (a) gender; (b) age group; (c) experience playing video games; and (d) boredom playing this particular game/performing this experience.

When grouping subjects by *experience* and *boredom* levels (Figs. 5c and 5d, respectively), results are not as clear-cut. Figures show an apparent score increase for higher Likert levels, though less distinctly for *boredom* due to lower score distribution at level 4 and lack of level 5 data. In both cases, the *p*-value is comfortably below the commonly used $\alpha = 0.01$ significance threshold, meaning that different levels of *experience* and *boredom* likely lead to different scores. Since the figures hint at a possible score increase trend, the Jonckheere-Terpstra trend test was applied using this assumption for the alternative hypothesis (the null hypothesis being that no upward trend exists). As shown in Table 2, the *p*-value for *experience* is borderline significant (in a $\alpha = 0.01$ scenario), while the *p*-value for *boredom* is considerably more significant, despite the score distribution dip at level 4 and lack of level 5 answers.

Finally, and given the possible association of both "experience" and "boredom" with higher scores, we were interested in determining a potential correlation between these two Likert scale-sourced variables. Kendall's rank correlation coefficient was calculated for this purpose, yielding $\tau = 0.25$, denoting a possible

Table 2. p-values denoting the differences and trends (or lack thereof) between the human player groups shown in Fig. 5. For the null hypothesis H_0 of groups having the same underlying distribution, the non-parameteric Mann-Whitney (two groups) and Kruskal-Wallis tests (more than two groups) were used. For H_0 that no ▲/▼ trend exists, the Jonckheere-Terpstra test was applied.

H_0	Dimension			
	Gender	Age group	Experience	Boredom
Same distribution	0.1918	0.0016	0.0013	0.0053
No ▲/▼ trend	—	▼ 0.0002	▲ 0.0094	▲ 0.0001

positive correlation. However, the associated hypothesis test yielded a p-value of 0.1114 under the alternative hypothesis that there is a positive correlation, which is insufficient to reject the null hypothesis that there is no correlation.

5   Discussion

When comparing human and AI levels of play, the main result to be highlighted is that both online and offline learning techniques, the NBC and GA, respectively, were able to attain human level without much difficulty: the NBC by observing 10 human-played game sessions, and the GA by evolving during 500 generations. These results are in accordance with existing literature for more complex games [10,11,13]. However, since humans were able to quickly master the game, with the NBC not far behind in imitating human play level, and the GA saturating at the same level of scores than both humans and NBC, it is likely that the proposed *Trash Picker* game in general, and the specific rules used here in particular, may be too simple to pose a real challenge.

Looking at results from a purely human perspective, this study mostly confirms previous findings in the literature, as is the case of no gender performance differences [28] and age-related performance decreases [31]. If we consider that the upward trend in score with *experience/boredom* does in fact occur (and that a correlation between *experience* and *boredom* exists), then this is also in line with recent literature, which underlines that bored players are generally those with more experience, which is one of the assumptions behind dynamic difficulty adjustment studies [4,17,25]. Therefore it should be expected that bored and more experienced players have higher scores in the *Trash Picker* game. However, closely observing Fig. 5c (*experience*) and Fig. 5d (*boredom*), it is possible to note that Likert level 3 yields the highest median scores in both cases. This suggests a possible alternative interpretation, in which more experienced and/or bored players will have lower scores due to playing faster, thus committing more errors. This is highly speculative of course, but opens the door to measuring play time, even though this is a turn-based game, to check if faster play leads to more errors and is in any way correlated with *experience* or *boredom*.

However, this work presents several limitations. Due to its exploratory nature, no research questions were specifically defined, other than determining to which point could relatively simple online and offline AI techniques reach or surpass human play level. The tested techniques are either very simple, as the case of NBC, or not thoroughly tested, i.e., GAs, in which we experimented with very few parameters. The human-specific analysis came as a bonus of the collected data. Results mostly confirm previous findings, although they also hinted at alternative interpretations, while pointing to several possible improvements and future investigations—discussed in Sect. 6—consisting of an interesting first step in that regard. Furthermore, the small sample size ($n = 18$), with various survey questions having small counts (or no counts, as is the case of "boredom" level 5), limits our confidence in the possible effects and correlations found.

In any case, we believe this exploratory work produced some interesting preliminary results, suggesting that an improved experimental design could lead to potentially finding more appropriate AI techniques to mimic human behavior in-game, or uncovering new relations between mental states and game performance, for example.

6   Conclusions and Future Work

This paper presented an exploratory study on assessing human player performance against online and offline AI learning techniques (NBC and GAs, respectively) using the simple *Trash Picker* turn-based game. An evaluation was also done on how the human participants perform according to gender, age, experience playing games, and self-reported boredom level during the game sessions. Within its limitations, this study showed that human players and both AI techniques attained statistically indistinguishable score distributions, and an analysis of human scores and post-game survey replies highlighted no significant differences in performance of male and female users. As for age, experience, and boredom, results largely confirmed what is described in recent literature, although leaving room for alternative interpretations and suggesting future directions.

For future experiments, GAs should be tested with more detail than what was done here. Nonetheless, various interesting alternatives exist, such as combining the NBC with GAs using a specific type of GA called Estimation of Distribution Algorithms (EDAs), namely the Univariate Marginal Distribution Algorithm, an EDA with independent variables [23], and the Bayesian Optimization Algorithm [26], more suited when variables have codependencies. Although EDAs can be used for offline learning, their probabilistic nature also makes them appropriate for online optimization. More recent state-of-the-art AI for games techniques could also be experimented with, namely (deep) reinforcement learning [20,38] and neuroevolution [24], which are widely used in games AI research [37]. It is debatable, however, if scores could be further improved with any of these techniques considering *Trash Picker*'s current rules. These should be revised to make the game more strategic and challenging for humans, while posing a more real challenge for AI techniques. Possibilities include further penalizing explicit movement, reducing penalties for random movement, or giving points for skipping a turn. In any case, current rules require a thorough revision.

Other research possibilities include comparing the sequence of actions taken by the AI players with those of the human players, evaluating if the algorithms are able to actually mimic the human playing style, other than obtaining equivalent scores. It would also be interesting to test human perception to game world edges, for example modifying the UI so the user cannot see the edges or immediately understand that the grid is toroidal. In such case, how would results compare with the current UI? Finally, measuring the time a person takes to play, and comparing it with the dimensions studied here—score, gender, age, experience, boredom—as well as other factors, also appears to be a compelling path forward.

References

1. Aliprandi, F., Nobre, R.A., Ripamonti, L.A., Gadia, D., Maggiorini, D.: Find, fuse, fight: genetic algorithms to provide engaging content for multiplayer augmented reality games. In: De Paolis, L.T., Arpaia, P., Sacco, M. (eds.) Extended Reality XR Salento 2022. LNCS, vol. 13446, pp. 178–197. Springer, Cham (2022). https://doi.org/10.1007/978-3-031-15553-6_14
2. Amrhein, V., Greenland, S.: Remove, rather than redefine, statistical significance. Nat. Hum. Behav. $2(1)$, 4 (2018). https://doi.org/10.1038/s41562-017-0224-0
3. Chan, A., Fachrizal, F., Lubis, A.: Outcome prediction using Naïve Bayes algorithm in the selection of role hero mobile legend. J. Phys: Conf. Ser. $1566(1)$, 012041 (2020). https://doi.org/10.1088/1742-6596/1566/1/012041
4. Chanel, G., Rebetez, C., Bétrancourt, M., Pun, T.: Boredom, engagement and anxiety as indicators for adaptation to difficulty in games. In: Proceedings of the 12th International Conference on Entertainment and Media in the Ubiquitous Era, MindTrek 2008, pp. 13–17. ACM, New York (2008). https://doi.org/10.1145/1457199.1457203
5. Fachada, N.: ColorShapeLinks: a board game AI competition framework for educators and students. Comput. Educ. Artif. Intell. 2, 100014 (2021). https://doi.org/10.1016/j.caeai.2021.100014
6. Fachada, N., et al.: Improving the CS curriculum of a top-down videogames BA. In: Proceedings of the 11th Computer Science Education Research Conference, CSERC 2022, pp. 62–63. ACM, New York (2023). https://doi.org/10.1145/3569173.3569183
7. Fachada, N., Barreiros, F.F., Lopes, P., Fonseca, M.: Active learning prototypes for teaching game AI. In: IEEE Conference on Games 2023, CoG 2023. IEEE, August 2023. https://doi.org/10.1109/CoG57401.2023.10333229. https://ieeexplore.ieee.org/document/10333229
8. Fachada, N., Códices, N.: Top-down design of a CS curriculum for a computer games BA. In: Proceedings of the 2020 ACM Conference on Innovation and Technology in Computer Science Education, ITiCSE 2020, pp. 300–306. ACM, New York, June 2020. https://doi.org/10.1145/3341525.3387378
9. Feldman, J., Monteserin, A., Amandi, A.: Detecting students' perception style by using games. Comput. Educ. 71, 14–22 (2014). https://doi.org/10.1016/j.compedu.2013.09.007
10. Fernández, A., Salmerón, A.: BayesChess: a computer chess program based on bayesian networks. Pattern Recogn. Lett. $29(8)$, 1154–1159 (2008). https://doi.org/10.1016/j.patrec.2007.06.013

11. García-Sánchez, P., Tonda, A., Fernández-Leiva, A.J., Cotta, C.: Optimizing hearthstone agents using an evolutionary algorithm. Knowl.-Based Syst. **188**, 105032 (2020). https://doi.org/10.1016/j.knosys.2019.105032

12. Jonckheere, A.R.: A distribution-free k-sample test against ordered alternatives. Biometrika **41**(1/2), 133–145 (1954). https://doi.org/10.2307/2333011

13. Katoch, S., Chauhan, S.S., Kumar, V.: A review on genetic algorithm: past, present, and future. Multimedia Tools Appl. **80**, 8091–8126 (2021). https://doi. org/10.1007/s11042-020-10139-6

14. Kaviani, P., Dhotre, S.: Short survey on Naive Bayes algorithm. Int. J. Adv. Eng. Res. Dev. (IJAERD) **4**(11), 607–611 (2017). http://ijaerd.com/index.php/ IJAERD/article/view/4155

15. Kendall, M.G.: A new measure of rank correlation. Biometrika **30**(1/2), 81–93 (1938). https://doi.org/10.1093/biomet/30.1-2.81

16. Kendall, M.G.: The treatment of ties in ranking problems. Biometrika **33**(3), 239–251 (1945). https://doi.org/10.1093/biomet/33.3.239

17. Klimmt, C., Blake, C., Hefner, D., Vorderer, P., Roth, C.: Player performance, satisfaction, and video game enjoyment. In: Natkin, S., Dupire, J. (eds.) ICEC 2009. LNCS, vol. 5709, pp. 1–12. Springer, Heidelberg (2009). https://doi.org/10. 1007/978-3-642-04052-8_1

18. Kruskal, W.H., Wallis, W.A.: Use of ranks in one-criterion variance analysis. J. Am. Stat. Assoc. **47**(260), 583–621 (1952). https://doi.org/10.1080/01621459. 1952.10483441

19. Mann, H.B., Whitney, D.R.: On a test of whether one of two random variables is stochastically larger than the other. Ann. Math. Stat. **18**(1), 50–60 (1947). http:// www.jstor.org/stable/2236101

20. Markovska, J., Šoberl, D.: Deep reinforcement learning compared to human performance in playing video games. In: Pečečnik, K.S., Jakus, G. (eds.) Proceedings of the 7th Human-Computer Interaction Slovenia Conference 2022, HCI SI 2022, vol. 3300, November 2022. https://ceur-ws.org/Vol-3300/short_8285.pdf

21. Millington, I.: AI for Games, 3rd edn. CRC Press, Boca Raton (2019). https://doi. org/10.1201/9781351053303

22. Mitchell, M.: Complexity: A Guided Tour. Oxford University Press, Oxford (2009)

23. Mühlenbein, H., Paaß, G.: From recombination of genes to the estimation of distributions I. Binary parameters. In: Voigt, H.-M., Ebeling, W., Rechenberg, I., Schwefel, H.-P. (eds.) PPSN 1996. LNCS, vol. 1141, pp. 178–187. Springer, Heidelberg (1996). https://doi.org/10.1007/3-540-61723-X_982

24. Ortega, J., Shaker, N., Togelius, J., Yannakakis, G.N.: Imitating human playing styles in Super Mario Bros. Entertain. Comput. **4**(2), 93–104 (2013). https://doi. org/10.1016/j.entcom.2012.10.001

25. Pagalyte, E., Mancini, M., Climent, L.: Go with the flow: reinforcement learning in turn-based battle video games. In: Proceedings of the 20th ACM International Conference on Intelligent Virtual Agents, IVA 2020, pp. 1–8. ACM, New York (2020). https://doi.org/10.1145/3383652.3423868

26. Pelikan, M., Goldberg, D.E., Cantú-Paz, E., et al.: BOA: the Bayesian optimization algorithm. In: Proceedings of the 1st Annual Conference on Genetic and Evolutionary Computation, GECCO 1999, vol. 1, pp. 525–532. Morgan Kaufmann Publishers Inc., San Francisco (1999)

27. Saini, S., Chung, P.W.H., Dawson, C.W.: Mimicking human strategies in fighting games using a data driven finite state machine. In: 2011 6th IEEE Joint International Information Technology and Artificial Intelligence Conference, vol. 2, pp. 389–393. IEEE (2011). https://doi.org/10.1109/ITAIC.2011.6030356

28. Shen, C., Ratan, R., Cai, Y.D., Leavitt, A.: Do men advance faster than women? Debunking the gender performance gap in two massively multiplayer online games. J. Comput.-Mediat. Commun. **21**(4), 312–329 (2016). https://doi.org/10.1111/jcc4.12159

29. Soares, E.S., Bulitko, V.: Deep variational autoencoders for NPC behaviour classification. In: 2019 IEEE Conference on Games (CoG), pp. 1–4 (2019). https://doi.org/10.1109/CIG.2019.8848095

30. Terpstra, T.J.: The asymptotic normality and consistency of Kendall's test against trend, when ties are present in one ranking. Indag. Math. **14**(3), 327–333 (1952)

31. Thompson, J.J., Blair, M.R., Henrey, A.J.: Over the hill at 24: persistent age-related cognitive-motor decline in reaction times in an ecologically valid video game task begins in early adulthood. PLoS ONE **9**(4), e94215 (2014). https://doi.org/10.1371/journal.pone.0094215

32. Unity Technologies: Unity®(2023). https://unity.com/

33. Van Hoorn, N., Togelius, J., Wierstra, D., Schmidhuber, J.: Robust player imitation using multiobjective evolution. In: 2009 IEEE Congress on Evolutionary Computation, pp. 652–659. IEEE, May 2009. https://doi.org/10.1109/CEC.2009.4983007

34. Wang, K., Shang, W.: Outcome prediction of DOTA2 based on Naïve Bayes classifier. In: 2017 IEEE/ACIS 16th International Conference on Computer and Information Science (ICIS), pp. 591–593. IEEE (2017). https://doi.org/10.1109/ICIS.2017.7960061

35. Weber, M., Notargiacomo, P.: Dynamic difficulty adjustment in digital games using genetic algorithms. In: 2020 19th Brazilian Symposium on Computer Games and Digital Entertainment (SBGames), pp. 62–70. IEEE, November 2020. https://doi.org/10.1109/SBGames51465.2020.00019

36. Wu, Y., Yi, A., Ma, C., Chen, L.: Artificial intelligence for video game visualization, advancements, benefits and challenges. Math. Biosci. Eng. **20**, 15345–15373 (2023). https://doi.org/10.3934/mbe.2023686

37. Yannakakis, G.N., Togelius, J.: Artificial Intelligence and Games. Springer, Cham (2018). http://gameaibook.org

38. Zhang, Y., Li, Z., Cao, Y., Zhao, X., Cao, J.: Deep reinforcement learning using optimized Monte Carlo tree search in EWN. IEEE Trans. Games (2023). https://doi.org/10.1109/TG.2023.3308898

An Evolutionary Approach for PCG in a Cooperative Puzzle Platform Game

José Bernardo Rocha[1,2]($\boxtimes$) (ID), Nuno Martins[1], and Rui Prada[1,2] (ID)

[1] Instituto Superior Técnico, Universidade de Lisboa, Lisbon, Portugal
{jose.b.g.rocha,nuno.lages.martins,rui.prada}@tecnico.ulisboa.pt
[2] INESC-ID, Lisbon, Portugal

Abstract. Procedural content generation (PCG) is a popular topic in game research and practice, however, the generation of content for cooperative games, specifically content that requires collaboration between both players to be completed, is still underdeveloped. In this work, we contribute to the body of knowledge of PCG for cooperative games, describing our approach for generating levels, for the cooperative game Geometry Friends, based on genetic algorithms and the definition of cooperative constraints. We present the evaluation conducted to test the quality of a sample of levels generated and the appropriateness of the constraints that define areas of reach for each player in the game. The evaluation showed that the constraints given to the generation algorithm are able to express different levels of cooperation in the levels generated, according to the subjective assessment of players.

Cooperation in games has been expressed in many different forms and requires additional design concerns not necessary in non-collaborative games. Developing games that focus on providing cooperative challenges that require two or more players to overcome can be very difficult due to the need to carefully design and test the game levels for the gameplay and experience emerging from the players' joint action. Some research has been conducted to help designers. Rocha et al. [9] defined several collaborative design patterns and challenge archetypes. These were later extended by Seif El-Nasr et al. [11], who also introduced cooperative performance metrics (CPM). Reuter et al. [8] proposed patterns for cooperation in gameplay sections. These patterns and guidelines are useful, but the industry relies more and more on procedural content creation (PCG) to develop games and the ideas that sustain the design of cooperative gameplay are not usually addressed in PCD research and practice.

In this paper, we propose a PCG solution to generate levels for cooperative games (in this particular case, a cooperative puzzle platform game - Geometry Friends[1] [10]) that takes into account the design specificities of cooperative games. Our approach uses the definition of areas of reachability of the players in the game world to convey different levels of cooperation and guide the generation algorithm to distinct levels.

---

[1] https://geometryfriends.gaips.inesc-id.pt/game.

© The Author(s), under exclusive license to Springer Nature Switzerland AG 2024
L. Vale Costa et al. (Eds.): VJ 2023, CCIS 1984, pp. 287–299, 2024.
https://doi.org/10.1007/978-3-031-51452-4_20

1   Related Work

Games like Minecraft[2], Risk of Rain[3], Valheim[4], Deep Rock Galactic[5] use Procedural Content Generation (PCG) to create their maps and levels, and have cooperative gameplay modes. However, these modes do not need cooperation, content can just be made easier by the players cooperating. The PCG process for these games does not take into account the design concerns of Cooperative Games and does not attempt to ensure that the experience is cooperative in nature, it comes down to the players to take a divide-and-conquer type of approach.

There has been little research on PCG for cooperative games. One of the few exceptions is the work by van Arkel et al. [1] that used PCG to generate levels for a 2D puzzle-platform game for two players. The objective of the game is to move from the start to the end of a level. The players can move, jump, stand on top of each other, and interact with levers or move objects in the game world. Their approach is based on design patterns that they defined following Reuter et al. [8] and Hullettand and Whitehead [4] proposals describing sections of gameplay. The generator combines such sections and generates gameplay situations. The work used Ludoscope [3] an AI-assisted level design tool.

A different approach was taken by Huimin Liu et al. [6]. In their work, first, a human game-level designer creates level chunks, that are evaluated by two AI agents playing through each chunk to determine the degree of collaboration required. Then, a simulated annealing algorithm was used to optimize a total cost function that encoded both the degree of collaboration required and other game-level design decisions, thus allowing the generation of a game level by combining the chunks.

Baek et al. [2] proposed four cooperation-level design patterns for the two-player cooperative game, Overcooked![6], and designed a controllable generator with a parameterized genetic algorithm that used these design patterns (e.g., items that players are required to interact, and the number of rooms) as inputs, and conducted a user study to validate the cooperation patterns by having users play and evaluate the levels previously generated.

2   Geometry Friends

To define the domain of application of our work, we start by describing the game Geometry Friends. It is a two-player cooperative puzzle platformer computer game that takes place in a 2D environment with simulated physics (with gravity

---

[2] Mojang Studios 2011, Minecraft video game, Multiplatform.

[3] Hopoo Games 2013, Risk of Rain, video game, Microsoft Windows, Chucklefish.

[4] Iron Gate Studio - early access 2021, Valheim, video game, Microsoft Windows, Coffee Stain Studios.

[5] Ghost Ship Games 2020, Deep Rock Galactic, video game, Multiplatform, Coffee Stain Studios.

[6] Ghost Town Games 2017, Overcooked! video game, Multiplatform, Team17.

and friction). The goal of the players is to gather a set of diamonds in the least amount of time. Each player controls one of the two playable characters, a yellow circle, or a green rectangle. Players control the motion of their characters, who are subject to certain restrictions. The rectangle moves by sliding to the sides (e.g., using a horizontal force). The circle moves by rolling (e.g., applying a torque to increase its angular momentum). Additionally, the rectangle can change its shape to a horizontal or vertical rectangle (with the same area), while the circle character is capable of jumping.

Levels are composed of a series of platforms and a variable number of diamonds that characters must collect to complete the level - the collectibles (Fig. 1 - Subfigure 4 shows a simple level). These collectibles often find themselves in places that require the cooperation of both characters or might need to be collected in a particular order.

Platforms in the game also contain different characteristics, some platforms can obstruct the movement of one player specifically or both. There are three kinds of platforms: black, yellow, and green platforms. The circle's (yellow) movement is obstructed by green and black platforms, while the rectangle's (green) movement is obstructed by yellow and black platforms. Levels containing these coloured platforms (or zones) create an additional layer of challenge between both players, however, in the current work we use only black platforms. The game itself consists of a series of levels, where the layout of the obstacles and the initial position of the characters and collectibles vary.

3   A Cooperative Game Level Generator

The generation process begins with the designer defining character reachability areas in the level. These can be reachable by the circle only, by the rectangle only, by both characters, or reachable by cooperation (i.e., the circle reaches with assistance from the rectangle). Figure 1 - Subfigure 1 shows an example of these input areas.

The input areas have implicit cooperative design principles. Exclusive areas for one character force the player to take responsibility for that area (e.g., getting the collectibles there), which can lead to divide-and-conquer cooperative situations but may create the feeling of playing alone if not properly balanced. The areas reached by both characters provide interaction but may not impose cooperation as any player can take responsibility for the area. The cooperative reach areas require the cooperation of the players, hence inducing shared responsibility for the challenge.

We believe that these areas support the specification of several cooperative situations and are a good candidate to use as a parameter in a PCG process where we wish to control the degree of cooperation of the levels generated.

The generation follows, based on the input areas, and outputs the level layout with the information of the platforms, the next step is placing the collectibles. These must be placed in reachable areas so that they can be collected by the players, as the level must be solvable. We chose to place one collectible in the reachable portions of the input areas.

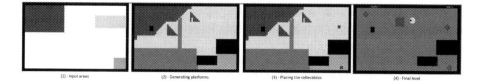

Fig. 1. The level generation from input areas to the in-game level: (1) the input specification, (2) the platforms generated and correspondent reachable areas based on the starting positions of the characters, (3) the level with the collectibles, and (4) the level in the game. Yellow areas are only reachable by the circle. Green areas are only reachable by the rectangle. Grey areas are reachable by both characters. Blue areas are only reachable by the circle with assistance from the rectangle. (Color figure online)

An overview of the level generation process, from initial input to an in-game level, can be seen in Fig. 1.

3.1   Generating the Level Platforms

Our approach uses a genetic algorithm (GA) to generate levels according to the specification of reachability areas. The genetic algorithm implementation was done in Python and by resorting to the PyGAD library[7]

The population of the GA represents candidate levels. The chromosome is a list of integers structured as follows:

$$[RectangleSpawn, CircleSpawn, PlatformArray]$$

The *Rectangle Spawn* represents the location where the Rectangle character will start the game. Similarly, the *Circle Spawn* is the starting position for the Circle character. The *Platform Array* contains all potential platforms in the level. We use a fixed-size chromosome, which requires limiting the size of the Platform Array - we restrict it to a maximum of 8 Platforms, which is enough to define interesting levels for the games, taking into account the human-defined levels that we have on the game. Each Platform in the *Platform Array* is structured as:

$$[Activation, Position, Width, Height]$$

The *Activation* determines if the platform is present in the level. This allows varying the number of platforms in the level (from 0 up to 8 platforms). If the *Activation* is on, the platform is placed in the level, otherwise, it will be ignored. This mechanism allows the composition of potential platforms that may be later expressed in the population, but are hidden during the evolution. It is also a simple way to deal with the removal of platforms. All values in the genes represent coordinates in the game world and are bounded by its size.

---

[7] PyGAD Library, https://pygad.readthedocs.io/.

The initial population is generated with random values, we simply specify the size of the population. Our fitness function evaluates an individual by comparing the reachability areas of the level it generates to the input that the designer specified. The function begins by determining what areas in the generated level are reachable by each character, using a flood-fill-like algorithm. Then it assumes that if the circle can reach the area of the rectangle, then above that there is a cooperative area beyond the circle's own reach (e.g., the circle can jump on top of the rectangle). To compute the fitness, it determines the intersections between the areas specified by the designer and the computed reachability areas (according to the type of reachability), as well as the sizes of these intersections. The fitness of a level is the percentage of overlap between the input reachability areas specified by the designer, by type and position, and the actual reachability areas of the generated level.

We used a discretization of the level that converts the original pixel space of the game into 16×16 cells. The reachability algorithm follows Martins et al. approach [7]. It calculates the positions where each character could fit and then simulates the movements they could make starting from their spawn position by considering only the positions where they can fit. Our solution added a step that extended the reach of the characters by traversing each position a character can reach and simulating having them placed there. This approach is heuristic and is only an approximation of the reachability of a level as if it was actually played. We avoid the complexity of running agents to solve the level (which is still an open problem in the game [10]).

This process outputs a grid that represents what are the reachable areas, by type, of the level. Figure 1 - Sub-figure 2 and 3 show a visual representation of such a grid.

After calculating the fitness of the individuals in the population, the parents are selected for crossover by using rank selection. We generated a single child from each pair of parents and used a uniform crossover. There was a 50–50 random chance of inheriting a specific gene from each of the parents. The population keeps 20% of the parents in the next generation. The mutation rate was 10%. If a gene is mutated, it gets a new random number.

3.2 Placing the Collectibles

The generation process is two-step. We separate the collectible placement from the platform generation, given that placing the collectibles is a natural result of the platforms that exist at the level. It also facilitates both procedures. The collectible placement was designed with the assumption that the input areas specify areas that are relevant to the gameplay. Hence, each should get a collectible. This also assures that the collectibles are placed in areas that are reachable, which is important for the level's solvability. The collectible is placed randomly inside the computed reachability area.

3.3   Level Generation Results

To test the output of the algorithm we defined three different level specifications (i.e., input areas) that express three different design goals in terms of cooperation:

- **Exclusive** - only rectangle-only and circle-only reachability areas. See (Fig. 2a and 2b).
- **Common** - at least half of the area can be reached by both characters and does not contain cooperative reachability areas. see (Fig. 2c and 2d).
- **Coop** - included at least one cooperation reachability area. See (Fig. 2e and 2f).

We expected the level of cooperation in the levels to be higher in levels with the **Coop** specification (due to the cooperation reachability), followed by the **Common** specification, which supported some shared areas, and by last the **Exclusive** specification.

We designed two level specifications for each specification (see Fig. 2. We used input areas with the same sizes, a similar number of input areas, and similar positions, to minimize differences unrelated to the type of input areas used.

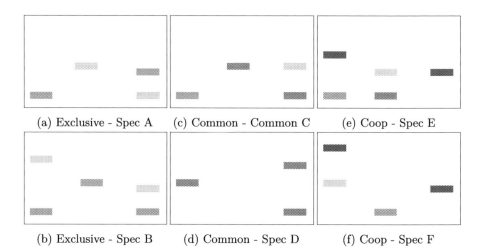

(a) Exclusive - Spec A   (c) Common - Common C   (e) Coop - Spec E

(b) Exclusive - Spec B   (d) Common - Spec D   (f) Coop - Spec F

Fig. 2. The specs (areas specified) for each of the design constraints. Yellow areas are only reachable by the circle. Green areas are only reachable by the rectangle. Grey areas are reachable by both characters. Blue areas are only reachable by the circle with assistance from the rectangle. (Color figure online)

To generate the levels we run the algorithm with a population of 50 for 500 generations, selecting 10 parents for crossover. With the exception of the **Exclusive** specifications, all specifications converge to the fitness of 1 (Spec A converged to 0.75 and Spec B converged to 0.6). The resulting reachability areas are shown in Fig. 3 and the final levels, after the collectible placement, are shown in Fig. 4. The level generated for the Exclusive - Spec B is not solvable, because the circle was placed on a platform, thus, unable to move. This reflects some potential problems with the discretization of the game world that we need to address.

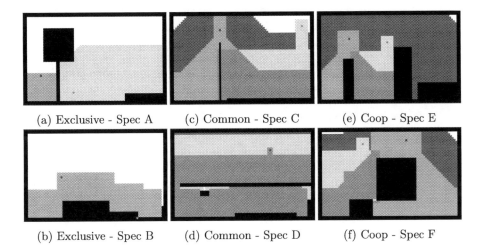

(a) Exclusive - Spec A   (c) Common - Spec C   (e) Coop - Spec E

(b) Exclusive - Spec B   (d) Common - Spec D   (f) Coop - Spec F

Fig. 3. Reachability of the best solution for each of the specs. Yellow areas are only reachable by the circle. Green areas are only reachable by the rectangle. Grey areas are reachable by both characters. Blue areas are only reachable by the circle with assistance from the rectangle. (Color figure online)

4   User Testing of the Generated Levels

To test the levels we conducted a user study. We measured the subjective experience of the gameplay affordable by each level. We measured the general user experience using the GUESS-18 questionnaire [5], and the level of collaboration that players experienced while playing, using the following questions:

1. I feel that I was collaborating with the other player;
2. I feel that the challenges required collaboration;

We ran the experiments in eight evaluation sessions with a total of 16 participants (81% male and 29% female, average age of 31.19 years). Participants were recruited at our university and the sessions were conducted in our lab. In each session, participants played in pairs the 6 levels. A random sequence of levels was generated for each session. At the beginning of the session, the game was explained by the experimenter, and the participants were allowed to experiment

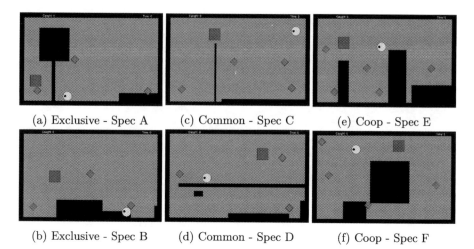

| (a) Exclusive - Spec A | (c) Common - Spec C | (e) Coop - Spec E |
| (b) Exclusive - Spec B | (d) Common - Spec D | (f) Coop - Spec F |

Fig. 4. The levels generated for each of the specs

with the game for a while to get used to the game controls. The session continued with the core testing phase. Each pair played the six levels sequentially until the end and respond to the questionnaire between levels. We collected in each session 12 measures (6 per participant).

We formulated the following hypotheses base on our design goals behind the three specifications. We also expect the more cooperative levels to provide a better user experience, given the cooperative nature of the game, which should influence the players' expectations.

1. Levels in the Coop condition will have a higher collaboration score when compared to the other conditions.
2. Levels in the Common condition will have a higher collaboration score when compared to the Exclusive condition.
3. Levels in the Coop condition will have a higher GUESS score when compared to the other conditions.
4. Levels in the Common condition will have a higher GUESS score when compared to the Exclusive condition.

4.1   Results

An overview of the results of the user testing of each level can be seen in Fig. 5. Unsurprisingly, level B (see Fig. 4b and Fig. 5b) was poorly evaluated in comparison with the remaining levels.

It is apparent, by comparing the figures in Fig. 5, and examining the more level-dependent factors (Usability, Play Engrossment, Enjoyment, Creative Freedom, Personal Gratification, Social Connectivity, Collaboration), that levels generated according to the Coop specification had higher ratings than the rest of the levels, and that levels generated according to the Common specification obtained higher ratings than the levels generated with the Exclusive specification (even when ignoring level B).

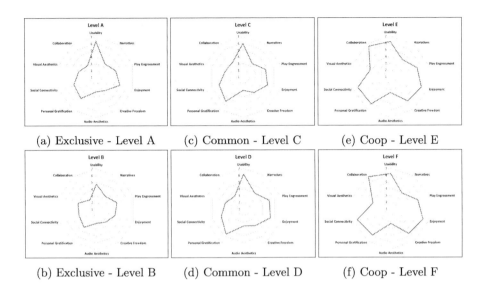

(a) Exclusive - Level A   (c) Common - Level C   (e) Coop - Level E

(b) Exclusive - Level B   (d) Common - Level D   (f) Coop - Level F

Fig. 5. The means of the GUESS-18 questionnaire subscales plus the collaboration subscale for each of levels generated

Figure 6 shows the average of the GUESS factors (excluding the Narratives, Audio Aesthetics, and Visual Aesthetics, because these are less related to the content that was generated) and the average of the collaboration metrics.

The chart shows clearly that levels of the Exclusive condition were evaluated more poorly than the rest of the conditions, and that the Coop condition presents better results, both in terms of user experience and in perceived collaboration.

We conducted a statistical analysis to check the significance of the results. To validate hypotheses 1 and 2 (related to the collaboration scores), we performed a Friedman test (due to lack of normality and sphericity) and found that there is a statistically significant difference in the Collaboration scores within at least two conditions ($p \leq 0.001$, see Table 1). We ran pairwise Wilcoxon tests (see Table 2) for further analysis, applying Bonferroni correction and Eta squared for determining the effect size type. We found a significant difference between the Coop condition and the Common condition ($mean(Common) = 3.516$; $mean(Coop) = 6.719$; $p \leq 0.001$), and a significant difference between the Coop condition and the Exclusive condition ($mean(Coop) = 6.719$; $mean(Exclusive) = 2.953$; $p \leq 0.001$). This supports hypothesis 1. Levels using the Coop input specifications provide higher Collaboration. However, there was no statistically significant difference between the Common condition and the Exclusive condition ($mean(Common) = 3.516$; $mean(Exclusive) = 2.953$; $p = 0.746$), hence, hypothesis 2 is not supported.

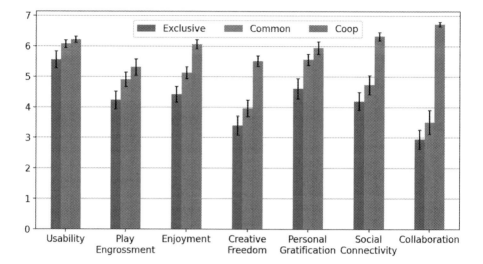

Fig. 6. Average user-evaluation results of the noteworthy GUESS subscales and the additional Cooperation subscale for both levels generated from each of the three Specs

Concerning hypotheses 3 and 4, a Friedman test found that there were statistically significant differences in the overall GUESS-18 scores within at least two conditions ($p \leq 0.001$, see Table 3). The pairwise Wilcoxon tests (see Table 4) show a significant difference between the Coop and the Common conditions ($mean(Common) = 41.219$; $mean(Coop) = 46.781$; $p \leq 0.001$), and the Coop and the Exclusive conditions ($mean(Coop) = 46.781$; $mean(Exclusive) = 36.844$; $p \leq 0.001$). This supports hypothesis 3. Levels generated with the input areas of the Coop conditions lead to a better user experience. However, hypothesis 4 is not supported because no statistically significant difference was found between the Common condition and the Exclusive condition ($mean(Common) = 41.219$; $mean(Exclusive) = 36.844$; $p = 0.157$).

Table 1. Collaboration score - Friedman test results for variable X (Design Specs)

Source	W	df	Q	p-unc
Condition	0.672	2	43.034	0.000

Table 2. Collaboration score - Post-hoc Pairwise Wilcoxon tests results for variable X (Design Specs)

Contrast	A	B	mean(A)	std(A)	mean(B)	std(B)	W-val	p-corr	eta-square
Condition	Common	Coop	3.516	2.234	6.719	0.420	0	0.000	0.498
Condition	Common	Exclusive	3.516	2.234	2.953	1.748	152	0.746	0.019
Condition	Coop	Exclusive	6.719	0.420	2.953	1.748	0	0.000	0.687

Table 3. GUESS-18 score - Friedman test results for variable X (Design Specs)

Source	W	df	Q	p-unc
Constraint	0.336	2	21.504	0.000

Table 4. GUESS-18 score - Post-hoc Pairwise Wilcoxon tests results for variable X (Design Specs)

Contrast	A	B	mean(A)	std(A)	mean(B)	std(B)	W-val	p-corr	eta-square
Condition	Common	Coop	41.219	6.746	46.781	4.726	77	0.002	0.186
Condition	Common	Exclusive	41.219	6.746	36.843	10.040	148.5	0.157	0.061
Condition	Coop	Exclusive	46.781	4.726	36.844	10.041	22.5	0.000	0.286

5   Discussion

In this paper, we proposed a level generator that provides cooperative challenges applied to the Geometry Friends game. The method for creating those levels used a genetic algorithm with a chromosome that represented the level as the solution. We separated our level generation into two steps, a platform generation step that used a genetic algorithm, and a collectible placement step that used a simpler approach. In our genetic algorithm implementation, we used a fitness function that received a set of areas that specify areas of reachability (exclusive, shared, and accessible by cooperation) within the game world, which is related to the solution of the game level. We can build different types of cooperative challenges by combining the different areas (e.g., based on individual or joint actions, or with more individual responsibility or more evenly distributed participation).

The generation algorithm was able to generate levels compatible with the input areas. The evaluation conducted in the user study confirmed our hypothesis that levels with areas that lead to gameplay that require joint action present higher perceptions of collaborative experience. In addition, having more areas with shared reachability, which grant more opportunities for interaction, even if not required for the solution of the puzzle, seems to lead to a higher sense of collaboration. These findings are not surprising but demonstrate that using the three different types of input areas is a good means to specify different levels of collaboration at a game level.

The user experience was aligned with the sense of collaboration (better in the levels that provided a better sense of collaboration), but this was expected given that the game was introduced to the participants as a collaborative game. Nevertheless, the user experience metrics were very positive for the levels generated, which affords the general quality of the levels generated.

6 Conclusions

The generation of cooperative levels is a complex problem that has not been extensively addressed in the research community. The generation needs to take into account the specificities of cooperative gameplay. It requires the inclusion of concerns for the actions, and experience, of all players in the game. Properties of joint interaction and coordination need to be used to guide the generation of the levels and be used in the evaluation of the levels' quality.

We propose the use of areas of reach (or action) as a way to guide the generation of cooperative gameplay. We applied this idea to the Geometry Friends game with promising results, despite some limitations on the implementation. The idea fits well with a 2D puzzle game, but we believe that the same approach can be applied to 3D games or other gameplay genres. The same type of input can be valid for other games as long as there exists a partition aspect of the characters' movement or action space.

Acknowledgments. This work was supported by national funds through Fundação para a Ciência e a Tecnologia (FCT) with reference UIDB/50021/2020.

References

1. Arkel, B.V., Karavolos, D., Bouwer, A.: Procedural generation of collaborative puzzle-platform game levels (2015)
2. Baek, I.C., Ha, T.G., Park, T.H., Kim, K.J.: Toward cooperative level generation in multiplayer games: a user study in overcooked! In: 2022 IEEE Conference on Games (CoG), pp. 276–283 (2022). https://doi.org/10.1109/CoG51982.2022.9893581
3. Dormans, J.: Engineering emergence: applied theory for game design. Universiteit van Amsterdam [Host] (2012)
4. Hullett, K., Whitehead, J.: Design patterns in FPS levels. In: Proceedings of the Fifth International Conference on the Foundations of Digital Games, FDG 2010, pp. 78–85. Association for Computing Machinery, New York, NY, USA (2010). https://doi.org/10.1145/1822348.1822359
5. Keebler, J.R., Shelstad, W.J., Smith, D.C., Chaparro, B.S., Phan, M.H.: Validation of the GUESS-18: a short version of the game user experience satisfaction scale (GUESS). J. Usability Stud. **16**(1), 49 (2020)
6. Liu, H., Choi, M., Kao, D., Mousas, C.: Synthesizing game levels for collaborative gameplay in a shared virtual environment. ACM Trans. Interact. Intell. Syst. (TiiS) (2022)
7. Martins, N.M.B.L.: Procedural Content Generation for Cooperative Games. Master's thesis, Instituto Superior Técnico, Universidade de Lisboa, January 2021
8. Reuter, C., Wendel, V., Göbel, S., Steinmetz, R.: Game design patterns for collaborative player interactions. In: DiGRA (2014)
9. Rocha, J.B., Mascarenhas, S., Prada, R.: Game mechanics for cooperative games (2008)

10. Salta, A., Prada, R., Melo, F.: A game AI competition to foster collaborative AI research and development. IEEE Trans. Games **13**(4), 398–409 (2021)
11. Seif El-Nasr, M., et al.: Understanding and evaluating cooperative games. In: Proceedings of the SIGCHI Conference on Human Factors in Computing Systems, CHI 2010, pp. 253–262. Association for Computing Machinery, New York, NY, USA (2010). https://doi.org/10.1145/1753326.1753363

Icarus, Towards Diplomatic Agents in Diplomacy

André Araújo[1,2], João Dias[2,3,4], and Pedro A. Santos[1,2(✉)]

[1] Instituto Superior Técnico, Universidade de Lisboa, Av. Rovisco Pais, 1049-001 Lisboa, Portugal

[2] INESC-ID, Rua Alves Redol 9, 1000-029 Lisboa, Portugal
pedro.santos@tecnico.ulisboa.pt

[3] Faculdade de Ciências e Tecnologia, Universidade do Algarve, Estr. da Penha 139, 8005-246 Faro, Portugal

[4] CCMAR, Universidade do Algarve, Campus de Gambelas, 8005-139 Faro, Portugal

Abstract. Diplomacy is a 7-player game where players (autonomous agents or human players) compete for territories but need teamwork and eventual betrayal to get an edge over their opponents. Agents in Diplomacy often neglect diplomatic interaction with other players, which is a missed opportunity in terms of creating interesting agents to play against. This paper explores how to create and train an agent that is able to perform diplomatic interactions with other players, such as proposing alliances. Towards this end, we explore recent deep learning techniques and architectures such as Transformers and LSTMs, and propose the Icarus architecture, a deep neural network with an explicit Diplomatic State representation.

Keywords: Socially Intelligent Agents · Diplomacy Game · Deep Learning · Supervised Learning

1 Introduction

Diplomacy is a seven-player game that features both cooperation and competition, where through careful planning, teamwork and betrayals a player can obtain an edge over his opponents. Given the strategic complexity of the game and the high number of players, sometimes it is hard to find other human players to play with, and thus the possibility of being able to play against interesting artificial intelligence opponents would be a nice addition to the game.

Furthermore, from an artificial intelligence perspective, the Diplomacy game provides a rich and complex environment for studying how artificial intelligence adapts to these kinds of social problems while still being contained and free from external variables. In addition to the complexity provided by diplomatic actions and interactions, even without communication (a Diplomacy game without communication is named No Press) the game is more complex than similar games used for the testing of intelligent agents like Chess and Go, as each of the seven players controls multiple units with a large number of possible actions and all of these actions are played simultaneously.

© The Author(s), under exclusive license to Springer Nature Switzerland AG 2024
L. Vale Costa et al. (Eds.): VJ 2023, CCIS 1984, pp. 300–314, 2024.
https://doi.org/10.1007/978-3-031-51452-4_21

The first attempts at creating Diplomacy agents have focused on rule-based agents, first only capable of playing the game without communication and then at a later stage, rule-based agents appeared with limited messaging capabilities. More recently a new wave of approaches based on machine learning has emerged but again mostly limited to the non-communication variant of the game.

In our work, we aim to explore the use of deep learning approaches to develop an agent that is able to perform some form of diplomatic interactions, in particular proposal and acceptance/rejection of peace and alliances, and proposal and acceptance/rejection of order suggestions.

However, our goal is not to create an artificial intelligence that plays the game better than humans, but that has a human-like level of play, while being able to perform diplomatic interactions.

2 Diplomacy and DAIDE

Diplomacy is a 7-player game where each player controls one of the seven "Great Powers of Europe" (Austria, England, France, Germany, Italy, Russia, and Turkey) in the years prior to World War I. These powers fight over 34 supply centers, scattered across 74 provinces, with the goal of owning 18 of these centers to win the game.

The way to interact with the game is by issuing orders to army and fleet units, that travel on land and seas or coasts respectively. The game is split into years where each year contains two phases where the orders are given and executed and one where the number of units is adjusted to match the number of controlled supply centers.

The four order types are Hold, where a unit protects its current province, Move, where the unit moves to another province and attacks it if it's defended, Support, where a unit supports an adjacent Move or Hold and Convoy, where a fleet unit transports an army unit across a sea.

Communication in the normal game is done with natural language, either with private or public messages. A Diplomacy game with such type of communication is called a Press game in the Diplomacy community, while a game without communication is called a No Press game.

The communication model used comes from DAIDE (Diplomacy Artificial Intelligence Development Environment), a research framework that enables bots to compete against each other as well as against human players. It introduces a simplified language for diplomatic negotiations between bots split into different communication levels that go from No Press (Level 0) to Full Press (Level 130+). We are mostly interested in exploring the first levels, Press 10 (Peace and Alliances), and Press 20 (Order Proposals).

2.1 Related Work

Many bots precede our work, from the first DAIDE bots to the more recent machine learning agents, and we used these as inspiration for our architecture and as benchmarks to test our agents.

Those old rule-based bots include RandBot [8], which plays random orders each turn, and DumbBot [8], which calculates values for each province and attacks the most valuable ones. Following those Albert [7] was released, a rule-based bot capable of Level 2 press, making it the best Press bot prior to the release of Cicero [4].

Later came the deep learning agents, mostly focused on No Press Diplomacy, DipNet [10], the pioneer of the machine learning agents, DeepMind's Best Response bot [1], and the FAIR team (Meta Fundamental AI Research) agents, SearchBot [6], DORA [2], and Diplodocus [3] the current No Press state-of-the-art. During the execution of our work, a new agent named Cicero [4] was released, a bot capable of playing Diplomacy at a high level while communicating with natural language, making it the current Press Diplomacy state-of-the-art.

3   Icarus

In order to present the architecture of our agent Icarus, we will start by describing a No Press variant of the architecture. The rationale for this approach was to determine if we were capable of creating and training a model able to achieve reasonable performance in the game without communication.

3.1   No Press Architecture

The base No Press model consists of encoding the game state information and feeding it to a policy network to obtain the orders to play in a given phase and the value of that state as seen in Fig. 1.

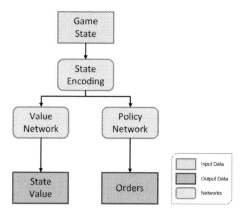

Fig. 1. General view of the No Press Model

The game state consists of the board state and the previous orders. The board state is a matrix where each line represents a province and contains 7 features represented by one-hot encoding (Unit Type, Unit Power, Buildable, Removable, Dislodged Unit Type and Power, Area Type, and Supply Center

Owner), creating a binary matrix. The previous orders use a similar matrix with a value for each province but use integer values instead of one-hot encoding to represent the unit type, the powers, and the locations related to the order for a total of 8 features (Unity Type, Order Type, Order Location, Target Location and Extra Locations 1 to 4).

The board state and previous order representations are then encoded using an encoder network (Appendix B, Fig. 5). This encoder imbues each location with information from the locations surrounding it thanks to the transformer-encoder used [12].

We then select the encoder's representation for each location that needs orders and feed it into an LSTM [5] that runs through them in order from the top-left corner of the map to the bottom-right to maintain some locality in the orders since they may rely on each other. It gives us the probability to play each order for every location with a unit.

We also trained a Value Network (Appendix B, (Fig. 6), mostly using linear layers, that gives us the probability of each power eventually winning the game at the given state.

3.2 Press Architecture

The complete Press architecture adds to the No Press base, with a message log, encoded into a Diplomatic State, and two message networks that send messages, reply to messages and encode this Diplomatic State. The general view is represented in Fig. 2.

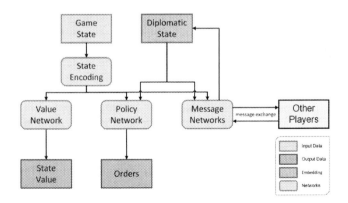

Fig. 2. General view of the Press Model

The message log consists of *message_log_size* message embeddings, default 20, each with size *message_embed_size*, default 100. These message embeddings are created by a PyTorch [11] Embedding module (Appendix B, Fig. 7).

These message networks (Appendix B, Fig. 8), are mostly comprised of linear layers, and besides giving us the probability to send each message and reply also give us the Diplomatic State, which is later used to improve the order selecting model (Appendix B, Fig. 9).

These networks are used to send messages at the beginning of the phase, and every time a new message is received they update the Diplomatic State, generate and send a response, send a new round of messages using the updated state, and finally update the Diplomatic State with the sent messages. This message flow is shown in Appendix B, Fig. 10.

4   Results

In order to achieve a human-like level of play we trained our models using supervised learning, using two different datasets, and measured the policy loss and the prediction accuracy while training. Additionally, we also paired our agents with previous Diplomacy bots, some rule-based and some using more recent machine learning architectures. Finally, we measured some relevant cooperation metrics for Press Icarus to understand how much of the press system he managed to grasp.

4.1   No Press Icarus Results

The No Press model used a human dataset with no messages provided to us by Philip Paquette, author of DipNet [10], of which we selected 122 993 games that used the standard map and some combination of rules that we felt didn't alter the core game too much. We then used supervised learning with Cross Entropy loss to learn how to predict the orders given a state. Additionally, we used a validation set of 200 games to better measure the progress of each epoch.

The results of this training can be seen in Fig. 3. For the games against other bots, we chose to use the model after 5 epochs since the training loss and accuracy plateaued at that stage and it was a peak of the validation set accuracy.

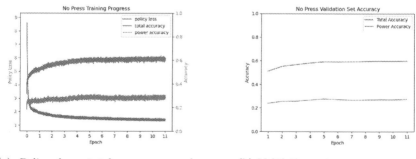

(a) Policy loss, total accuracy, and power accuracy of predictions per epoch for the No Press model

(b) Validation set accuracy per epoch for the No Press model

Fig. 3. No Press Training Results

To test the performance of our models we played multiple matches of 100 games against 5 different bots, all described in Sect. 2.1, and the results can be seen in Table 1. We can see that the No Press model managed to consistently beat RandBot but unfortunately failed to beat DumbBot and the No Press Albert variant. The bot is also unable to beat any of the more advanced DipNet models [10] so we didn't test against the later machine learning agents as the result would surely be the same.

Table 1. Icarus No Press win rate against the various other bots in 1 vs 6 games, based on 100 games per match. In a balanced match, the bot with one agent should win around 14.29 games and the six agents 85.71.

Match	Wins	Draws
6 vs 1 RandBot	99	1
1 vs 6 RandBot	97	1
6 vs 1 DumbBot	10	0
1 vs 6 DumbBot	0	4
6 vs 1 (No Press) Albert	24	0
1 vs 6 (No Press) Albert	0	0
6 vs 1 DipNet SL	4	0
1 vs 6 DipNet SL	0	1
6 vs 1 DipNet RL	1	0
1 vs 6 DipNet RL	0	0

4.2   Press Icarus Results

The complete Press-capable model is also trained using supervised learning using Cross Entropy loss but uses a dataset we generated with 264 games of Albert vs RandBot since we needed messages only up to Level 2 press (explained in Sect. 2) which is what Albert is capable of using. Given the smaller size of the dataset, we used only 20 games for our validation set.

Again we kept track of the loss and order accuracy, now adding message loss and f1-score (not accuracy since the large number of messages not sent would always result in large accuracies). These results can be seen in Fig. 4. Like the No Press model, the loss starts decreasing and the accuracy increasing, however, due to the small dataset and the limited training time, there is no obvious plateau so the latest epoch model, epoch 16, was used for the bot games described below.

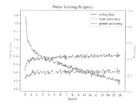

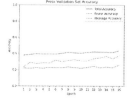

(a) Policy loss, total accuracy, and power accuracy of predictions per epoch for the Press model

(b) Message loss and f1-score per epoch for the Press model

(c) Validation set accuracy per epoch for the Press model

Fig. 4. Press Training Results

The matches played to test Press Icarus performance were the same as the ones used for the No Press counterpart but the addition of messages meant we could run some games with press on to see if that would give an edge to our model. These games are displayed in Table 3. The press variant, even though it seems to give a slight advantage of a game or two for Press Icarus against Press Albert compared with the No Press Albert variant, seems to have little

Table 2. Press Icarus win rate against the various other bots in 1 vs 6 games, some with press and some without, based on 100 games per match. In a balanced match, the bot with one agent should win around 14.29 games and the six agents 85.71.

Match	Press On	Wins	Draws
6 vs 1 RandBot	Yes	99	1
6 vs 1 RandBot	No	99	1
1 vs 6 RandBot	No	86	12
6 vs 1 DumbBot	Yes	0	0
6 vs 1 DumbBot	No	0	0
1 vs 6 DumbBot	No	0	2
6 vs 1 (No Press) Albert	Yes	4	0
6 vs 1 Albert	Yes	5	0
6 vs 1 Albert	No	1	0
1 vs 6 Albert	Yes	0	0
1 vs 6 Albert	No	0	0
6 vs 1 DipNet SL	Yes	1	0
6 vs 1 DipNet SL	No	0	0
1 vs 6 DipNet SL	No	0	0
6 vs 1 DipNet RL	Yes	0	0
6 vs 1 DipNet RL	No	0	0
1 vs 6 DipNet RL	No	0	0

to no impact on the results as those few winning games could easily be due to random chance. The bot does however retain the capacity to win against RandBot, meaning the addition of press doesn't alter its No Press performance.

4.3   Cooperation Metrics

To determine Icarus' true cooperation capabilities we analyzed the 100 games between 6 Press Icarus and 1 Albert bot shown in Table 3 to determine how these agents use orders and messages to coordinate between different powers and amongst their own units. We did this by looking at the messages they sent, the agreements they accepted, and the support orders they issued. Here we will talk about peace (PCE), ally (ALY), order suggestion (XDO), and demilitarized zone (DMZ) messages, for more detail on these messages see the DAIDE syntax document [9].

We started by looking at the number of messages each agent, Icarus and Albert, sent per phase, confirming that both sent about the same number of messages each phase, mostly sending messages in the first one to establish peace and alliances.

We then looked at propositions (PRP) sent and received and the corresponding acceptance rates (Table 3) extracting the following conclusions. Icarus learned how to reply to certain agreements as the acceptance rate, 51,72%, is higher than the 33% it would have been if it randomly responded with YES, REJ, or by ignoring the message. It also never learned how to use DMZ and XDO messages, sending less than one DMZ per game and no XDO across the 100 games, this is likely due to the large amount of variations these orders have, DMZ having one for each location and combinations of up to two powers and XDO having a different message for each order, making it so our small dataset

Table 3. Statistics on the average amount of sent and received propositions in the 100 games with 6 Press Icarus vs 1 Albert

Player	Message	Average Sent PRP	% of Sent PRP Accepted	Average Received PRP	% of Accepted PRP
Press Icarus	PCE	3,68	76,10%	3,20	76,90%
	ALY	6,95	35,98%	6,01	40,00%
	DMZ	0,97	45,38%	1,89	53,49%
	XDO	0,00	–	2,41	45,86%
	Total	11,60	49,50%	13,51	51,72%
Albert	PCE	2,80	75,00%	5,67	72,84%
	ALY	8,36	58,13%	1,37	7,30%
	DMZ	6,84	51,17%	14,01	38,62%
	XDO	14,50	45,86%	0,00	–
	Total	32,50	52,65%	21,05	45,80%

likely contained only a very small percentage of those variations. And finally, we observed that Icarus is much more likely to accept ALY and DMZ propositions than Albert which may be due to some imbalance in the dataset prone to accepting propositions in general or specifically those two types of agreements.

We also explored how messages and alliances affected the orders played. By alliances here we mean PCE or ALY agreements sent by one power and accepted by another that were broken when one of those powers tried to move into a supply center controlled by the allied power. In these games alliances were very short, Icarus agreeing to around 3,59 alliances per game and breaking 2,47 of them after roughly 3,57 movement phases, while Albert made 8,12 alliances and broke 2,55 after 5,27 turns, having only a 31.4% break ratio to Icarus' 68,80%, telling us that Icarus didn't fully grasp the concept of alliances.

Unfortunately, it seems it didn't understand supports either since his self-support moves had only a 17,1% chance of being successful, in the sense that the move being supported was actually ordered, while Albert of course had 100% successful self supports since it controlled both the unit supporting and the unit moving. This coupled with the poor understanding of agreements meant that alliances had no effect on the cross-power supports, in fact, there was less than one support made to allies per game in the 100 games played.

Looking at the other agreements like DMZ and XDO we can again see that Press Icarus has very little understanding of their meanings. It agreed to 496 DMZs across the 100 games and of those he broke 343 after about 4,35 turns, a 69,15% break ratio. The bot also sent no XDOs as seen above (Table 3) and from the 653 sent by Albert and agreed to by Icarus it played only 12.

4.4   Discussion

Starting with the No Press model, looking at both the training results and the performance against other bots (Fig. 3 and Table 1) we see that it was capable of learning the game to a certain degree, beating out RandBot and winning some games against Albert and DumbBot, but still being considerably weaker than the state-of-the-art machine learning bots. We attribute this to our lack of time and resources compared to the state-of-the-art agents, limiting our ability to experiment with more complex models and to tune the parameters of the networks. However, the fact that it can win against the simpler bots means we have a working baseline that allows us to experiment with different Press mechanisms.

The full Press-capable model suffered similar issues, it also obtained a basic grasp of the game, again beating RandBot in both 6v1 and 1v6 matches, and managed to work with the press side of the game to an extent, being able to send and agree to peace and alliances, but it still lacked the understanding for both applying those agreements to the orders played and to process the more complex proposals like the demilitarised zones and the suggested orders.

The Press model had the same limitations on time and scope as the No Press model, for example, we chose a pretty simple network to process the messages consisting mostly of linear layers, that while quick to train, which was necessary for the available hardware, made it so the message understanding of our model was also pretty basic. One of the biggest issues was perhaps the dataset, consisting of only 264 games generated by Albert, making it so not only the model would likely never be able to beat Albert, given that it was learning directly from its games without improvement, but also the limited amount of data made it so the model only saw a very small percentage of the thousands of possible messages, making it practically impossible to obtain a good grasp on the press system.

Our initial plan was to follow the supervised learning procedure with a reinforcment learning one, as was done in the state of the art bots. Unfortunately lack of computer resources did not allow to do this training in a reasonable amount of time. We can however determine from the limited success of the model, namely the capability to ask for alliances and peaces early and to reply appropriately to incoming propositions, that our system, consisting of generating a Diplomatic State from the previous messages and using it to choose messages to send and orders to issue, is a good structure for a capable Press-capable bot.

5 Conclusion

In this work, we developed an agent capable of playing Diplomacy, both with and without communication. This agent, Icarus, is capable of beating some simple bots in the No Press variant of the game, as well as sending and accepting proposals for peace and alliances with other players, like Press-capable bots.

To obtain a human-like level of play we trained this agent using Supervised Learning in a human dataset, as well as a dataset composed of games from a rule-based Press-capable bot. Our model employs state-of-the-art network architectures like Transformers [12].

Icarus' structure, consisting of encoding the game state and the diplomatic state of the game in order to improve the network's decisions, proved capable of both commanding the bot's units and trading messages with other Press-capable bots, even if at a basic level, showing that with some improvements it could lead to interesting diplomatic agents capable of playing the game at a high level using machine learning.

6 Future Work

Our project opens the door to many future works dealing with Press systems for the Diplomacy Game. Some of the improvements we suggest involve the initial No Press dataset, for example, it could be balanced and filtered based on player skill. Likewise, for the Press dataset, a new approach should be used, either generating more bot games or upgrading the model to Full Press and using a human expert dataset. In terms of the model, we propose experimenting with different architectures and input shapes to improve the results as well as remove some limitations we imposed on the models, like DMZs with only one location. The use of Reinforcement Learning after the Supervised Learning could also greatly improve the bot's results. Finally, after obtaining a bot with better Press capabilities it would be interesting to pit the agent against human players, both new and experienced, to evaluate how users perceive the bot's Press mechanics.

Acknowledgements. This work received Portuguese national funds from FCT - Foundation for Science and Technology through projects: UIDB/50021/2020 and UIDB/04326/2020, UIDP/04326/2020, LA/P/0101/2020 and SLICE PTDC/CCI-COM/30787/2017.

Appendix A   DAIDE Press Messages

Here are detailed the messages used for reaching agreements between powers for Level 10 and Level 20 Press in the DAIDE framework. For simplicity we will focus on the negotiation messages represented by the keyword **press_message** and ignore the ones pertaining to communicating with the server and order submission, so there are no relevant messages in Level 0 (No Press) since there are no direct messages between players. For a more detailed description of all messages one can consult the DAIDE syntax document [9].

- **Level 10**
  - Proposing an Arrangement:
    * **press_message = PRP (arrangement)**: The sending power is proposing an arrangement. Unless otherwise specified an agreement, formed by accepting an arrangement, lasts for one turn. For the agreement to be valid all receiving powers have to reply using the **YES** token. An **arrangement** can be in the forms described bellow.
    * **arrangement = PCE (power power power ...)**: Arrange Peace between the listed powers. The arrangement is continuous, that is, it lasts for more than the current turn.
    * **arrangement = ALY (power power ...) VSS (power power ...)**: Arrange an Alliance between the powers in the first list. The second list is the powers to ally against. The arrangement is continuous.
    * **arrangement = DRW**: Arrange a Draw. In the case of a game that accepts partial draws this may also be DRW (power power power ...). The list of powers must include at least two powers. This does not immediately draw the game if accepted, it is only a proposal, to actually request a draw one would use **DRW** while this command would be **PRP(DRW)**.
    * **arrangement = SLO (power)**: Propose a Solo (solo win by capturing 18 SCs) to the specified power. Note that the client can't actually order a solo - but may be able to order its units in a way that causes one to occur.
    * **arrangement = NOT (arrangement)**: All of the available arrangements can have **NOT** placed in front of them to mean the opposite.

* **arrangement = NAR (arrangement)**: All of the available arrangements can also have **NAR** placed in front of them. This represents the lack of an arrangement, so the arrangement can or not be followed. **NAR** is most commonly used in order to undo a previous arrangement.
- Replying to a message:
  * **reply = YES (press_message)**: Accept the arrangement
  * **reply = REJ (press_message)**: Reject the arrangement
  * **reply = BWX (press_message)**: Refuse to answer. None of the sending power's business.
- Canceling a proposal:
  * **press_message = CCL (press_message)**: A press message which proposes an arrangement can be canceled before the arrangement has been agreed, using a **CCL** message. This can also be used to cancel a **YES** reply to a proposed arrangement, before all parties involved in the proposal have replied. A **CCL** message which is sent after the arrangement has been agreed has no effect, and **CCL** may not be used to cancel a message which is not attempting to form an agreement.
- Making a statement:
  * **press_message = FCT (arrangement)**: This message states that **arrangement** is true. This is generally used either to pass information, or to unilaterally override a previously made agreement. There are no defined replies to **FCT**, although of course, a **FCT** message may cause other statements or proposals to follow.
- **Level 20**
  * **arrangement = XDO (order)**: This is a arrangement for the given order to be ordered. **order** uses the same format as the normal order submissions. An **XDO** arrangement applies to the next turn in which the order type is valid, Hold, Move, Supply and Convoy for the Movement Phase, Retreat or Disband for the Retreat Phase and Build, Remove or Waive for the Adjustment Phase. Replies use the format described in Level 10.
  * **arrangement = DMZ (power power ...) (province province ...)**: This is an arrangement for a demilitarized zone, meaning the listed powers should remove all units from the listed provinces, and not order to move, support, convoy to, retreat to, or build any units in any of these provinces. The arrangement is continuous. Replies use the format described in Level 10.

Appendix B   Network Graphs

This appendix contains graph representations of the various networks used in this project along with a flow graph of the message system.

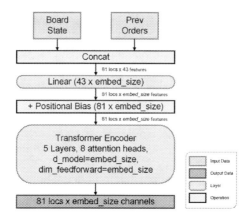

Fig. 5. Architecture of the Encoder Module

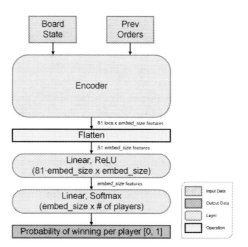

Fig. 6. Architecture of the Value Network

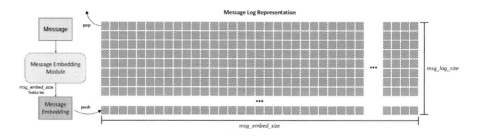

Fig. 7. Message Encoding and Message Log Representation

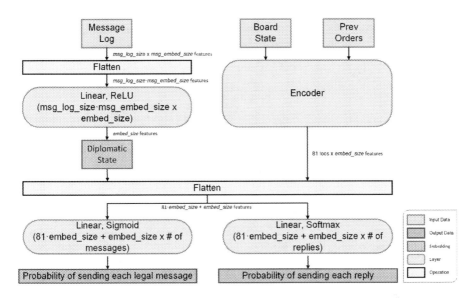

Fig. 8. Architecture of the Press Model's Message Networks

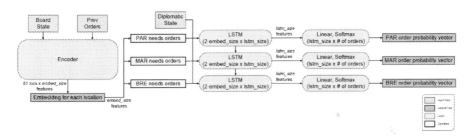

Fig. 9. Architecture of the Press Model's Policy Network

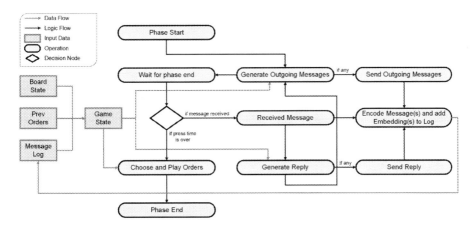

Fig. 10. Data and State Flow of the Press Model

References

1. Anthony, T., et al.: Learning to play no-press diplomacy with best response policy iteration. Adv. Neural. Inf. Process. Syst. **33**, 17987–18003 (2020)
2. Bakhtin, A., Wu, D., Lerer, A., Brown, N.: No-press diplomacy from scratch. Adv. Neural. Inf. Process. Syst. **34**, 18063–18074 (2021)
3. Bakhtin, A., et al.: Mastering the game of no-press diplomacy via human-regularized reinforcement learning and planning. arXiv preprint arXiv:2210.05492 (2022)
4. Fair, M.F.A.R.D.T., et al.: Human-level play in the game of diplomacy by combining language models with strategic reasoning. Science **378**(6624), 1067–1074 (2022)
5. Graves, A.: Long short-term memory. In: Supervised Sequence Labelling with Recurrent Neural Networks, pp. 37–45 (2012)
6. Gray, J., Lerer, A., Bakhtin, A., Brown, N.: Human-level performance in no-press diplomacy via equilibrium search. arXiv preprint arXiv:2010.02923 (2020)
7. van Hal, J.: Diplomacy AI - albert (2013). https://sites.google.com/site/diplomacyai/
8. Norman, D.: Daide client downloads (2023). http://www.daide.org.uk/clients.html
9. Norman, D.: Diplomacy AI development environment message syntax (2010). https://shorturl.at/auAI8
10. Paquette, P., et al.: No-press diplomacy: modeling multi-agent gameplay. In: Advances in Neural Information Processing Systems, vol. 32 (2019)
11. Paszke, A., et al.: Pytorch: An imperative style, high-performance deep learning library. In: Advances in Neural Information Processing Systems, vol. 32, pp. 8024–8035. Curran Associates, Inc. (2019). http://papers.neurips.cc/paper/9015-pytorch-an-imperative-style-high-performance-deep-learning-library.pdf
12. Vaswani, A., et al.: Attention is all you need. In: Advances in Neural Information Processing Systems, vol. 30 (2017)

Unlocking the Untapped Potential of Video Game Data: A Case Study of Aim Trainers

Jan Rejthar$^{(\boxtimes)}$ ⓘ

Department of Econometrics, Prague University of Economics and Business, Nám. Winstona Churchilla 1938/4, 120 00 Prague, Czechia
rejj02@vse.cz

Abstract. This paper shows that video games data may offer great opportunity to study human behavior. It demonstrates it by utilizing data from KovaaK's aim trainer to test the Hot Hand hypothesis. The findings indicate that even phenomena traditionally associated with sports can be better studied using video games. Specifically, the paper concludes that there is no evidence of the hot hand effect among KovaaK's players. Moreover, it argues that the data obtained from KovaaK's is of exceptionally high quality, surpassing previously utilized non-experimental data in the Hot Hand literature.

Keywords: the Hot Hand · aim trainers · entropy · video games

1 Introduction

In their aptly named article, Bar-Eli et al. [1] argue, that sports offer a unique opportunity to test economic theories, or as they put it, *an excellent laboratory to study human behavior in real competitive environments.* I propose that video games may present even greater opportunities and I will demonstrate it using the example of the Hot Hand phenomenon. Although the Hot Hand is commonly associated with sports, where the term originates from, and heavily recognized by fans and coaches [2], the data derived from sports encounter constraints that makes the analysis of the Hot Hand challenging. I will demonstrate how data from aim trainers can be valuable in surmounting these limitations.

While the classification of video games as sports remains a topic of ongoing debate [3], I will refrain from taking a stance and instead adhere to the conventional differentiation, treating video games and sports as separate domains of human endeavor.

2 The Hot Hand

Referring to a player as having Hot Hands typically implies that the player is experiencing a notable streak of success. This expression has become ingrained in the sports lexicon and has expanded beyond sports, being used as a synonym for psychological

This work was supported by The Internal Grant Agency of Prague University of Economics and Business under Grant VŠE IGS F4/52/2023.

© The Author(s), under exclusive license to Springer Nature Switzerland AG 2024
L. Vale Costa et al. (Eds.): VJ 2023, CCIS 1984, pp. 315–321, 2024.
https://doi.org/10.1007/978-3-031-51452-4_22

momentum in areas like finance or marketing [4]. The Hot Hand phenomenon has gar-
nered considerable attention in the academic literature ever since Gilovich et al. [2]
called its existence into question and classified it as a cognitive fallacy. Although the
existing research has been inconclusive, recent studies tend to lean towards supporting
the legitimacy of the Hot Hand phenomenon [1]. However, the disciplines employed
in the literature exhibit notable drawbacks, which can be categorized into four distinct
areas.

First and foremost, many research papers rely on data from sports such as basketball, baseball, or football, where players constantly interact with each other, leading to
numerous instances of complex endogeneity [5]. Secondly, there is often a disregard for
the heterogeneity of attempts. Each shot, swing, or match is treated as if it is identical to
all others, without considering the contextual factors that may significantly influence the
outcome [6]. Thirdly, number of papers suffer from limited data sequences. For example,
sports like football, ice hockey, basketball, and even bowling may yield only a few points
or shots for analysis [7]. And fourthly, the temporal aspect is frequently ignored. Shots
or swings are seldom uniformly distributed over time due to the natural progression of
the match, breaks, or time-outs, and matches are often spaced days or even weeks apart,
which may overlook potential cooling effects (e.g. [1] and [7]).

Efforts have been made to tackle these challenges, such as using bowling to avoid
player interactions [8], taking difficulty and timing of the shots into account [6], or
aggregating multiple matches or tournaments to increase the number of shots in the
sequences [9]. However, to the best of my knowledge, the only successful attempts in
addressing all of the aforementioned concerns have been achieved through controlled
experiments (e.g. [10]). This implies that sports might not be as ideal of a laboratory as
[1] suggest. In my argument, I will assert that data obtained from aim trainers possess
the capability to address all of the aforementioned limitations. Therefore, aim trainers
can offer data of experimental quality while circumventing the drawbacks associated
with conducting traditional experiments.

3   Aim Trainers

An aim trainer is a specialized software primarily developed to improve players' aiming
skills in shooter games or enhance their mouse control. Among various aim trainers
available, I selected KovaaK's for the analysis due to its feature of locally storing data
from each individual run of a scenario. Furthermore, all runs receive a score, and players' personal records are showcased on the leaderboards, introducing an element of
competitive pressure. KovaaK's provides a wide range of tens of thousands of practice
scenarios, each varying in several aspects. However, for the purpose of this paper, only
the scenarios pertinent to the analysis will be elucidated.

In the specific scenarios under consideration, players aim at stationary balls or cubes
of consistent size and strive to hit as many of them as possible. Consequently, there
is no interaction between players within these scenarios. After each shot or within a
brief predefined time frame, the target disappears, only to be replaced by a new one.
This ensures that the difficulty of the shots remains nearly identical, if not entirely so.
Each scenario has a fixed duration of either 30 or 60 uninterrupted seconds, yielding an

average of over 74 hits per run. As a result, the shots are distributed close to or exactly uniformly over time, effectively circumventing potential momentum disruptors such as breaks or time-outs.

4 Data

Data collection from players was conducted through the official KovaaK's Discord platform. Participants were provided with instructions to upload their data voluntarily and anonymously using a Dropbox link. A total of 53,345 runs were collected, out of which 77 runs met the criteria for inclusion in the analysis resulting in sampling rate of 0.1%.

Players were requested to provide their entire playing history rather than just usable runs for two main reasons. Firstly, this approach simplifies the data gathering process for the players, placing the burden of filtering on the researcher. Secondly, it helps to minimize sampling error by reducing self-selection.

The selected runs for the analysis are limited to scenarios described in the previous section with accuracy levels ranging from 20% to 90%. Table 1 provides a summary of the statistical information related to the selected runs.

Table 1. Summary statistics of the runs

	Number of runs	Mean	Median	St. Dev	Min	Max
Number of shots	77.000	74.117	73.000	11.227	33.000	94.000
Accuracy	77.000	0.616	0.644	0.154	0.219	0.890

In the sample, the shortest sequence consists of 33 shots, surpassing the number of throws in a typical bowling game and falling just short of the number of shots taken by NBA all-star players in a match. Conversely, the longest sequence is 94 shots long with the average exceeding 74. The average surpasses what is typically observed in most disciplines. Furthermore, considering that the shots occur in rapid succession, the quality of the data becomes unparalleled.

5 Methodology

Similar to Zhang et al. [11], my approach to the Hot Hand phenomenon does not solely rely on considering it as a player being on a streak of successive hits. Instead, I adopt the perspective that the Hot Hand can be observed as a clustering of hits, indicating a departure from stationarity rather than dependence. This viewpoint allows for the interpretation of the Hot Hand as a manifestation of momentum or *being in the zone*, as it is commonly described in the sports jargon. Consequently, a single missed shot does not necessarily imply that the hands fully *cooled down*. Consistent with [11], I employed entropy as the metric to measure the degree of clustering and a test for the presence of the Hot Hand within the KovaaK's data.

Let us define a vector X_i of length n representing the sequence of shots, where $X_i = 1$ indicates a hit and $X_i = 0$ indicates a miss. Additionally, let's define a vector d_j of length m representing the inter-event times. In the case of a uniformly discrete distribution of shots, the time between shots can be calculated as the difference between their respective indexes in the vector X_i. Consequently, d_1 represents the distance between the starting point and the first hit, d_m represents the distance between the last hit and the endpoint, and d_j, where $j \in \{2, 3, ..., m - 1\}$, represents the distance between two closest hits. Figure 1 provides an illustrative example of how the vector d_j can be constructed based on a vector X_i of length 10, where black dots represent hits and white dots represent misses.

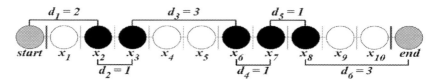

Fig. 1. Example of inter-event times calculation for a vector of length 10

For instance, $d_1 = 2$ because the second shot corresponds to the first hit, $d_2 = 1$ because the second hit immediately follows the first one, and $d_3 = 3$, because the second and third hits occur on the third and sixth shots respectively, resulting in $d_3 = 6 - 3 = 3$ etc. The entropy of the vector d_i can then be calculated using the following formula:

$$H(X_i) = -\sum_{j=1}^{m}(d_j)\log(d_j) \tag{1}$$

To evaluate the presence of the Hot Hand phenomenon, the null hypothesis stating that X_i is i.i.d. is tested using Monte Carlo permutation tests with 1,000,000 repetitions.

To control for the possibility of false positives resulting from simultaneous inference, two controls are employed. Firstly, the Family-wise Error Rate (FWER) is controlled at 5%, ensuring no false positives occur at this level. This is accomplished using the step-down Holm-Šidák procedure, which maintains the FWER at 5% precisely when all null hypotheses are true [12].

However, controlling for FWER is a highly conservative approach that reduces statistical power [13]. Therefore, a False Discovery Rate (FDR) control is also employed, which is less conservative and increases statistical power. FDR allows for a certain percentage of discoveries to be false positives. In this paper, the FDR is set at 5% using the Benjamini-Hochberg procedure.

By incorporating these controls, this research provides a comprehensive evaluation of the Hot Hand phenomenon while minimizing the risk of drawing incorrect conclusions.

6 Results

Let us examine an example of a run that potentially exhibits the Hot Hand. Equation 2 represents the vector X_i with shots from run number 3.

$$X_i = 0, 1, 0, 0, 0, 0, 0, 0, 0, 1, 0, 0, 0, 0, 0, 1, 1, 0, 0, 0, 1, 0, 1, 1, 1, 0, 1, 1, 1, 0, 1, 1,$$
$$0, 0, 0, 0, 0, 0, 0, 0, 0, 0, 0, 0, 0, 0, 0, 0, 0, 1, 0, 0, 1, 0, 1, 1, 1, 0, 0, 0, 1, 0, 0, 1 \tag{2}$$

Figure 2 shows a histogram of entropies calculated for 1,000,000 permutations if X_i, as well as the entropy of the run itself. The entropy of the run is -107.9, which falls below 99.4% of the permuted entropies Therefore, the run is deemed statistically significant at the 5% and even 1% levels.

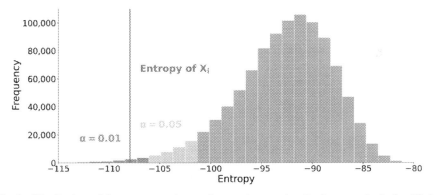

Fig. 2. Distribution of the entropy estimator for a string number 3 of a scenario *Reflex Flick - Fair*.

Table 2 presents the outcomes of the significance tests conducted on the 77 individual hypotheses. Out of the 77 individual hypotheses examined, seven were found to be statistically significant at a significance level of 5%. However, when controlling for simultaneous inference and considering either the Family-wise Error Rate (FWER) or the False Discovery Rate (FDR), none of these hypotheses retain its significance. Based on these results, it can be inferred that the hands of KovaaK's players do not get *hot*.

Table 2. Results of the permutation tests

Number of runs	Number of hypotheses rejected at 0.05		
	Individual testing	Simultaneous testing	
		FWER	FDR
77	7	0	0

7 Discussion

The results of the study provide insights on two levels of interpretation. Firstly, they contribute to our understanding of the existence of the Hot Hand phenomenon. The findings suggest that players of KovaaK's do not experience the Hot Hand. While it is challenging to extrapolate this conclusion and categorically assert that the Hot Hand is solely a cognitive misperception, the results imply that the phenomenon might not exist as a universal principle where success leads to further success. Therefore, it is possible that certain conditions need to be present for psychological momentum to manifest itself.

Secondly, the study demonstrates the significant potential of video games as a platform for studying human behavior. Even in situations where the advantages of video games may not be immediately apparent, such as the absence of human error in refereeing, they offer unique advantages over other data sources. The utilization of KovaaK's data in this research showcases the quality and value that even non-experimental data from video games can provide, surpassing the capabilities of previous non-experimental data used in the Hot Hand literature. This highlights the promising opportunities that video games offer for studying various aspects of human behavior.

8 Conclusion

This research paper demonstrates the effectiveness of utilization of video game data to test theories from other fields. The findings highlight the potential superiority of video game data over other non-experimental designs. Furthermore, the study concludes that players of KovaaK's do not exhibit the Hot Hand. Although it is challenging to definitively claim that the Hot Hand is solely a cognitive misperception based on these findings, they strongly indicate that the phenomenon may not exist as a general principle of success leading to further success in and of itself. This paper can thus be considered as a spiritual successor to [1] and [14].

References

1. Bar-Eli, M., Krumer, A., Morgulev, E.: Ask not what economics can do for sports - ask what sports can do for economics. J. Behav. Exp. Econ. **89**, 101597 (2020)
2. Gilovich, T., Vallone, R., Tversky, A.: The hot hand in basketball: on the misperception of random sequences. Cogn. Psychol. **17**(3), 295–314 (1985)
3. Tjønndal, A.: 'what's next? calling beer-drinking a sport?!': Virtual resistance to considering eSport as sport. Sport, Bus. Manage. Int. J. **11**(1), 72–88 (2020)
4. Morgulev, E.: Success breeds success: physiological, psychological, and economic perspectives of momentum (Hot Hand). Asian J. Sport Exerc. Psychol. **3**(1), 3–7 (2023)
5. Iso-Ahola, S.E., Dotson, C.O.: Psychological momentum: why success breeds success. Rev. Gen. Psychol. **18**(1), 19–33 (2014)
6. Lantis, R., Nesson, E.: Hot shots: an analysis of the 'hot hand' in NBA field goal and free throw shooting. J. Sports Econ. **22**(6), 639–677 (2021)
7. Avugos, S., Bar-Eli, M., Ritov, I., Sher, E.: The elusive reality of efficacy–performance cycles in basketball shooting: an analysis of players' performance under invariant conditions. Int. J. Sport Exerc. Psychol. **11**(2), 184–202 (2013)

8. Dorsey-Palmateer, R., Smith, G.: Bowlers' hot hands. Am. Stat. **58**(1), 38–45 (2004)
9. Cotton, C.S., McIntyre, F., Nordstrom, A., Price, J.: Correcting for bias in hot hand analysis: an application to Youth Golf. J. Econ. Psychol. **75**, 102091 (2019)
10. Miller, J.B., Sanjurjo, A.: Surprised by the hot hand fallacy? A truth in the law of small numbers. Econometrica **86**(6), 2019–2047 (2018)
11. Zhang, Y., Bradlow, E.T., Small, D.S.: New measures of clumpiness for incidence data. J. Appl. Stat. **40**(11), 2533–2548 (2013)
12. Ritzwoller, D.M., Romano, J.P.: Uncertainty in the hot hand fallacy: detecting streaky alternatives to random Bernoulli sequences. Rev. Econ. Stud. **89**(2), 976–1007 (2022)
13. Benjamini, Y., Hochberg, Y.: Controlling the false discovery rate: a practical and powerful approach to multiple testing. J. Roy. Stat. Soc.: Ser. B (Methodol.) **57**(1), 289–300 (1995)
14. Wagner, M.G..: On the scientific relevance of eSports. In: Proceedings of the 2006 International Conference on Internet Computing & Conference on Computer Games Development, pp. 437–442, CSREA Press, Las Vegas (2006)

ChemXP AR Edition, A Serious Game

Mário Bandeira[1]([✉]), Mário Vairinhos[1], Paulo Dias[2], Raquel Soengas[3],
and Vera Silva[4]

[1] Department of Communication and Art, University of Aveiro, Aveiro, Portugal
`mariobandeira@ua.pt`
[2] Department of Electronics, Telecommunications and Informatics, University of Aveiro,
Aveiro, Portugal
[3] Faculty of Chemistry, University of Oviedo, Oviedo, Spain
[4] Department of Chemistry, University of Aveiro, Aveiro, Portugal

Abstract. This project presents the design and development of a Serious Game,
that utilizes Augmented Reality (AR) technologies, aimed to involve and engage
students in Organic Chemistry. The game's core features encompass several missions, and a tutorial, specifically targeting the challenging concept of determining
the R/S Configuration of enantiomers. It also includes a physics-based molecular
creation tool, using the attraction and repulsive forces. Two rounds of usability
tests were carried out, where most participants were students from Digital Game
Development and Multimedia. These tests would help to prepare the game for
the end users—students of organic chemistry. So, the first round of usability tests
involved eight students, which provided invaluable insights, as they gave suggestions, identified bugs and issues, resulting in a neutral-to-positive user experience
(UX). The second round, consisting of fifteen participants, resulted in positive
feedback, along with even more suggestions for further improvement. The game
mode that was most liked by the participants was the Sandbox due to the freedom
of building molecules and visualizing the smooth animations of atoms moving
into their places. Also, for future work, tests will be carried out with the end users,
the organic chemistry students, and will cover real-world usage scenarios.

Keywords: Organic Chemistry · Serious Game · Augmented Reality

1 Introduction

Organic Chemistry isn't an easy subject, and for a long time, students have struggled
with it, considering it a complex scientific field of study [1–4], where even the students,
who scored good grades, couldn't deny the difficulty [3]. So, this subject can be difficult
at times, particularly when visualizing molecular structures while solving exercises.
The main problem, as the starting point that led to the origin of this project, was due to
the general difficulty felt among organic chemistry students, as stated by two members
of the team, who are Organic Chemistry teachers. Furthermore, it is also mentioned
that, sometimes, it is difficult to explain organic chemistry concepts through a two-
dimensional (2D) environment, hence the objective of the creation of an interactive tool.

© The Author(s), under exclusive license to Springer Nature Switzerland AG 2024
L. Vale Costa et al. (Eds.): VJ 2023, CCIS 1984, pp. 322–336, 2024.
https://doi.org/10.1007/978-3-031-51452-4_23

Not forgetting the incorporation of game aspects since it could be an effective tool to improve learning outcomes.

The proposal was the design and development of a serious game that addresses the problem, offering a tool for visualization, which could potentially help the students' involvement in Organic Chemistry, and find the extra motivation.

The team is composed of five members, collectively possessing expertise in the fields of Digital Game Development, Multimedia, Informatics, and Organic Chemistry.

This paper is divided into multiple sections. The first section is the introduction. The second section, the theoretical framework, provides knowledge about common problems faced by students in Organic Chemistry and discusses solutions such as gamification and serious games. The third section explains the project phases. The fourth section offers a brief overview of the current prototype. The fifth section presents the results of the usability questionnaire answered by the participants after testing the game. Finally, the sixth section includes the conclusion and addresses future work.

2 Theoretical Framework

There are several reasons why Organic Chemistry can be a difficult subject. The first one is that students have trouble visualizing three-dimensional molecular structures from a two-dimensional drawing [1,3]. This difficulty of visualization can be felt, for example, when asked if two enantiomers have the same R and S Configuration, where the chemist has to mentally rotate the molecule to come to an answer [3,5]. However, this mental activity is taught to students by drawing molecules in different positions [5,6], which is related to spatial ability, and affects students' performance in tests [6]. An example of a practical exercise, where the student has to determine R and S Configuration of two simple molecules, can be observed on Fig. 1, which is already the end result to the exercise asked.

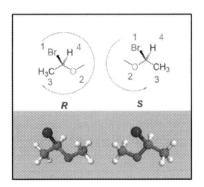

Fig. 1. R and S Configuration of two molecules

Another reason for Organic Chemistry to be a difficult subject, is the low intrinsic motivation to learn it among the students [3,7], where it is recommended the use of creative motivational techniques to increase students' interest, confidence, and competence in science [2]. In Organic Chemistry, the student must think critically, rather than memorizing, and the approach to every organic problem must be tailored to it [7,8]. Also, they should learn to visualize spatially and to recognize patterns [3,7,8], by incorporating scientific practices into everything that the students do [8]. An example is ensuring that the students use their knowledge daily on tasks like predicting, modelling, explaining, arguing and others (Cooper et al., 2019). Also, wherever necessary, Organic Chemistry teachers should design activities, and integrate them inside their usual classroom [3]. Given that, exercises can be adapted to students' level of cognitions and experiences, which can be done by adjusting or modifying instructions, adjusting materials, and designing tasks to engage students in process-based learning [2]. Additionally, students should start engaging and practicing problems as soon as possible, in the beginning of the semester, where a positive impact can be seen [9].

2.1 Gamification and Serious Games

There are other solutions, which appeals the gamification, and the use of Serious Games to teach students. In short, gamification is defined as the use of "game-based mechanics, aesthetics, and game thinking to engage people, motivate action, promote learning, and solve problems." [10, p.10]. According to [17], Serious Games are games who have an "explicit and carefully thought-out educational purpose" [17, p.9], adding that they "are not intended to be played primarily for amusement" [17, p.9]. Still, several authors provide similar definitions, as there isn't one that can describe what serious games truly are. For example, [18] defines that "a serious game is a digital game created with the intention to entertain and to achieve at least one additional goal" [18, p.3]. Furthermore, "the characterizing goals of serious games can be matched to competence domains" [18, p.9], such as "cognition and perception, emotion and volition, sensory-motor control, personal characteristics, social attitudes, and media use" [18, p.9].

Several studies have shown to have positive impact when teaching students with the use of both gamification and serious games. For example, a study made by [11], which they use an app called "MILAGE LEARN +", as a complementary teaching and learning tool, to help students by providing motivation, while facilitating the learning process and improving outcomes. The results were positive. Additionally, other studies show that games have positive impacts effects such problem-solving, achievement, and engagement in task learning [12–15], and on tests and performance on the final exam [12,14,16].

3 Method

The project is divided into two phases. In the first phase, we focus on designing and developing a serious game centered around Organic Chemistry. The main objectives include visualizing molecules and engaging students in exercises like "finding the R/S Configuration of an enantiomer." To enhance student engagement, we plan to incorporate various mechanics and features such as a narrative, badges system, and points system. The game will be accessible on Android devices, necessitating careful consideration of performance optimization.

Additionally, participants will play the game on their personal devices, emphasizing the importance of seamless performance on the Android platform. Furthermore, the serious game is mainly designed to be played using Augmented Reality (AR) technology.

In the second phase, usability tests were conducted to verify and validate all game features and system functionalities. These tests allowed us to assess various variables, including the game's intuitiveness, performance, user satisfaction, and overall enjoyment. Additionally, the tests helped identify issues and bugs to fix them in future updates. Importantly, participation in the usability tests did not require a deep understanding of Organic Chemistry.

4   Prototype, ChemXP AR Edition

ChemXP AR Edition is a serious game developed for this study, and as seen in Fig. 2, the game starts with the initial menu screen.

Fig. 2. ChemXP AR Edition, Initial Menu Screen

The game offers a short narrative, which starts as soon as the player starts a new game. To summarize, the player is the main character, who works mainly on repairing and configuring machines, while travelling across the galaxy to meet the needs of his customers. However, this game has a focus solely on a new client, Robot Robert, supervisor of ChemXP Company, who called the player asking for help to configure the machines to produce organic compounds. Throughout the game, players will encounter numerous dialogues that allow them to get to know more about the characters, as there are a total of six characters. Figure 3 showcases the initial encounter between the player and the company's supervisor.

The company can be seen in Fig. 4, who is the game main menu, where the player can access the several game features, for example, the missions, the sandbox, the tutorial, and even check the badges unlocked.

Throughout the game, players can play with AR mode or screen mode. This strategic choice ensures that students can engage with the game even if their personal devices do not support the AR technology.

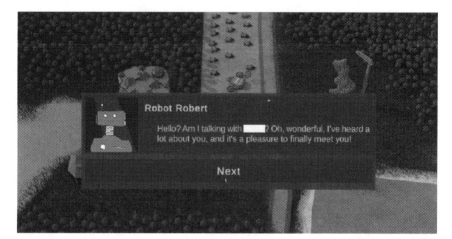

Fig. 3. ChemXP AR Edition, Dialogue with a Character

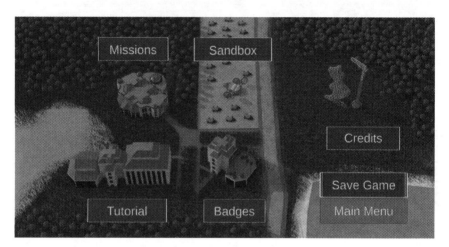

Fig. 4. ChemXP AR Edition, Game Menu

The tutorial is the place where players can learn how to solve the exercise "Determine the R/S Configuration of an enantiomer", so that they can mentally apply the rules to the missions, to achieve victory. As observed in Fig. 5, an enantiomer was generated, and the exercise can be started. Throughout the exercise, hints and tips will be provided.

The sandbox is a game mode in which the player can freely build molecules to visualize them, and since the game has physics such the attractive and repulsion forces, smooth animations are provided. So, as seen in Fig. 6, a random molecule was created to visualize. The atoms smoothly move into their positions, and the bond angles are calculated based on the atom configuration. There are several limitations, for example, experiencing some lag during the process, as the molecule grows bigger, the system performance decreases. However, the performance depends on the system requirements

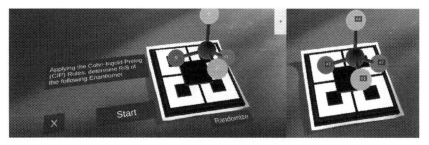

Fig. 5. ChemXP AR Edition, Tutorial to Determine R/S Configuration of an Enantiomer

of the device, and lag would only be noticed if there are a lot of atoms spawned into the scene, causing a lot of calculations to happen.

Fig. 6. ChemXP AR Edition, Sandbox AR Mode

Figure 7 shows us a screen with the game missions, having only 2 categories, the "Atoms" and the "R/S Configuration". New levels can be unlocked after completing the previous one, and the difficulty will progressively increase. At the beginning of each mission, a dialogue with one of the characters will occur, and at the end, if the player achieves victory, another dialogue will appear.

Figure 8 shows us a level of the mission "R/S Configuration", where the player must do two tasks: Build the Enantiomer and determine its configuration. Each mission the player will have a time limit, and a quantity of attempts, which fails the task if one of them reaches zero.

The player will unlock new badges, as can be seen in Fig. 9, which is another way to show the game progress.

Missions can be replayed to set new records, based on attempts and time spent. In Fig. 10, the left side illustrates a new mission being started, displaying the current best record. On the right side, after completing the mission, the mission completion window is shown, featuring rewards and the new best record.

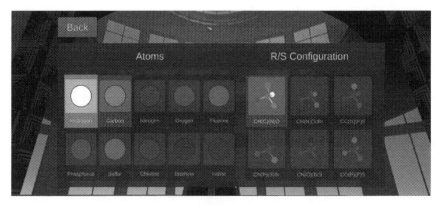

Fig. 7. ChemXP AR Edition, Missions Screen

Fig. 8. ChemXP AR Edition, R/S Configuration Mission

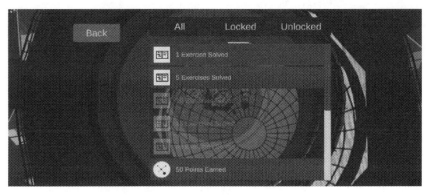

Fig. 9. ChemXP AR Edition, Badges Screen

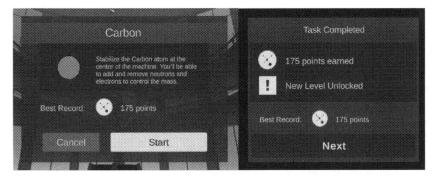

Fig. 10. ChemXP AR Edition, Badges Screen

Also, several features were added after each round of usability tests, which were asked for by the participants. For example, to add a screen "How to Play" before each mission started, as seen in Fig. 11.

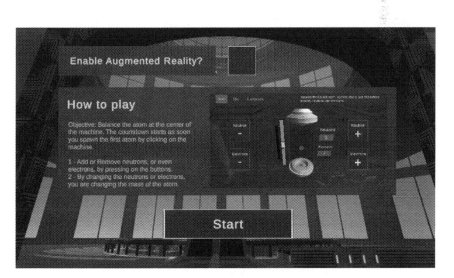

Fig. 11. ChemXP AR Edition, "How to Play" Screen before a mission starts

Figure 12 illustrates another addition, demonstrating the improvement of atom visualization by featuring the atomic symbol in front of the atoms, making identification easier. Additionally, bugs and other issues were fixed, preparing the prototype for round 2.

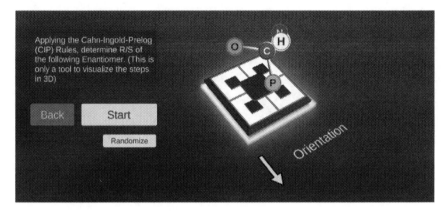

Fig. 12. ChemXP AR Edition, Molecule Visualization Example

5   Results

There were two rounds in total, with the first round having eight participants and the second round having fifteen participants. All the recruited participants were students from University of Aveiro and University of Coimbra, including colleagues, which most of them are pursuing master's degrees in digital game development, Multimedia, Informatics, and even Organic Chemistry. The participants were informally invited to participate in the usability tests through face-to-face interactions and text messaging. Those who expressed interest were recruited after checking their availability and were then assigned to a session in pairs. The sessions primarily took place in two different rooms within the Department of Communication and Art at Aveiro University: an empty study room and the lounge area.

The questionnaire results on the first round varied from neutral to positive, all of which were carefully analyzed. In the second round of usability tests, there were significant improvements in the results. Bugs and issues identified during the first round were fixed, and enhancements were successfully implemented.

5.1   Session Planning and Execution Overview

A round would have several testing sessions, each with two participants, lasting approximately one hour each. At the start of each session, participants were given a brief explanation of the research objective, the game concept and, finally, how to install the game on their devices with a brief tutorial. If the participants' device did not support AR, they would have the option of using an alternative device with the game already installed. Additionally, they would have to fill out a paper about the Informed Consent, granting permission for audio recording solely for research purposes. They would also consent for photographs to be taken during the session, for use in this paper and other scientific publications. As the tests would be carried out in pairs, communication between the participants regarding the game was encouraged, providing their insight and feedback. During all rounds, instructions were given to the participants, for example, everyone was asked to start with the tutorial, making their way through the several features, and then into the other game modes. Figure 13 shows a participant heading to the missions and being asked to activate the AR mode.

Fig. 13. Usability Tests Session, the Participant is enabling AR Mode

At the end of the session, users were asked to complete a usability questionnaire, divided into several sections, taking around fifteen minutes. The 5-point Likert scale was used in most questions, but open questions could also be found in each section, allowing the participants to provide additional feedback. Although the questionnaire is about usability, there was also a section about AR technology, where data regarding the participant's experience with AR could be obtained. All the data gathered, using both a questionnaire and observation, would always be analyzed at the end of each round, which then creates a new backlog of tasks to implement for the next update. At the end of the session, there was a small snack for them, to thank them for their time.

5.2   Usability Tests—Round 1

Figure 14 shows that one participant wasn't familiar with this technology AR, and three of them have never used it before, on Graphs 1 and 2, consecutively. Therefore, both parties, those who have never used it and those who have, could provide feedback based on their own experience with AR, even if they have none. Following Graphs 3 and 4, those who used AR, play with it more but rarely or only once a week. However, the ones that do use it a few times a week, use it for work and study.

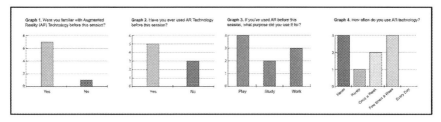

Fig. 14. Usability Tests, Round 1—Graphs—The use of AR technology

According to Fig. 15, both graphs were positive, where most of the testers found the tutorial to be intuitive and easy to follow. However, one participant thought the tutorial to be difficult, as shown in both Graphs 5 and 6, where the tester was blocked due to a bug, and said that the tutorial didn't really explain the exercise rules. Additionally, the tester reported that it looked more like an exercise rather than a tutorial, since there wasn't any visual guidance, but only tips based on text. Furthermore, several participants proposed adding visual cues to make the tutorial intuitive and explain the exercise rules in a deeper level. While all participants successfully completed the tutorial, step by step, they all thought it difficult to apply the tutorial's concepts during the game missions.

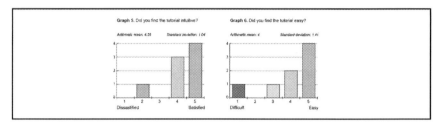

Fig. 15. Usability Tests, Round 1—Graphs—Tutorial

In Fig. 16, both Graphs 7 and 8 were somewhere between positive and neutral consecutively, where some testers claimed the objective was self-explanatory. By that, they mean they already knew a sequence needed to be entered to build a molecule. Also, three participants reported that it was difficult to visualize the molecule being built, as their attention was primarily focused on interacting with the buttons. Graph 9 demonstrates a positive score, where some testers interacted easily with the system, but others had trouble. They thought that, to select a molecule, they needed to drag it into the machine instead of clicking. Sometimes, the click would also fail as the molecules were travelling fast in the treadmill, and the colliders were small. After selecting a molecule, the testers were also able to rotate it, although there was no information saying that they could, which can also be confirmed in Graph 10, as they even said it was easy to visualize. They gave suggestions such as adding visual information, showing that it is possible to rotate the molecule to further analyze it. Participants wanted the timer to start counting down only after they interacted for the first time with the level.

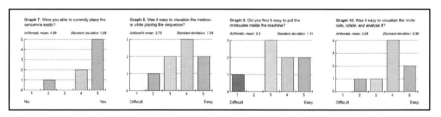

Fig. 16. Usability Tests, Round 1—Graphs—Mission RS Config

The Sandbox Mode, which can be seen in Fig. 17, almost all participants said to be their favorite part of the game, being the place where testers could build molecules, and visualize them in real-time. A few players, even in jest, tried to create gigantic molecules, testing the system at its maximum capacity, quickly creating atoms after atoms. The only issue reported by the participants by doing it so, was that the game started to get laggy. So, as can be seen in Graph 11, the testers found it easy to create atoms, and gave suggestions to make the colliders bigger, making it easier to spawn new atoms. Although the participants had no trouble visualizing the molecule, in Graph 12, a few of them said that it could be difficult to see a specific atom because of the material (Oxygen was red, Bromine was dark red). Some participants asked for the Undo button as they wanted to remove the last added atom.

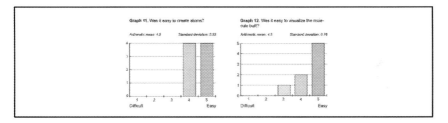

Fig. 17. Usability Tests, Round 1—Graphs—Sandbox

As seen in Fig. 18, the User Interface had positive results, where a few issues were found. For example, creating a new game would freeze the game during the fade screen, or button names could be misleading ("Player Ship" as the Sandbox, or "Quests" as some sort of achievements). Nevertheless, users enjoy the consistent buttons position to efficiently navigate between screens, making it faster and intuitive. Some of them even associate colors with a certain functionality (Dark Blue to Confirm an action, and Red to Cancel). The UI was considered pleasant, where both the color palette, the minimalist design, and the element positioning, made the positive impact. Still, the UI was harder to read in some devices, and sometimes, the text overlapped the 3D scene, making it difficult to distinguish the UI from the background scene. Additionally, the UI elements were almost outside the screen boundaries.

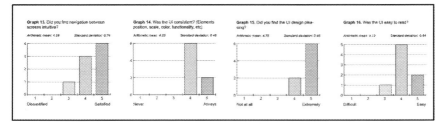

Fig. 18. Usability Tests, Round 1—Graphs—User Interface

5.3 Usability Tests—Round 2

As observed in Fig. 19, the participants appear to use more AR than the participants from the previous round (Fig. 14). Still, in Fig. 19, Graph 19 shows that the majority use AR to play and work, but only 1 use it for study purposes. Furthermore, graph 20 reveals a balance between testers with and without prior AR experience.

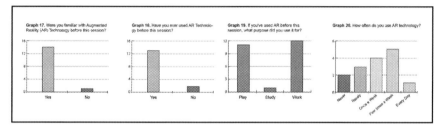

Fig. 19. Usability Tests, Round 2—Graphs—The use of AR technology

As seen in Fig. 20, the arithmetic means from all the graphs increased, from neutral to positive, in comparison with the last round. However, a few more issues were detected, which will be implemented in the next update. For example, visual or audio information to alarm the player about the time limit or number of attempts left, as well as the other timer limit that the player must analyze and insert the molecule into the machine.

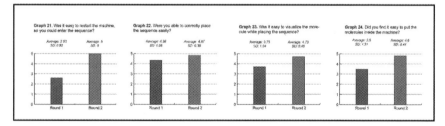

Fig. 20. Usability Tests, Round 2—Graphs—Mission RS Config

The sandbox also received positive results, as observed in Fig. 21, in which after the addition of the Undo button, the participants were able to go back a few steps, and create a different molecule. A few testers reported that sometimes could be hard to identify a specific atom, for which they provided the suggestion of adding the atomic symbol, as an element of UI in front of the atoms. All these suggestions can be implemented into the next update.

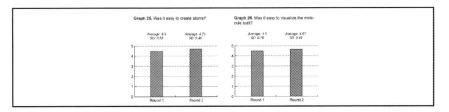

Fig. 21. Usability Tests, Round 2—Graphs—Sandbox

6 Conclusion

Usability testing played an important role in improving the game's design and functionality. All the insights obtained from the two rounds of testing, which involved a total of twenty-three participants, made it possible to identify issues, resulting in a user experience that went from neutral to positive. The positive feedback received in the second round, together with suggestions, highlights the potential of this serious game in the field of organic chemistry.

For future work, tests will be carried out with the end users, the organic chemistry students, and will cover real-world usage scenarios. Thus, both classroom settings and autonomous learning environments will be opted, enabling students to study and engage with the serious game. Also, more suggestions made by participants could be implemented. For example, the addition of different tasks, making it less repetitive, where other subjects in organic chemistry could be addressed.

References

1. Abdinejad, M., Talaie, B., Qorbani, H.S., Dalili, S.: Student perceptions using augmented reality and 3D visualization technologies in chemistry education. J. Sci. Educ. Technol. **30**(1), 87–96 (2021). https://doi.org/10.1007/s10956-020-09880-2
2. Ali, T.: A case study of the common difficulties experienced by high school students in chemistry classroom in Gilgit-Baltistan (Pakistan). SAGE Open **2**(2), 215824401244729 (2012). https://doi.org/10.1177/2158244012447299
3. Eticha, A.T., Ochonogor, C.: Assessment of undergraduate chemistry students' difficulties in organic chemistry (2020). https://uir.unisa.ac.za/handle/10500/19962. Accessed 16 Dec 2022. https://www.researchgate.net/publication/344179315
4. Grove, N., Bretz, S.L.: CHEMX: an instrument to assess students' cognitive expectations for learning chemistry. J. Chem. Educ. **84**(9), 1524 (2007). American Chemical Society (ACS). https://doi.org/10.1021/ed084p1524
5. Habraken, C.L.: Perceptions of chemistry: why is the common perception of chemistry, the most visual of sciences, so distorted? J. Sci. Educ. Technol. **5**(3), 193–201 (1996). https://doi.org/10.1007/bf01575303
6. Bongers, A., Beauvoir, B., Streja, N., Northoff, G., Flynn, A.B.: Building mental models of a reaction mechanism: the influence of static and animated representations, prior knowledge, and spatial ability. Chemis. Educ. Res. Practice **21**(2), 496–512 (2020). Royal Society of Chemistry (RSC). https://doi.org/10.1039/c9rp00198k
7. Lynch, D.J., Trujillo, H.: Motivational beliefs and learning strategies in organic chemistry. Int. J. Sci. Math. Educ. **9**(6), 1351–1365 (2011). https://doi.org/10.1007/s10763-010-9264-x

8. Cooper, M.M., Stowe, R.L., Crandell, O.M., Klymkowsky, M.W.: Organic chemistry, life, the universe and everything (OCLUE): a transformed organic chemistry curriculum. J. Chem. Educ. **96**(9), 1858–1872 (2019). American Chemical Society (ACS). https://doi.org/10.1021/acs.jchemed.9b00401

9. Szu, E., et al.: Understanding academic performance in organic chemistry. J. Chem. Educ. **88**(9), 1238–1242) (2011). American Chemical Society (ACS). https://doi.org/10.1021/ed900067m

10. Kapp, K.M.: The Gamification of learning and instruction: game-based methods and strategies for training and education (1st ed.). Pfeiffer (2012)

11. Fonseca, C.S.C., Zacarias, M., Figueiredo, M.: MILAGE LEARN+: a mobile learning app to aid the students in the study of organic chemistry. J. Chem. Educ. **98**(3), 1017–1023 (2021). American Chemical Society (ACS). https://doi.org/10.1021/acs.jchemed.0c01313

12. Lima, M.A.S., et al.: Game-based application for helping students review chemical nomenclature in a fun way. J. Chem. Educ. **96**(4), 801–805 (2019). American Chemical Society (ACS). https://doi.org/10.1021/acs.jchemed.8b00540

13. Robertson, J., Howells, C.: Computer game design: opportunities for successful learning. Comput. Educ. **50**(2), 559–578 (2008). Elsevier BV. https://doi.org/10.1016/j.compedu.2007.09.020

14. Stringfield, T.W., Kramer, E.F.: Benefits of a game-based review module in chemistry courses for nonmajors. J. Chem. Educ. **91**(1), 56–58 (2013). American Chemical Society (ACS). https://doi.org/10.1021/ed300678f

15. Westera, W., Nadolski, R.J., Hummel, H.G.K., Wopereis, I.G.J.H.: Serious games for higher education: a framework for reducing design complexity. J. Comput. Assist. Learn. **24**(5), 420–432 (2008). Wiley. https://doi.org/10.1111/j.1365-2729.2008.00279.x

16. da Júnior, J.N., de Lima Castro, G., Junior, A.J.M.L., Monteiro, A.J., Alexandre, F.S.O.: Gamification of an entire introductory organic chemistry course: a strategy to enhance the students' engagement. J. Chem. Educ. **99**(2), 678–687 (2022). American Chemical Society (ACS). https://doi.org/10.1021/acs.jchemed.1c00766

17. Abt, C.C.: Serious games. University Press of America (1987)

18. Dörner, R., Göbel, S., Effelsberg, W., Wiemeyer, J.: Serious games: Foundations, concepts and practice (2016). https://doi.org/10.1007/978-3-319-40612-1

Author Index

A

Andrade, Bruno 150
Araújo, André 300

B

Bandeira, Mário 322
Barroso, Ivan 49
Berkman, Mehmet İlker 72
Bootes, Robin 217
Bostan, Barbaros 59
Boussejra, Hakim 174
Brandão, André Luiz 103

C

Castro, Diego 134
Choueib, Ahmed 72
Cocco, Chiara 150
Costa, Liliana Vale 86
Crowley, Saul 150

D

de Assunção, Carina 33
de Marchi, Alessio 103
Dias, João 300
Dias, Paulo 322
Duradoni, Mirko 59

F

Fachada, Nuno 272
Fernandes, Carlos M. 272
Fernandes, Pedro M. 3
Ferreira, João L. A. P. 166

G

Gama, Sandra 103
Guazzini, Andrea 59
Gursesli, Mustafa Can 59

H

Hassan, Lobna 19

I

Inácio, João 272

K

Kubik, Darjan 187

L

Lopes, Manuel 3
Lopes, Richard da Cruz 103
Lu, Chien 19

M

Marques, João A. B. T. 166
Martins, Nuno 287
Masti, Federica 59
Matos-Carvalho, João P. 272
McNally, Brenda 150
Mejía-Alandia, Diego A. 202

P

Passos, Ana 86
Pinto, Valéria Moreira 118
Prada, Rui 3, 287

R

Rejthar, Jan 315
Ristić, Tatjana 187
Rocha, José Bernardo 287
Roque, Licínio 118

S

Santos, Flávia de Souza 103
Santos, Pedro A. 300
Scott, Michael James 33
Seiça, Mariana 118
Silva, Frutuoso G. M. 166
Silva, Vera 322
Soengas, Raquel 322
Sousa, Carla 49
Sousa, Micael 257

© The Editor(s) (if applicable) and The Author(s), under exclusive license
to Springer Nature Switzerland AG 2024
L. Vale Costa et al. (Eds.): VJ 2023, CCIS 1984, pp. 337–338, 2024.
https://doi.org/10.1007/978-3-031-51452-4

Summerley, Rory K.   33
Sungu, Ertugrul   59
Surinx, François-Xavier   238

V
Vairinhos, Mário   322
Vittori, Karla   103

W
Werner, Claudia   134

X
Xexéo, Geraldo   134

Y
Yasui, André Kazuo   103

Z
Zagalo, Nelson   86
Zilbeyaz, Pervin Cagla   59

Printed in the United States
by Baker & Taylor Publisher Services